Urban Policy Issues

Canadian Perspectives

Second edition

Edited by

Edmund P. Fowler
and David Siegel

OXFORD
UNIVERSITY PRESS

OXFORD
UNIVERSITY PRESS

70 Wynford Drive, Don Mills, Ontario M3C 1J9
www.oupcan.com

Oxford University Press is a department of the University of Oxford.
It furthers the University's objective of excellence in research, scholarship,
and education by publishing worldwide in

Oxford New York

Athens Auckland Bangkok Bogotá Buenos Aires Cape Town
Chennai Dar es Salaam Delhi Florence Hong Kong Istanbul Karachi
Kolkata Kuala Lumpur Madrid Melbourne Mexico City Mumbai Nairobi
Paris São Paulo Shanghai Singapore Taipei Tokyo Toronto Warsaw

with associated companies in Berlin Ibadan

Oxford is a trade mark of Oxford University Press
in the UK and in certain other countries

Published in Canada
by Oxford University Press

National Library of Canada Cataloguing in Publication Data
Main entry under title:
Urban policy issues: Canadian perspectives
2nd ed.
First edition edited by: Richard A. Loreto, Trevor Price.
Includes bibliographical references and index.
ISBN 0-19-541593-0
1. Urban policy – Canada. I. Fowler, Edmund P. (Edmund Prince), 1942–   .
II. Siegel, David.

HT127.U72 2001   307.76'0971   C2001-930624-5

Cover Image: Brown W. Cannon III/Stone
Cover & Text Design: Brett J. Miller

1 2 3 4 - 05 04 03 02
This book is printed on permanent (acid-free) paper ∞.
Printed in Canada

Contents

About This Book

This is the second edition of a book originated by Richard Loreto and Trevor Price in 1990. At that time it filled a significant vacuum. There were several reasonably comprehensive textbooks on local government on the market, and there were numerous books and government reports devoted to particular issues, especially in such areas as planning and housing, but there was no book geared to undergraduate students or to the general public that provided an introductory survey of the range of policy fields for which local governments are responsible. Loreto and Price's book was a well-received contribution that fit into that niche. We are very pleased that they have allowed us to follow in their tradition and take over editorship for this edition. We feel that there is still as much need for this book now as there was ten years ago.

All the contributions in this book were prepared especially for this edition. The focus of the book is on public policy, with individual chapters devoted to specific issues; however, the objective of the first four chapters is to provide some broad context for the environment in which these policies are made. Thus, these chapters discuss determinants of policies, the demographic and financial backgrounds of urban policy, and changing municipal structures. It would be advisable for readers to read these four chapters first before moving on to the chapters on policy. The policy chapters are presented in no particular order. Each is free-standing, so that the chapters can be read in any order. Of course, no policy is totally free-standing, and the various authors point out how their policy fields interact with others, but this is all the more reason why it is impossible to specify a preferred order.

Acknowledgements

An edited book always accumulates a greater debt to others than a single-authored book. Obviously, our greatest debt is to the authors of the chapters, who did such an excellent job of producing clear and enlightening discussions in their policy areas. We appreciate their informing us about aspects of their areas that would be useful in our introductory chapter, and they were invariably kind in the give and take that always goes on between editors and authors of chapters of books like this.

We owe a particular debt of gratitude to Richard Loreto and Trevor Price, who co-edited the first edition of this book and did quite a bit of preparatory work for the second edition. The entire local government community should be grateful that they had the foresight to understand the need for a book of this sort, and the current editors are especially appreciative of the early work they did on this book.

Fowler acknowledges the generous support of Glendon College's Research Grants Committee toward meeting the costs of preparing the manuscript for publication.

The book also benefited a great deal from the suggestions offered by the anonymous reviewers and by Oxford's editor, Stephanie Fysh. Finally, Phyllis Wilson and Len Husband of Oxford University Press were especially helpful in shepherding the book through the production process with great dispatch.

About the Authors

Caroline Andrew is Professor of Political Science at the University of Ottawa.

Donna Cardinal is a cultural consultant to municipalities and organizations and a lecturer in cultural policy in the Canadian Studies Program at the University of Alberta.

Barbara Wake Carroll is Professor of Political Science at McMaster University.

David K. Foot is Professor of Economics at the University of Toronto.

Edmund P. Fowler is Associate Professor of Political Science at Glendon College, York University.

Rodney Haddow is Associate Professor of Political Science at St Francis Xavier University.

Trevor Hancock is a public health physician and health promotion consultant focusing on healthy cities and communities.

Franz Hartmann is Environmental Advisor to Councillor Jack Layton of the City of Toronto. He teaches in the Environmental Studies Program at Innis College, University of Toronto.

Jack Layton is a city councillor in Toronto. He teaches at the University of Toronto's Innis College in the Environmental Studies Program.

Christopher Leo is Professor of Political Science at the University of Winnipeg and Adjunct Professor of City Planning at the University of Manitoba.

Jeff Morrison is the Public Affairs Officer at the Association of Universities and Colleges of Canada in Ottawa.

Trevor Price is retired from the Department of Political Science at the University of Windsor.

Donald G. Reid is Professor in and former Director of the University School of Rural Planning and Development at the University of Guelph.

Andrew Sancton is Professor and Chair, Department of Political Science, University of Western Ontario.

David Siegel is Professor of Political Science at Brock University.

Bryan J.A. Smale is Associate Professor in the Department of Recreation and Leisure Studies and Associate Dean of Computing and Special Projects in the Faculty of Applied Health Sciences at the University of Waterloo.

Peter Woolstencroft is Associate Professor of Political Science at the University of Waterloo.

Introduction: Urban Public Policy at the Turn of the Century

Edmund P. Fowler and David Siegel

There are a number of ways of studying local government. We could look at the politics of local government (voter turnout, candidate recruitment, party politics), the legal environment of local government (limits on municipal authority, planning regulations), relationships with provincial governments (the role of departments of municipal affairs, financial regimes), structures of governance (one tier versus two tier), or internal administrative organization (the role of the mayor and the chief administrative officer). Instead we have chosen to focus on the public policies produced by local governments. These policies tell us a great deal about local governments because they are the outcomes of the interactions of all the factors mentioned above. Policies are also important because they define how local governments interact with their citizens. As far as citizens are concerned, the policies local government adopts are the 'face' of local government.

There are many factors that will influence local policy-making in the twenty-first century, and they will be constantly changing. This is especially clear in the first four chapters of this book, which deal either with the environment in which local governments operate or with the structures of local government within which local policies are made. This introductory chapter provides an overview of some of the influences on these policies. The second chapter, David Foot's on demographics, discusses the impact of changes in population on government policies. David Siegel's chapter on finance outlines how municipalities obtain their funds and where they spend them. Andrew Sancton's chapter discusses the characteristics of alternative organizational structures and the advantages and disadvantages of each; Sancton also details the significant structural changes that occurred during the 1990s.

These chapters provide a backdrop for the remaining chapters, each of which discusses a different policy field in which local governments are involved. The editors did not specify a standard format for the policy chapters. This would have been impossible: every policy field has its unique characteristics. Nonetheless, each author has provided a portrait of a different policy field, with background about how the current state of affairs developed and where developments are headed in the future. This was a very difficult task because each province's municipal system is different and summarizing findings across ten different systems is not easy. As editors, we were fortunate to be able to assemble a strong field of policy experts who were able to do this. The authors' approaches to their subject varied: some chose a descriptive style, while others consciously argued a particular point of view. We feel that this variation in approach adds to the book's vitality while in no way detracting from its scholarship.

The purpose of this introduction is to pull together a number of themes that cut across all the chapters and to highlight their significance in defining the changing environment of urban policy-making in the twenty-first century. First, however, we want to examine what is meant by *public policy*.

What Is Public Policy?

What is public policy? It has a number of different definitions, all perfectly legitimate in their proper context (Hogwood and Gunn 1984). For instance, 'housing' is a policy field, as is 'the Constitution' or 'the environment', but a housing policy could be defined either as a general commitment to encourage the private sector to build more housing at moderate prices or as a more specific program to give low-income families extra money to cover their rent. Furthermore, there is considerable slippage throughout the process of policy formation and implementation: a program to fine companies responsible for toxic effluent from factories could be called a policy (see Price's chapter), but so could aggressive cuts in the number of inspectors to enforce the law, as could a pattern of decisions not to prosecute companies who have been breaking the law. These scenarios are common. The links between stated intent (or goals), actual legislation, implementation of legislation, and final outcome—all termed *policy*—can be exceedingly tenuous (Hogwood and Gunn 1984; Kernaghan and Siegel 1999).

Several authors in this volume, in fact, raise the issue of whether public policy is an end in itself or the means to a further end. For example, Smale and Reid suggest that recreation policy is less important in itself than as a way to help citizens enrich their quality of life in different ways. Hancock remarks that economic development is instrumental in the same way. It is a long way from identification of an issue or problem area to collective action that actually has an effect on that issue or problem. Many of our contributors give histories of governments' stated policies to, say, alleviate housing shortages, improve social services, or implement far-reaching recreational or cultural policies; nonetheless, more and more Canadians live on the streets, use food banks, or spend most of their leisure time in front of the television set watching American sitcoms.

Analyzing public policy requires attention to the way policy issues are defined. In general, as Smale and Reid note in their chapter, public policy is directed at goods and services that the market either does not provide or provides unequally; that is, it is directed only to those able to afford the good or service. For instance, if the consensus of the political system is that services such as education, or goods such as parkland, should be available to all regardless of their ability to pay, then those goods and services are provided collectively and financed by taxation. Frequently, such *public goods*, as they are called, are indivisible, meaning that if they are provided at all, then by their nature, no one can be excluded (at least practically) from their use; such goods would include streets or parkland. Some of the most contentious issues in public policy are focused, in fact, on whether what is supposed to be an indivisible service—such as police protection—is in fact equally available to all. Thus, public policy issues are usually defined in the context of these principles of the collective provision of public goods.

Considerable work has been done on why issues are raised at specific times (Howlett 1998; Kingdon 1984; Soroka 1999) and why they are defined the way they are (Rochefort and Cobb 1994). For example, Andrew and Morrison's chapter shows that priorities for infrastructure investment have been defined in terms of roads and sewers, whereas more awareness of the importance of culture and recreation to the quality of life shifts infrastructure priorities to theatres and arenas. Fowler and Layton suggest in their chapter that transportation issues be redefined from better roads and greater mobility to improved access to services—which implies building cities that are compact and diverse.

Hancock's chapter on public health illustrates a similar redefinition. There is a hot debate in Canada over the survival of medicare. Hancock points out that public health programs, which concentrate on sickness prevention rather than on after-the-fact care, make a significant contribution to the health of the nation even though the medicare debate has focused attention on the higher profile areas of hospitals and doctors' services. There is no doubt that one dimension of health policy should be equal and effective services to all patients, but Hancock reminds us that the major determinants of health are a nutritious diet, regular exercise, unpolluted air and water, and rewarding social relationships. He also argues that the redefinition of health care policy to promote these factors is long overdue.

One step removed from how a policy issue is defined is whether it is defined at all. Most of the chapters in this book make the point that public attention to particular issues rises and falls over time. There is, in fact, a debate as to how predictable those variations in attention are (Baumgartner and Jones 1993; Howlett 1998; Soroka 1999)—a debate that often ignores the crucial issue of problem definition. As Price's chapter points out, worries about the health of the biosphere reached a fever pitch in the late 1980s but receded before worries about the health of the human economy during the recession of the early 1990s.

How policies are defined, or whether they are defined, is affected by the accumulation of past decisions that leave tangible legacies such as bureaucracies and habitual ways of solving problems. Sometimes, when a specific solution is found, policy-makers apply that 'solution set' to other contexts, even when it is inappropriate (Jones and Bachelor 1993). Thus, policy-making has a recursive character: previous definitions define the limits of imagination in current policy controversies.

Take the case of infrastructure. The investment of billions of dollars into arterial roads and distribution of services (fire, police, education, electricity, sewage, waste disposal) has resulted not only in massive amounts of immovable concrete, but also in engineers and other technicians on permanent government salary trained to turn out more of the same even if it is no longer sensible—and there is much evidence to show that some of it is not, as Price's and Andrew and Morrison's chapters show.

Contrasts among Levels of Government

Another recurring theme—central to any study of municipal politics—is the question of which level of government is best equipped to carry out which function. For instance, although most of us believe that the federal government should be handling foreign policy, there is growing evidence that municipalities are already involved in making foreign policy (Magnusson 1996). Haddow's chapter argues that municipalities are ill-equipped—and even unwilling—to provide most social services equitably and that these functions should be performed by the federal and provincial governments.

The legal status of local governments differs in important respects from that of provincial and federal governments, whose separate functions are defined by the Canadian Constitution. By contrast, municipalities are hardly mentioned in that document and are, in fact, corporations created—and sometimes abolished—by provincial legislatures. And whereas provinces can bargain as equals with the federal government, municipalities have no such prerogative and are often characterized as mere administrative agents of the provinces. Although this status clearly circumscribes their discretion, they are often creative and intelligent formulators of public policy.

Each level of government has its own policy-making processes, and these different processes have an effect on how issues are defined and what policies are adopted. For example, contrast the political process employed in parliamentary systems at the federal and provincial levels with the system employed at the local level. Although a number of Canadian cities have political parties, cities usually operate according to a presidential structure, with the mayor—the system's chief executive—elected separately from council members. The chief executive in a parliamentary system is head of the majority party, and all parties in the system define and structure policy issues by constructing platforms, contesting elections, holding caucus and cabinet discussions on policy, and voting as disciplined groups in the legislature. These practices mean that many policies are defined and implemented as much to advance the political fortunes of a party as to solve substantive problems. Sancton points out in his chapter that former premier John Savage of Nova Scotia and Premier Mike Harris of Ontario argued during their election campaigns that amalgamation was an unintelligent direction for municipal reorganization; nevertheless, on becoming premier, each amalgamated the largest city of his province over the significant vocal opposition of residents of those cities. Andrew and Morrison make it clear that the federal government's infrastructure initiative for municipalities in the late 1990s owed much to the approach of national elections.

A major distinction between the styles of municipal and provincial governments is that between the politics of places and the politics of parties. The partisan scenario is often not appropriate for the local level. When the controversy of whether or not to build the Spadina Expressway into the heart of Toronto's downtown reached the provincial cabinet, it split both the governing Tories and the Liberals. Support for the project was determined by the location of an MPP's riding, not by ideological principles.

Places are in fact the central concern of local governments. The basic functions of police and fire protection, waste management, transportation, parks and recreation, and public health are services to places. People could not reside, conduct their businesses, shop, or hold meetings in buildings without the efficient provision of over a dozen services by municipalities to each of those buildings. That is why local governments also concern themselves with land use policy, which involves the sensible coordination of services and human purposes in a single place. Such coordination requires an intimate knowledge of how places and people fit together, not in the abstract, but on a place-by-place basis. Provincial and federal governments cannot have the in-depth knowledge needed to effect this coordination, a major reason why they decentralize responsibility to municipalities. In fact, many large cities also have difficulty with this spatial coordination. A theme that recurs through most of the chapters in this book is the interrelationships among all the policy areas: Smale and Reid make this point explicitly with recreation; Fowler and Hartmann and Price, with environmental policy; Hancock, with public health; and Woolstencroft, with education. Coordinating these interrelationships makes more policy sense at the local level.

From afar, the intricate ways that places and people fit together are incomprehensible. These intricacies are not mysterious, though, to those of us who know the places. Large-scale regional and provincial governments are not, as we have mentioned, insensitive to this fact. Hollick and Siegel (2001), in their analysis of amalgamations in Ontario, remark on the earnest attempts by the province to let each area negotiate its own model of consolidation.

Large governments, however, have a way of applying general rules willy-nilly to a wide variety of heterogeneous places. The results have not been pretty. For example, Price reminds us in his chapter of the massive costs of urban sprawl—economic, social, even psychological. This form of development did not just happen: it was fuelled by everything from the tax and fiscal policies of the federal government to provincial subsidies of roads and trunk sewers (Fowler 1992). Such practices made a mockery of municipal boundaries, caused us to spend billions of extra dollars on infrastructure, and created grievous damage to our personal health and to the environment. Without denying local governments' complicity in the process, we would argue that the partisan, as opposed to place-oriented, character of policy-making at the provincial and federal levels was at least partially responsible for this mess.

This said, it would be a mistake to conclude that there are no ideological or abstract principles that structure local policy controversies. For instance, spending money on daycare or public transit can be seen as a way of favouring the working class, whereas charging for recreational services does the opposite. Similarly, council debates often manifest splits between those who are anxious to give full rein to developers and their proposals and those who have other priorities and different philosophies of service delivery (public, private, or partnership).

Nevertheless, policy definition seems to be linked to the level of government making the policy. Both Carroll, writing on housing, and Hancock, writing on public health, give examples that show the contrast between the types of policies framed by provincial governments and those framed by local governments. Hancock shows that public health agencies at the local level deal more with such non-medical—and often place-oriented—health issues as clean soil, water, and air, whereas the debates at higher levels of government focus on the funding of hospitals and doctors who treat people who are already sick.

Local governments also face a significant problem of organizational fragmentation. Many urban policy fields are the responsibility of agencies that are semi-independent from city council, such as police and transit (Richmond and Siegel 1994). Some fields are shared between levels of government in ways that lead to fragmentation. Although there are many independent boards and commissions at the provincial and federal levels, these governments have total control over what functions remain 'independent' and what functions do not. Local governments have no such power. Some local and regional governments are so large that coordination among their constituent parts is also a challenge. The structure of local government can thus affect policy-making in a negative way. Amalgamation is only a solution up to a certain scale; after that, local bureaucracies become as huge and impenetrable as provincial and federal ones.

To summarize, any evaluation of urban public policy requires intelligent awareness of how the policy problem has been defined and what agency is making and implementing policy. With these considerations about the definition of public policy and contrasts between levels of government in mind, we discuss in the rest of this chapter a number of factors that have been influential in the determination of public policies by and for local governments.

Determinants of Local Public Policy

The Demographic Context

One set of variables with a powerful influence on urban policy-making is the relative distribution, growth, and composition of the Canadian population. David Foot's chapter outlines some of the policy implications of variations in these demographic factors in cities and through time. For example, some cities are growing much faster than others, and that growth can be skewed toward the younger generation or toward seniors. In the former case, spending on schools, sports arenas, and daycare facilities might preoccupy city councils; with a growing older population, policy concerns will centre on health services, heritage conservation, and housing for smaller family groupings. Some cities have more of both young and old people, making their dependency ratio (the proportion of people outside the normal age of the working population) high. The theoretical significance of this ratio is, however, based on the assumption that work is the same as a paid job; in fact, most significant economic work is done outside the money economy, although the amount of unsalaried work will depend on the culture (Brandt 1995).

Culture is, in fact, another demographic variable of great significance. Various chapters in this book show that the growing cultural diversity of the Canadian population has the potential to cause considerable controversy in the fields of education, support for cultural programs, housing patterns, and preferences for recreation and leisure activities. In education, for instance, there is a constant debate over whether curriculum and holiday celebrations should reflect the students' many different backgrounds or attempt to integrate students into traditional Canadian culture (see Woolstencroft's chapter).

Culture is also a factor in one of the most significant demographic variables, population density. North American culture's preference for single-family dwellings on large lots has resulted in urban sprawl, and most of the chapters in this book have something to say about the social, economic, and political consequences of sprawl. Many of the debates over how metropolitan regions should be governed (see Sancton's chapter) stem from the spread of subdivisions across municipal boundaries. Our suburban culture has little use for public transit or for many of the social problems of Canadian cities' downtowns. Carroll notes, as well, that once suburban housing (and its supporting infrastructure; see Andrew and Morrison's chapter) is in place, it is 'non-adaptive and immobile' and has a long-term physical inertia that may not be responsive to demographic shifts in the Canadian population. Smale and Reid point to a similar situation in the field of recreation policy.

Thus, population patterns such as the baby boom and increasing cultural diversity must be part of the context of policy-making in the twenty-first century. But they are only part of the mix. Decisions in the fields of policy covered in this book should be seen as part of a dynamic relationship between the demographic context—variations in age, density, multiculturalism, and territorial distribution of the Canadian people—and the formulation of ideals about the kind of cities we want to live in.

Municipal Restructuring

Policy-making in Canadian cities has been significantly affected by changes in the structure of municipal governments in recent years. These restructurings will have an important impact on urban decision-making well into the twenty-first century.

The trend toward consolidation of local authorities of all kinds has been underway for at least thirty years, but the pace and scope of this process accelerated during the 1990s, as Sancton's contribution on multi-purpose municipal governments and Woolstencroft's on education make clear. The trend in areas such as education, health, and social services has been toward fewer, larger agencies with responsibilities for millions of people in some cases. For the proponents of consolidation, the advantages include greater equity in service provision, similar service standards (see Haddow's chapter on social services), and greater efficiency—better service for less money. Cardinal's chapter on culture and the arts suggests that amalgamating these functions in Halifax and Toronto has proven beneficial. Larger jurisdictions could also coordinate land use policies to discourage urban sprawl (see Leo's and Fowler and Hartmann's chapters).

Nevertheless, one might question whether the legacy of consolidations from the last decade of the twentieth century has provided a healthier institutional context for the formulation of public policy. Sancton shows that the projected financial savings of municipal amalgamations seldom materialize and that these amalgamations have exacted a heavy toll on public participation in policy-making (see below). Consolidations also highlight the tensions between local governments as political entities, with their own political traditions and cultures, versus local governments as administrative arms of the province, implementing policy that has been made elsewhere. This theme is revisited at the end of this chapter.

Although a definitive judgement on the benefits conferred by these amalgamations will have to await future assessments, it is clear that these new structures will have an impact on the way policies are made, as indicated in a number of chapters.

The Impact of Other Levels of Government: Who Does What

Local government is considered to be the most junior level of government. Although this terminology seems demeaning, it is an inescapably apt description of where local governments fit in the policy process. The federal and provincial governments have strong legal, constitutional mandates and the money to follow through on those mandates. Local governments have frequently viewed themselves as the recipients of policies passed down from above, rather than as policy-makers. Later in this chapter we shall suggest that that role is changing, but it is clear that many of the local government policies discussed in this book are heavily influenced by the actions of federal and provincial governments.

Siegel's chapter on finance illustrates clearly how dependent local governments have been on provincial governments for funding and also how that relationship is changing. As local governments receive less funding from the province, they will become less dependent on senior governments and more autonomous in terms of making their own decisions. Government influence is not, however, just a matter of financial levers. As just noted, some provincial governments have exercised their constitutional right to create, restructure, and abolish local governments in order to radically change the local government map. For now, provincial governments still have the greatest impact, although Andrew and Morrison's chapter on infrastructure shows that federal government funding programs can also have an influence on local governments' policy deliberations.

Various chapters also provide a number of examples of the way in which policies adopted by senior governments have a major influence on how policies are delivered by local governments. Hancock's chapter illustrates how provinces have completely restructured public health services, raising serious concerns about accountability. According to Fowler and Layton, Toronto's attempts to make decisions about rapid transit lines in the 1990s were constantly frustrated by provincial directives that told the City to build first more, then fewer lines. Ottawa's Unemployment Assistance Act, Haddow tells us, allowed provinces such as Ontario to make local governments pay for '20 per cent of assistance cost . . . and to absorb all administrative costs'. In addition, all but one province has legislated minimum welfare rates. This reminds us of the influence of both provincial and federal policies. Price's discussion of environmental issues shows local governments caught in a web of international pressures and of all sorts of federal and provincial government policy priorities.

This does not mean that municipalities are completely devoid of power. Clearly, in some aspects of policy fields such as environment, social services, and housing, municipalities have acted in very innovative ways within the framework set by other governments. Carroll's chapter gives the example of Montreal, which proposed a neighbourhood revitalization program to the province in 1995. The program was approved, and by 1997, 5,500 units had been renovated or created. There are also areas in which municipalities have rather broad scope for policy-making, as noted in Cardinal's chapter on culture and the arts and in Smale and Reid's chapter on recreation and leisure.

In general, the intergovernmental dynamic has been changing; several provinces have reviewed the division of responsibilities between provincial and local governments and have tried to rationalize this division through a process known as *service exchange* or *local service realignment*. This process, the outcome of which is reflected in a number of chapters, involves an attempt to eliminate the confusion of shared authority by allocating responsibility for particular services unequivocally to one level of government. This promises to give local governments greater scope for action in areas that have been allocated to them. This process will be discussed in more detail later in this chapter.

In July 2000, Toronto city council voted 'to demand special charter status and put an end to what it sees as provincial government interference in its affairs' (Moloney 2000). This initiative is a reminder that other cities in Canada have charter status, such as Vancouver and Saint John, New Brunswick. One implication of charter status for the policy process is that, for example, Vancouver is not required to have its official plan approved by the province.

Federal and provincial governments have always had a significant impact on local government policies. A number of chapters in this book document the way in which this is changing. Developments in this area could have a major impact on the role of local government in the coming years.

New Public Management

New Public Management is an approach to governance that has become very influential in the last few years (Charih and Daniels 1997; Kernaghan and Siegel 1999). As with most new trends, it is difficult to define it precisely, but some of its elements that have affected local government are these:

- *Orientation to citizen service.* A traditional critique of many organizations is that they are organized to serve the interests of the employees of the organization and not the interests of the citizens who receive the services of the organization. New Public Management emphasizes service to the public as an important organizational value.
- *Alternative service delivery.* Traditionally, governments have been concerned with both steering (policy-making) and rowing (service delivery) (Osborne and Gaebler 1993). New Public Management suggests that governments should focus on steering and consider alternative ways of delivering services. These alternatives could take the form of traditional approaches such as contracting out, or they could take the form of innovative activities such as partnerships.

Local governments were using many of the principles of New Public Management before they became fashionable elsewhere. For example, contracting out has long been used by some local governments, and partnerships have a long history in such areas as social housing. The chapters in this book provide many examples of the way in which local governments have extended this approach as a result of the New Public Management.

Local government restructuring, as described in Sancton's chapter, is frequently done with a clear focus on making the new organization more client-centred. Partnerships are becoming much more common in such areas as culture and recreation. The Healthy Cities approach, an alternative delivery system that involves citizens in making decisions and carrying out some aspects of those decisions (see Hancock's chapter), is a way of breaking out of the bureaucratic box in an attempt to prevent problems from developing rather than treating them after the fact.

Globalization

Local government policies are not influenced only by federal and provincial governments. The concept of globalization is a reminder that local governments are also part of a much larger system. Leo discusses the importance to municipalities of retaining and attracting businesses that are transnational in scope, both for the property taxes they pay and for the jobs they provide to residents. Andrew and Morrison argue in their chapter that maintaining a proper infrastructure is also important in attracting these new businesses. Municipalities must be aware of the impact on business of such policies as the level of property and other taxation, the type of regulatory environment, and the general quality of municipal services. This requires municipalities to do some difficult balancing between the interests of existing individual citizens and the interests of new businesses. Some municipalities are so focused on attracting new businesses that they forget the needs of citizens who are already living and working there (see Leo's chapter).

Another aspect of globalization is the manner in which new knowledge is transmitted rapidly. If citizens learn through television or the Internet that a city in Germany or Australia has developed an innovative solution to a problem, they might feel that their municipality should adopt the same innovation (Magnusson 1996). Price's chapter on the environment provides a number of illustrations of the manner in which innovations are transmitted rapidly through international networks of interested people. This rapid communication challenges politicians and administrators to stay informed about worldwide developments.

Environmental issues discussed by Price and by Fowler and Hartmann provide another perspective on globalization. Pollution is not a problem that can be easily compartmentalized within one municipality. Price points out in his chapter that a large urban area's footprint extends far beyond its political boundaries.

Public Participation

Most of the chapters in this book have comments on public participation in policy-making, on its breadth and its impact on the final product. The structural changes referred to in this chapter resulted in what many authors consider to be greater barriers to public participation in defining and shaping public policy. For example, assigning public health responsibilities to regional health boards—a move that has occurred in most provinces—prompts Hancock to express concern about accountability. Regional boards are elected, but turnout for these elections is very low; furthermore, as independent agencies, public health boards are not easily held accountable for policy decisions. In the field of education, Woolstencroft argues that consolidation of school board districts and the centralization of education policy-making to the provincial level—a clear trend in the 1990s—have made it more difficult for the public to participate in decisions on education policy. Sancton echoes Woolstencroft's concerns: citizens, he points out, are finding it difficult to identify with larger municipalities, whether these are two-tier or amalgamated. Hollick and Siegel (2001) found that there was only a limited amount of public participation in the local government restructurings that they examined.

At the level of informal power structure and contrary to the oft-expressed belief that local government is more democratic, Andrew and Morrison state categorically that policy decisions about infrastructure are dominated by elite interests, with little public input (see also Franklin 1991). Fowler and Layton confirm this assessment in their discussion of transportation policy. Smale and Reid report that although principles on recreation policy framed by provincial governments back in the 1970s stressed the need for local neighbourhood involvement, local governments have tended to pre-empt policy initiatives in this field. In Smale and Reid's opinion, leisure and recreation practices should be defined, and even implemented, more by the local community than by municipal government.

At the local level, disciplined parties with the ability to direct authoritative government action are rare. Municipal policy-making does involve some fairly informal committee work, in which deputations clash and in which councillors ponder issues and actually change their minds without a party whip leaning over their shoulders. Good ideas can come out of the direct interchange between policy-makers and citizens. This interchange occurs in part because local governments are generally smaller, so that it is easier to talk to representatives face to face. However, caution is required in stereotyping local governments as small. Urban governments generally encompass quite large areas, and the recent trend to amalgamations with reduced numbers of councillors has increased the number of residents per councillor and, therefore, increased the distance between councillor and citizen.

Local government structure encourages more participation, not in voting (local turnout is usually low), but in committees, hearings, and other public venues (Graham and Phillips 1998). Cardinal demonstrates convincingly that cultural policy in large Canadian cities was made in part by their citizens because local governments genuinely included them in the policy-making process.[1] The result was not only more creative cultural policies, but also a more vital local political process.

This is not a trivial finding. The conventional view is that 'too much participation' slows down the efficiency of the policy-making process; the scene typically conjured up is of sophisticated experts, politicians, and civil servants twiddling their thumbs while one screwball after another wastes their time with off-the-wall opinions and irrelevant facts and figures. This stereotype needs debunking. Interviews with Toronto councillors by Fowler revealed that council's deliberations benefited enormously from constant interchange with constituents, not only on city-wide matters but also on very local ones. The key to the value of this interchange is that intelligent urban policies on housing, transportation, land use, and social services depend on balancing the particular with the general, the local with the city-wide, and that which applies only to particular places with general principles that are accepted by all.

The councillors interviewed were expressing the dynamic between the function of representing unique places and people and the function of making collective decisions for the public good. Political parties can interfere with this dynamic, no matter how useful they are in aggregating opinions, developing platforms, getting out the vote, and forming governments (Siegel 1987).

Overall Impact of Recent Changes in Intergovernmental Relations

It is very difficult to summarize all the changes that are described in the chapters of this book, but one major theme that runs through several chapters is the withdrawal of provincial control over municipalities in some areas and the increasing amount of local autonomy this creates. Siegel's chapter on finance describes the reduction in the level of conditional grants, which provide funds to municipalities with very detailed conditions attached. Sancton's chapter on restructuring points to the creation of larger units of government that will be better able to control their own destiny. Carroll's chapter on housing suggests that federal and provincial governments are increasingly turning this field over to municipalities. Many other chapters echo this same theme.

The withdrawal of provincial control creates both a challenge and an opportunity for local governments, which have traditionally been controlled very firmly by provincial governments. This firm control has created animosity on the part of local governments, who resent being treated in this way; but it has also served as a protection for local governments who have not had to make many of their own decisions. Although local governments railed against provincial controls, there was also comfort in knowing that they could frequently hide behind the defence of 'the province made us do it'.

The greater autonomy that local governments will have is, then, a two-edged sword that will both give them considerably more scope to make their local decisions and remove the shield of provincial control. The question is: Are local governments ready to meet this challenge?

Challenges to Urban Governments

Local governments have frequently been viewed as service-delivery agents for policies set elsewhere. Municipalities have bridled at their limited role, but they have been unable to escape it. With the changing environment described in this book, local governments will now need to develop the ability to make and implement their own policies. This book suggests that there are a number of obstacles standing in their way.

One challenge is the consequence of urban sprawl, whose negative impact is documented in this volume (see especially Leo's chapter). As development spills out over the countryside, there is always more territory to be serviced with schools, roads, and police protection. The boundaries of built-up areas are constantly changing, so that policy-makers are facing a moving target. Fragmented local governments that make up metropolitan areas seem to be both the cause and the effect of this sprawl (Razin and Rosentraub 2000). One of the largest problems facing urban governments is the coordination among themselves of sensible policies to contain development and to make it economically and environmentally sustainable.

Another serious challenge is the fragmentation of the policy process itself. Several chapters lament the fact that policies frequently seem to be made in isolation from one another. This has come about because individual municipal departments have become too accustomed to receiving their marching orders as much from a provincial government department as from their own council. As a result, departments have sometimes had a tendency to operate as separate fiefdoms controlled by the chair of the relevant council committee and the commissioner of the department, with funding obtained through conditional grants. This has given rise to the term *silo management*: each department operates in its own silo with little contact with or regard for what happens in adjacent silos.

This problem is exacerbated by a lack of focus within councils. Unlike parliamentary forms of government, which are controlled by a cabinet of reasonably like-minded people—or at least of people who are members of the same political party—councils are sometimes referred to as 'groups of anarchists held together by a common parking lot'. If councils are to become real policy-making bodies, they will have to learn to function in a more coordinated way. Canadians have traditionally resisted having political parties in local government (although Vancouver and Quebec's larger cities could be considered an exception to this generalization), and there are some sound arguments against local parties; but if local councils start to become policy-making bodies, there might be more pressure to develop parties.

More emphasis on policy-making at the municipal level could also have an impact on the role of public involvement in the policy process. Local governments have traditionally had much more direct public participation than other levels, but there is some concern about how truly effective this participation is. Sometimes local governments are not really open to participation, and sometimes citizens are not prepared to participate as effectively as they could. A stronger policy-making role for local governments could make the role of citizens more important. If this is to work effectively, then both citizens and local governments will need to change their attitudes to public participation.

There will also need to be changes in the way in which local public servants function. Local governments have generally been blessed with very high quality staff, but the emphasis of this staff has been on management of the service. Local governments generally have a very limited capacity for policy analysis or policy advice, with the possible exception of larger cities such as Vancouver, Toronto, and Montreal. In the past, there has been no need for this capacity, because most policies have been handed down from senior governments. In the future, local governments will need to have the capacity to develop, analyze, and evaluate policies within their own governments. This will require a significant reorientation of the perspective both of municipal councillors, who will be expected to make more policy decisions, and of municipal staff, who will be required to function more as policy advisors.

The current changes in the municipal system seem to be producing the most basic changes in municipal government since its origins in the nineteenth century. It seems unlikely that provincial governments will accede to pressure from municipalities to be given full constitutional status. However, the current changes, particularly the increase in the size and scope of municipal governments through restructuring and the devolution of responsibilities, will likely result in a significant increase in the power of the municipal level of government. In carving out new arenas of policy, municipalities could literally create power where it did not exist before. This is, in fact, how the US federal government created a centralized system out of a constitutionally decentralized one (Riker 1964). Stone (1989) has described how the City of Atlanta was able to increase its power significantly by the creation of a regime that included many of the most powerful elements in society. The convergence of the various trends discussed throughout this book could mean that local governments will gradually obtain a de facto status as real governing and policy-making bodies, which provincial governments would never allow them to attain de jure.

Notes

1.   There are, of course, many cases of purely symbolic hearings and consultations that have no impact on public policy (Arnstein 1969).

References

Arnstein, Sherry. 1969. 'A Ladder of Citizen Participation'. *Journal of the American Institute of Planners* 35: 216–24.

Baumgartner, Frank R., and Bryan D. Jones. 1993. *Agendas and Instability in American Politics*. Chicago: University of Chicago Press.

Brandt, Barbara. 1995. *Whole Life Economics: Revaluing Daily Life*. Philadelphia: New Society.

Charih, Mohamed, and Arthur Daniels, eds. 1997. *New Public Management and Public Administration in Canada*. Toronto: Institute of Public Administration of Canada.

Fowler, Edmund P. 1992. *Building Cities That Work*. Montreal: McGill-Queens University Press.

Franklin, Ursula. 1991. *The Real World of Technology*. Toronto: CBC Publications.

Graham, Katherine A., and Susan D. Phillips. 1998. *Citizen Engagement: Lessons in Participation from Local Government*. Toronto: Institute of Public Administration of Canada.

Hogwood, Brian W., and Lewis A. Gunn. 1984. *Policy Analysis for the Real World*. London: Oxford University Press.

Hollick, Thomas R., and David Siegel. 2001. *Evolution, Revolution, Amalgamation: Restructuring in Three Ontario Municipalities*. London, ON: Local Government Program, University of Western Ontario.

Howlett, Michael. 1998. 'Predictable and Unpredictable Policy Windows: Institutional and Exogenous Correlates of Canadian Federal Agenda-Setting'. *Canadian Journal of Political Science* 31: 495–524.

Jones, Bryan D., and Lynn W. Bachelor. 1993. *The Sustaining Hand: Community Leadership and Corporate Power*. 2nd ed. Lawrence, KS: University Press of Kansas.

Kernaghan, Kenneth, and David Siegel. 1999. *Public Administration in Canada: Selected Readings*. 4th ed. Scarborough, ON: Nelson.

Kingdon, John W. 1984. *Agendas, Alternatives, and Public Policy*. Boston: Little Brown.

Magnusson, Warren. 1996. *The Search for Political Space: Globalization, Social Movements, and the Urban Political Experience*. Toronto: University of Toronto Press.

Moloney, Paul. 2000. 'Council Demands New Status for City'. *The Toronto Star*, 7 July.

Osborne, David, and Ted Gaebler. 1993. *Reinventing Government: How the Entrepreneurial Spirit is Transforming the Public Sector*. New York: Penguin.

Razin, Eran, and Mark Rosentraub. 2000. 'Are Fragmentation and Sprawl Interlinked? North American Evidence'. *Urban Affairs Review* 35: 821–36.

Richmond, Dale, and David Siegel, eds. 1994. *Agencies, Boards and Commissions in Canadian Local Government*. Toronto: Institute of Public Administration of Canada.

Riker, William. 1964. *Federalism: Origin, Operation, Significance*. Boston: Little Brown.

Rochefort, David A., and Roger W. Cobb, eds. 1994. *The Politics of Problem Definition: Shaping the Policy Agenda*. Lawrence, KS: University Press of Kansas.

Siegel, David. 1987. 'City Hall Doesn't Need Parties'. *Policy Options* 8(5): 26–8.

Soroka, Stuart. 1999. 'Policy Agenda-Setting Theory Revisited: A Critique of Howlett on Downs, Baumgartner and Jones, and Kingdon'. *Canadian Journal of Political Science* 32: 763–72.

Stone, Clarence. 1989. *Regime Politics: Governing Atlanta, 1946–1988*. Lawrence, KS: University Press of Kansas.

Van Kempen, Eva T. 1997. 'Poverty Pockets and Life Chances: On the Role of Place in Shaping Social Inequality'. *American Behavioral Scientist* 41: 430–49.

Zussman, David, and Robin Ford. 1997. *Alternative Service Delivery: Sharing Governance in Canada*. Toronto: Institute of Public Administration of Canada.

CHAPTER 2

Urban Demographics in Canada

David K. Foot[1]

Introduction

People are the centrepiece of all urban and rural areas. They purchase goods and services from governmental as well as non-governmental entities. They provide the revenues, either through purchases or through taxes, that enable goods and services to be provided, and they constitute the workforce that produces the goods and services.

The scientific study of human populations is called *demographics*. This discipline examines the various socio-economic characteristics of the population. *Social characteristics* include age, gender, marital status or living arrangements, ethnic origin, and mother tongue, and *economic characteristics* cover such items as occupation, employment status, income, and sometimes housing and household details.

In North America, demographic data are collected primarily by means of a census of the population. The most recent censuses were in 2000 in the United States and in 1996 in Canada. The next census for Canada is scheduled for 2001. Annual estimates of the population, both intercensal and post-censal, are based on these census data.

Census information provides the regional residence of the respondent (by means of the postal code), and this information is used to measure population size on a regional basis and to define urban areas. Statistics Canada, the collector and publisher of census data on behalf of the nation, defines a *Census Metropolitan Area (CMA)* as a regional agglomeration of people constituting a defined area with a high degree of economic and social integration and with more than 100,000 persons resident within its contiguous boundaries. As of 1996, there were twenty-five CMAs in Canada. In addition, a further nine urban areas with populations of 100,000 or more persons could be identified in 1996. These are the urban areas referred to in this chapter.

This chapter starts with a brief review of the major characteristics and trends in the Canadian population. Of particular interest are the definition of what have been called the *boom*, *bust*, and *echo* generations (Foot with Stoffman 1996, 1998) and the identification of the aging of the Canadian population. The demographic characteristics of Canada's major urban areas are examined in the context of the national data. Increasingly, dependency ratios have been used as key demographic indicators in economic and policy analyses, so a subsequent section defines, displays, and discusses dependency ratios for Canada's urban areas. Since individuals' needs for public (and private) goods and services vary predictably over the life cycle, demographic changes—especially population aging—can be expected to affect many public-sector programs and policies. This chapter therefore concludes with some brief observations on the potential relevance of these demographic data for a variety of public programs and policies, including education, housing, crime, and health care.

Demographic Definitions

Table 2.1 summarizes the age–gender characteristics of the Canadian population as of July 1, 1996, when 29.672 million persons lived in the Canadian provinces and ter-

Table 2.1: Population (Thousands) by Age and Gender, Canada, 1996

Age Group	Male	Female	Total
0–4	1,007.0	958.3	1,965.3
5–9	1,033.3	984.0	2,017.2
10–14	1,031.4	977.8	2,009.2
15–19	1,035.0	978.0	2,013.0
20–24	1,023.9	986.7	2,010.6
25–29	1,093.7	1,069.8	2,163.5
30–34	1,306.2	1,276.2	2,582.4
35–39	1,317.8	1,308.5	2,626.3
40–44	1,184.6	1,190.8	2,375.4
45–49	1,065.0	1,066.8	2,131.8
50–54	825.7	830.3	1,656.0
55–59	659.3	672.1	1,331.3
60–64	593.6	614.2	1,207.8
65–69	533.2	590.1	1,123.3
70–74	426.2	540.7	967.0
75–79	282.4	407.0	689.4
80–84	170.3	287.3	457.6
85+	103.1	241.6	344.7
Total	14,691.8	14,980.1	29,671.9

Note: Components may not sum to total because of independent rounding.
Source: Statistics Canada.

ritories. Canada was then a statistically female-dominant population, with a slight majority (50.5 per cent) of its population being female. By 1996, the male-to-female sex ratio was 0.981, which means that there are 981 males for every 1000 females. The sex ratio, however, varies noticeably by age. In the younger age groups, it is higher than average, reflecting a male-dominant sex ratio at birth. For example, the sex ratio of the preteen group (aged 0 to 12 years) is 1.052. On the other hand, it is lower than average in the older age groups, reflecting the greater longevity of females. By 1996, life expectancy at birth in Canada was over 75 years for males and over 81 years for females. Consequently, the sex ratio in the elderly senior population (85 years and over) was 0.427 (or approximately 234 females for every 100 males). These figures have numerous implications for the delivery of social and other services and for relationships between the genders.

This discussion of sex ratios underscores the importance of age distribution in the interpretation of demographic data and in the development of policies in the public and private sectors. In 1996, there were over one million more people in the 30- to 39-year age group than in the 10- to 19-year age group, even though the probability of death increases with age beyond infancy. With such dramatic variations in the Canadian demographic profile, primarily as a result of the dramatic rise and subsequent fall in post-war fertility, age is probably the single most important demographic variable in understanding historical trends and, incidentally, in anticipating future trends. It is for this reason that the remainder of this section is devoted to a careful review of the age structure of the Canadian population.

The dominant feature of the Canadian population is the large 'bulge' of people who by the mid-1990s were in their thirties and forties. These people are often referred to as the *baby boom* generation (colloquially, the *boomers*). A careful review of the single year-of-age data underlying Table 2.1 shows the numbers of people decreasing noticeably between 49 and 50 years, thereby establishing the front end of the boomer generation as having been born in 1947 (and hence aged 49 in 1996). The numbers then keep increasing to a maximum of 537,729 thirty-five-year-olds. These people were born in 1961.[2] The numbers then start to decline rapidly, with a noticeable drop occurring between 30 and 29 years of age. These features provide a convenient quantitative definition of the baby boom generation in Canada. According to Table 2.1, its members were aged 30 to 49 years in 1996 and hence were born between 1947 and 1966. In 1996, they totalled 9.7 million persons or 32.7 per cent of the Canadian population. Being twenty years in duration, this definition is close to the usual sociological definition of a generation.

The deduction of birth years from the 1996 data is, of course, based on the truism that every year an individual gets one year older (the unpalatable alternative of death being ignored). Consequently, it is easy to be forward-looking in this context. The first boomers in Canada reached age 50 in 1997. At the turn of the century (2000), boomers were aged 34 to 53 years. They will enter the traditional retirement age of 65 years commencing in the year 2012 and will continue to retire over the subsequent twenty-year period. This is what has given rise to increasing concerns regarding the viability of pensions and health care in Canada.

Declining fertility over the 1960s and 1970s—the Canadian fertility rate fell from a high of almost 4 children per woman in the late 1950s to level off at around 1.7 children per woman by the mid-1970s—created what demographers have called the *baby bust* generation. The smallest single-year cohort in this group was aged 22 in 1996 and hence was born in 1974. There are 395,122 persons in this cohort, which is almost 26.5 per cent less than in the peak boomer cohort. By the late 1970s, births began to increase as the boomers started to have their children. This group is called the *baby boom echo* (or just *echo*) generation.

It is difficult to identify the echo generation in Canadian data because some regions (notably in eastern Canada) do not have an echo, whereas in other regions (notably in Ontario and most of western Canada) the echo is very apparent. Again using single year-of-age data, there were 5,000 more 16-year-olds than 17-year-olds in 1996, which identifies the echo as having started in 1980. Consequently, its members reached school age (6 years) in 1986 and became teenagers in 1993. By the turn of the century (2000), the first of the echo were 20 years of age.

Also clearly apparent from the 1996 data is that the peak of the echo has now passed. Births peaked in Canada in 1990 and declined over the 1990s as boomer mothers aged into their lower-fertility years. For example, a peak boomer born in 1960 was aged 36 in 1996 and by 2000 was entering her forties, when it becomes increasingly difficult to have children. This decline in the number of births over the 1990s and beyond has important implications for the education system in the new millennium, just as it did thirty years ago. Since there were over 10,000 fewer 3-year-olds than 4-year-olds and almost 10,000 fewer 2-year-olds than 3-year-olds in 1996, the end of the echo generation for Canada can be identified as having been in 1993.[3]

Given these definitions, in 1996, there were 9.72 million boomers, 5.37 million busters, and 5.65 million echo children in a population of almost 29.67 million. Together, these three groups comprise 20.7 million people, or 70 per cent of Canada's population.

Although there are many more people in the younger age groups, public policy is also affected by those born ahead of the boomers. The first decade of the 1900s was relatively buoyant, while the second decade was characterized by World War I, resulting in fewer births over the period 1915–19. These people were aged 77 to 81 years in 1996. The 'Roaring Twenties' followed, and births rose again, only to be followed by a decline over the Depression era in the 1930s. A minimum occurs for those aged 62 years in 1996, who were born in 1934.[4] Thereafter, World War II acted as a transition to the post-war baby boom. Births increased gradually during the war, reflecting in part the effect of postponed fertility during the 1930s, improved economic activity as a result of supporting the war effort in Canada, and, of course, the fact that hostilities did not take place on North American soil. These factors also set the scene for the post-war baby boom.

This Canadian demographic profile is relatively unique in the developed world. Post-war fertility in Europe, although generally increasing, did not reach Canadian levels, and the post-war emigration of persons of childbearing age from Europe had a moderating effect on European births and an accelerating effect on births in North America. Consequently, the baby boom in Europe is much less noticeable than in North America. Meanwhile, the dramatic increases in births in the immigrant-receiving countries of Canada, the United States, and Australia reflected both a favourable age structure and growing incomes that enabled children to be affordable. Even in the United States, however, fertility peaked in 1957 at 3.58 children per woman, below Canadian levels, which reached 3.94 children per woman in 1959; this difference means that the US baby boom is a somewhat smaller percentage of the US population compared to Canada. But since US fertility has been noticeably higher than Canadian fertility over the 1980s and 1990s, the echo generation is comparatively larger there. Australian fertility peaked at 3.54 children per woman in 1961, below both Canadian and US levels, but continued at comparably higher levels over the 1960s, so that the Australian baby boom, being spread out over approximately thirty years, is not nearly as concentrated as in North America.

In summary, the Canadian demographic profile reflects the numerous important historical events that have shaped the development of the country over the twentieth century. Consequently, it is unique to Canada. The only other country with a similar demographic profile is the United States. The only other developed country with a substantial baby boom is Australia, but there it was spread over thirty years (1947–76) and is not as peaked as the Canadian and US profiles. Contrary to many claims, there is no sizable baby boom in Europe when viewed from a North American perspective. It is the massive size and concentrated shape of the boomer generation, the subsequent bust, and the echo children in Canada that makes demographics particularly important in understanding Canadian policy issues, including urban policy.

Urban Demographics

As indicated in the previous section, the updating and projecting of demographic data is a relatively easy exercise, being based on the truism of each person's aging one year every year. In 1996, the boomers were aged 30 to 49 years, the busters were aged 17 to 29 years, and the echo generation was made up of those aged 3 to 16 years. Table 2.2 lists the twenty-five Census Metropolitan Areas (CMAs) in Canada with estimated populations of 100,000 persons or more in 1996.[5] The largest was Toronto, with 4.403 million persons, having passed Montreal (with 3.394 million persons) in the 1970s. Third in size was Vancouver (1.912 million), followed by Ottawa-Hull (1.038), Edmonton (0.885), Calgary (0.845), Quebec City (0.684), and Winnipeg (0.679). The smallest, but not the newest, CMA was Saint John (0.128), followed by Thunder Bay (0.129), Trois-Rivières (0.142), and Sherbrooke (0.150).

Over the post-war period, CMAs in eastern and central Canada, such as Chicoutimi-Jonquière, Quebec City, St Catharines–Niagara, Saint John, and Windsor, have been losing ground, while those in western Canada, such as Calgary, Edmonton, and Saskatoon, have been moving up in the rankings. This reflects in large part the westward drift of the Canadian population. There are, however, some

Table 2.2: Demographic Indicators, Census Metropolitan Areas, Canada, 1996

CMA	Population (thousands)				Percentage			Young Dependency Ratio	Seniors Dependency Ratio	Total Dependency Ratio
	Total	0–14 years	15–64 years	65+ years	0–14 years	15–64 years	65+ years			
Calgary	845,493	179,353	593,481	72,659	21.2	70.2	8.6	0.302	0.122	0.425
Chicoutimi–Jonquière	162,949	31,385	114,085	17,479	19.3	70.0	10.7	0.275	0.153	0.428
Edmonton	885,123	191,207	608,508	85,408	21.6	68.7	9.6	0.314	0.140	0.455
Halifax	341,463	67,147	240,301	34,015	19.7	70.4	10.0	0.279	0.142	0.421
Hamilton	642,729	126,741	428,024	87,964	19.7	66.6	13.7	0.296	0.206	0.502
Kitchener	395,208	84,523	268,346	42,339	21.4	67.9	10.7	0.315	0.158	0.473
London	410,407	83,333	276,005	51,069	20.3	67.3	12.4	0.302	0.185	0.487
Montreal	3,393,739	632,546	2,356,645	404,548	18.6	69.4	11.9	0.268	0.172	0.440
Oshawa	277,073	64,661	185,515	26,897	23.3	67.0	9.7	0.349	0.145	0.494
Ottawa–Hull	1,037,853	210,376	723,208	104,269	20.3	69.7	10.0	0.291	0.144	0.435
Quebec City	683,741	118,352	486,356	79,033	17.3	71.1	11.6	0.243	0.163	0.406
Regina	199,527	43,567	132,821	23,139	21.8	66.6	11.6	0.328	0.174	0.502
Saint John	128,029	25,857	86,138	16,034	20.2	67.3	12.5	0.300	0.186	0.486
Saskatoon	225,963	50,612	150,480	24,871	22.4	66.6	11.0	0.336	0.165	0.502
Sherbrooke	150,098	27,808	104,097	18,193	18.5	69.4	12.1	0.267	0.175	0.442
St Catharines–Niagara	382,813	72,889	248,336	61,588	19.0	64.9	16.1	0.294	0.248	0.542

St John's	177,054	34,410	125,121	17,523	19.4	70.7	9.9	0.275	0.140	0.415
Sudbury	165,009	31,718	114,125	19,166	19.2	69.2	11.6	0.278	0.168	0.446
Thunder Bay	129,089	24,873	86,295	17,921	19.3	66.8	13.9	0.288	0.208	0.496
Toronto	4,403,092	873,957	3,053,580	475,555	19.8	69.4	10.8	0.286	0.156	0.442
Trois-Rivières	142,234	25,033	98,618	18,583	17.6	69.3	13.1	0.254	0.188	0.442
Vancouver	1,912,120	345,002	1,345,738	221,380	18.0	70.4	11.6	0.256	0.165	0.421
Victoria	316,828	51,828	209,468	55,532	16.4	66.1	17.5	0.247	0.265	0.513
Windsor	287,486	56,917	193,968	36,601	19.8	67.5	12.7	0.293	0.189	0.482
Winnipeg	679,174	136,159	453,459	89,556	20.0	66.8	13.2	0.300	0.197	0.498
Total CMAS	18,374,294	3,590,254	12,682,718	2,101,322	19.5	69.0	11.4	0.283	0.166	0.449
Total non-CMAS	11,297,598	2,401,552	7,415,377	1,480,669	21.3	65.6	13.1	0.324	0.200	0.524
Canada	29,671,892	5,991,806	20,098,095	3,581,991	20.2	67.7	12.1	0.298	0.178	0.476

Source: Statistics Canada. 1997. *1996 Census.* As compiled by Strategic Projections Inc.

notable exceptions. Oshawa has been consistently moving up in the rankings, while Winnipeg has been sliding. Many others, such as Halifax (number 13), Trois-Rivières (number 23), Vancouver (number 3), and Victoria (number 14), have remained remarkably stable in the rankings over this period.

The majority of Canadians now live in a CMA. This has not always been true. As recently as 1951, less than one-half (46 per cent) of the Canadian population lived in a CMA. This proportion has been gradually increasing over the post-war period as more and more of the population has been attracted to urban locations. By 1996, 61.9 per cent of the Canadian population lived in a CMA.

The trend of the increasing urbanization of the Canadian population reflects increasing productivity in agriculture, which has resulted in the depopulation of rural areas and increasing economic activity in urban areas. It also reflects the age structure of the population. Young people are attracted to cities, and as the boomers matured over the 1960s and 1970s, they moved to the major urban centres. As they matured into their family formation ages over the 1980s and 1990s, however, they moved out to the suburbs, resulting in an increasing suburbanization of the population. Since the definition of a CMA includes both the core and the surrounding suburbs, this relocation within the CMA is not captured by urbanization measures based on CMA definitions. It does, however, have profound implications for urban policies.

Table 2.2 also summarizes the estimated age structure of Canadian CMAs in 1996. Approximately one-fifth (20.2 per cent) of the Canadian population were aged zero to 14 years. These were predominantly members of the echo generation. The CMA with the largest share of preschool- and school-aged children (aged 0 to14 years) was Oshawa (23.3 per cent), followed by Saskatoon (22.4), Regina (21.8), Edmonton (21.6), Kitchener (21.4), and Calgary (21.2). This suggests that preschool and school programs are in the greatest need in these communities, whereas they are relatively less important in those urban areas with lower population shares in these ages, such as Victoria (16.4), Quebec City (17.3), Trois-Rivières (17.6), Vancouver (18.0), Sherbrooke (18.5), and Montreal (18.6). Schooling needs reflect not only higher fertility in the locations with the largest share of preschool- and school-aged children, but also an age distribution of the population that favours family formation.

As noted previously, population aging is reflected not only in the Canadian data, but also in urban area data. Some CMAs are older than others. Besides having a lower share of younger people in their communities, these older CMAs also tend to have a higher share of people in the older age groups. For example, the CMAs with the highest shares of 45- to 64-year-olds are all in Quebec. They are indicative of concerns often raised in that province that aging is detrimental to the continued survival and regeneration of the francophone culture.

Probably the most commonly used indicator of age and aging is the proportion of a community's population that is in the traditional retirement age range of 65 years and over. In 1996, 12.1 per cent of the Canadian population was in this age group. Not surprisingly, the oldest CMA by this criterion was Victoria, with 17.5 per cent of its population in these senior ages. Victoria was followed by St Catharines–Niagara

(16.1), Thunder Bay (13.9), and Hamilton (13.7). These CMAs are all in the province of Ontario, and the 1996 data reflected the earlier migration of economic activity and people to that province. The data also suggest that the provision of health care and other services used by seniors is likely to be relatively more important in these CMAs, whereas they will be relatively less important in the Calgary (8.6), Edmonton (9.6), Oshawa (9.7), St. John's (9.9), Halifax (10.0), and Ottawa-Hull (10.0) CMAs.

In general, Canada's CMAs have a smaller proportion of young persons aged 0 to 14 years compared to non-CMAs (19.5 per cent versus 21.3 per cent). This is because fertility levels tend to be lower in urban areas. This noticeable difference suggests that smaller communities, on average, are under relatively greater pressure to provide young people's services, such as education and recreation, than are larger communities in Canada. However, Canada's CMAs also have a smaller proportion of seniors aged 65 years and over compared to non-CMAs (11.4 per cent versus 13.1 per cent), because those of working age tend to migrate to urban areas. This means that Canada's CMAs have a higher proportion of persons in their working ages (15 to 64 years) than do non-CMAs (69.0 per cent versus 65.6 per cent), which in turn means that it is comparably easier to raise taxes in urban than in non-urban areas, at least from a demographic perspective.

It is also worth noting that although Canada's registered Native population tend not to live in urban areas and make up only a small percentage (2.1) of the total Canadian population, they do make up more than 7 per cent of the populations of Manitoba and Saskatchewan (and approximately 25 per cent of the populations of the territories of Yukon, the Northwest Territories, and Nunavut). Since the registered Native population is noticeably younger than the Canadian population, with 31.8 per cent aged 0 to 14 years (compared to 20.2 for Canada) and only 4.2 per cent aged 65 years and over (compared to 12.1 for Canada), this can affect the demographics of urban areas, especially those in which Native populations are concentrated.

Dependency Ratios

Demographers have used dependency ratios, based on age distribution data, to indicate not only the need for the provision of goods and services in a community, but also the community's ability to produce or pay for those needs. This is not a new idea. Any society can be divided into three groups: current producers; the young, or producers of the future; and the elderly, or producers of the past. To a very large extent, both the young and the elderly depend on the current producers for their current needs, be these in the form of food in a traditional agrarian society or in the form of income in a modern society. This dependency is also the basis for the extended family, in which goods and services are shared according to the ability to provide. It also provides a rationale for the redistributive function of government.

The same idea can be extended to a modern society. The young in a community represent the future, but they currently need food and education in order to mature to the point when they can assume the role of provider. In a modern capitalistic society, food is provided by the family and education is provided by the community, that is, by the private and public sectors respectively. There is no reason in principle why the reverse could not be the case. Any society can choose what needs will be provided collectively (in the public sector) and what needs will be provided individually (in the private sector).

The same logic applies to the seniors, or elders, in a modern society. Their past provision of goods and services to the current producers gives seniors a legitimate claim on some of the current production to satisfy their current needs. Note that in a modern society, this claim may be in the form of pensions or interest payments on past investments. It may or may not include the provision of health care. Health care is primarily provided in the public sector in Canada, whereas it is provided in the private sector in the United States. Once again, any society can choose the extent to which seniors' needs are provided for by collective as opposed to individual sources.

These responsibilities to the young and seniors represent a claim on current production and hence a 'burden' on the current producers. Obviously, if there are relatively few people in each of these 'dependent' groups, then the burden on society is relatively light. On the other hand, if these groups are relatively large in number, then the burden on society is heavy. The demographic dependency ratio is one measure of this burden.

A society usually chooses a government of one form or another to ensure the collective provision of goods and services. In a modern market economy, transfers between producers and dependents can occur 'in kind' or as income transfers, because income provides the recipient with a claim on current production. Consequently, governments levy taxes on current producers, on production, or on both to generate the revenues to produce goods and services, such as education and health, and to fund income transfers, such as welfare and pension payments, in order to ensure that the dependent members of the society are looked after. The dependency ratio provides an indicator of this tax burden.

To calculate the dependency ratio, the population is divided into the three groups mentioned above: the dependent young and seniors, and working-age producers. These divisions are inherently arbitrary. A convenient approach, given the data in Table 2.1 and Table 2.2, is to define the young as aged 0 to 14 years, those of working age as aged 15 to 64 years, and seniors as aged 65 years and over. Those of working age are the potential taxpayers and become the denominator in the ratio calculations (see Foot 1989). Note that according to this definition, the boomers are now in their potential tax-paying ages and their echo children are largely the young dependents.

A *young dependency ratio* is the number of young people (Y) divided by the number of working-age people (W), while a *senior dependency ratio* is the number of senior people (S) divided by the number of working-age people. These are often called the *child* and *old-age dependency ratios* respectively. The total dependency ratio (D) is the sum of these two ratios, that is

$$D = (Y/W) + (S/W) = (Y + S)/ W$$

Note that since all variables on both the numerator and denominator of D can be divided by the total population (Y + W + S), the dependency ratio can also be expressed as a ratio of the respective shares in the population. Table 2.2 presents these calculations for the Canadian CMAs as of 1996. As a group, their young dependency ratio was 0.283, which means that for every 1,000 persons of working age, there were 283 young persons (aged 0 to 14 years). Not surprisingly given the above discussion, Oshawa had the highest young dependency ratio, with 0.349, followed by Saskatoon (0.336), Regina (0.328), Kitchener (0.315), Edmonton (0.314), and Calgary (0.302). Note that these are Ontario and western-Canadian CMAs, where the echo generation is most apparent. The lowest young dependency ratio CMAs were Quebec City (0.243), followed by Victoria (0.247), Trois-Rivières (0.254), Vancouver (0.256), Sherbrooke (0.267), and Montreal (0.268), which are in the retirement haven of British Columbia or in Quebec. These results reflect, in part, the migration patterns of the Canadian population over the post-war period.

In 1996, Canadian CMAs as a group had a senior dependency ratio of 0.166, or 166 seniors (aged 65 years and over) for every 1,000 persons of working age. The highest senior dependency ratio occurred in Victoria, where there were 265 seniors for every 1,000 persons of working age, followed by St Catharines–Niagara (0.248), Thunder Bay (0.208), Hamilton (0.206), Winnipeg (0.197), and Windsor (0.189). The lowest senior dependency ratios were to be found in Calgary (0.122), St John's (0.140), Edmonton (0.140), Halifax (0.142), Oshawa (0.145), and Ottawa-Hull (0.144).

Combining these two component ratios gives the total dependency ratio. For Canadian CMAs as a group, the total dependency ratio in 1996 was 0.449, which means that there were 2.23 persons of working age for every person of non-working age. The CMA with the highest total dependency ratio was St Catharines–Niagara (0.542), followed by Victoria (0.513), Regina (0.502), Saskatoon (0.502), and Winnipeg (0.498). The CMAs with the lowest total dependency ratios were Quebec City (0.406), St John's (0.415), Vancouver (0.421), Halifax (0.421), Calgary (0.425), and Chicoutimi-Jonquière (0.428). Of the three largest CMAs in Canada, Toronto (0.442) was ranked sixteenth, Montreal (0.440) appeared as eighteenth, and Vancouver (0.421) was twenty-third.

A comparable analysis of all urban areas with populations of at least 100,000 persons introduces nine additional urban areas, the largest being Kingston (143,400) and the smallest Brantford (100,215).[6] The highest total dependency ratios are all new additions, namely Peterborough (0.592), followed by Abbotsford (0.577), Kelowna (0.574), and Brantford (0.564). Barrie (0.539) follows the previous high, St Catharines–Niagara (0.552). For Peterborough, Kelowna, and St Catharines–Niagara, these high dependency ratios were primarily attributable to relatively higher senior dependency, whereas for Abbotsford, Brantford, and Barrie, they were primarily attributable to relatively higher young dependency. Also, it is interesting to note that these high-dependency urban areas are all in the provinces of Ontario and British Columbia. The urban areas with the lowest total dependency ratios were as before, namely Quebec City (0.406), St John's (0.415), Halifax (0.421), Vancouver (0.421), Calgary (0.425), and Chicoutimi-Jonquière (0.428). In the ranking of the thirty-four largest urban areas, Toronto was ranked twenty-fourth, Montreal was ranked twenty-seventh, and Vancouver was ranked thirty-first, all well into the bottom half of the list (see Strategic Projections [2000] for more details).

A number of authors have pointed out the limitations of demographic dependency ratios for policy analysis. For example, I have noted (Foot 1982) that as indicators of tax rates, they implicitly assume that a child and a senior cost the same to society. They do not take into account that in modern society, the costs of raising the young tend to be largely borne by the family or household—that is, in the private sector—but increasingly, the costs of supporting seniors (primarily pensions and health care) tend to be borne by society, that is, in the public sector. Canadian data suggest that it costs approximately 2.5 times more to support a senior on public-sector programs than a young person. Moreover, this ratio varies noticeably by level of government, with the ratio being highest for the federal government and lowest for local governments (Foot 1984). In essence, within the Canadian Constitution and its various interpretations, local governments have been primarily responsible for the delivery of public programs used mainly by the young, such as schooling, libraries, and recreational facilities, whereas the federal government has been primarily responsible for programs oriented to seniors, such as old age security, the guaranteed income supplement, and some health care.

A further criticism of demographic dependency ratios as indicators of economic pressures in society focuses on the definition of *dependency*. For example, there are many members of the working-aged population who are dependent on society. The unemployed and those not able to seek positions in the paid labour force, such as some persons with disabilities, come readily to mind. There are also some seniors who continue to work and, therefore, are not dependent on society. In general, as shown by Foot (1989), such adjustments raise dependency ratios because they allocate people who are not employed from the denominator to the numerator of the calculation. Despite these shortcomings, however, demographic dependency ratios provide a useful starting point for jurisdictional comparisons and policy analysis. The important message, as with all policy indicators, is to apply them wisely.

As indicated above, there are numerous implications of these data for urban policy. The following section briefly outlines some of these implications for a selection of policy areas. More detailed descriptions of specific policy areas can be found in other chapters.

Policy Implications

Although demographic dependency ratios provide an overview of the economic pressures in a community, it is important to remember that these pressures come from a variety of sources and will vary across communities. One useful disaggregation has already been provided, namely, the young and senior dependency ratios.

Generally, new communities have high young dependency and low senior dependency ratios, whereas mature communities experience the opposite. This is a reflection of the fact that migrants tend to be in the youngest working ages, which are the prime family formation years. This is true for all migrants, whether they move within the community, from one community to another, or from one country to another. For example, Oshawa would be an example of a CMA with relatively high young dependency ratio and a low senior dependency ratio, while the Victoria CMA would be an example of the opposite.

There are, of course, urban areas that do not fit this pattern. Recently rejuvenated areas may experience both high young and high senior dependency ratios, whereas areas characterized by low fertility and low life expectancy face the opposite. The Winnipeg and St John's CMAs are, respectively, examples of these contrary trends.

Beyond these general indicators of economic pressures in communities, there are numerous specific programs that are influenced by demographic considerations. The following is an illustrative, but by no means exhaustive, list of policy implications for specific program areas that are clearly influenced by the demographic composition in the community. In general, the discussion is ordered from programs oriented to the young to those oriented to seniors.

Daycare

Demographics can have a major impact on policies affecting preschool-aged children, such as daycare. With the boomers having their children during the 1980s, it was not surprising to see daycare emerge as a major issue on the agendas of all levels of government over that decade. Both programs and facilities were developed to meet this expanding need. Although daycare programs remain an important component of many communities in Canada today, especially in western Canada, the growth in demand levelled off and began declining over the 1990s, reflecting in large part the declining numbers of births in the 1990s. Future daycare needs are likely to be declining in most communities in Canada, even in those communities that experienced the echo boom in the 1980s.

School Enrolment

Since school attendance is compulsory up to the mid-teen years in Canada, school enrolment is an area in which demographic analysis has been used to plan facilities and staffing at a community level. Certainly, the education of the massive baby boom generation in elementary and secondary schools during the 1950s and 1960s led to an ever-expanding system, which then found itself with considerable excess capacity when the baby bust generation entered in the 1970s and early 1980s. Facilities were closed, hiring was frozen, and early retirement and similar packages were developed to deal with the teacher surplus. Then in the mid-1980s, in many communities, the echo generation commenced their education and enrolment started to rise again. Over the subsequent decade, schools were taken out of mothballs or reconverted to schooling use and new facilities were built. Urban land was often allocated for more schools. But in the early 1990s, the number of births started to decline. The peak echo children born in 1990 reached their mid–elementary school age in 1999 and will reach their mid–high school age in 2005 or 2006, so it was predictable that school enrolment would begin to decline by the late 1990s in many communities and, once again, facilities and staff will gradually become redundant. Since school enrolment spills over into other policy areas, such as land use and transportation (school bus) policies, there are important implications for these issues as well. Once again, demographics plays a crucial and predictable role.

It is important to note one significant difference between the schooling and day-care applications of demographics. In the case of schooling, everyone in the relevant age groups must attend by law. In the case of daycare, utilization is the choice of the parents, which means that the facilities do not have to be made available and that the number of preschoolers is indicative of only the potential need in the community. Nonetheless, demographics can provide a powerful indicator of the growth and decline in need, both historically and into the future, in both applications.

Colleges and Universities

While almost all urban areas have daycare and school facilities, not all urban areas have a college or university located within their boundaries. But many do, and in these urban areas, the institutes of post-secondary education often make important contributions to the community not only as providers of various services within the community, but also as employers and consumers of many goods and services in the community. Demographics has a lot to say about post-secondary educational enrol-ment. The first boomers reached college age in the mid-1960s, and that is when the post-secondary system expanded. Expansion continued through the 1970s and into the 1980s as the last of the boomers entered their post-secondary education ages. By then, the early boomers were in their graduate school ages and enrolment was rising among the older students, both graduate and part-time.

Unfortunately, colleges and universities often do not make it particularly easy for older students with other responsibilities in their lives, both at home and at the office, to take courses, especially upper-level courses, on a part-time basis. Admission is often a cumbersome procedure, especially if one is not continuing directly from lower-level courses; lectures are not offered at convenient times and often may not be related to the 'real world'; and classrooms are uncomfortable at best and back-breaking at worst. The aging boomers continue to need education—education is a life-long process—but post-secondary institutions have been slow to recognize the needs of the older student. Perhaps they do not have to worry. The echo generation appeared on their doorsteps by the late 1990s, and once again, colleges and universities can concentrate on educating the traditional young, full-time student, at least for the first decade of the new millennium. Meanwhile, who will provide education to the aging boomers, who still have an average of twenty years of working life before them? Perhaps this will be an opportunity for the private sector and for forward-looking colleges and univer-sities, especially in those urban areas where the echo does not exist.

Housing and Offices

Housing and office construction strikes at the core of land-use policies. The first boomers born in the late 1940s began entering the job market in the mid-1960s and leaving home to establish their own households in the late 1960s. For the next twenty years, the labour force grew dramatically and, along with it, the need for new office space. The busters started entering the labour market in the late 1980s; the demand for new office space slackened, with disastrous results for many construction companies. A depressed economy in the early 1990s intensified this trend, but it would have been noticeable regardless of economic factors. The echo generation start to enter the labour force over the first decade of the new millennium, which means that after a decade or more of office vacancies, demand will gradually pick up again. New work arrangements, such as telecommuting, may modify this conclusion but are unlikely to substantially change it.

As for rental housing, the first boomers started leaving home in the late 1960s. Vacancy rates decreased, rents increased, and rent controls appeared in many jurisdictions. This situation continued for two decades as the rental housing market absorbed the boomers. Then the rental market crashed in the late 1980s when the busters appeared. The first of the echo generation start to leave home and enter the rental housing market at the turn of the century, at which time demand will increase again, resulting in falling vacancies and rising rents; but this will be nothing like the boom of the 1970s and 1980s, because the echo generation is noticeably smaller than the baby boom generation.

The next logical step in life is to an owner-occupied dwelling. Demand from front-end boomers started rising by the early 1980s and then burst forward over the mid-1980s. A housing boom appeared as much of the baby boom attempted to secure their homes at the same time. It should have continued into the early 1990s, but an economic recession cut it short. The demand appeared from the tail-end boomers, often called Gen-Xers, in the late 1990s, which is why pressures for more suburban developments did not disappear until the end of the decade. Thereafter, the busters enter the housing market, and here the story becomes familiar. Zoning, land use, sewerage, and transportation planning, for example, should reflect these predictable demographic trends.

Transportation

The peak use of public transportation occurs in the late teenage years, when individuals are independent enough to move around on their own but before they have purchased their own automobiles. Moreover, public transportation is relatively cheap, and money is certainly scarce when a person is young. By their thirties, individuals have probably married, moved out to the suburbs, started a family, and are commuting to the office. Time is at a premium. The automobile offers a faster, usually more comfortable, and much more flexible commute compared to public transportation.

Over the 1960s and 1970s, the boomers were young and using public transportation. Then in the 1980s, they started moving out to the suburbs, raising families, and commuting by automobile to work. The growth in demand for public transit ceased, and in many communities, public transit use declined and the roads became crowded. This is the pervasive impact of demographics once more. The decrease in demand for public transit has little to do with the prices of bus, rail, or subway tickets or of gasoline. And the 'problem' cannot be solved by attempting to modify behaviour regarding auto use, including car pools, or by building more bicycle paths. Regardless of their obvious environmental benefits, neither provides a necessary service or a quality transportation medium, which is what the aging and busy boomers require.

This does not mean that public transit had no future, because in the mid-1990s, the echo generation started to enter their prime transit-using ages, which gradually stimulated demand in a system operating well below capacity. As a result, it is important to invest in maintenance but not in new capacity, except in those areas where it can be justified. The peak of the echo generation reach their late teens toward the end of the first decade of the new millennium, after which public transit will once again be challenged. Meanwhile, the aging boomers, driving their families and themselves, are crowding the roads and are becoming 'eyesight-challenged', which will increase the demand for larger and clearer road signs, not to mention large print maps and so forth.

Crime and Drugs

Most crime is committed by teenagers. Consequently, communities with higher shares of teens in their populations generally experience higher crime rates. As the criminal ages, criminal activity generally declines but the crimes become more serious. Consequently, as the boomers aged through their youth ages over the 1960s and 1970s, the crime rate increased. Then in the mid-1980s, as the boomers aged further, the crime rate stabilized; and in the 1990s, it started to decline in many communities. Not surprisingly, however, the crimes that were committed were more serious; for example, armed robbery replaced breaking and entering. These trends had little to do with the quality of law enforcement in the community. Once again, the subtle influence of demographics was at work.

What is the outlook for the future? Because the echo generation began entering their youth ages in the mid-1990s, a return to a rising crime rate would not be surprising. Meanwhile, the aging boomers, who can no longer run as fast, move into 'white collar' crimes; credit-card and other types of fraud are on the rise. These trends have numerous implications for policing policies. For example, given these trends, law enforcement training in forensic accounting would seem to be advisable.

Just as with criminal activity, there is a life cycle in drug use. Glue sniffing is followed by 'soft' drugs, which in turn are followed by 'hard' drugs. Hence, the boomers were sniffing glue in the 1960s, smoking pot in the 1970s, and shooting crack in the 1980s. However, the drug preferences of those in their forties moves away from illegal drugs to legal drugs, such as tranquilizers and sleeping pills. If this pattern remains, the 'drug problem' gradually moves off the streets and into the traditional health care system, that is, from an illegal problem to a legal problem. While this may be pushing the application of demographic life-cycle analysis to its extremes, these trends have quite dramatic implications for the direction of policies related to drugs. In this case, both the policing and the health care sectors are directly involved.

Leisure and Recreation

A general finding in most research on leisure and recreation activities is that individuals do less of everything the older they become. In addition, the nature of the activity gradually changes with age. Recreational activity tends to move from arenas and tennis courts to gardens and birding preserves. It also moves from popular music to symphonic music and from rock concerts to musicals. Therefore, a population filled with young people will be more sports-oriented and less culture-oriented than an older community. In general, population aging is gradually moving the nation and its communities away from sports and toward more cultural activities. Theatres and museums are becoming of increasing interest to the aging boomers in their forties and fifties as they gradually slow down physically and spend time educating their growing families. Football, volleyball, and hockey are being replaced by golf, darts, and curling. Running is being replaced by walking. Gender bonding for men increasingly takes place at the hunting lodge not at the hockey arena and, for women, at the ballet or opera.

The implications of these trends for both private and public policies are dramatic. It is better to be selling golf clubs than tennis racquets. It is better to be constructing walking trails that can double as birding and cross-country trails than to be constructing new arenas, football fields, or downhill-skiing slopes. More of the recreational budget should be directed to local cultural facilities, such as theatres, museums, and music halls. It is also important to maintain the sports facilities for use by the echo generation, but the impact of this generation on the growth in recreational demand is not likely to be so large or so noticeable as that of the boomers, who are moving into more sedate activities as they age.

Health Care

One policy area that has received increased attention from a demographic perspective is health care. By the late 1970s, policy analysts and governments became increasingly aware of the impacts of population aging on health care costs. Because, on average, people in their senior ages make greater per capita use of physicians, hospitals, and drugs, it became increasingly apparent that an aging population would make greater demands on these programs in the future. By the mid-1990s, this emerged as a major topic of Canadian public policy. The debate has many dimensions: what services should be covered (the public–private mix debate), at what cost (the user-fees debate), and who should be covered (the universality debate)?

Regardless of the outcome of these important discussions, it is clear that communities with higher senior dependency ratios are likely to find health care issues to have higher priority in their discussions and budgets than are communities with lower senior dependency ratios. Moreover, these discussions are likely to transcend the traditional health care sector and move into housing policies, such as the location of retirement homes and villages, and community service policies, including such programs as home care, meals on wheels, and other senior-support programs.

Seniors are not the only users of the health care system. Communities with high birth rates also need health care services, both pre- and post-natal, although, in general, these needs will be relatively less important in the future. Although often delivered in the same facilities, the type of services required by the various users are quite different from those needed by seniors. The service mix will need to change in an aging population. Once again, demographic dependency ratios can provide a general guide, but relevant programs need to be tailored to the specific needs of each community. There is no doubt, however, that population aging is likely to place upward pressure on health care service provision and costs in all communities in the years ahead, although the major impact is still more than a decade into the new millennium when the boomers reach their senior years.

Conclusions

Changes in demographics affect many urban policies. A review of the age structure of the population, characterized in Canada by the baby boom, baby bust, and echo generations, reveals both similarities and differences between urban communities and their needs. All communities in Canada are experiencing the effects of an aging population, but some communities are much younger than others. A convenient overview can be obtained using demographic dependency ratios, but the implications of these data for program policies are best seen by examining individual program areas. A variety of program areas, from housing to health care, from daycare to drugs, and from education to recreation, provide illustrative examples of the application of demographics to urban policy issues. In all cases, both a retrospective and a prospective analysis are possible. Demographic life-cycle projections based on the truisms that 'every year a person gets one year older' and that average people 'tend to act their age' provide the urban policy-maker with a firm foundation for historical analysis and a future vision.

Notes

1. The author thanks Tom McCormack of Strategic Projections Inc. for useful discussions and the preparation of Table 2.2. Thanks are also extended to Richard Loreto and to the editors for their helpful comments in the preparation of this chapter.
2. The peak number of births in Canada occurred in 1959, but subsequent augmentation of the population by immigrants, who tend to be younger, has moved the peak back two years. So it is often convenient to use 1960 (the average) as indicative of the peak of the baby boom generation.
3. In Ontario and western Canada, the echo generation lasts into the mid-1990s and, therefore, is relatively larger in these regions.

4. Another dip occurs for those aged 59 years in 1996, who were born in 1937.
5. These CMA data are supplied by Tom McCormack of Strategic Projections Inc. (2000) and are adjusted for the census undercount, estimated at 2.86 per cent for Canada in 1996. These upward adjustments occur primarily to those of working age.
6. Statistics Canada does not make adjusted data publicly available for non-CMAs. Consequently, to be comparable, these dependency ratios are calculated with unadjusted data and are slightly higher than those reported previously (see note 5).

References

Foot, David K. 1982. *Canada's Population Outlook: Demographic Futures and Economic Challenges.* Toronto: Lorimer for the Canadian Institute for Economic Policy.

———. 1984. 'The Demographic Future of Fiscal Federalism in Canada'. *Canadian Public Policy* 10: 406–14.

———. 1989. 'Public Expenditures, Population Aging and Economic Dependency in Canada, 1921–2021'. *Population Research and Policy Review* 8: 97–117.

Foot, David K., with D. Stoffman. 1996. *Boom, Bust & Echo: How to Profit from the Coming Demographic Shift.* Toronto: Macfarlane Walter & Ross.

———. 1998. *Boom, Bust & Echo 2000: Profiting from the Demographic Shift in the New Millennium.* Toronto: Macfarlane Walter & Ross.

Strategic Projections Inc. 2000. *Tomorrow's Markets Today 2000: Canada's Metropolitan Area Prospects to 2021.* Oakville, ON: Strategic Projections Inc.

CHAPTER 3

Urban Finance at the Turn of the Century: Be Careful What You Wish For

David Siegel

Introduction

I guess we all remember our parents threatening us with the old saying 'Be careful what you wish for: you might get it'. The last decade of the twentieth century saw a major change in the provincial–municipal relationship, particularly as manifested in the financial relationship between the two levels of government. As a result of these changes, municipalities have now received at least a part of what they were wishing for and are left wondering if they really wanted it. This chapter will argue that these major changes in provincial–municipal financial and other relationships will be a major boon for municipalities in the long run, although they are causing a great deal of pain in the short term.

Municipalities have always wanted more control over their own destinies. Particularly, they have wanted to have more autonomy in delivering services as they saw fit without having to labour under the constraints imposed by conditional grants and other forms of provincial controls. The 1990s saw a reduction in the level of provincial grants that has disentangled the provincial–municipal relationship somewhat, although at least some local governments wish that they had not been so successful in liberating themselves from provincial funding assistance. This trend varies somewhat by province; but for reasons that will be discussed later in this chapter, almost all provinces have been reducing their transfers to local governments, although they are doing it in different ways and at differing speeds.

This chapter will begin by discussing where local government fits in the overall system of public finance. The next two sections will discuss sources of local revenue and objects of expenditure. The final section will analyze trends identified in the first two sections to determine their effect on the future of local government.

Local Government in the Intergovernmental Context

Figure 3.1 provides a historical overview of expenditures of all three levels of government as a percentage of gross domestic product (GDP). GDP is a measure of the size of the total Canadian economy. Looking at government expenditure as a percentage of GDP is more illuminating than looking at dollar figures because the GDP measure shows how the size of government has changed in relation to the total Canadian economy. Focusing on changes in dollars can be misleading because these figures are influenced by inflation and changes in total population.

Figure 3.1 indicates that the increase in the size of government in the post-war period can be attributed almost entirely to the growth of the federal and provincial governments. Local government grew slightly at the beginning of this period but has levelled off since then. This graph also indicates that local government has played a relatively limited role in the overall governmental scene as measured by expenditure. This will likely change somewhat because of the provincial downloading of some service responsibilities, as discussed in this chapter.

Sources of Revenue

Figure 3.2 shows the sources of local government revenue. The three main sources have always been the property tax, user charges, and transfers from provincial gov-

Figure 3.1: Government Expenditure as Percentage of GDP

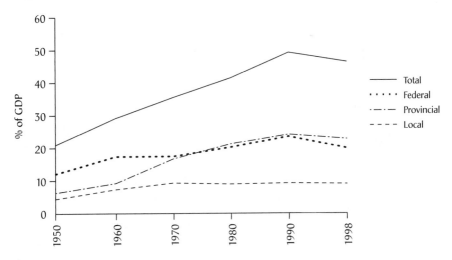

Source: Karin Treff and David B. Perry. 1999. *Finances of the Nation.* Toronto: Canadian Tax Foundation.

Figure 3.2: Sources of Local Revenue

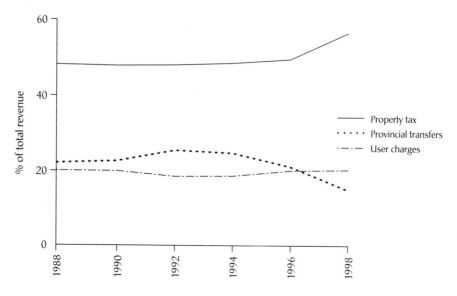

Source: CANSIM matrix numbers 7093–7100 and 8489–91.

ernments, but the relative importance of these sources has changed rather dramatically over the relatively short period shown in the graph. Funding from provincial governments has fallen significantly in the last few years, and the main source that has been used to make up that reduction has been the property tax. Property tax and user charges are commonly called *own source revenue* because municipalities have direct control over the level of these sources. This differs from provincial transfers, for which municipalities are at the mercy of provincial policies. Although local governments can lobby to receive more provincial funds, the provincial government makes the final decision. There are also, however, practical and political limits on the level of control that local governments have over own source revenue. Local media and taxpayers generally watch closely the taxation levels in other municipalities; these serve as political limitations on local decisions about own source revenue.

The figures for all ten provinces can sometimes mask major differences between provinces; but, in this case, the trend lines are fairly similar for all provinces except Quebec and Manitoba. In Manitoba, there was virtually no change in the relative shares of revenue from 1988 to 1998. Quebec was the only province in which there was an increase in the proportion of local revenue provided by provincial transfers.

The reduction in provincial transfers is the result of a series of events that started in the mid-1980s. At that time, the federal government was beginning to feel a great deal of pressure to reduce its deficit. One of the first places the federal minister of finance looked for expenditure reduction was federal transfer payments to the provinces. This was an attractive course for the federal government because it would not have to bear the direct consequences of these reductions itself and most provinces were in a fairly good economic position.

When the shock hit the provinces, they had to find ways to reduce their expenditures. Provincial treasurers then did to municipalities what the federal government had done to the provinces: reduce transfer payments. Figure 3.3 illustrates why cutting back on payments to municipalities was attractive. From the 1950s to the mid-1980s, local governments had collectively registered very small deficits,[1] but this turned around to surpluses from the mid-1980s onward. In other words, local governments were in quite a good financial condition compared to senior levels of government, which were fighting years of accumulated deficits. On the one hand, local governments should be congratulated for their fiscal responsibility. On the other hand, the price of their fiscal responsibility was that they were vulnerable to provincial cutbacks, because they could bear them better than other levels of government. It was this dynamic involving all three levels of government that led to the decrease in provincial transfers and the relative increase in the importance of the property tax.

Property Tax

Property tax is imposed on all real property, that is, on land and buildings, but not on personal property, such as equipment, vehicles, and store fixtures. The property

Figure 3.3: Local Government Revenue and Expenditure

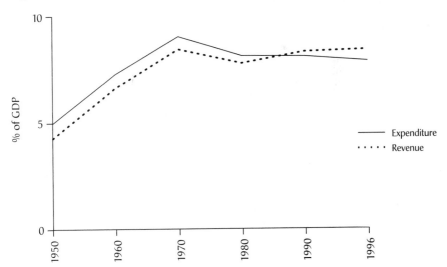

Source: Karin Treff and David B. Perry. 1999. *Finances of the Nation.* Toronto: Canadian Tax Foundation.

tax is a major source of revenue for local governments, and it has also been a very controversial form of taxation in recent years. This section will first review the mechanics of calculating the tax and determining the tax base and then proceed to a discussion of some of the controversial aspects of the property tax.

Calculation of the tax

The calculation of the property tax is really quite simple. First, an *assessed value* is determined for each property in the municipality. Next, each year the council strikes a *mill rate*, which is applied to the assessed value; the result is the amount of tax payable in that year. The mill rate is so called because it is expressed as a certain number of mills (one-tenth of a cent) per dollar of assessed valuation. Alternatively, some people view the mill rate as dollars per thousand dollars of assessed value. Mathematically, either calculation produces the same result.

The assessment system

Assessment is the assigning of a value to a particular property. The usual principle is that the assessed value of a property is its fair market value (i.e., the price determined by a willing buyer and a willing seller operating at arm's length), although this section will discuss a number of quirks in the assessment system.

In most provinces, properties are divided into three broad categories: residential, commercial/industrial, and farm. The effect of most provincial systems is that commercial/industrial properties bear a greater property tax burden than residential or farm properties. The situation in British Columbia is fairly typical in that the property tax is applied to 100 per cent of the value of commercial/industrial properties but to only 50 per cent of the value of residential properties (Kitchen 1992).

There seem to be two rationales for this favouritism. It could be purely political in that it is an attempt to favour residential property owners who are voters. Or it could be explained by the fact that property taxes on commercial and industrial properties are deductible as expenses for income tax purposes, whereas individual homeowners enjoy no such benefit.

Farmland is assessed on the basis of its value for farm purposes rather than on its potential value in its highest possible use, which would sometimes be as fully developed land, that is, subdivisions. There is frequently a big difference between the actual and the potential value of farmland. Assessment at the farm use value reduces the farmer's taxation and reduces the pressure to convert from farm to other uses, which is a way of preserving farmland, or at least slowing its conversion to more developed uses.

Property assessment is usually done by a provincial department or a semi-autonomous agency, although a few of the large cities in some provinces handle their own assessment. Provincial assessment ensures that there is a uniform basis of assessment throughout an entire province.

Ontario had severe problems with its assessment system in the recent past because it allowed the system to get out of date, which created serious problems in that properties were not assessed on an equitable basis (Ontario, Fair Tax Commission 1993;

Soroka and Spiece 1995). When it tried to update the system, which was as much as fifty years out of date in some places, there were major political repercussions from people who saw sudden increases in their tax bills. The province has now updated the system, but there is a lesson here: it is easier to maintain a fair assessment system on an ongoing basis than to play catch-up when a system has been allowed to fall out of date. There will be a more in-depth evaluation of the efficacy of the property tax system later in this chapter, but the system certainly has the ability to achieve equitable results if the assessment system is fair and up-to-date.

Exempt properties

Not all properties are subject to taxation. The specific exemptions vary by province, but they generally relate to property owned and used by governments and by educational, charitable, and religious institutions (Kitchen 1992). Property of the federal government is exempt from all provincial and municipal taxation because, under the terms of the Constitution Act, no other government can impose a tax on the federal government. In all provinces except Prince Edward Island, provincial property is also exempt under terms of provincial legislation. Property owned by charitable and religious institutions and used for charitable or religious purposes has traditionally been provided an exemption because these organizations are usually considered to be deserving of government support.

Federal and provincial governments normally make a voluntary payment to local governments, referred to as a *grant* or *payment in lieu of taxes*. Municipalities frequently complain that this payment is not equal to the full amount of taxes that would have been imposed on the property. This concern has heightened in recent years as both federal and provincial governments have made major cutbacks in the level of these grants. Charitable and religious organizations do not provide such payments.

Exempt property does not just reduce a municipality's tax take; it can also create inefficient land use patterns. Organizations that benefit from exemptions feel little pressure to economize on the use of even very expensive land. Municipalities have argued that the tax exemption for some organizations ought to be terminated and replaced by cash grants. If this were to happen, these exempt organizations would probably find ways of using less (or less-expensive) land in order to reduce their property tax burden. In turn, municipalities would benefit from the release of new land for development purposes. For practical political reasons, this is unlikely to occur. Providing overt subsidies to religious organizations would be such a contentious activity that politicians would rather these subsidies remain hidden like they currently are.

The benefits of the property tax

The property tax has traditionally been a very attractive tax for local governments. It is efficient to administer because it attaches to the land and buildings and so is virtually impossible for taxpayers to evade. The property tax is also easy to compute, which makes it easy for taxpayers to understand, compared to the income tax, for example.

One traditional theoretical justification for the property tax flows from a distinction between services to property and services to people. The argument is that the property tax should bear the cost of services to property, that is, 'hard' services, such as sewers, water, and roads. The rationale for this is that provision of these services increases the value of property; therefore, the cost of providing them ought to fall on the property benefited. The corollary to this is that services to people, that is, 'soft' services, such as education, health, and social services, should be funded through income-based taxes, which have a greater ability to redistribute income.

The difficulty with this argument is that all services are ultimately services for people. Making the distinction between services to people and services to property is not always an easy task. For example, education would seem to be a classic service to people, but a glance at the 'House for Sale' listings in the newspaper suggests that proximity to a school will increase the value of a property.

Another argument in favour of the property tax stems from the adage that 'an old tax is a good tax'. This has two complementary interpretations. One is that taxpayers have become accustomed to an old tax and so will offer less political resistance to it than to a new form of taxation. The second, economic interpretation of this statement is that old taxes have become built into price and market structures over time. New taxes can have unpredictable consequences on prices and markets. In short, there are a number of factors that make the property tax a very attractive tax, but there have been some problems with its use in the last few years.

Level of the property tax

A great many taxpayers complain about the amount of the property tax and its presumed escalation in recent years. However, perceptions are not always reality. Many people are keenly aware of the increase in the dollar amount of the property tax but forget that some of that increase is caused by inflation and so could be offset by increases in their incomes. A more meaningful way of considering levels of the property tax would be to relate it to ability to pay as measured by personal income. Figure 3.4 indicates that property tax declined slightly as a percentage of personal income in the latter part of the period from 1992 to 1997.

The high level of dissatisfaction voiced about the property tax likely stems from the fact that it is a highly visible tax that must be paid in a lump sum, unlike federal and provincial taxes, which are either deducted at source before taxpayers are aware they have the money (income tax) or paid daily in such small amounts that no one is aware of the total annual amount paid (federal GST and provincial sales taxes). You might try an experiment with people you know who own property: ask them if they know how much property tax they pay to the nearest ten dollars; they will likely know exactly. Then ask them if they know how much federal income tax they pay to the nearest thousand dollars. Not many people know that because it is deducted at source. This difference in visibility is one reason why there is so much more resistance to the property tax than to other taxes.

Incidence of the property tax: regressive, proportional, or progressive?

The incidence of the property tax has been another source of controversy. *Incidence* refers to the technical question of who actually bears the burden of a particular tax.

Incidence can be very difficult to determine because the people who ultimately bear the tax are not necessarily those who pay it in the first place. For example, manufacturers must pay an income tax on their profits, but the amount of that tax is usually added to the price of the product, so that the ultimate consumer really bears the cost of the corporation income tax. In economic parlance, the manufacturer pays the tax, but the incidence of the tax falls on the final consumer.

A *regressive tax* is a tax that falls proportionally more heavily on low-income taxpayers.[2] Conversely, a *progressive tax* falls proportionally more heavily on high-income taxpayers. For example, on the surface, the income tax is a progressive tax because higher incomes are taxed at higher rates than lower incomes. A *proportional* tax is borne equally by taxpayers in all income groups. It is usually argued that progressive forms of taxation are more desirable than regressive ones because progressive taxes involve a redistribution from the rich to the poor.

Traditionally, the property tax has been considered to be regressive because regardless of how low a person's income is, he or she must still purchase some minimum amount of shelter. A person pays the property tax either directly to the municipality (if he or she owns the property) or indirectly when the landlord adds in the property tax to arrive at the monthly rent. In economic terms, this scenario assumes that the landlord is able to shift the tax to the renter. The argument continues that as a person's income increases, he or she spends a lower percentage of income on shelter, which is taxable, and more on luxuries, such as yachts or jewellery, which do not attract an annual tax. Thus, the argument goes that the property tax ought to be minimized because it is regressive.

There have been several empirical studies of this question (Bird and Slack 1978). The basic problem in arriving at a conclusion about the regressivity of the property

Figure 3.4: Property Tax as a Percentage of Personal Income

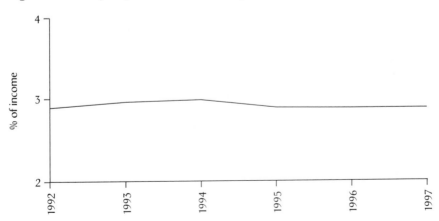

Source: CANSIM matrix numbers 7093–7100 and 8489–91.

tax is that no definitive answer is available about the question of shifting. For example, sometimes the entity that pays the tax is able to shift the real burden of the tax to someone else as when a manufacturing company factors the cost of the property tax into the prices it charges for its goods. A comprehensive study by Meng and Gillespie (1986) suggested that the property tax is generally regressive over all income levels and in all regions of the country. A more recent study, which deals only with Ontario, arrives at the same conclusion (Ontario, Fair Tax Commission 1993).

The public policy implications of this question are enormous. One of the strongest arguments that local politicians have made against the property tax is that it is regressive and that society ought not rely too heavily on a regressive form of taxation. If, however, the property tax is actually progressive or proportional, then it becomes a very attractive form of taxation because of its ease of administration.

Sharing the property tax base

Another problem with the property tax is that a number of different units of local government must share the same tax base. In a few provinces, this includes the provincial government, but more generally it would include a metropolitan or regional government, a lower-tier municipal government, several school boards, and possibly some other special purpose bodies. Each of these bodies can have the right to impose a property tax without consulting any of the other organizations.

This problem is particularly acute for the lower-tier municipalities, because they must usually collect taxes on behalf of the other units. This creates confusion in the minds of the general public and forces lower-tier municipal governments to shoulder much of the blame for tax increases that are actually the shared responsibility of several governments.

The consequences of the property tax

The property tax is by far the largest tax over which councillors have control. Because councillors want to avoid increasing the tax rate, the only way to increase the yield of the tax is to increase the assessment base. Councillors' sometimes desperate attempts to do this can have undesirable consequences: they begin to feel that any form of development on any terms is desirable. This view is supplemented by a general bias in favour of growth as a measure of how well a council is performing.

Councillors who follow this line of thinking are implicitly assuming that municipal expenditure is a fixed amount and that any increase in assessment will spread this fixed expense over a larger base and so reduce the taxes of all ratepayers. The obvious flaw in this logic is that the presence of additional properties using municipal services will normally (although admittedly not always) increase the expenditure side of the budget as well as the revenue side (Kushner 1992).

The overwhelming desire on the part of councils to maximize the assessment base can be dysfunctional in a number of ways. In some provinces, municipalities can provide bonuses to taxpayers in the form of tax reductions or sale of land at less than market value. Where this is not legal, municipalities are frequently pressured to bend zoning requirements or waive various rules to encourage development. The excessive desire on the part of some municipalities to maximize assessment can lead to bad decision-making. For example, it can lead to too much commercial and industrial zoning in inappropriate locations.

The property tax has been the topic of much debate and criticism, not all of it particularly enlightened. There are some advantages to the use of the property tax, and some of the disadvantages have been overstated. However, considering the strength of the criticism, it is not surprising that local governments have begun to search for other sources of revenue.

User Charges

User charges are fees imposed on users of services where the fee imposed bears some relation to the benefit enjoyed. The most obvious examples are transit fares, water rates, sewer charges, and fees to use recreational facilities. These have traditionally been a rather limited source of local government revenue, but councils seem to be turning to them more frequently in recent years as a response to financial restraint (Ridler 1984). In some cases, user charges are being imposed for the first time for services that had previously been considered 'free'.[3] In other cases, charges that were simply token amounts have been increased to reflect the full cost of providing the service.

Bird and Tsiopoulos have argued that 'whenever it is possible and appropriate public services should be charged for rather than given away. The main economic reasons for levying user charges on the direct recipients (whether individuals or businesses) of benefits from particular public services is to make governments' use of scarce public resources more efficient' (1997: 36). They argue that user charges promote efficiency in two ways: '(1) by providing information to public sector suppliers about how much clients are actually willing to pay for particular services and (2) by ensuring that citizens value what the public sector supplies at least at its (marginal) cost' (Bird and Tsiopoulos 1997: 36).

User charges promote economic efficiency because they act as signalling devices to local councils to identify which services are in greatest demand. Where services are provided free, the demand is likely to be unlimited; the imposition of some price helps to determine whether people are really interested enough in a service to pay for it.

User charges can also be used to influence citizens' behaviour and to ration the use of resources. A classic example is the recent interest that many municipalities have taken in charging for the collection and disposal of solid waste. If people must pay for each bag of garbage they deposit at the curb, then they will be more likely to recycle or to take other measures that will lengthen the life of municipal landfill sites.

However, there are also certain negative aspects of user charges. Charging for solid waste disposal can lead to more illegal roadside dumping. User charges for municipal services such as recreational facilities can be a political minefield. In some municipalities, sports groups, such as hockey and softball leagues, are very well organized and are in a good position to bring strong pressure to bear on councillors who want to increase user charges. Even focusing on unorganized groups can be dysfunctional. Who wants to be responsible for beginning to charge six-year-olds to use the municipal swimming pool?

Probably one of the greatest concerns about user charges is their distributional effects. Some services are provided by government precisely because society does not like the distribution of the good that would occur if it were provided on an ability-to-pay basis. For example, if families were forced to purchase education for their children, some would not be able to afford it. Most would agree that this circumstance is undesirable.

In sum, user charges can be desirable from both equity and efficiency viewpoints and as a source of new funds, but they have serious distributional consequences. Politicians have learned that they must proceed very carefully in this area because of the strength of some organized groups.

Development Charges

Some provinces allow municipalities to impose development charges or lot levies on new properties as they are being developed. New development imposes a significant cost on the municipality in terms of roads, sewer and water mains, parks, and other hard services. Large developments will also require new schools, community centres, libraries, and fire and police stations. These costs could simply be added to the property tax and be paid for by all ratepayers in the municipality. The purpose of development charges is to impose those costs on the developer instead. The development charge will usually be stated as a certain amount per lot, or it could be based on the frontage of the lot. It is set at a level to cover the cost of providing the service.

The charge is levied on the developer in the first place, but it will usually be added to the cost of the lot and passed on to the ultimate purchaser. This increases the cost of the lot and drives up the cost of housing and commercial development. For this reason, some municipalities reduce or waive this charge as a way of encouraging development. Although waiving development charges will almost certainly be successful in reducing the cost of developed land, it will impose an additional tax burden on all ratepayers in the municipality because someone must pay for the new infrastructure.

Development charges have been quite contentious in some municipalities. On the one hand, the municipality would like to maximize the amount of the charge in order to cover the full cost of new services. On the other hand, developers see development charges as an onerous burden that either reduces their profits or increases the price of their products. Even though development charges are not a major source of revenue for the entire municipal system, they are an important way for a growing municipality to offset the high cost of infrastructure associated with rapid growth.

Transfer Payments

Transfer payments are payments that are made to local governments by federal or provincial governments and that are not made for the provision of any current good or service; the government providing the transfer payment is receiving nothing in exchange and is under no legal obligation to make the payment. Because the federal government has only limited contacts with local governments, most transfer payments are provided by provincial governments.

There are two types of transfer. *Unconditional transfers* can be used for any purpose desired by the recipient government. *Conditional transfers* can be used only for the purposes specified by the government providing the transfer.

There are a number of rationales for these transfers (Boadway 1980). The main rationale for unconditional transfers is simply to deal with the inability of local governments to raise enough funds to cover their cost of operations. This is why these types of transfers frequently have equalization factors to provide more funding to municipalities with lower resource bases. The level of unconditional grants has traditionally been quite low compared to that of conditional grants.

Conditional transfers are provided to local governments with strings attached. At minimum, the grant must be spend on the identified service, but there are frequently other conditions, such as maintaining minimum standards for the service, providing an accounting for funds spent, and so forth.

The main rationale for the use of conditional transfers is to compensate a municipality for interjurisdictional spillovers or for externalities that occur when expenditures made by one locality benefit other jurisdictions. Some examples are the cost of educating a young person who then moves to another area and the cost of pollution control that benefits downstream municipalities. Municipal councillors are understandably reluctant to spend money on programs that benefit other jurisdictions; however, the provincial government is aware that these expenditures are necessary for the good of the entire province. The higher level of government, therefore, provides a conditional transfer to offset this spillover and so encourage municipalities to spend more on the service.

Provincial governments also use conditional grants to encourage or enforce standardization of services across the entire province. Following this rationale, provincial transfers are used to encourage municipalities to provide services up to a provincially defined standard level. An example of this would be a transfer payment for roads that a municipality would receive only if it maintained its system up to the provincial standard.

The final rationale is to encourage municipalities to undertake new initiatives. In some cases, this is just a matter of smoothing over a situation in which a province wants municipalities to do something that the province is unwilling to fund in its entirety. Grants to encourage municipal involvement in recycling are examples of this.

One of the major problems with provincial transfers, from the standpoint of municipalities, is that the province has absolute control over the level of these payments so that the level can change significantly without warning from one year to the next. In the past few years, provincial governments have dealt with their financial problems by reducing transfer payments to municipalities. These cutbacks are attractive from the standpoint of the provinces because they do not have a direct impact on services provided by the province, but they play havoc with the ability of municipalities to engage in long-term planning.

Local governments are always pleased to receive funds, but conditional transfer payments are sometimes a mixed blessing. One of the most frequent complaints is that conditional transfers skew the priorities of the recipient government. For example, where the province shares 75 per cent of the cost of a program, the argument is usually made that the program is really spending only 'twenty-five cents', that is, that each twenty-five cents of municipal expenditure results in one dollar of total expenditure on the program. This makes programs that receive conditional transfers more attractive than those that do not. And this, in turn, means that municipal governments sometimes bend their priorities to attract these transfer payments.

When this occurs, municipalities are vulnerable to shifts in provincial priorities. The provincial government could be very interested in a program for a number of years and encourage municipalities to develop extensive delivery systems on which local citizens become dependent. Later, provincial priorities could change, resulting in a reduction or total withdrawal of provincial funding for this service. The municipality, however, cannot shift gears so easily because it has an extensive delivery system in place and a clientele that has come to rely on the service. Thus, the municipality must continue to provide the service without provincial assistance.

This points to another problem with conditional transfers: they tend to muddle accountability. Stripped of all the administrative niceties, a transfer payment is basically one level of government spending money that was raised by another level of government. If the service is not provided properly, whose fault is it? Did the government making the transfer provide too little funding or impose inappropriate conditions? Or did the recipient government use the funds unwisely? It is very difficult for a citizen to know which government should be held accountable for problems.

There can also be significant administrative costs associated with conditional transfers. Municipalities must maintain records to prove that they have spent the funds in accordance with the sometimes very detailed conditions of the program. Then the provincial government must establish a group of auditors and program specialists to check up on municipalities to ensure that they are complying with the conditions of the transfer. Conditional grants can be difficult and expensive to administer for both levels of government.

New Revenue Sources

Revenue sources other than property taxes, user fees, and grants have been explored, but the small size of municipalities eliminates some potential taxes because they can be avoided too easily. For example, a municipal sales tax would simply encourage people to shop in neighbouring municipalities with a lower tax rate or no tax whatsoever. A tax on hotels and amusements seems very attractive at first because most of it would be paid by non-residents of the community; the problem is that it could cause tourists to avoid the community. Likewise, a municipal income tax could cause people to shun living in a community, and it also raises assessment and collection problems. Municipalities receive limited revenue from the licensing of ventures related to the recent increasing interest in gambling; however, most of this rapidly increasing source of revenue has been appropriated by the provinces. For example, municipalities get a portion of bingo funds, but provinces receive most of the revenue from casinos.

Municipalities are looking for additional sources of revenue, but provincial rules and more practical problems of avoidance make it difficult to identify lucrative new sources of revenue.

Objects of Expenditure

An examination of expenditure is a good place to look at the different sizes of local governments in the different provinces. Figure 3.5 shows the per capita municipal expenditure in each province. The use of per capita figures illustrates the different sizes of the local sector in the various provinces. For example, it is clear that the local government sector provides more services in Ontario, Alberta, and British Columbia than it does in Newfoundland, Prince Edward Island, and New Brunswick. Some of the variance among provinces is caused by the disparity in the wealth of provinces and by the differences in demographic factors discussed by Foot in his chapter; however, most of the variation is reflective of different divisions of responsibilities between local and provincial governments in different provinces. In some provinces, local governments have a major role in providing services; in other provinces, the provincial role is so significant that there is less scope for local government activity.

Figures 3.6a and 3.6b illustrate the relative expenditure by local governments on various services. There is greater disparity among provinces on the expenditure side than on the revenue side, but some generalizations can be made when Ontario is treated separately. Figure 3.6a shows the level of expenditures for all provinces excluding Ontario.

The two major areas of expenditure are environment and roads. Environment expenditures are predominately on sewers, water, and solid waste. These two classic

Figure 3.5: Per Capita Municipal Expenditure, 1998

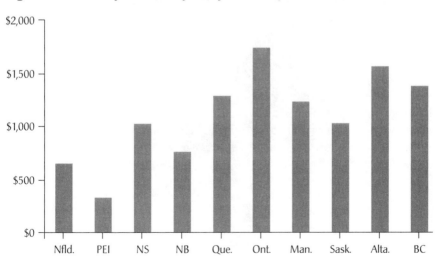

Source: CANSIM matrix numbers 7093–7100 and 8489–91.

Figure 3.6a: Municipal Expenditure, 1998 (Excluding Ontario)

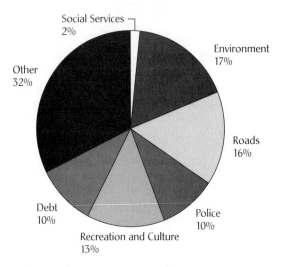

Source: CANSIM matrix numbers 7093–7100 and 8489–91.

hard services constitute about one-third of total local government expenditure. Recreation and culture is the third-largest category, and it has been one of the fastest-growing areas. This reflects a changing role that citizens see for local government. Police and fire also account for major portions of local expenditure, but these have

Figure 3.6b: Municipal Expenditure, 1998 (Ontario)

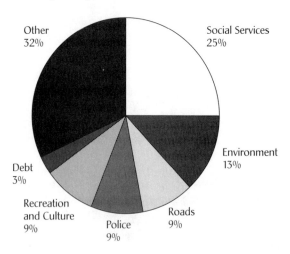

Source: CANSIM matrix numbers 7093–7100 and 8489–91.

not been growing in recent years. Debt services includes both interest and payments on principal; this percentage is considerably lower that the comparable figure for the federal and most provincial governments.

The Ontario situation as depicted in Figure 3.6b is similar, with one major exception: Ontario is the only province in which local governments are still expected to provide a significant contribution to social assistance expenditures. In all other provinces, most or all of such expenditures are funded by the province. Social assistance accounts for the single largest expenditure by Ontario municipalities: one-quarter of total expenditure. When this difference is accounted for, the remainder of the picture for Ontario is similar to other provinces. However, debt is also considerably lower in Ontario than in the composite of the other nine provinces.

This provides a quick overview of levels of expenditure. Most of the services mentioned will be discussed in more detail later in the various chapters of this book.

The Future of Local Government

This chapter has referred to a number of major changes in the provincial–municipal relationship. Figure 3.2 illustrated the shift away from provincial transfers as a revenue source and the attendant need for additional own source revenue to fill the gap. Another major shift has been the transfer of services between the provincial and local levels of government. This has occurred so recently that its effect does not appear in the graphs, but future analyses will probably show significant shifts in levels of expenditure. The avowed purpose of these shifts has been to disentangle provincial–municipal relations and to shift responsibility for a service to the level of government that is best able to deliver it. For example, in Ontario, the provincial government is now funding a much higher portion of education expenditure, but municipalities will be responsible for a variety of services, such as ambulance service and social housing, that were formerly funded by the province.

This shift of responsibilities has led to considerable tension between provincial and local governments; the Ontario government contends that the shift is revenue-neutral and uses phrases like 'service exchange' or 'local service realignment', whereas local governments question whether this is revenue-neutral and complain of downloading. These shifts are causing local governments a great deal of stress as they restructure themselves to deal with the major reduction in funding and the major increase in responsibilities. This restructuring has taken the form of amalgamations, such as those discussed in Sancton's chapter, as well as internal re-engineering in some municipalities.

It will take some years for the outcomes of the various initiatives to be determined; however, this short-term pain might be beneficial in the long run for both municipalities and citizens. It is nice to receive the funds associated with conditional grants, as municipalities have for so many years, but these grants bring several problems with them: they skew the priorities of the recipient government; they can be expensive to administer; and from the standpoint of citizens, they muddle accountability. The greater reliance by municipalities on own source revenue will give them greater control over their own futures.

The service exchange between the two levels of government can result in a better allocation of responsibilities, although there are still some problems. The fact that Ontario municipalities are still responsible for social services is one glaring example of a misallocation of responsibilities. Still, the service exchange has resulted in improvements.

It will require some time to determine the overall impact of these major changes; however, it seems already that the disentanglement and the greater reliance by local governments on own source revenue should provide local governments with considerably more autonomy. This autonomy is both an opportunity and a challenge. At the opening of this chapter, I referred to the expression 'Be careful what you wish for, you might get it'. Municipalities have long argued for the increased autonomy that is now being thrust upon them. There will certainly be some initial problems while municipalities attempt to digest the new services for which they will be responsible and as they deal with a new financial regime. This autonomy is causing some indigestion in the short run, but in the long run, it will benefit municipalities.

Career Opportunities in Finance

Pursuing a career in the field of finance generally requires a specialized background in accounting, as evidenced by two credentials. The first is either a university degree or college diploma with a specialization in accounting. The second is one of the accounting designations: Chartered Accountant (CA), Certified General Accountant (CGA), or Certified Management Accountant (CMA). Obtaining the CA designation generally requires a university degree, experience working for a CA firm, and a stringent examination. The requirements for the other two designations are a bit more flexible. They each have correspondence programs that can be completed while a candidate is gaining the required experience in an accounting environment (not necessarily in a CA firm). They also require a stringent examination.

Accounting is sometimes looked down on as uninteresting because it involves numbers. In fact, because the treasurer is involved in preparation of the budget and other financial statements, he or she obtains a broader overview of the entire operation of the municipality than most other staff in the municipality, except the chief administrative officer (CAO). This is probably the reason that one of the most common routes to the CAO's position is through the treasury function. Because of the level of expertise required, the treasurer is also one of the most highly paid department heads. The accounting field provides good entry-level opportunities because there is always a need for people in this area even when most other areas are experiencing serious cutbacks.

Working in the finance function requires a level of comfort with numerical analysis and an attention to detail. Most of the work is done in the office, as compared to recreation or some aspects of engineering, but it is not as desk-bound as some might think. It involves frequent contact with other units of the organization, which requires diplomatic skills. In sum, finance is an interesting career path with fairly open career opportunities that pays well; however, it requires a fairly high level of specialized expertise.

Notes

1. As will be discussed later, local governments are not allowed to budget for a deficit in their current expenditure; however, they are allowed to borrow for capital expenditures. This is likely what was happening in the earlier period.
2. Conventionally, the regressivity of a tax is measured by the relationship between the amount of the tax payable and the taxpayer's income. In the case of the property tax, an argument could be made that the more relevant measure is the relationship between the amount of the tax and the taxpayer's accumulated wealth. Many would say that a retired person with low current income but significant accumulated wealth would be better able to pay the property tax than a young family with higher current income but little accumulated wealth.
3. One of the major obstacles to the introduction of some kinds of user charges is that citizens see them as charges for services that had previously been free. Obviously, the services were not free before; however, because they were paid for from general taxation, the true cost of providing the services was hidden.

References

Bird, Richard, and N. Enid Slack. 1978. *Residential Property Tax Relief in Ontario.* Toronto: University of Toronto Press.

Bird, Richard M., and Thomas Tsiopoulos. 1997. 'User Charges for Public Services: Potential and Problems'. *Canadian Tax Journal* 45: 25–86.

Boadway, Robin W. 1980. *Intergovernmental Transfers in Canada.* Toronto: Canadian Tax Foundation.

Kitchen, Harry M. 1992. *Property Taxation in Canada.* Toronto: Canadian Tax Foundation.

Kushner, Joseph. 1992. 'The Effect of Urban Growth on Municipal Taxes'. *Canadian Public Administration* 35: 94–102.

Meng, Ronald, and W. Irwin Gillespie. 1986. 'The Regressivity of Property Taxes in Canada: Another Look'. *Canadian Tax Journal* 34: 1417–30.

Ontario. Fair Tax Commission. 1993. *Fair Taxation in a Changing World: Report of the Ontario Fair Tax Commission.* Toronto: University of Toronto Press.

Ridler, Neil B. 1984. 'Fiscal Constraints and the Growth of User Fees among Canadian Municipalities'. *Canadian Public Administration* 27: 429–36.

Soroka, Lewis, and Carey Spiece. 1995. 'Market Value Assessment in Niagara: The Regional Dimension'. *Canadian Tax Foundation* 43: 401–14.

Treff, Karin, and David B. Perry. 1999. *Finances of the Nation.* Toronto: Canadian Tax Foundation.

CHAPTER 4

Metropolitan and Regional Governance

Andrew Sancton

Introduction

The simple way of organizing municipal government for large cities is to establish one municipality for the whole built-up area. In most cities, however, simple arrangements seem not to be possible—they might not even be preferable. The main objects of this chapter are to examine the theoretical arguments about how the municipal government system can best be organized for large cities and then to explore the extent to which these methods of organization have been implemented in Canada by looking in some detail at the structural arrangements for our major urban areas.

This chapter does not focus on the structural makeup of individual municipalities. The legal authority of the mayor, the size of the municipal council, the organization of the administrative units—these and other like factors are important for municipal government in general, but they are largely irrelevant to the subject of 'metropolitan and regional governance'. The key concepts for this subject are boundaries, functions, special purpose bodies, and tiers. Each will briefly be defined in the paragraphs that follow.

All Canadian municipalities are corporate entities established as a result of provincial or territorial legislation. By definition, they must have exact, legally defined boundaries that encompass the territory within which they can exercise their legal authority. Major urban municipalities in Canada are called *cities*, although the new Halifax Regional Municipality is an exception. For most (but not all) of our major cities, the actual urbanized area associated with the city extends far beyond its legal boundaries. It is the governance of this wider area that is the concern of this chapter. We call it *metropolitan and regional governance* to distinguish it from the governance of individual, incorporated cities. The use of the term *metropolitan* corresponds to the use of *Census Metropolitan Area (CMA)* by Statistics Canada to refer to continuous built-up areas of over 100,000 people living in a number of distinct municipalities.

Municipalities can serve no useful purpose unless they are assigned particular governmental functions for which they are responsible. Normal municipal functions in Canada include such items as building and maintaining local roads and sewers, collecting and disposing of solid waste, and regulating the use of land. The central problem of metropolitan and regional governance is that existing municipal boundaries usually do not define the most efficient territories for the carrying out of assigned municipal functions. There is often pressure to change boundaries so that functions can be performed more efficiently. Such pressure is usually exerted on provincial governments, and it is in this way that the issue of metropolitan reorganization usually appears on the public policy agenda.

An alternative to changing the boundaries is to establish an intermunicipal *special purpose body*. Such bodies take over a particular municipal function on behalf of two or more contiguous municipalities. They are usually controlled by representatives from the affected municipalities. The organizational mechanism adopted to deliver particular services often has a profound impact on decisions that are taken about such services. For example, special purpose bodies are more likely to be easily influenced by technical experts than are directly elected municipal councils, probably because the latter are subject to more intense media scrutiny and councillors are anxious to demonstrate that they are serving popular interests rather than those of the experts. Another organizational variable is size: organizations that cover larger territories and include more people are likely to use more advanced technologies and more sophisticated management practices than are those covering smaller territories.

So far, we have assumed that there is just one tier of municipal government. But sometimes, instead of setting up a number of special purpose bodies covering the same municipalities, a new tier or level of municipal government is established. An upper-tier municipal government includes within it a number of distinct lower-tier municipalities and is charged with carrying out a number of functions deemed to be intermunicipal in nature.

Now that some of the basic definitions have been established, we can proceed to examining two distinct approaches, consolidationist and 'public choice', to organizing metropolitan and regional governance (Keating 1995). We shall then describe the implementation of the two-tier compromise in parts of Ontario and in British Columbia and Quebec. The final section explores how the consolidationist position has won the day in Winnipeg, Halifax, Toronto, Ottawa, Hamilton, and Sudbury.

The Consolidationist Approach

Consolidationists want to keep things simple. 'One metropolitan area, one municipal government' is their slogan. They believe that such an arrangement leads to stronger and more accountable municipal government, greater efficiency in the delivery of services, and more fairness in allocating costs to residents.[1]

Canadians instinctively understand the consolidationist position. Most of us would likely assume that, given a single metropolitan area, it would be better to have one municipal government than ten. The conventional view is that one government would be more efficient because we would need fewer politicians and fewer bureaucrats. Surely it is better, we often believe, to have just one mayor, one city engineer, and one city clerk.

Arguments about consolidation can become highly technical. Engineers, for example, often claim that it is more efficient to have one integrated sewer and sewage-treatment system for a whole urban area than to have each municipality operate its own. They are usually not especially concerned about which politicians formally control the single, integrated system—they just want to be able to design, build, and manage it. The engineers might well be happy with an intermunicipal special purpose body for sewage. But at this point, other concerns enter the picture. A special purpose body might weaken the affected municipalities involved, because they would then have one less function for which they were directly responsible. Their residents would not be so sure whom to hold accountable for the sewer system. Better, say the consolidationists, to merge all the affected municipalities so that the new consolidated municipality can directly control the sewers itself. An added advantage is that now the new municipality can itself better plan for urban growth in the area because it directly controls a service of government that is essential to such growth. Words like *coordination* and *planning* are always present in the consolidationists' vocabulary.

The word *fairness* is equally important. Consolidationists worry about externalities, or spillovers. For example, one municipality might own and operate a beautiful park that is often used by residents of adjoining municipalities who pay nothing toward its upkeep. Or another municipality might, because of its location in the metropolitan area, attract a disproportionate number of poor people, drug users, or petty thieves, all of whom make abnormally high demands on municipal welfare or police services. Why should this unfortunate municipality be stuck with all the costs when these sorts of problems are a function of the metropolitan area itself, not of a particular municipality? Finally, some municipalities are blessed with strong property tax bases (valuable commercial and industrial property, expensive houses), while others have weak tax bases (rundown commercial buildings, cheap homes). Consolidationists argue that tax bases should be pooled and services made uniform throughout each metropolitan area so that everyone is treated fairly. The only effective way to do this, they say, is to create one consolidated municipality.

The 'Public Choice' Approach

The 'public choice' approach is largely an invention of academic economists, mainly in the United States. The approach is rarely, if ever, propounded by Canadian politicians or civil servants at any level of government. Nevertheless, it does provide a serious intellectual counterweight to the consolidationist position and deserves attention for that reason alone.

Advocates of public choice do not accept the general proposition that one government for a given territory is necessarily going to be more efficient than multiple governments. They believe that the competition generated by multiple governments will lead to more cost savings than could ever result from consolidation. Indeed, they suggest that administrative complexities could well make a single consolidated government more costly than multiple governments.

They acknowledge that some services can be provided most efficiently for territories larger than those of individual municipalities. For these functions, they see nothing wrong with creating intermunicipal special purpose bodies. Such a system does get complicated, but, for public choice advocates, this is a small price to pay for having a system with units whose territories are appropriate for the services they are providing. Perhaps because of its origins in economics, the public choice approach sees accountability not so much in terms of politics and elections as in terms of markets. If residents of a particular municipality are dissatisfied with living conditions or taxation levels, then their ability to move to another nearby municipality is a potentially more useful personal response than is the ability to vote against the incumbent councillors at the next election.

Advocates of public choice are not especially interested in planning and coordination. This is because they have little faith in the ability of large governments to adopt and implement policies that are generally beneficial to society as a whole. Government monopolies are to be feared more than continuous intermunicipal bickering and occasional deadlock. To the extent that fairness is a concern within a given society, the public choice position is that equalization and redistribution schemes must be implemented by central rather than local governments in order to achieve the desired results.

Whenever consolidationist policies are proposed in Canadian metropolitan areas, there is inevitably considerable local opposition, especially in outlying suburbs and nearby rural areas. But such opposition is rarely, if ever, explicitly expressed in the terms used by public choice advocates. Instead, we hear apparently self-serving claims that existing small municipalities are indeed efficient and that they respond more effectively to citizen concerns than do larger governments. Sometimes anti-consolidationists even employ arguments that are antithetical to public choice, such as Magnusson's (1981) point that democratic decision-making by small, self-defined territorial communities is a crucial mechanism for helping build a new kind of society that is less (not more) dependent on global market forces. In many parts of Canada, local opponents of consolidation have not fared very well, in part because their position usually seems self-serving and incoherent. Employing the public choice approach could at least provide coherence.

The Two-Tier Compromise

In the real world of politics, it is the middle position between two extremes that often emerges triumphant (Sharpe 1995). The middle position between the consolidationist and public choice positions on metropolitan and regional governance is the two-tier compromise. A multi-functional upper-tier government is established to provide intermunicipal functions for the entire metropolitan area or region, while smaller lower-tier municipalities continue to provide more local services. Exactly which services belong to which level and how the two interact with each other are the central problems of two-tier structures.

Two-tier municipal systems in rural parts of Ontario and Quebec date back to the mid-nineteenth century. Upper-tier counties build and maintain major roads and some other intermunicipal services, while towns, villages, townships, and parishes look after such matters as local streets, concession roads, and recreation facilities. One of the main reasons why larger urban areas wanted to become incorporated as cities (rather than remain as towns) was that cities were not part of this two-tier system, even if they were completely surrounded geographically by a single county. Prior to 1954, all cities in Ontario and Quebec (and elsewhere in Canada) were, by definition, one-tier municipal systems. When they required more land to accommodate urban development, they annexed land from adjoining rural municipalities, usually by applying to provincial authorities who, if necessary, adjudicated between the conflicting parties.

Metropolitan and Regional Government in Ontario

The creation of the Municipality of Metropolitan Toronto (Metro) on 1 January 1954 marked the first and most significant change in this traditional system. During the period of rapid post-war suburban growth, the rural townships of Etobicoke, North York, and Scarborough were incapable of financing the required urban infrastructure. They appealed to the province for help. Meanwhile, the financially healthy City of Toronto claimed that it would come to the rescue by annexing the rural townships and nine other smaller towns and villages in the area. The provincial cabinet turned the issue over to a quasi-judicial agency, the Ontario Municipal Board (OMB), for investigation. It was the OMB that designed the Metro solution that was subsequently approved by the Ontario legislature.

Metro originally consisted of the City of Toronto and twelve other municipalities. Although the City contained more than half the areas's population and tax base, it was allocated twelve seats on the governing council and each of the other municipalities (regardless of population) was allocated one each. There was a provincially appointed chairman. Metro was essentially charged with building the required new infrastructure: roads, sewers, water supply, and (through a new Metro school board) new suburban schools. Because costs were allocated in accordance with each municipality's share of the total tax base, the City of Toronto was the main contributor.

Until the mid-1960s, the system worked well. The required infrastructure (including the Don Valley Parkway and the Gardiner Expressway) was built with a minimum of difficulty. Problems emerged when the Metro suburbs became more populous than the City and when urban growth began to expand far beyond Metro's borders. In 1965, a one-man royal commission was established to investigate these concerns. Carl Goldenberg recommended that the number of Metro municipalities be reduced, that they be represented on Metro council roughly in accordance with their population, and that Metro's borders not be extended. In 1966, the provincial legislature enacted the most important of the Goldenberg recommendations (Rose 1972). There were then six constituent municipalities, and the City was allocated fewer than half the council seats. A few years later, two-tier systems similar to Metro's (called *regional governments*) were established covering the nearby counties of Halton and Peel to the west, York to the north, and Durham to the east.

Meanwhile, between 1969 and 1974, the province also established similar two-tier regional systems in Niagara, Ottawa-Carleton, Sudbury, Hamilton-Wentworth, Waterloo, and Haldimand-Norfolk. By 1975, more than half of Ontario's population lived within these restructured urban two-tier systems. Provincial authorities claimed that the systems were necessary to control and finance urban development in the most rapidly growing areas of the province. Despite the establishment of two-tier systems, the provincial position was distinctly consolidationist, especially since the creation of each of the new regional systems also involved massive lower-tier municipal consolidation of the type Metro did not experience until 1966. Much of the opposition to regional government was not concerned with the new upper-tier authority but with the consolidation of long-standing towns, villages, and townships into larger lower-tier units with which many citizens could not identify. Because the introduction of the new system took place at the same time as the high inflation of the early 1970s, there was also a perception—usually caused by increased salaries for top administrators—that the new system was very expensive. In any event, the creation of new two-tier regional governments had stopped in Ontario by 1975.

One long-standing concern about Metro was that its chairman and staff were not really subject to effective political control. Its council (except for the chairman) was made up only of politicians who were elected first and foremost to serve at the lower tier. Voters knew little about Metro, and their voting decisions had little to do with Metro issues. Arguments were constantly being made that Metro deserved its own directly elected council. Indeed, when the Regional Municipality of Niagara was established, the council was set up such that it was made up of the twelve lower-tier mayors and sixteen other members directly elected to serve only at the regional level. It was hoped that the sixteen directly elected members would not only monitor regional issues more carefully, but also serve to integrate a highly diverse area. The argument was that because they did not also have to sit on a lower-tier council, they would be more likely to act in the interests of the region as a whole.

In 1977, another one-man royal commission recommended that Metro adopt the Niagara system. Such a system was finally implemented in 1988 (Mellon 1993). In Hamilton-Wentworth and Ottawa-Carleton, the decision was made to have the chair of the regional council directly elected by all regional voters in the same way as a mayor is. Once again, the idea was to attempt to get voters to focus on regional issues rather than local ones. In 1994, Ottawa-Carleton adopted a regional system unprecedented in Ontario: all regional councillors (including the chair) were directly elected to serve only at the regional level, and lower-tier mayors were excluded. In some cases, the boundaries of the regional wards crossed the boundaries of the lower-tier municipalities.

Ontario went a long way to establish Metro and the regions as an entirely distinct level of urban municipal government. By implementing direct election, the province invited increased political wrangling between the two tiers, as each group of politicians tried to protect its turf. Ironically, a two-tier system of the type established for Ottawa-Carleton existed in Winnipeg between 1961 and 1971, but one of the reasons the Winnipeg system was abolished was that political conflict between the two levels became too destructive of effective government. As of 2001, Ontario's two-tier systems in Toronto, Ottawa, Hamilton, and Sudbury had experienced the same fate, and largely for the same reasons.

Regional Districts in British Columbia

Two-tier urban government of a much different kind came to British Columbia between 1965 and 1967. At that time, the provincial government established regional districts throughout the entire province, including large areas that previously had no form of municipal government at all. The boards of directors that govern regional districts are made up of representatives from the councils of the constituent municipalities and by members directly elected by voters in the unincorporated areas. Because the provincial government has been reluctant even to acknowledge that regional districts constitute an additional level of government, there has never been any move to have municipal representatives directly elected. In many respects, the regional districts are little more than a gathering together under one umbrella of pre-existing special purpose bodies. They are so loose and flexible in their structure that they often have different boundaries for different functions. Board members whose areas are not served for a particular function by the regional district simply do not participate in that part of the decision-making process—nor do their constituents pay. Keeping track of who actually does what might be relatively complex, but municipalities generally maintain the freedom to decide the best way to provide services to meet their own special needs (Bish and Clemens 1999). These facts, combined with the absence of any attempt at lower-tier consolidation, probably explain why regional districts have been much less unpopular politically in British Columbia than regional governments have been in Ontario.

Not surprisingly, it is in Vancouver that the regional district system has been under most pressure. Established in 1967, the Greater Vancouver Regional District (GVRD) includes almost all the area of the Vancouver CMA. In contrast to the Ontario experience, some outlying suburban municipalities have been anxious to join the GVRD so as to benefit from its sewer and water supply systems. GVRD membership currently stands at eighteen municipalities and three unincorporated areas. In the public's mind, the GVRD is mainly associated with two ambitious attempts (in the 1970s and the 1990s) at regional planning, both of which were aimed primarily at restricting and channelling urban growth so as to protect Vancouver's remarkable natural environment. Such planning is carried out within the framework of tight provincial control over the conversion of agricultural land for urban use. One pecu-liarity of the GVRD is that it has no direct control over public transit, a function run, until recently, directly by the provincial government (Oberlander and Smith 1998). In functional terms, the GVRD is so weak that it barely qualifies as a distinct tier of government (Lightbody 1997).

Urban Communities and MRCs in Quebec

Two-tier urban government came to Quebec in 1970. Prior to then, there had been a great deal of talk but little action, even though there had been a 'metropolitan com-mission' concerned with intermunicipal financial issues in Montreal as early as 1921. In late 1969—in the aftermath of a police strike in the City of Montreal—the Quebec National Assembly approved legislation establishing urban communities for Mon-treal and Quebec City and a regional community for the Outaouais (Sancton 1985).

The Montreal Urban Community (MUC) includes all the municipalities on the Island of Montreal and two adjoining island municipalities (now twenty-eight in total). Because the City has always had more than half the population and because all its council members (now fifty-nine) sit on the council along with twenty-six suburban mayors, the voting system for the MUC council contains elaborate provi-sions for weighted votes and double majorities. This has been one reason why the MUC has never been especially effective in shaping Montreal's urban development. In a very real sense, that was never its purpose. Unlike Metro Toronto, in which the City of Toronto tended to subsidize the building of suburban infrastructure, the main original reason for the MUC was to force the nearby suburbs to share the heavy finan-cial burden of the City of Montreal's expensive police force. In 1973, all municipal police forces in the MUC were integrated into one, as they were for Metro in 1957.

In the early 1980s the provincial government established a network of *municipal-ités régionales du comté* (MRCs) throughout all the populated parts of Quebec not already included within the urban or regional communities (Quesnel 1990). Unlike regional governments in Ontario, their boundaries were usually quite different from the old county boundaries drawn in the nineteenth century. The MRCs are actually quite similar to the regional districts in British Columbia in that their constituent municipalities have considerable freedom to opt in and out of various MRC services.

Within the Montreal CMA—whose territory, like that of Toronto's, extends far beyond that of the metropolitan government—thirteen separate MRCs were estab-lished (Sancton 1994). By 1992, the provincial government realized that there were serious problems. It established a twelve-person task force, chaired by Claude Pichette, to study the municipal system in the entire region. The task force concluded in 1993 that a new metropolitan authority was needed to cover all 102 municipali-ties within the CMA. The MUC and the MRCs would be downgraded to 'intermunici-pal service agencies'. Lower-tier municipal consolidation was seen as desirable, but no specific proposals were presented. In May 2000, the Quebec minister of munici-pal affairs introduced legislation to establish an upper-tier Montreal Metropolitan Community covering the entire CMA. Meanwhile, the mayor of Montreal, Pierre

Bourque, was conducting a campaign to merge all of the MUC municipalities into an expanded City of Montreal (Sancton 2000). Despite considerable protest, the provincial government has gone ahead with legislation to amalgamate both the MUC and the Quebec City urban community as of 1 January 2002.

Single-Tier Systems

Outside Ontario, Quebec, and British Columbia, there are no Canadian two-tier municipal systems. This means, by definition, that major cities in other provinces are governed by single-tier systems. Prior to the creation of Toronto's 'mega-city' in 1998, the most populous of these single-tier municipalities was the City of Calgary, a municipality that has continuously annexed large tracts of rural land so that it now includes almost 95 per cent of the population of the Calgary CMA (Sancton 1994).

The third most populous Canadian single-tier municipality was Edmonton. Its annexations have been more contentious. In 1980, the City proposed an annexation involving all of the neighbouring County of Strathcona and the City of St Albert near its northwest boundary. After both sides spent about $7 million presenting their cases, the Local Authorities Board ruled largely in Edmonton's favour, only to be overruled by the provincial cabinet. St Albert survived, and Edmonton was allowed to annex only part of the county. One of the subjects in dispute was how regional land-use planning could be carried out if Edmonton's proposal were denied. An Edmonton Metropolitan Regional Planning Commission was established on which the City had only one-third of the votes even though its residents comprised 80 per cent of the population in the commission's defined area (Lightbody 1983). The representation problem was solved in 1994 when the Alberta legislature abolished all such regional planning commissions throughout the province. But problems of regional coordination remained; in 1999/2000, a provincially appointed task force was examining possible new organizational mechanisms to enable area municipalities to better cooperate with each other.

Winnipeg, the second most populous single-tier Canadian municipality prior to Toronto's mega-city, is a special case because its structural evolution has been much more complex. As indicated previously, between 1961 and 1971, there was a two-tier system covering the central City of Winnipeg and eleven suburban municipalities. In 1971, the NDP provincial government led by Premier Ed Schreyer published a proposal for a new 'Unicity' into which all existing municipal governments would be merged. In many respects, the government's case was a classic exposition of consolidationist principles. All the elements were there, especially an emphasis on fairness and equity. The NDP government was particularly concerned about apparent inequities of services and taxes between the wealthier suburbs and the inner city (Brownstone and Plunkett 1983). Since the Unicity system began in 1972, suburban residents have no longer been able to separate themselves from the problems of the central city through the artifices of municipal boundaries. They have, however, been able to elect councillors who have leaned toward capital investment in the suburbs rather than central-city rejuvenation (Axworthy 1980). In this sense, Unicity has not worked out quite as its proponents had expected or hoped.

One crucial element of the Unicity scheme was to compensate for the abolition of the twelve lower-tier municipalities by establishing a large Unicity council comprising a directly elected mayor and fifty councillors elected from small, single-member wards. Councillors in adjacent wards were grouped together to form community committees to consider matters of concern to particular neighbourhoods before these concerns were passed on for final decision to the council as a whole. Each committee was supposed to consult regularly with a residents' advisory group that was directly elected at community meetings open to all residents in the area. This system was supposed to be a breakthrough in participatory municipal government. On closer analysis, it was apparent that the residents' advisory groups had no real power because they advised community committees that were themselves only advisory.

By 2000, the number of Unicity councillors had been reduced to a more conventional fifteen, and the community committees and the residents' advisory groups had been completely abolished. In the final analysis, Winnipeg's Unicity can best be described as Canada's most massive and significant municipal consolidation (until 1998, at least). But in 1991, residents of Headingley in the western portion of Unicity convinced the provincial government to hold a referendum about secession. Headingley voters demonstrated overwhelmingly that they wanted out, and the provincial government obliged in 1992 (Sancton 1994). One of Canada's most notable examples of consolidation also produced a rare example of deconsolidation.

Halifax

A single-tier metropolitan government was created for Halifax in 1996. In terms of population, the Halifax CMA ranks thirteenth in Canada, but it is the largest in the Atlantic region. Prior to the amalgamation, the central city comprised only 35.7 per cent of the total CMA population (Sancton 1994). In fact, Halifax County, the 'rural' municipality surrounding the city, itself had a greater population than the central city. The other two urban municipalities surrounding Halifax harbour are Dartmouth and Bedford, the latter of which was incorporated as a town as recently as 1980.

The first serious proposals to amalgamate all the municipalities in the Halifax area were made in the 1974 report of the Nova Scotia Royal Commission on Education, Public Services, and Provincial–Municipal Relations. The plan was not pursued until 1991, when the minister of municipal affairs in the Progressive Conservative government led by Premier John Buchanan created a Task Force on Local Government charged with making recommendations to improve efficiency, accountability, and accessibility. In ten lines of a forty-six-page report, the task force recommended that the four Halifax-area municipalities be merged. In late 1992, Buchanan's colleague and successor, Donald Cameron, announced that the merger would take place prior to the 1994 municipal elections. He appointed a Halifax Metropolitan Municipal Reform Commissioner to oversee the process. But in May 1993, a provincial election intervened and Cameron was replaced by a Liberal premier, John Savage, the former mayor of Dartmouth, who stated during the campaign that he would not force a Halifax municipal consolidation and that it was 'a crazy idea' (Cox 1994). Meanwhile, in July 1993, the commissioner produced an interim report claiming that there would be annual savings from amalgamation of $9.8 million (Sancton 2000).

By October 1994, as part of an overall strategy to reduce government spending, Premier Savage announced that he now favoured amalgamation (Cox 1994). In April 1995, legislation was introduced to create a single-tier Halifax Regional Municipality. It was approved within a few weeks. The Progressive Conservatives could scarcely object because they had campaigned for amalgamation in the previous election. Some suburban Liberal backbenchers were obviously unhappy, but they tended to absent themselves from voting rather than launch a full-scale rebellion against a government that was already in political difficulty on other matters.

In municipal terms, there is (as of 1 April 1996) no longer a City of Halifax, only a Halifax Regional Municipality. Its area is about the same size as that of Prince Edward Island, stretching along the Atlantic coast for a straight-line distance of well over 100 kilometres. Tourists in Halifax are now able to leave their downtown hotel, make the round trip to the picturesque fishing village of Peggy's Cove, stay within the same municipality all day long, and still have traversed only a small portion of its total area.

It is obvious that in many respects the new Halifax municipality is closely modelled on Unicity Winnipeg. For example, community councils have been established that are very similar to Winnipeg's old community committees, except that they have real authority over local zoning issues. There is another crucial difference between the two systems: Unicity was consciously designed as an urban government. The original boundaries did take in rural areas of suburban municipalities, but there was a reasonable expectation that, over time, they would be developed for urban use. There can be no such expectation for most of the land included in the Halifax Regional Municipality, which has had to work out ways of serving both urban and rural residents simultaneously.

The Ontario Amalgamations

Since Mike Harris's government came to office in Ontario in 1995, there have been single-tier amalgamations in four major metropolitan areas: Toronto, Ottawa, Hamilton, and Sudbury. The Toronto merger, in which the two-tier Metro system was collapsed into a single new City of Toronto, was the most shocking. Such a plan had not been part of Harris's electoral platform, nor had any public inquiry or report ever recommended such a course of action. The plan was announced in late 1996, accompanied by a hastily completed report from a large consulting firm, KPMG, claiming that amalgamation would save $300 million annually.

Opposition to amalgamation emerged in all parts of Metro, but was especially intense within the central city, where the concern seemed to be that neighbourhoods would be threatened by insensitive decisions taken by a suburban majority on the new amalgamated council. The mobilization of opposition to amalgamation was greatly aided by the fact many Toronto citizens were also upset by a wide range of other government policies that were being proposed at the same time: the reorganization of school board boundaries and finances, increased municipal fiscal responsibility for welfare assistance, and a new assessment system for property tax purposes that involved dramatically higher taxes for residents of older single-family homes in the central city. Amalgamation was rejected by a large majority of voters in referendums conducted—with varying degrees of procedural rigour—in all six Metro municipalities. But the government went ahead anyway. On 1 January 1998, the new City of Toronto—the 'mega-city'—came into being.

In 1999, the new City was claiming that amalgamation was saving $150 million annually. In fact, the real amount was considerably less. A true accounting will not be possible until after we know how wage and salary levels are harmonized, a process still not complete by mid-2000 (Sancton 2000).

In 1998, legislation was approved to establish the Greater Toronto Services Board (GTSB), a body encompassing the new City of Toronto and the regions of Halton, Peel, York, and Durham. Its main functional responsibility relates to commuter trains, and for this purpose it also includes Hamilton. In general, however, the GTSB is weaker as a metropolitan authority than even the GVRD in Vancouver. In part because the new City of Toronto represents almost half the population within the GTSB, it is proving extremely difficult for members of the board to arrive at agreement on any items of area-wide significance. Political disagreements around a wide range of issues between the new City of Toronto and the so-called 905 area (the number comes from the telephone area code) are intense. (Second area codes are being introduced for both the City and the 905 area in 2001.)

During the Ontario provincial election of 1999, municipal amalgamations were not a significant issue. Opposition had died down in Toronto, probably because the new mega-city council—with financial assistance from the province—had succeeded in preventing any increase in its average property tax rates. In some parts of the province, including Hamilton, government candidates pledged that there would be no forced amalgamations. Nonetheless, almost immediately after the election, the government took steps to replace each of the two-tier systems in Ottawa, Hamilton, and Sudbury with one new, single-tier municipality. By the end of 1999, the legislation had been passed, causing one newly re-elected Harris conservative from the suburban Hamilton area to resign from the legislature in protest. The new single-tier municipalities came into existence on 1 January 2001.

Conclusion: Is Bigger Better?

This new Canadian phenomenon of combining a major city and large areas of rural and non-developable land into a single municipality—apparent to a lesser extent in Calgary and Edmonton than in Halifax, Ottawa, Hamilton, and Sudbury—deserves careful attention because it is such a radically different approach to metropolitan and regional governance. The traditional view, still reflected within Ontario's remaining two-tier regional governments, is that there must be some form of municipal division between urban and rural because their interests in land use regulation and municipal services are fundamentally different. Furthermore, since there will always be more urban voters than rural ones, rural concerns will likely be ignored. It is precisely such worries that led the Nova Scotia government to include the provisions for community councils and community committees within its amalgamation legislation. But will they work? Evidence from Winnipeg suggests not.

If rural and urban can successfully be brought together, then it seems that there is no need for all the complexity and duplication inherent in the two-tier systems of Ontario, Quebec, and British Columbia. This was precisely the point that was advanced repeatedly by proponents of amalgamation in Halifax, Ottawa, Hamilton, and Sudbury. It is still far from clear, however, that non-urban areas can maintain their identity within consolidated urban-rural municipalities.

In the current political context, the biggest issue relating to amalgamations involves cost savings. From what we know so far, it seems that accountants and consultants have been remarkably unsuccessful in their attempts to project savings accurately. The problem is that most such studies are static. They work from existing expenditure data for each municipality, carefully listing costs that appear to be duplicated by other municipalities. The sum total of all the costs on the list is then presented as the savings to be gained from amalgamation. No consideration is given to the new ongoing expenditures that the consolidated system itself will generate, such as those that result from attempting to prove to both residents and remaining employees that amalgamation is not making anyone worse off. One of the reasons for having community councils and committees within amalgamated municipalities (as in Halifax and Toronto) is to provide a mechanism through which local neighbourhoods can fight to get a larger share of the whatever financial resources are available. Many such councils and committees—and individual councillors—will always argue that their areas should have service levels that are similar to the best that exist elsewhere within the municipality. They will want municipal personnel physically situated in their communities to respond to citizen needs. In some cases, these will be precisely the same positions that the accountants assumed would be cut when they made their cost-savings calculations. To the extent that the amalgamated council satisfies some of these demands in order to prevent the complete alienation of underserviced areas, the anticipated cost savings will never be realized.

This same 'levelling up' process applies to wage levels as well. Whereas the accountants generally assume that wage levels for workers in amalgamated municipalities will be near the average level for the former municipalities, unions generally have different ideas. They insist that no workers should have their wages reduced, which means that all wages should rise to the highest level. Both Halifax and Toronto have experienced municipal strikes around exactly such issues. Total costs of the settlements have not yet been tabulated. When they are, much of the projected saving from the amalgamations will have disappeared

A public choice analysis would present additional reasons why expenditures are likely increase in consolidated municipalities. Instead of a few smaller bureaucracies that are relatively easy to understand and control, there is only one large one, all the activities of which no one person—even the one in charge—can really grasp. The information about how the system really works is buried deep in the lower levels. Competition among municipalities in the same area to provide higher levels of service at lower costs is removed. Citizens can no longer point to neighbouring municipalities and say 'If they can do it this way, why can't we?' In short, there is a reduction in the number of governments without necessarily reducing the overall size of government.

While Canadian governments responded desperately to demands for reduced spending, we all wanted to believe that there were at least some easy savings to be made through reorganization. Municipalities squabbling with each other in the same metropolitan area were easy targets. By consolidating them into one, we could surely eliminate the squabbling and reduce the size of government. If only it were so easy! What consolidation does is to make the squabbling less visible while limiting our opportunities for democratic decision-making.

Given the right circumstances, the arguments for some forms of municipal consolidation can be convincing. The creation of Unicity in Winnipeg and of the Montreal Urban Community did promote fairness and equity within the metropolitan regions. The creation of the Municipality of Metropolitan Toronto did help create a better-planned, better-serviced urban area; it was a significant factor in developing Toronto's reputation as a city that works. At the top of the political agenda today, however, are concerns about economic development and cutting the cost of government. There is precious little evidence that these concerns can be helpfully addressed through municipal consolidation (Sancton 1999). As we think about metropolitan and regional governance, it is time once again to think about how we can best enhance democratic and equitable decision-making within our diverse territorial communities. In so doing, we shall make a greater contribution to efficient local government than any accountant who searches municipal financial statements for overlap and duplication.

Notes

1. For a recent American approach, see Rusk (1995).

References

Axworthy, Lloyd. 1980. 'The Best Laid Plans Oft Go Astray: The Case of Winnipeg'. In *Problems of Change in Urban Government*, ed. M.O. Dickerson, S. Drabek, and J.T. Woods. Waterloo: Wilfrid Laurier University Press.

Bish, Robert, and Clemens, Eric G. 1999. *Local Government in British Columbia*. 4th ed. Richmond, BC: Union of British Columbia Municipalities.

Brownstone, Meyer, and Plunkett, T.J. 1983. *Metropolitan Winnipeg: Politics and Reform of Local Government*. Berkeley: University of California Press.

Cox, Kevin. 1994. 'Halifax-Area Leaders Fuming over Plans for Supercity'. *The Globe and Mail* (28 October).

Keating, Michael. 1995. 'Size, Efficiency and Democracy: Consolidation, Fragmentation and Public Choice'. In *Theories of Urban Politics*, ed. David Judge, Gerry Stoker, and Harold Wolman. London: Sage.

Lightbody, James. 1983. 'Edmonton'. In *City Politics in Canada*, ed. Warren Magnusson and Andrew Sancton. Toronto: University of Toronto Press.

———. 1997. 'A New Perspective on Clothing the Emperor: Canadian Metropolitan Form, Function, and Frontiers'. *Canadian Public Administration* 40: 436–56.

Magnusson, Warren. 1981. 'Community Organization and Local Self-Government'. In *Politics and Government of Urban Canada: Selected Readings*, 4th ed., ed. Lionel D. Feldman. Toronto: Methuen.

Mellon, Hugh. 1993. 'Reforming the Electoral System of Metropolitan Toronto: Doing Away with Dual Representation'. *Canadian Public Administration* 36: 38–56.

Oberlander, H. Peter, and Patrick J. Smith. 1998. 'Restructuring Metropolitan Governance: Greater Vancouver–British Columbia Reforms'. In *Metropolitan Governance Revisited: American/Canadian Intergovernmental Perspectives*, ed. Donald N. Rothblatt and Andrew Sancton. Berkeley: Institute of Governmental Studies Press, University of California.

Quesnel, Louise. 1990. 'Political Control over Planning in Quebec'. *International Journal of Urban and Regional Research* 14: 25–48.

Rose, Albert. 1972. *Governing Metropolitan Toronto: A Social and Political Analysis, 1953–1971*. Berkeley: University of California Press.

Rusk, David. 1995. *Cities without Suburbs*. 2nd ed. Washington, DC: Woodrow Wilson Center Press.

Sancton, Andrew. 1985. *Governing Montreal: Language Differences and Metropolitan Politics*. Berkeley: University of California Press.

———. 1994. *Governing Canada's City-Regions: Adapting Form to Function*. Montreal: Institute for Research on Public Policy.

———. 1999. 'Globalization Does Not Require Amalgamation'. *Policy Options* 20(9): 54–8.

———. 2000. *Merger Mania: The Assault on Local Government*. Westmount, QC: Price-Patterson.

Sharpe, L.J., ed. 1995. *The Government of World Cities: The Future of the Metro Model*. Chichester, UK: Wiley.

CHAPTER 5

Housing Policy in the New Millennium: The Uncompassionate Landscape

Barbara Wake Carroll

Introduction

Housing policy and housing problems are largely urban phenomena. Housing is one of the more important urban policy areas because it is an essential good that defines people and their lifestyles, because it absorbs scarce resources at the household level and at all levels of government, and because its visibility and durability mean that the quality and appearance of the housing stock shape our current and our future urban environments. Housing policy also forms a good microcosm of public policy because it involves both economic and social policy, thus providing a reflection both of the interventionist strategies of the 1960s and 1970s and of the small, non-interventionist strategies of the late 1980s and 1990s, as well as of the current trend toward federal disentanglement and provincial downloading.

This chapter focuses on trends in housing policy since the second world war, interprovincial and municipal variations, and the current problems that exist within housing markets. In the late 1940s and 1950s, the policy strategists and planners in the federal housing agency, the Canada Mortgage and Housing Corporation (CMHC), developed a dream of the ideal city, eloquently described by the late Humphrey Carver in his book *Compassionate Landscape* (1975). This chapter analyzes Canadian housing policy in the last half of the twentieth century and concludes that as we move into the new millennium, the early promise of a compassionate landscape has gone unfulfilled. We begin with a discussion of the nature of housing and housing markets.

Housing Markets and Forms of Intervention

The characteristics of housing that are important for understanding housing policy are the complexity of housing markets, the durability and immobility of the housing stock, and the mixed public/private nature of housing as a good. Bourne (1981) uses the expression 'bundle of services' as a way to conceptualize housing as a good. It is an economic good, both as a source of personal investment to individual homeowners and as an important part of the economy. It is a physical good in terms of providing shelter and in terms of its appearance, which makes up a large portion of the urban environment. It is also a 'social' good, providing status and satisfaction to individuals—it is a commonplace to describe people in terms of where they live—and establishing the setting within which much of the social interaction among people takes place.

At the same time, the housing market is subject to a number of economic, social, and demographic influences on both the demand and supply sides that are highly interdependent and not well understood (Bourne 1981). The demand for housing is dependent on demographic factors such as the age of the population, the number and size of households, and the ability of households to purchase or rent housing. Houses are also durable, non-adaptive, and immobile. New additions to the stock of existing housing represent a very small proportion of the total market. The housing stock, therefore, adjusts very slowly to changes in demand or taste.

Changes in housing demand (and taste) can also be met through renovation, conversion, and gentrification, as well as through the filtering down of the existing stock. In fact, investment in renovation now exceeds investment in new housing starts. This means that building housing for future adaptability is even more critical now than when new starts made such a large contribution.

Canada has what is referred to as a *mixed allocation system* for the provision of housing. This means that although most of the housing is allocated within the private market for those who can afford to purchase their own choice of housing goods, there is a separate, parallel public allocation system that provides housing at subsidized levels for those who cannot afford to purchase enough housing for themselves or their families. This latter type of housing is often referred to as *social housing* because its allocation is based upon social need rather than market demand. Most of the housing in Canada, however, is delivered through the private market according to economic demand. This market for housing is a highly segmented series of linked and interdependent sub-markets differentiated by geographic area, age, house type, size, and type of tenure. Changes in demand within these sub-markets can be met only by incremental additions of new housing. But the number of new housing units provided is affected less by the individual demand for units than by overall economic conditions, especially the level of interest rates and the availability of land. At the same time, not only does it take a considerable period of time to actually build the units, but housing requires expensive and extensive infrastructure services in the form of transportation systems, schools, sewer and water services, and recreational services. The result is a significant lag between shifts in demand and the ability of the market to respond, with corresponding cyclical swings in availability and price.

Each of the economic, the social, and the physical characteristics of the housing market has led to some form of government intervention. This intervention has been justified as part of economic policies designed to create employment, to compensate for economic cycles, and to protect financial investment in the residential mortgage market. Policy initiatives also have been directed, as part of social welfare policies, to meet the needs of those who cannot compete in the private market and those who have special needs that the market does not meet. Thus, although most housing demand is met through the private market, historically some has also been provided through the public sector on the basis of social need rather than economic demand. Finally, planning policies and housing standards regulations, which greatly affect the physical location and design of houses, have been used to compensate for externalities and to ensure minimum health and safety standards.

To some extent, types of policy coincide with the jurisdictional responsibilities of the levels of government in Canada. The federal government has constitutional responsibility for monetary and fiscal policy and the provinces for property and social welfare, whereas municipalities have been delegated responsibility for many of the physical aspects of property. As with most policy areas in Canada, however, the actual divisions have not been so clear-cut, particularly when we consider that the ultimate outcome of these policies is the single housing unit—your home. For example, policies intended to protect mortgage investment affect the type of physical product that is produced, and, by stipulating mortgage conditions, these policies also determine the income level necessary to purchase the house. Similarly, a municipal planning decision that allows, for example, the building of only single-family detached houses on large lots affects the level of investment in, and the social makeup of, that community, while a decision to regulate builders in order to control housing quality leads to higher levels of market concentration and, in some cases, prices (Carroll 1988, 1998). Perhaps ironically, although housing forms the major physical and financial component of our urban areas, in the last half of the twentieth century, municipal governments have played only a minor, primarily reactive role in the development and implementation of housing policy (Carter and McAfee 1990). The main, and very important, role played by municipalities with regard to housing is in planning where housing is to be developed and in regulating building and occupancy standards. Even in these areas, however, municipalities have also often simply complied with senior government requirements.

The policy instruments used have also been extensive and varied, from the regulation of land use, building standards, and price levels, to the regulation of the family structure of occupants, and, indirectly, to the allowable income levels of occupants. There have been grants, subsidies, and forgivable and non-forgivable loans at varying levels of market and non-market interest rates; variations in sales, income, and property tax treatments; and direct involvement by all levels of government in the owning and building of housing (Carroll 1989). The legislature of Upper Canada passed legislation for the first public housing project in Toronto in 1840. Nonetheless, if one looks at our urban landscape, from the suburban 'monster' homes ('monster' in the sense of being both large and ugly) on tiny lots, a three-hour commute on a freeway to and from work, to the cardboard box on a street heating grate, it is clear that we have not done a very good job of dealing with housing issues.

As with other types of public policy, the forms of intervention that have developed are a response to the demands of the individuals and groups involved in the market, each wanting housing policies to reflect their own preferences. Organized interest groups, such as the Canadian Home Builders Association, have tended to concentrate their efforts at the provincial and federal levels, advocating policies for economic intervention or reduction in regulation; social advocacy groups, such as the Canadian Council on Social Development, have pressed for the reintroduction of low-income housing; others, such as the Cooperative Housing Foundation of Canada and its seventeen affiliated organizations, have advocated only one type of program alternative; while one-issue NIMBY ('not in my backyard') groups have been primarily concerned with a single project or planning decision.

All governments respond to those demands that are important to their political fortunes, but the importance of these types of groups and their impact vary among levels of government. Municipal governments dependent upon the property tax are more open to one-issue problems, having to trade off the demands of groups such as residents wanting to protect their lifestyles and investments by opposing lower standards of housing or additional growth with the demands of developers wanting to develop and build (Fowler 1992). Federal and provincial governments are more open to broader social and economic pressures and to the influence of large organized interests. One-issue groups tend to exert pressure at the federal or provincial level only when the problem affects a large bloc of voters, such as renters or new-home buyers. Municipalities are supposed to regulate land use, but outside of a few major centres, they have shown little concern for housing other than as a means of shoring up their tax base and responding to development interests. Even the much vaunted 'new urbanist' movement, a form of 'back to basics' in housing, has been largely developer-driven (see Leo's chapter).

Thus, policies intended to meet the underlying problems of the housing market became complicated as different levels of government attempted to respond to the demands of competing interests and to resolve problems caused by intervention at another time or for another purpose. What evolved was a range in the type of intervention that covered almost every aspect of housing and every level of government and that used a bewildering array of policy instruments. At the same time, we have seen a wide variation in the amount of intervention, from large-scale financial loans and grants in the 1970s to the current inertia that constitutes a retreat from intervention, a retreat consistent with other initiatives to dismantle the welfare state (Mishra 1990). One indication of the magnitude of this change is that in the 1970s, the federal government was willing to invest more than $1 billion per year in new investment in housing, but by 1997 it had reduced its commitment for new investment to zero. The federal government still spends $1.9 billion per year in operating costs and subsidies from previous investment, but that amount is also expected to fall as the operating agreements to fund these costs expire (Carroll and Jones 2000).

Stages of Housing Policy Since 1945

Contemporary Canadian housing policy began with the establishment of Canada (then Central) Mortgage and Housing Corporation, with a very specific mission to build a great deal of housing in order to meet the pent-up demands of the returning war veterans and create a building industry. Although its main focus was on private-market housing, in later years it also played a leading role in land use planning and development and in the provision of subsidies for social programs. Between that post-war period and the present, there have been five stages in housing policy. These are highlighted in Table 5.1. (For a more detailed description of the programs themselves, see Rose [1982] and Sayegh [1987].)

Each of these stages developed in response to different demographic and economic conditions, was driven by differing ideological values, fit within the more general changes in the pattern of intergovernmental relations in Canada, and was not dissimilar to the pattern of other social welfare policies (see Haddow's chapter; Banting 1990; Mishra 1990). The stages have also been marked by shifts in the patterns and trends of the policies rather than by changes in the specifics of particular programs. Throughout all of the stages, the building of new suburban homeowner developments has continued on a cyclical, but steady scale. The major difference in the subdivisions over the period has been in their density. Initially, in the post-war era, they were modest houses on modest lots; this gave way in the 1960s and 1970s to larger houses on larger lots and then to the current pattern of larger houses on smaller lots.

The economic development stage from 1945 to 1968 was driven by the economic and demographic pressures of economic reconstruction, the needs of returning veterans, and the pent-up demand from the 1930s and 1940s. The goal was the development of a large-scale housing industry. This produced large-scale, medium-density, suburban homeowner developments with infrastructure projects to service them. It was a time of federal leadership, with federal money used to provide direct loans and grants. In this post-war era, there was a belief in the efficiency of the private market and in the ability of government planners to direct growth in the best way. Canadians wished to become a nation of homeowners. Thus, primary emphasis was placed on the provision of single-family detached owner-occupied housing for middle-income families, under the assumption that low-income problems could be solved through filtering. That is, the middle-income groups who moved to the suburbs would vacate smaller, older, cheaper housing closer to the urban core, making it available for lower-income groups. The programs were national in scope, with little flexibility for regional or provincial needs.

The second stage of social development dated from 1968 and evolved from the Hellyer Report, named after the minister responsible for housing, Paul Hellyer. It was assumed that comprehensive planning could solve policy problems through rational problem-solving techniques and that it was possible to develop and implement a blueprint, or vision, of what our urban areas should look like. These were the urban reformers at the short-lived Ministry of State for Urban Affairs (MSUA), whose goals included cooperating with other levels of government rather than imposing policies

Table 5.1: Phases of Canadian Housing Policy

Characteristics	Economic Development (1945–68)	Social Development (1968–78)	Financial Restraint (1978–86)	Disentanglement (1986–94)	Disengagement & Privatization (1994–present)
Economic conditions	reconstruction and prosperity	prosperity and inflation	recession and recovery	high government deficit	economic growth, widening social gap
Major demographic force	pent-up demand, returning veterans	baby boom	aging population, single families	40- & 50-somethings dominant	smaller, non-traditional family unit
Overall goals	economic development	social reform	financial restraint	reduced government presence	rediscovery of social needs
Market philosophy	filtering and infrastructure support, planned urban landscape	intervention, participation, flexibility	reduced intervention	free-market privatization	neo-liberalism, globalization
Housing goals	industrial development, suburban development, physical planning	community development, income integration, demand support	supply support	deconstructionism, 'fix up, patch up'	unclear
Delivery instruments	direct federal loans and grants	cost-sharing direct subsidies, loans	loan guarantees, mortgage insurance	co-production, private-sector partnership	volunteers, local government
Intergovernmental	federal leadership	tri-level consultation, 'province-building'	provincial leadership	solely provincial	solely provincial
Outcomes	large projects, 'corporate city'	widespread, uncontrolled subsidies	administrative overlap	non-policy, small-scale intervention	unclear

upon them. These goals also reflected the social and environmental reform movements of the 1960s and 1970s.

By 1968, it was also necessary to sustain the house-building industry, whose structure had been defined in the immediate post-war years, while also meeting the needs, values, and high expectations of the baby boom generation. This necessity led to home ownership assistance programs for medium-density townhouses and apartment condominiums, neighbourhood improvement and rehabilitation programs, income-integrated housing, housing for senior citizens, and, in the latter years, energy conservation programs. Later programs, such as rent control, responded to the inflation of the 1970s but continued to cater to the expectations and demographic demand of the baby boomers (Miron 1988). All of the programs were developed in cooperation with the provinces in an era of province-building, when the provinces were attempting to bolster their autonomy. Indeed, this period also saw provincial initiatives, as many of the provinces, most notably British Columbia, Ontario, and Quebec, developed and funded their own initiatives for home ownership and social housing, which sometimes complemented and at other times competed with federal programs.

Whereas the first two stages emphasized building, the latter three stages have been more concerned with constraint and targeted assistance. The financial restraint stage, from 1978 to 1986, responded to the desire for government restraint and reduced spending. Funding was passed to the private sector, with senior governments providing mortgage insurance and subsidies. During this period, there was a reduction in programs along with the reduction in government spending, which was increasingly targeted to low-income families, and the passing of program delivery to provincial and municipal governments. The main continuing programs were for non-profit social housing and housing rehabilitation (Carroll 1993). Then, in 1986, the federal government appeared to lose interest in housing: it was no longer an agenda item. In fact, in the Charlottetown Accord of 1986, it was proposed to give sole jurisdiction for housing to the provinces. The more recent Social Accord does not even mention housing.

This led to the fourth stage, disentanglement, which was a reflection of the desire to reduce government presence in housing markets and of the perceived need for deficit control. The federal government signed agreements with the provinces by which the federal government agreed to continue to share the cost of the subsidies for non-profit social housing and for rehabilitation programs on a 75:25 ratio, with the condition that funds were to be primarily targeted to those most in need. Provincial allocations would be based on housing need, with specific allocation rules laid out. There was little in the way of national standards, so provinces could vary program features. Alberta, Quebec, and Ontario opted for a 60:40 split, which meant a bigger program with more provincial financing. This stage ended in 1994 when the federal government announced the ending of all new federal funding for housing. They would continue to fund commitments only under pre-existing agreements (Banting 1990). The federal budget of that year placed additional financial restrictions on the senior government's obligations, with a $2.13 billion cap on housing expenditures. In 1995/96, the amount was further reduced to $2.026 billion, and in 1996/97 to $1.942 billion.

The fifth stage, divestment and disengagement, has developed since then. This most recent phase reflects a non-interventionist ideology, with a bias toward privatization and devolution, and a reduction of the government presence in markets. Indeed, the Ontario government is on the verge of selling its public housing stock altogether (Galloway 2000). This strategy has reflected in part a recognition of the failure of large-scale intervention into housing markets to solve problems of low-income housing needs. This is not just a reduction in funding. It seems to carry with it a belief at the federal level and among some provinces that the state should play a more limited role in housing markets. Policy decisions, to the extent that they are made at all, are made in isolation. The closely tied policy networks that had developed in housing over the 1960s and were sustained through the 1970s and 1980s seem to have atrophied. Finally, despite economic growth, there has been a widening income gap between the rich and the poor. Demographically, this stage has been marked by smaller, non-traditional family units and an aging population.

The clearest pattern across the five phases has been in the delivery of programs. Initially, the federal government funded and delivered programs. As programs gained acceptance, the federal government would gradually withdraw, passing the financing costs to the private sector and the delivery and regulation costs to the provinces. Increasingly, the momentum moved to municipalities, the private sector, and various forms of community partnership. This policy was exaggerated in the 1990s when 'partnerships' were everything. The reasons for these later changes were threefold. In the first place, that demographic blitzkrieg, the baby boomers, were housed and moving into their second homes. They did not require, or demand, intervention. Secondly, a non-interventionist political ideology had become dominant. Finally, and perhaps most important, there was, belatedly, some recognition that spending large amounts of scarce resources on housing programs had not alleviated housing problems (Cooper and Rodman 1992).

In summary, the early phases emphasized social involvement and rational planning within the context of the economic prosperity and inflation of the 1960s and 1970s. The growing assertiveness of the provinces was responded to by increasing their responsibility for program delivery. The 1980s reflected a concern with cost containment and disentanglement in the face of rising budgetary deficits at both the federal and provincial levels. The pattern of development and turnover continued, but in the 1980s, social policy lobbying and province-building combined to produce programs that were both inefficient and ineffective at meeting needs (Canada, Task Force on Program Review 1985; Ontario, Office of the Provincial Auditor 1992). Finally, we have rethinking of the role of government, disengagement, and some smaller-scale, non-government intervention.

Provincial Variations

To this point, the emphasis of this chapter has been on broad national problems and trends. There are, however, important variations across provinces in housing conditions and programs. Directly after World War II, the provinces had little involvement with major housing initiatives, their role being responsive and limited to cost-sharing. During the 1970s and early 1980s, they became more active but still largely responded to federal initiatives. The major solely provincial initiative was a flirtation with rent-control legislation in the mid-1970s that mirrored to some extent the federal initiative on wages and prices controls. This initiative, the major impact of which was to bring to a halt the building of privately financed rental housing, had largely died out by the 1980s, although rent review, the 'child of rent control', started to be phased out in Ontario only in 1998. After 1986, the provinces had sole operating responsibility for housing. For the first years after 1986, they continued to deliver the same programs that they had inherited from the federal government. Gradually, however, as changes in governments occurred at the provincial level, more variations across provinces have begun to appear.

The provinces started to look at ways of meeting the needs of an aging population and an aging housing stock (CMHC 1994) in a period of financial restraint. 'New' programs tended to consist of small loan or grants for home repair or rehabilitation or for upgrading to existing standards (Keyes 1990). Many of these were targeted at senior citizens in an effort to maintain their housing independence. In terms of delivery, greater emphasis was put on municipalities, public/private partnerships, and community involvement, particularly greater tenant involvement in management.

British Columbia has followed a somewhat similar path, trying to 'strengthen communities through local solutions' (Ramsay 1995) and has produced new forms of tenancy arrangements, such as land lease and tenant purchase. Manitoba has emphasized tenancy innovations and the revitalization of its urban cores. It was one of the first provinces to become involved with 'life-lease' rental projects for senior citizens, although it is notable that it does not, as Ontario does, require that tenants sit on a project's board of directors. Indeed, Manitoba allows non-profit housing groups to have bylaws that expressly prohibit the tenants who have invested in a project to sit on the board of directors (Garrity 2000).

Newfoundland and Labrador, Prince Edward Island, and Quebec have also continued to make use of the private rent supplement program in which the government pays a private landlord the difference between the market rent of the unit and the tenant's ability to pay. This program, originally introduced in the late 1970s, has always been one of the most flexible, cost-efficient programs available.

Ontario, under the NDP, tied housing to job creation programs through the construction of non-profit and cooperative rental projects. These programs were terminated and rent review is being phased out by the Conservative government. Most important, the government has tabled legislation that will download all responsibility for and costs of social housing—both the public housing stock and the responsibility for non-profit and cooperative housing—to the municipalities (Ontario, Ministry of Municipal Affairs and Housing 2000). The goal is for the transfer of all 'public housing business, assets and employees to new municipally-controlled local housing corporations, effective January 1, 2001' and 'the transfer of responsibility for non-profit and co-op housing administration . . . through a negotiated process over the next 18 months' (Fenn 2000). This downloading is viewed by municipal planners and housing analysts as, at the least, a major challenge to and, at the most, a fiscal disaster for municipalities. The municipalities are limited to a tax base that is inelastic and highly susceptible to poor economic conditions and faced with a responsibility that becomes more costly in economic downturns. (See Siegel's chapter on the nature of municipal financing.)

Most provinces have also embarked on various renovation and repair strategies in order to meet the needs of people who require accommodation and to deal with an aging social housing stock. Saskatchewan, Manitoba, and Quebec have programs specifically dedicated to upgrading projects in urban settings, most of which are variations on the older, federal rehabilitation program, which the federal government continues to fund. Others, such as British Columbia, New Brunswick, and Nova Scotia, have focused on the promotion of urban growth by changing zoning bylaws and assisting in land servicing.

In summary, most provinces, while recognizing that they cannot replace the loss of federal resources, have introduced some small-scale, often experimental programs that reflect their own demographic and housing needs in a climate of fiscal restraint. There are only limited signs, however, that provinces have started to grapple with the problem that will be facing our urban centres over the next decade or two, namely an imbalance between the housing that is needed and the housing stock that is available.

Urban Form and Variations

So what does the housing in cities look like? Although there are some variations based on the age of the city, on geographic features that limit or constrain growth, and on the dominant industry of the city, most cities in Canada have similar features. Except where the city has grown to incorporate an existing town, such as St Albert in the case of Edmonton, the city will evolve in more or less concentric rings from the urban core, with the newest housing on the periphery. These rings will actually be more like diamonds as the development tends to move close to transportation corridors, such as tramways, rail lines, or highways. Edmonton and Winnipeg are good examples of cities that developed in this way because there are no natural barriers, whereas cities such as Halifax, Toronto, Hamilton, and Vancouver have barriers to growth in some direction.

In the downtown core, there are high-density, high-rise apartments. The core will be surrounded by older residential neighbourhoods, some dating from the turn of the last century, but somewhat older in the Maritimes and somewhat younger in parts of the West. Many of these buildings will be multiple-storey and may now be rental or hostel housing. Mixed in will be brick apartment buildings and some houses from the post–World War I era. One of these neighbourhoods will be of very large houses, the mansions of the wealthy then and now. These are areas such as Rosedale in Toronto, Inglewood in Hamilton, Tuxedo in Winnipeg, and Shaughnessy Heights in Vancouver.

Still within walking or inner-city transit commuting distance will be the post-war suburbs. These are bungalows and one-and-a-half- or two-storey houses, of less than 1000 square feet, although most now will have additions. Beyond this come the suburbs of the 1960s and 1970s, with curved streets and large lots. In some cases, these are further out from the city, as the development was built originally as a 'new town' or planned community some distance from the city. These are neighbourhoods such as Kanata in Ottawa and Sherwood Park in Edmonton. Next, there will be the townhouses and single-family houses of the later 1970s. Here there is also some high-rise development, usually centred on shopping centres. Finally, there are the large subdivisions with smaller lots and larger houses.

Not every city is precisely like this—there will be pockets of in-fill housing or renewal where some areas were torn down and rebuilt, and the size of each section will depend upon the growth rate of the city at the time—but there is a distinct pattern. Smaller centres tend to have developed in a similar fashion, without the high-rise apartments in the core. There, apartments will be more on the periphery. Whereas overall, 60 per cent of Canadians own their own home and 40 per cent rent, the proportion of renters is slightly higher in large urban centres and rental stock tends to be more concentrated toward the centre of the city.

There are, however, variations in housing policy and needs between urban centres. These are primarily variations between large and small urban centres in their housing requirements, in their ability to meet these requirements, and in their ability to influence the type of assistance available. In earlier periods, large metropolitan centres, such as Toronto, Vancouver, Winnipeg, and Montreal, moved beyond a reactive role to become facilitators in defining their own needs and working with senior governments to develop programs and projects. Smaller centres had neither the financial nor the political capability to undertake major social programs or to withstand development pressure. The major centres, which had benefited earlier from urban renewal and public housing programs, were also able to make use of programs, such as non-profit and neighbourhood-improvement programs, that required a local delivery capacity. Smaller urban centres were more dependent upon externally initiated programs, such as public housing for senior citizens. Most small centres have some public housing, mainly for senior citizens, but usually run by a housing authority rather than by the municipality itself. Larger cities also established municipal non-profit corporations to compete with private non-profits for federal and provincial funding. The first of these was Cityhome in Toronto, which was established in 1974 and now owns and manages more than 7,000 housing units. But for the most part, 'municipal actions are regulatory in nature and are designed to ensure that safety standards are met, infrastructure and community services are provided, and the operations of the market are controlled to the extent that housing is appropriately located relative to other land uses' (Carter and McAfee 1990: 229).

As mentioned earlier, there was some municipal activism under the various federal-provincial programs until the 1990s (Carter and McAfee 1990). Encouragingly, some urban centres have stepped into the housing policy vacuum. Four of these initiatives, in Montreal, Hamilton, Calgary, and Vancouver, will be briefly outlined. It is clear that each city is responding to its own unique housing problems, but the variations also highlight the differences between the problems of rapidly growing cities and the problems of those that are static or in decline.

Montreal

In April 1995, the City of Montreal proposed a program to the Province of Quebec that was intended to revitalize some of the most rundown neighbourhoods in the city. The goals of the program were to increase the density of the areas, providing needed housing while combatting some of the effects of urban sprawl. The provincial government approved the program, and by the end of 1997, Phase I of the project had provided more than 5,500 units. About half the units and the bulk of the money went into the five targeted inner-city communities. The rest was spread across other targeted zones, mainly for the recycling and renovation of existing buildings. Although the provincial government originally agreed to put up $50 million (cost-shared with Ottawa), which the City was to match, in the end only $40 million in public money was used in the first phase. Private investment provided the great bulk of the funds for the $200-million program.

The program was intended to be flexible and innovative, and the range of actions taken provides examples: 20 boarded-up buildings were recycled, creating 500 new units; 840 in-fill units were built; 470 sheds that were unsightly fire hazards were demolished; and 4,200 dwellings were renovated. Most important, the program increased the number of owner-occupants living in these core neighbourhoods, which provides greater stability, brought an influx of medium- to high-income families back to the inner city, and improved the quality of existing affordable units. It has also had a dramatic impact on the liveability of the city.

Montreal has, moreover, the advantage of having two universities within the urban core. Cities that have institutions in their downtowns have the advantage that institutional expansion can drive inner-city renewal and provide a population to maintain the viability of the commercial core (City of Montreal, http://www.ville. montreal.qc.ca/habitation/engl, accessed 31 March 2000).

Hamilton

Hamilton is almost a classic case of the hollowing out of the urban core. It once had a vibrant downtown, but suburban sprawl has occurred, primarily above the Niagara Escarpment, which, although it provides a striking geographic feature for the city, tends to discourage people who live on the 'Mountain' from coming into the downtown to shop. Urban renewal was tried but resulted in empty shops because the office towers did not generate enough trade. There have been a number of attempts in the past to revitalize the downtown, none of which has been successful.

A more recent initiative seems to hold considerable promise. In 1998, the City Council adopted a strategy to encourage private investment and improve public infrastructure through road and 'streetscape' changes. Key initiatives were the devel-

opment of a community-inspired vision statement for the downtown and the establishment of the 'Hamilton Downtown Partnership', a not-for-profit corporation with
a board of business and political leaders.

One key goal is residential development in the downtown core, in a way not dissimilar to Montreal's in its focus on intensifying residential development in the
downtown core and its emphasis on the heritage aspects of some of the existing
buildings (Hamilton, Community Planning and Development Division 1999). One
aspect of this strategy is the funding of studies such as one carried out by the local
homebuilders association, which looked at the residential potential of existing building in the downtown core (HHHBA 1999). The other aspect of this strategy is to provide for the funding of new city-sponsored programs such as the Convert/Renovate
to Residential Loan Program, which provides zero-interest loans to convert non-res-
idential space in commercial buildings into rental housing.

Some successes have occurred. One of the first is City Places, a low-rise, mixed-
use building being developed on the site of several commercial old buildings and a
parking lot. It is an initiative of the City of Hamilton's Housing Corporation and is
intended as a demonstration project to show that there is a demand for commercial
market and affordable housing and that they can coexist in the urban core. The
financing is split 50:50 between the City and private investment (Arnold 1999). The
second success really consists of two projects, both private but benefiting from pref-
erential zoning and bylaw treatment, aimed toward the younger, urban demographic
group, many of whom may be people working in Toronto but who are now commuting from Hamilton on the recently extended GO train service. One of the projects
is a warehouse conversion, the other a newly built condominium. Both are being
marketed as 'luxury downtown living'.

The City has also changed street patterns to make the core more compact and less
of a route to somewhere else. (See Fowler and Layton's chapter on this concept of the
city street.) This is the smallest of the four initiatives, in part because Hamilton does
not have the tax base for large-scale subsidies; but it is an example of a municipality
willing to take the initiative and do it alone without large-scale support from other
governments or agencies.[1]

Calgary

Calgary's needs are quite different again. The city is growing quickly and there is a
critical need for affordable housing. In 1998, there were 1,000 people in the city identified as being homeless, and many of the emergency shelter facilities were taken up
by people who were working but could not find a place to live. The City has identified the need for over 3,000 new housing units, both shared social housing units for
hard-to-house individuals and single rooms and apartments for employed and
unemployed users of emergency shelters. The City wants to build new housing
because it recognizes that the current shortage is not a short-term problem. There
are almost no private rental units coming on stream, the vacancy rate is low, and it
is unlikely that net migration to the city will become negative in the near future.

To deal with the problem, the City is, in 2000, in the midst of identifying potential housing sites from within its own land inventory and has asked the provincial and federal governments to do the same. It issued a call for proposals for meeting the housing need with a minimum of 50 per cent equity in the project. The proposal contained detailed cost and recovery estimates based upon the type of housing and the percentage of affordable units within each type of project, whether the project consists of walk-up apartments, townhouses, or some form of shared accommodation. None of the last is expected to rent at market rents, although it is possible that there are people who would pay market rents for this type of accommodation. This project is still, in 2000, in the development stage, but it does represent an attempt to take action to solve the problem (City of Calgary 2000; Jack Layton, personal communication, 30 October 2000).

Vancouver

The City of Vancouver may be one of the most activist municipalities in the area of housing, although its policies have changed considerably over time (Carter and McAfee 1990). The major route used by the City is to lease city-owned land for social housing. But it has a number of other programs/policies. The City works with developers of large, private-market projects to gain more social housing either by incorporating it within the project or by the developers paying into the Affordable Housing Fund. For large projects, the policy has been to have 20 per cent of the units as some form of affordable housing. There are 800 units of such housing currently under development. In established neighbourhoods, the City has a special development levy, with some of the money directed to affordable replacement housing in that area.

The funds from the Affordable Housing Fund and the rest of the levy are used to provide funds for projects built on City-owned land. The Neighbourhood Housing Demonstration Program provides funds from an endowment to encourage demonstration projects to increase housing density and funds two programs to encourage rental housing: the Assured Moderate Rental Housing program, which involves private-public partnerships to build market rental units on City-leased land, and the Downtown Low-Income Housing program, which provides replacement for lost single-room-occupancy units in the downtown core (City of Vancouver, http://www.city.vancouver.bc.ca/commsvcs/housing, accessed 1 April 2000).

Conclusions

What these four urban areas have in common is a desire by the municipality to solve a housing need and a willingness to take the initiative and to provide financial incentives for partnerships with private interests. Although this is admirable, none of these municipalities has solved the problems of homelessness or urban sprawl. It is not a coincidence that what all urban areas have in common, albeit to varying degrees, is a reliance upon the property tax base and a political system that makes them the level of government at which private interests are most influential. Urban governments are, therefore, the least able to withstand private pressures for development, the least able to underwrite the social costs of housing, and the least able to withstand local resistance to social housing in particular locations—the familiar NIMBY syndrome. It is important to keep this political context in mind as we turn to a brief overview of the challenges that cities presently face in the field of housing policy.

Current Problems

In fifty years, Canadian housing policy has come almost full circle. Federal activity has been reduced to the role of mortgage insurer, and the broader responsibility for housing policy has been left to the provincial and municipal governments. This raises the questions of what intractable, or 'wicked',[2] problems these governments are facing and how they will cope with them. Solutions have certainly eluded us in the past. In the fifty years of activism, there were nearly 300,000 units of social housing and 200,000 units of public housing created (CMHC 1999; Sewell 1994). But at the end of this period, there were still a million urban households in Canada living in what the CMHC calls 'core need', that is, living in housing that 'needs major repair, lacks adequate bathroom facilities, is overcrowded and/or costs 30 percent or more of their incomes, and the household would have to spend 30 percent more of its income to pay the average rent of alternative local market housing that meets standards' (CMHC 1999: 7). In some cities, such as Vancouver in 1991, the last year for which census information is available, 22 per cent of households were living in such circumstances, and the numbers have been increasing, not decreasing, since that time (CMHC 1999; Layton 2000). More important, there seems to be little commitment on the part of any government to try to deal with this problem, perhaps with the exception of the cities mentioned above.

The housing problem facing our urban areas is not just core need and a shortage of rental housing. There are also the physical problems of obsolescence and urban sprawl, the changing demographic composition of our population, and the problems of affordability and homelessness.

We have had fifty years of building low-density suburban developments on the urban fringes to meet the aspirations of an affluent middle class. The services for these developments were paid for by federal and provincial grants and by the property tax, which is regressive. The provision of services for low-density developments represents a redistribution from lower- to higher-income groups and from owners of older homes to owners of new homes (Hill, Wolman, and Ford 1995). A high proportion of this Canadian housing stock—rental and homeowner, publicly and privately owned—is also over twenty years old and in need of upgrading and rehabilitating. Similarly, municipal infrastructure and urban renewal projects also require replacement or upgrading. In addition, the mortgages on the social housing stock built in the 1960s and 1970s are close to being repaid. The federal government has said that there will be no money for renovations or modernizations of these projects, some of which are over thirty-five years old. A major rethinking is needed of how urban centres are to cope with rebuilding their infrastructure and upgrading and altering their housing stock.

The 1994 federal infrastructure program might have provided such an opportunity, but many of these expenditures were used for shorter-term job creation projects.

Not only is the Canadian population aging, but household size is declining. Families are having fewer children and more single-parent families are being formed. At the same time, 'Generation X', as it is called, has not moved into the housing market as previous generations have done. Possibly for economic reasons, or possibly because of differences in values, the age at which people are buying their first home is rising (CMHC 1994). This has major implications for the effective use of the existing housing stock and for the type of new housing that will be needed (Burns and Grebler 1986). Much of the newer housing stock is large suburban bungalows. As the baby boom generation reach their sixties, there will be increasing demand for smaller urban dwellings with convenient shopping and transportation, that is, a movement back to the urban core. But what will we do with the aging suburbs and the monster homes?

Particularly in urban areas that are not growing, there is the question of who will live in these suburban houses as family size declines and the age of households increases. But in those areas that are still growing, another important effect is the continued consumption of recreational and agricultural land for residential purposes to satisfy the short-term development needs of municipalities and the building industry. Once the land is taken up for housing, it is difficult, if not impossible, to return it to its original use.

Finally, despite the efforts of governments over the last forty years, large numbers of Canadian households, particularly those with children, still do not have the earning capacity to provide themselves with this essential good. Even those who can afford it often have difficulty finding suitable rental housing, as the supply of rental housing stock other than subsidized social housing has remained almost static for twenty years. Although affordability is tied to the question of expectations, there is still a substantial group who require some form of assistance. It is accepted that the large-scale social housing programs of the 1970s and 1980s were both inefficient and ineffective. But that does not mean that nothing can, or should, be done. There have been innovative programs suggested that would provide affordable housing at little or no cost to government. One, for example, involves the purchase and renovation of existing homes as affordable homeowner and rental housing. The houses would be developed by non-profit building co-ops using apprenticeship labour and donated building materials. Rental units could be built within the units to assist the low-income homeowner with the mortgage. Costs could be kept low by buying houses at property tax sales or in the more rundown parts of the inner city. Government mortgage insurance would be needed for the completed unit, but costs would be well below the value of a new home or one renovated on the market. A similar program in Toronto much earlier produced some 1,000 units without government subsidies.

Within this problem of affordability is the major crisis of actual 'homelessness'. Given our climate, ours is not a country where people can live easily on the streets. Yet increasingly that is what is happening as governments withdraw from providing housing assistance. Measuring the amount of homelessness, or the number of homeless—even defining what homelessness is—is a difficult problem (Jack Layton, personal communication, 30 October 2000). Jack Layton, chair of the National Housing Policy Options Team of the Federation of Canadian Municipalities, has estimated that 200,000 Canadians 'experience homelessness at some time during the year' (Layton, personal communication, 30 October 2000). Using the same definition, the estimate for the United States was 1,200,000 in the 1980s. At the same time, it has been estimated that the number of individuals who live in temporary shelters or on the streets is between 250,000 and 500,000 (Layton, personal communication, 30 October 2000), an estimate that remained reasonably stable from the 1970s to the 1990s, with the homeless becoming being more visible as the kind of person who is homeless has changed (Maier 1995). It should be noted that there are parts of the United States where the climate makes it possible to live outdoors year-round. This is not true anywhere in Canada.

Homelessness is not just a housing issue. Some of the people currently without homes have social or mental health problems, and their being on the street is a by-product of the de-institutionalization of the 1970s, whereby people who had lived in protected environments were cut loose to fend for themselves. Others are children running away from abusive relationships. But a large number are those who simply do not have enough money for shelter, the so-called near homeless, who are placed in temporary accommodation. The welfare costs of looking after these people, particularly women with children, are high. In Toronto, for example, many are warehoused in motels, where the short-term costs are high and the living conditions poor. Some attempts to move these families to lower-cost cities where social housing was available were made, but this solution only works if the individuals have family support in the smaller centres.

Although there are some admirable volunteer and municipal actions to try to assuage the problem of homelessness and near homelessness, the problem is worsening, which raises the more fundamental issue of whether or not we are a compassionate society. The inertia of the federal and provincial governments and the passing of the responsibility for housing to municipalities leaves this area in the hands of the level of government least able to withstand the private pressures against social intervention and with a tax base which cannot be expanded in the event of economic downturns.[3]

Conclusion

Housing is an area that exemplifies the '"tragedy of the commons" in which behaviour that is perfectly rational for the individual, or the group, becomes extremely dysfunctional for the society as a whole' (Peters 1989: 22). The competing interests within the housing market all make legitimate claims; but the pressures of self-interest groups tend to lead to reactive and visible rather than viable solutions. In the same way, the pressures of electoral politics have led to short-term solutions.

For example, although the short-term interests of municipalities and of the development industry and the private interests of one sector of the public are met by the provision of new suburban housing, 'practical housing policy is much more about the management of an existing stock than it is about anything else' (Laver 1986: 180).

Greater concern with the management of the existing stock could do more to alleviate the problems that have been discussed in a cost-effective way. As the head of one provincial housing agency put it, 'While these existing units form a large part of the solution to housing those in need, they also present a key challenge for the future. The maintenance and regeneration of this stock will place an additional burden on already tight resources in years to come' (Noseworthy 1995).

In 1946 and 1969, there was a consensus on the problem to be dealt with and on the general direction for action. Both consensuses lasted for twenty years before reactive pressures caused distortions sufficiently visible to spark a major overhaul of the policies and the development of a new set of programs to attempt to rectify these distortions. Each time, this was achieved by imposing on existing institutions a coordinating mechanism with a defined perception of the future.

In the past, the distortions and drift that programs created were addressed by new programs and more elaborate program mechanisms. Unfortunately, this produced complex, high-cost programs that were cumbersome in achieving their goals. The consensus today is to try to achieve action within the market, without the expenditure of government funds. At the same time, the federal mechanism that in the past was able to ensure some degree of equity and coordination is now concerned primarily with being an enabling rather than a lead agency, with programs to encourage municipalities to develop more innovative solutions to zoning obstacles and density issues (CMHC 2000).

The lack of central coordination could have opened up opportunities for innovation. (See Haddow's chapter for discussion of this point.) The nature of the policy process, and the use of national programs that assumed a uniformity of housing problems, caused some of the difficulties that we currently face. Both provincial and larger urban governments could have responded with coordinated, small-scale initiatives that allowed for some experimentation, but there has been little action (Carroll and Jones 2000). What is lacking is leadership in terms of restructuring the home-building industry and changing the reliance of municipalities on 'new' development. This is a priority because errors in housing policy, once they are translated into the physical form, form a part of the urban environment for decades. We seem to have moved a long way from Carver's eloquent plea for a 'compassionate landscape' in the 1970s. The last decade has seen an increase in the development of ugly suburban subdivisions and an acceptance of people living in squalor or on the streets. We seem to have taken the compassion out of our urban living space.

Career Opportunities in the Field of Housing

Besides the most obvious careers of engineering, architecture, and the skilled building trades, such as electricians, plumbers, and carpenters (who make a great deal more money, and have a great deal more job satisfaction, than many people would expect), there are many careers related to housing policy. Most municipalities have urban planners who took a graduate planning degree. Building inspectors, who consider whether houses are up to building standards, are employed by municipalities and also by mortgage lenders and mortgage insurers, or they work as independent consultants. This profession involves technical training at a community college. For those who like working with numbers, appraisers, who determine the value of a building, are employed by banks, provinces, and insurance companies, although they increasingly work as private consultants. They usually have a university degree, with additional courses to get their appraisal accreditation. Then there are real estate agents, real estate brokers, property managers, and mortgage underwriters, all of whom have a designated accreditation with or without an undergraduate degree. All of these have professional associations that can give details on how to achieve accreditation.

Notes

1. Much of the information on Hamilton is based upon a 2000 case study, 'Intensification of the Downtown Core: Surveying Origins, Initiatives and Progress in the City of Hamilton' (Landes 2000).

2. 'Wicked' policy areas are those that Harmon and Myer (1986) define as having no solutions, only temporary and imperfect resolution, because of their high degree of complexity, and an unclear or rapidly changing consensus on goals.

3. The March 2000 Liberal policy convention passed a resolution for the federal government to reintroduce housing policies to deal specifically with the issue of homelessness. A federal–provincial meeting of housing ministers was held in Fredericton, New Brunswick, in the fall of 2000. The author was unable to find any press reports of the outcome of the meeting. Housing was not an issue in the federal election held in November 2000.

Bibliography

Arnold, Steve. 1999. 'Comeback in the Core'. *The Hamilton Spectator* (28 May).

Banting, Keith G. 1990. 'Social Housing in a Divided State'. In *Housing the Homeless and Poor: New Partnerships among the Private, Public, and Third Sectors*, ed. George Fallis and Alex Murray. Toronto: University of Toronto Press.

Bourne, Larry S. 1981. *The Geography of Housing*. London: Edward Arnold.

Burns, Leland S., and Leo Grebler. 1986. *The Future of Housing Markets: A New Appraisal*. New York: Plenum.

Canada. Task Force on Program Review. 1985. *Housing Programs: In Search of Balance. A Study Team Report to the Task Force on Program Review*. Ottawa: The Task Force.

Canada Mortgage and Housing Commission (CMHC). 1994. 'The Long-Term Housing Outlook: Preliminary Projections, 1991–2016'. *Research and Development Highlights*. Ottawa: CMHC.

———. 1999. *Evaluation of the Urban Social Housing Programs*. Ottawa: CMHC, Audit and Evaluation Services.

———. 2000. *The Evaluation Study of the Affordability and Choice Today (ACT) Program*. Ottawa: CMHC, Audit and Evaluation Services.

Carroll, Barbara W. 1988. 'Market Concentration in a Geographically Segmented Market: The Residential Home Building Industry in Ontario'. *Canadian Public Policy* 14: 296–306.

———. 1989. 'Post-War Trends in Canadian Housing Policy'. *Urban History Review* 18 (June): 64–74.

———. 1993. *The Allocation of a National Housing Budget: And Consequences Thereof.* Toronto: Institute of Public Administration of Canada.

———. 1998. 'Size and Response to Environmental Change in the Residential House Building Industry: Ontario 1978–1984'. *Canadian Journal of Urban Research* 6(1): 1–27.

Carroll, Barbara Wake, and Ruth Jones. 2000. 'The Road to Innovation, Convergence or Inertia: Devolution in Housing Policy in Canada'. *Canadian Public Policy* 26: 227–93.

Carter, Tom, and Ann McAfee. 1990. 'The Municipal Role in Housing the Homeless and Poor'. In *Housing the Homeless and Poor: New Partnerships among the Private, Public, and Third Sectors,* ed. George Fallis and Alex Murray. Toronto: University of Toronto Press.

Carver, Humphrey. 1975. *Compassionate Landscape.* Toronto: University of Toronto Press.

City of Calgary. 2000. 'Meeting the Critical Need for Affordable Housing in Calgary'. Accessed 15 February 2001: http://www.gov.calgary.ab.ca/community/publications/hcritical.html

Cooper, Matthew, and Margaret Rodman. 1992. *New Neighbours: A Case Study of Cooperative Housing.* Toronto: University of Toronto Press.

Fenn, W. Michael. 2000. 'Social Housing Reform Act, 2000'. (Memo to all Ministry of Municipal Affairs and Housing Staff, 12 October).

Fowler, Edmund P. 1992. *Building Cities That Work.* Montreal: McGill-Queen's University Press.

Galloway, Gloria. 2000. 'Poor Ask Where They'll Go'. *Hamilton Spectator* (23 March).

Garrity, K.M. 2000. 'Information Form: Life Lease Tenants in Occupancy'. Winnipeg: Fred Douglas Place, Inc. Mimeographed.

Hamilton. Community Planning and Development Division. 1999. *Design Strategy: Downtown Hamilton Secondary Plan.* Hamilton, ON: Urban Strategies.

Hamilton-Halton Home Builder's Association (HHHBA). 1999. *Downtown Hamilton: Residential Redevelopment Opportunities.* Hamilton, ON: HHHBA.

Harmon, Michael M., and Richard Myer. 1986. *Organization Theory for Public Administration.* Boston: Little, Brown.

Hill, Edward W., Harold L. Wolman, and Coit Cook Ford III. 1995. 'Can Suburbs Survive without Their Central Cities?' *Urban Affairs Review* 31: 147–74.

Keyes, Langley. 1990. 'The Private-Sector Role in Low-Income Housing'. In *Housing the Homeless and Poor: New Partnerships among the Private, Public, and Third Sectors,* ed. George Fallis and Alex Murray. Toronto: University of Toronto Press.

Landes, Megan. 2000. 'Intensification of the Downtown Core: Surveying Origins, Initiatives and Progress in the City of Hamilton'. Honours thesis, McMaster University, Hamilton, ON.

Laver, Michael. 1986. *Social Choice and Public Policy*. Oxford: Basil Blackwell.

Layton, Jack. 2000. *Homelessness: The Making and Unmaking of a Crisis*. Toronto: Penguin.

Maier, Mark H. 1995. *The Data Game: Controversies in Social Science Statistics*. 2nd ed. New York: M.E. Sharpe.

Miron, John. 1988. *Housing in Postwar Canada: Demographic Change, Household Formation, and Housing Demand*. Kingston, ON: McGill-Queen's University Press.

Mishra, Ramesh. 1990. 'The Collapse of the Welfare Consensus? The Welfare State in the 1980's'. In *Housing the Homeless and Poor: New Partnerships among the Private, Public, and Third Sectors*, ed. George Fallis and Alex Murray. Toronto: University of Toronto Press.

Noseworthy, Robert. 1995. Letter to the author. (7 June).

Ontario. Ministry of Municipal Affairs and Housing. 2000. 'Guide to Social Housing Reform'. Accessed 15 February 2001: http://www.mah.gov.on.ca

Ontario. Office of the Provincial Auditor. 1992. *Annual Report of the Auditor General of Ontario, 1992*. Toronto: Queen's Printer of Ontario.

Peters, B. Guy. 1989. *The Politics of Bureaucracy: A Comparative Perspective*. 3rd ed. New York: Longman.

Ramsay, Shayne. 1995. Letter to the author. (11 May).

Rose, Albert. 1982. *Canadian Housing Policy 1945–1980*. Toronto: Butterworth.

Sayegh, Kamal S. 1987. *Housing: A Canadian Perspective*. Ottawa: Academy Book.

Sewell, John. 1994. *Houses and Homes: Housing Canadians*. Toronto: Lorimer.

CHAPTER 6

Municipal Social Security in Canada

Rodney Haddow

Introduction

Research on urban politics in Canada is now assessing the significance of economic globalization for local governance. If globalism is emasculating the nation-state, as is now argued by many political scientists, will this allow sub-national structures, including municipalities, to become more important political actors? Because local governments are closer to citizens than are national and provincial ones, might this development not represent an opportunity to democratize our politics precisely when we thought that popular control of economic and social life had become impossible? These questions are of particular interest for the study of social security because it is in this field more than any other that the twentieth-century nation-state extended its involvement with the lives of its citizens while powerfully curtailing the role of local governments; and it is in this field, too, that the nation-state's weakness in the face of global economic forces has been most evident.

This chapter addresses the above questions with particular reference to the social security role of Canadian municipal governments.[1] The first section traces the history of the municipality's role in providing social security to Canadians, documenting the precipitous decline of this role as the federal and provincial governments took on more responsibilities during the twentieth century and detailing their social security activities as they were in the mid-1990s. The second section documents important trends since the 1970s that reflect globalism, including cuts in federal social programs and changing patterns of inequality and poverty; it then assesses the impact of these developments on municipal social security measures since the mid-1990s and on the incidence of need in Canada's urban centres. In light of this evidence, the third section evaluates the contrasting arguments that have been put forward by observers of Canadian municipal politics about whether local governments should now play an important role in providing social security.

Municipal Social Security in Historical Perspective

If advocates of ample social security also support a wider municipal role in dispensing it, they are unlikely to base their case for the latter on the historical social policy record of local governments. In Canada's early history, municipal social provision was punitive and benefits were meagre and uneven; the story of the marginalization of municipal social security is also a tale of the gradual ascendency of federal and provincial governments in this area, an ascendancy that broadened and improved the social security net. When circumstances have occasionally increased the social security burden faced by local governments, they have often favoured punitive measures in order to lighten the load. Nor have municipalities resisted their loss of authority in this field; overly reliant on unpopular property taxes and often poorly equipped to administer sophisticated social benefits, they have generally ceded ground gladly. Where municipalities still perform an important role in dispensing social aid, they often continue to provide benefits that are less uniform and more parsimonious than those available from programs administered by more senior governments.

In Canada, municipal institutions were the primordial home of the welfare state. Until the second decade of the twentieth century, 'relief' was the main form of social security. This provided limited help to the most needy, whose qualification for benefits was determined by applying some form of means test to ensure that all other means of subsistence had been exhausted.[2] The British Poor Law of 1601, which required local governments to assume responsibility for relief, was adopted in Nova Scotia and New Brunswick during the eighteenth century (Guest 1980). Mandatory municipal provision was not the norm in other Canadian provinces, but most also assigned relief to local institutions of some type. In Ontario, a tradition of voluntary relief by local charities emerged; municipalities were nevertheless extensively involved in providing relief by the middle of the nineteenth century (Splane 1965). In all four western provinces, relief was generally provided by municipalities, with more limited involvement by private charities (Cassidy 1945). Only in Quebec, Prince Edward Island, and Newfoundland did municipalities not emerge as the main purveyors of relief. Until World War II, most relief in Quebec was distributed by religious organizations through their network of local parish branches (Cassidy 1945). In Newfoundland, it was dispensed by the colonial government (Godfrey 1985).

Relying almost exclusively on these relief arrangements, social security in Canada very much conformed to a 'residual' model before World War I. Social protection was seen as a stop-gap, needed to provide for people who, because of infirmity or temporary unemployment, were unable to provide for themselves and their families through employment in the market economy; such employment was seen as the normal and proper source of a livelihood. This market orientation was reflected in a key feature of relief provision in almost all provinces: with the possible (and partial) exception of claimants considered to be particularly 'deserving', recipients of relief received limited benefits and were subject to demeaning administrative practices, so that their circumstances would be 'less eligible' (less desirable) than those of persons employed in the labour market at the lowest available wages (Guest 1980). Administration by municipalities had clear advantages from this residual perspective: it permitted the merits of claims for relief to be assessed by local administrators who were well-acquainted with local employment prospects and wage levels and, frequently, with the personal circumstances of the claimant. In this respect, administration by local branches of religious charities in Quebec and by provincial politicians in tiny Prince Edward Island could accomplish the same end.

The exigencies of 'less eligibility' in the quite different labour markets that existed in different communities, along with the variable fiscal and administrative capacities of municipalities, an equally variable cost of living, and diverse local politics, were responsible for another common feature of early municipally administered relief: eligibility criteria and benefit levels often varied substantially from one community to another (Cassidy 1945).

Municipal administration was much less compatible with the institutional conception of social security that made its first tentative appearance in Canada during and after World War I than it was with the residual model. One reason for this was administrative: an institutional approach sees social security as a first line of defence for all citizens, protecting them against infirmities and risks associated with life in market society. From this perspective, social security is no longer conceived of as a temporary measure, available to a few exceptional individuals; it becomes an integral part of everyday life for the broad mass of citizens, who receive benefits as a matter of right. To accomplish this, institutionalized social security measures must be widely available and granted according to comparable standards of benefit and eligibility. It therefore makes more sense to provide them through national and provincial governments that can avoid the inconsistencies that were always the hallmark of municipal relief.

A second reason for the incompatibility of municipal administration with institutionalized social security was financial. As broader forms of provision began to emerge, the cost of Canada's social security system grew rapidly. Health and social welfare expenditures of all types, for all levels of government, totalled only $15.2 million in Canada in 1913, when the welfare state consisted almost entirely of relief; by 1940/41, they totalled $255.1 million, and had been considerably higher during the Depression years of the 1930s (Guest 1980). Municipalities lacked the financial capacity, or the will, to undertake such expenditures. Canadian municipalities have always relied heavily on property taxes as their main own source revenue (i.e., revenue not received in the form of transfer payments from other governments, usually the province). This remains true today: in 1998, 68 per cent of own source revenues, for all Canadian municipalities, came from property taxes.[3]

As Siegel points out in his contribution to this volume, municipalities are loath to extend the use of this tax: they claim that it is a crude instrument whose incidence is not always related to ability to pay; it is highly visible; property tax receipts are sensitive to the business cycle, so that revenues decline precisely when the need for social expenditures is likely to be rising; and finally, it is commonly feared that if a municipality raises its property taxes much above those of its neighbours, it will experience a flight of employment-creating firms (Tindal and Tindal 1990).

As the institutional welfare state advanced, therefore, municipalities did not resist their own marginalization. On the contrary, periodic fiscal crises in the municipal welfare state—in the 1930s and in the early 1960s—led to a chorus of appeals for senior governments to relieve local governments of the burden (Sancton 1986). Where municipalities continue to play an important role in financing social programs, as in Ontario, an elimination of this responsibility remains their preferred option.

Workers' compensation and mothers' allowances were Canada's first significant steps in the institutional direction; most Canadian provincial governments created programs of these two types during the 1910s and 1920s. The federal Old Age Pension Act of 1927 represented Ottawa's first ongoing social security commitment; like mother's allowances, this means-tested pension relieved municipalities of a part of their relief expenses.

Ottawa and many of the provinces were less willing to accept responsibility for relief of the unemployed at the beginning of the Great Depression of the 1930s. But the manifest incapacity of local governments to meet the enormous demands put on them at that time drew the senior governments into a series of ad hoc commitments to finance unemployment assistance and relief work, although administration frequently remained in municipal hands. The municipal share of health and social welfare expenditures by all levels of government, which had been 54 per cent in 1913, fell to 20 per cent in 1930, and to 15 per cent in 1940 (Guest 1980).

In the wake of the Great Depression and of the war that followed it, Canada made its fullest commitment to the institutional approach, although its welfare state has always remained more market-oriented, and its benefits less generous, than those of most Western European countries. The federal government launched an Unemployment Insurance (UI) program in 1941 and, at the end of the war, committed itself to universal health insurance and to a major public pension initiative; fulfilling these commitments was Ottawa's main social policy preoccupation between 1945 and 1971. The UI program and Ottawa's commitment at the end of the war to conduct a Keynesian economic policy to minimize unemployment were considered likely to reduce municipal relief (by then commonly called 'social assistance') to a very secondary place in Canada's welfare state. Indeed, municipal assistance for employable persons was unavailable in Ontario and in some other provinces during most of the 1950s; employable claimants were considered to be a federal responsibility (Struthers 1994). The financing and administration of benefits for many unemployable persons were also taken on by the more senior governments after Ottawa introduced categorical assistance programs for blind and disabled persons in the early 1950s. In 1953/54, municipal health and social welfare expenditures of all kinds amounted to less than 5 per cent of such expenditures by all three levels of government (Guest 1980).

Unemployment rates began to rise during the mid-1950s, and unemployed persons who were ineligible for UI frequently had to turn to private charities for assistance. Ottawa eventually passed an Unemployment Assistance Act, sharing equally with the provinces the cost of assistance for this group. This new legislation actually amounted to a new burden for municipalities in those provinces where it was to be administered by them. In Ontario, for instance, local governments were expected to cover 20 per cent of assistance costs under the new legislation and to absorb all administrative costs; these were expected to rise rapidly under the new program (Struthers 1994). During the late 1950s and early 1960s, the effect of this was aggravated because unemployment levels were rising and because municipalities had to absorb a share of cost increases resulting from a rash of extensions in provincial programs for unemployable recipients (Struthers 1994). Municipal health and social security expenses rose from $78.4 million in 1953/54 to $117.3 million in 1962/63 (Guest 1980). Alarmed at this, municipalities in several provinces, especially Ontario and British Columbia, attempted to curtail their assistance rolls through 'work for relief' arrangements (compelling employable recipients to provide work in exchange for their benefits), a practice that had been commonly adopted during the Depression. When the federal government ruled that work for relief could not be covered by the Unemployment Assistance Act, municipal associations in these provinces demanded unsuccessfully that the Act be amended (Haddow 1993).

Municipal pressure for such punitive options subsided by the mid-1960s, in part because the burden on municipalities was again lightened—and their role in the Canadian social security system reduced to its present level—by a final round of reforms in federal and provincial assistance arrangements in the 1960s and early 1970s. Under the Canada Assistance Plan (CAP) of 1966, the federal government extended cost-sharing to virtually all then-existing provincial and municipal assistance programs. This extension was intended to permit provinces to move toward a more integrated approach to providing assistance, instead of assigning various categories of recipients to different programs. Integration was thought to be likely to reduce the inequities in access to benefits that were long associated with the categorical approach (Haddow 1993).

This integrative philosophy led four provinces where municipalities had historically administered most assistance—British Columbia, Alberta, Saskatchewan, and New Brunswick—to merge their municipal income assistance programs with the provincially administered programs that had grown up since World War I in a unified, provincially administered and financed program.[4] Eliminating municipal assistance was a particularly effective way of reducing inequities in access to benefits: municipal benefits were usually lower than those for provincially administered categorical programs and municipal benefits varied widely from one community to another, as they always had. During the Quiet Revolution, meanwhile, Quebec took over the assistance responsibilities that it had previously assigned to religious charities (Sancton 1986; Baccigalupo 1990).[5] Prince Edward Island and Newfoundland also modernized their provincially administered programs (Godfrey 1985).

In the wake of these reforms, only Ontario, Nova Scotia, and Manitoba continued to assign part of their income assistance regimes to municipal governments. Even in these provinces, most social assistance was now administered directly by the province, which also financed between 75 per cent and 80 per cent of assistance costs for what was left of the municipal tier (HWC 1988).

With grants from the provinces playing such a prominent role in financing municipal income assistance by the early 1990s, two of these provinces now exercised considerable influence over rates and eligibility criteria for the smaller municipal tier. But to the extent that municipalities still controlled some of their assistance rates, they continued to provide widely varying levels of benefits. In Ontario, the province's Family Benefits program provided assistance to unemployable persons; municipally administered General Welfare Assistance (GWA) was available for employable claimants. Uniform rates for basic coverage under GWA were set by the province; '[there was] wide variation, however, with respect to the provision of special assistance, which [was] the sole responsibility of Ontario municipalities' (NCW 1994: 10).

In Manitoba, the province established minimum rates for municipal assistance in 1992; in 1996, it then assumed responsibility for administering all assistance in Winnipeg, the provider of most municipal assistance in the province (NCW 1999b). Nova Scotia alone continued, until the mid-1990s, to exercise little influence over rates— or even eligibility criteria—for municipal assistance. Access to municipal assistance and available rates varied substantially across Nova Scotia; rates were also significantly below those for provincial assistance (Blouin 1992).

The municipal role in social services (i.e., in-kind social assistance rather than cash) was also curtailed in the wake of CAP. Five provinces (Newfoundland, Prince Edward Island, New Brunswick, Saskatchewan, and British Columbia) now provide almost all such services either through regional branches of provincial departments or through private agencies that are largely financed and controlled by the province. In Quebec, many health and social services are administered by a network of regional service councils (CLSCs) around the province. The elected councils were introduced in the early 1970s to integrate service provision at the local level and to provide more local control of services, but CLSCs are largely beyond the influence of municipal governments, elections to them have inspired little interest, and they are often seen as essentially controlled by the province (Wharf 1990; Sancton 1988). Among provinces that have eliminated municipal income assistance, Alberta alone grants a noteworthy role to municipalities in administering services; local governments there oversee family and community services (Masson 1994).

The municipal role in social services is now most extensive in Ontario and Nova Scotia. In each, municipalities administer or oversee daycare centres, some seniors' services, and homes for special care; they share with the province the cost of some child custody services (Canadian Tax Foundation 1992; Sancton 1988). As Foot's contribution to this volume suggests, the burden that these costs represent for municipalities varies significantly across Canada because of variations in the size of relevant dependent populations (primarily, youth and the elderly). In Ontario, the proportion of social services that is under municipal control nevertheless declined substantially between the mid-1960s and the mid-1980s (Sancton 1986). It is too soon to forecast whether the complex service exchange launched in Ontario in 1998 (see later in this chapter) will further lighten or additionally burden its municipalities.

The very marginal role that Canada's municipalities now play in providing both income assistance and social services is clearly reflected in expenditure data. As Siegel's analysis in this volume makes clear, these social security costs are not now a significant component of municipal expenditures in most provinces. In 1996/97, the net cost to Canadian municipalities of income assistance and related social services was $1.01 billion out of a total for all three levels of government of $20.56 billion; the municipal share was approximately 5 per cent. The majority of these municipal expenditures (almost $1 billion) were in Ontario, where they represented over 12 per cent of expenditures of this kind by the three levels of government and where these municipal costs had risen steeply between 1985 and 1995 (peaking at $1.13 billion in 1994/95) before falling over the next two years in the wake of restrictions legislated by the province. The only other province where net municipal income assistance and related service expenditures represented over 1 per cent of the total for all three levels of government was Nova Scotia; net municipal costs there were $61 million, or 11 per cent of the total, in 1996/97. Even before Manitoba assumed responsibility for Winnipeg's assistance tier in 1996, the province had effectively relieved municipalities of almost all costs associated with that tier.[6]

Reduced to such a lowly status, Canadian municipalities are now much less active in providing social security than are local governments in many other countries, especially in Western Europe. Over half of all public-sector employment in Norway and Denmark is at the municipal level; the municipal share rises to more than 80 per cent in Sweden, where local governments are responsible for delivering most of the country's ample health and social service programs. German and Dutch municipalities also play an important role in delivering services. Even in France, once renowned for its highly centralized system of government, administration of income assistance was decentralized to regional governments in the 1980s. In these countries, municipalities have access to greater financial resources than in Canada; they must observe national standards in administering social benefits, but they frequently have some discretion to adjust programs to local needs (Gilbert and Stevenson 1993). British and American municipalities have fewer social security responsibilities than their Continental counterparts, but they also retain more authority than do Canadian local governments (Manga and Muckle 1987; Sancton 1986).

Globalization and Contemporary Municipal Social Security

Since the 1970s, many Western countries—above all, the United States—have experienced significant increases in their rates of inequality and poverty. Until the mid-1990s, Canadian data revealed a more ambiguous pattern: inequality and poverty would have grown significantly if this had not been prevented by income security benefits; in effect, Canada's welfare state compensated less advantaged Canadians as they lost their ability to sustain their standard of living in the market economy. The most recent available poverty statistics, for 1997, suggest that Canada is now moving closer to the American pattern in the wake of substantial cuts in many income security measures since 1990. After reviewing evidence of these patterns, the second part of this section explores their implications for municipalities.

A Changing Socio-Economic and Policy Setting
There is clear evidence of a significant increase in inequality of earnings among Canadians between the early 1970s and the late 1980s (Morrissette, Myles, and Picot 1995).

But, unlike in the United States, Canada's income security programs were able to prevent this growth in earnings inequality from being translated into a comparable growth in inequality of total family incomes. The most important of these programs were social assistance, unemployment insurance (UI), and the family allowance (Blank and Hanratty 1993). These were also responsible for the fact that the incidence of poverty among Canadians did not grow steadily between the 1970s and the late 1980s (NCW 1995).

Beginning in 1990, both Conservative and Liberal federal governments in Canada significantly curtailed the income security benefits that played such a crucial role in the previous decade. UI was cut severely in 1990 and 1995. Other cuts in the late 1980s and early 1990s transformed the universal Family Allowance into a selective benefit and 'clawed back' benefits from the universal Old Age Security pension for middle-class individuals (Muszynski 1995). In 1995, the Liberal government terminated the CAP, cut back significantly on the money it transfers to all provinces for social assistance, and folded this money into the previously separate fund used to assist provincial health and post-secondary education programs; the new transfer, entitled the Canada Health and Social Transfer (CHST), came into effect on April 1, 1996. A predictable result followed these cuts: in 1997, well into an economic upturn, poverty rates remained well above pre-recession levels; 17.2 per cent of all Canadians were poor in that year, according to the National Council of Welfare's measures, compared to 13.6 per cent in 1989 (NCW 1999a).

These socio-economic and policy changes have all been linked, by governing politicians and by academic commentators on both the political right and the left, to globalization. Growing inequality in earned income in developed economies is traced to the disappearance of high-wage, low-skill manufacturing jobs, which have been decimated by growing competition from low-wage countries, and by the resulting need to increase productivity in these industries. Social security cuts are regarded as a necessary response to this more competitive global environment. And global competition is thought to preclude raising taxes to sustain existing provision in the face of rising need; on the contrary, it has been used to justify significant reductions in taxes on corporations and upper-income earners (McBride and Shields 1993).

Local Impact

If the most recent cuts are evidence that the Canadian nation-state—like others in the developed world—cannot defend its institutionalized welfare state against global forces, can municipalities step into the breach to prevent a resulting rise in inequality and poverty, already the evident consequence in the United States of miserly social security arrangements?

In fact, during the early 1990s, local governments were asked to do this in Ontario and Nova Scotia, the two provinces where municipalities retained an important role in financing social assistance. Assistance was the central element in Canada's welfare state that allowed the government to play its compensatory role in the 1980s. Even as the economy recovered from the recession of the early 1980s, many Canadians who had been thrown onto social assistance during the downturn remained there in the subsequent expansion: the number of welfare recipients in Canada, which reached a peak of 1.9 million in 1985, declined only to 1.8 million by 1988. With the onset of the next recession, social assistance dependency rates exploded, hitting 3.1 million in 1994 and 1995. Caseloads thereafter began to fall, especially in Ontario, which launched its restrictive new workfare program during that year. In 1997, 2.8 million Canadians depended on assistance (NCW 1987, 1992, 1998). The cost of assistance programs in the ten provinces also rose during the first half of the 1990s; from $5.4 billion in 1984/85, their cost reached $14.3 billion in 1994/95 before falling to $11.9 billion in 1997/98 (Statistics Canada 1998).

In the wake of these developments, the municipal cost of social assistance and related services in Nova Scotia rose from $76 million in 1985/86 to $134 million in 1993/94 before falling considerably after the province agreed to absorb a larger share of these costs in 1994 (Statistics Canada 1998). In 1995/96, Nova Scotia finally took steps to terminate its two-tier assistance system. It assumed control of municipal assistance in industrial Cape Breton and in Halifax and moved to integrate the two assistance tiers elsewhere in the province in 1997 (Nova Scotia, Department of Community Services 1997). In many parts of the province, elimination of the municipal tier was expected to lead to a significant increase in benefit levels (Nova Scotia, Department of Community Services 1998). Municipalities were initially required to continue paying a share of caseload costs, but Nova Scotia later agreed to phase out these charges over a four-year period. If this transition is completed, the province will have met a long-standing demand of the Union of Nova Scotia Municipalities that it assume responsibility for all assistance program costs (UNSM 1997).

The most dramatic effect on municipal finances was experienced in Ontario, where provincial initiatives gave rise to a protracted debate about the future of municipal assistance. Municipal assistance and related service costs in Ontario rose from $465 million in 1985/86 to $1.13 billion in 1994/95 before falling to $935 million in 1996/97 in the wake of welfare cuts introduced by Mike Harris's Conservative government after it came to power in 1995 (Statistics Canada 1998).

Between the late 1970s and the early 1990s, social assistance costs rose more rapidly than any other category of expenses for Ontario municipalities (Ontario, Advisory Committee to the Minister of Municipal Affairs 1991). There has been much discussion of the merits of integrating the province's two assistance tiers. In 1988, *Transitions*, a set of reform proposals drafted by a committee of non-governmental experts, recommended integration of the two tiers, with financing by the province (Ontario, Social Assistance Review Committee 1988). In 1991, Ontario's municipalities used the Hopcroft Report to indicate their desire to be unburdened of financial responsibility for assistance; the report was prepared by a committee dominated by municipal politicians and staff (Ontario, Advisory Committee to the Minister of Municipal Affairs 1991). By 1992, the cost spiral was clearly taking its toll on municipalities' ability to maintain existing benefit levels; even relatively large and affluent regional municipalities, such as Metropolitan Toronto and Ottawa-Carleton, cut benefits (NCW 1992). Municipal leaders were further upset when Ontario's NDP government introduced its Social Contract in April of that year, cutting transfers to the municipalities substantially.

Transfers from the province were cut even more deeply—by more than 20 per cent in some cases—by the Harris government in June 1995. The cuts were accompanied by changes in provincial legislation that extended the right of municipalities to charge user fees for daycare and other services (Mittelstaedt 1995; Rusk 1995). In 1996, the municipalities' remaining social security responsibilities became caught up in a massive provincial restructuring exercise. A government-appointed panel reiterated earlier demands that Ontario assume responsibility for the financing and administration of income assistance, as well as employment and child care services (Ontario, Ministry of Municipal Affairs and Housing 1996). But in May 1997, the province decided upon a quite different course: it would integrate about half of the clients from the provincially administered assistance tier (mainly sole-support parents) with the municipally administered tier in a new 'Ontario Works' program that would be administered entirely by municipalities, who would also fund 20 per cent of its benefits costs. Municipalities were expected to fulfill the new program's objective of returning recipients to work by providing job search assistance, basic literacy, referral to training opportunities, or community placements or by finding them a job. Municipalities also would fund 20 per cent of benefits costs for disabled persons, for whom assistance would remain under provincial administration in a separate program. The administrative costs for both programs would be shared between the province and municipalities on a 50/50 basis (Ontario, Ministry of Municipal Affairs and Housing 1999).

In exchange for the implied additional fiscal burden on municipalities (of funding one-fifth of benefit costs and one-half of administrative costs for the entire assistance regime, rather than for aid to just short-term recipients, as they had previously), the provincial government assumed responsibility for financing half of the costs of primary and secondary education, in effect reducing substantially the burden that education represented for local property taxes. The province also accepted full financial responsibility for two social services that had previously been partly municipal responsibilities: Children's Aid Societies and women's shelters. On the other hand, the municipal role was expanded in respect of child welfare services (Ontario, Ministry of Municipal Affairs and Housing 1999). The Association of Municipalities of Ontario (AMO) expressed concern that its members might—contrary to the province's claims—incur an additional financial burden because of this exchange. But these decisions did respond to some AMO apprehensions regarding the burden that social security costs represented for the property tax base. The AMO did not oppose the changes (AMO 1997). Table 6.1 summarizes the social security role of Ontario municipalities in the wake of these changes.

This recent crisis of social security in the two provinces where municipalities remained most active in its financing reflected the pressures of globalization discussed earlier in this chapter. Only in Ontario will municipalities retain an important social security role in the wake of this crisis. Beyond its direct impact on municipal assistance costs, is globalization having other consequences for municipalities? For instance, was the growth of the assistance-dependent population during the early 1990s accompanied by the expansion of an urban 'underclass', concentrated, perhaps, in Canadian

Table 6.1:   Municipal Income Assistance and Child Care Responsibilities, Ontario, 2000

Program Type	Program Costs and Responsibilities Assigned to Municipalities
Income assistance' for employable persons (Ontario Works)	
Assistance costs	20%
Employment services	20%
Administrative costs	50%
Administering jurisdiction	municipal
Income assistance for disabled persons (Ontario Disability Support Program)	
Assistance costs	20%
Administrative costs	50%
Administering jurisdiction	provincial
Child care services	
Program costs	20%
Administrative costs	50%
Administering jurisdiction	municipal

Source: Ontario. 1999. *Local Services Realignment: A User's Guide.* Toronto: Queen's Printer for Ontario, A16, A28.

inner cities? It has been argued by urban geographers that throughout the cities of the developed world, globalization is shifting employment from manufacturing to services, causing a polarization of incomes within these cities (Sassen 1998).

If this pattern is emerging in Canadian cities, then it would have clear implications for municipalities: it would mean that compensatory income security programs have not been as successful in urban areas as they have been nationally and that levels of social privation in cities are therefore rising. Certainly there are visible indications—for instance, the proliferation of food banks and some evidence of a rising incidence of homelessness—that in urban centres, particularly those with a large and aging inner city, an underclass is emerging. Milroy, for instance, documented the limited ability of Ottawa-Carleton's regional government during the 1980s to deal with what was perceived to be a problem of increasing homelessness (Milroy 1991). In keeping with this view, when Toronto launched an 'Action Plan' to combat homelessness in 1999, it stressed that 'The City of Toronto . . . cannot tackle the larger issues—poverty and the lack of affordable and supportive housing; these areas are the responsibility of the provincial and federal governments' (Toronto 2000).

There is little hard evidence, however, that widespread pauperization is in fact occurring in Canadian inner cities, though the phenomenon is well advanced in some American urban areas (Bourne 1993). Instead, pauperization, gentrification (upper-income families displacing disadvantaged residents), and polarization each appear to be occurring in various Canadian cities (Ley 1994). Indeed, Bourne has argued that these processes often coexist in the same communities: 'The conundrum is one of a persistent if not deepening level of social deprivation and poverty, co-existing with—but worlds apart from—areas of extensive revitalization and gentrification in the inner city' (Bourne 1993: 1313). There is not yet evidence that the gap between these affluent and poor districts is increasing significantly in most cities. But since the 1990s, cuts in federal and provincial income security measures have, as we have seen, begun to produce more polarized final incomes; in Ontario, at least, one would expect that municipal services of various kinds will eventually experience an additional burden.

Whither Municipal Welfare States?

Among observers of Canadian municipal politics, there is a long tradition of advocating greater social policy responsibilities for municipalities. This position was given a qualified endorsement by Cassidy in 1945. He anticipated most of the arguments now commonly made by proponents of municipal control: 'Local administration permits . . . some variation from place to place, to take account of differences in local conditions'; it 'permits experimentation by progressive communities'; it also facilitates the 'co-ordination of health and welfare services with other aspects of municipal administration', as well as enhancing 'co-ordination with private services and the mobilization of community resources' (Cassidy 1945: 205); and citizens can become more involved in social administration if it is done locally. Above all, 'there are important democratic values in the local administration of the health and welfare services. . . . Their retention at the local level tends to strengthen local government, which is potentially one of the chief foundations of a democratic system' (Cassidy 1945: 207).

This final argument has remained central to the thinking of contemporary champions of local control. 'Local government studies', Magnusson observes, 'are still shaped by the nineteenth-century ideal of municipal self-government: in other words, by the belief that every substantial local community—and especially every city—ought to have its own autonomous government. In the ideal, such an authority is sovereign within its own sphere' (Magnusson 1985: 576). Cassidy's arguments that municipal governments are particularly well qualified to coordinate local public and private services and that they can integrate these services around objectives defined through 'social planning' also remain popular (Manga and Muckle 1987; Wharf 1990).

Contemporary advocates of local control, such as Gilbert and Stevenson, have made an additional argument: the contention, referred to at the beginning of this chapter, that economic globalization is emasculating the nation-state and necessitating the emergence of competent local decision-making arenas to take their place—'both the public and private sectors are . . . increasingly operating within a context of "thinking globally and acting locally"' (Gilbert and Stevenson 1993: 76). They go on to recommend 'that social assistance programs be administered by local or regional governments—to permit easier integration with locally based programs and thus allowing . . . economies of proximity' (Gilbert and Stevenson 1993: 85). Effective municipal administration would require continued financial assistance from the more senior levels of government, but preferably on a less conditional basis than at present.

But the evidence surveyed in the first two sections of this chapter casts some doubt on the argument that social security can benefit from greater municipal direction. To begin with, the historical experience of municipal relief provision in Canada gives little indication that local governments, however 'democratic', can be counted on to meet recipients' needs any better than their national or provincial counterparts. Progress toward an institutionalized welfare state in Canada entailed a movement away from local control—and from the parsimonious and erratic benefits that typified municipal relief. And there is good reason to believe that when municipalities control benefits and must also finance a significant part of them from their own revenues, benefits will usually be quite stingy. Sancton observes that 'since social services are always consumed by a powerless minority and paid for by a sceptical majority, the dangers inherent in opening up the private world of social services to the local democratic process are obvious. There is much to be lost at the hands of the cost-slashing politician, particularly the inhabitants of city halls' (Sancton 1986: 61). Local politics is especially susceptible to these pressures because of a simple economic logic: 'If a city expands its services to needy citizens, it only increases its attractiveness as a residence for the poor. Other things being equal, consistent, concentrated pursuit of such a policy leads to bankruptcy' (Peterson 1981: 210). This preference for economic over social responsibilities is likely to be particularly strong in Canada, where municipalities have historically been 'mainly confined to service and regulation of the urban property industry—or real property more generally' (Magnusson 1985: 587). It is therefore understandable that Canadian municipalities have usually sought to abandon their social security responsibilities to more senior governments. If globalization is now eroding the capacity of nation-states to sustain institutionalized social benefits in the face of low-cost competition from abroad, there is every reason to believe that this logic has been even more compelling—for a much longer time—for municipalities.

Municipalities will have less reason to be stingy if the cost of benefits is borne almost entirely by more senior governments; this approach has permitted many of the European countries discussed earlier to reconcile municipal administration with generous provision. But, as Gilbert and Stevenson (1993) observe, substantial reliance on grants has been accompanied by often restrictive national standards in Europe (as it has in Canada). Grant-financing of local services is also objectionable on accountability grounds, an issue that is returned to later in this chapter.

The argument that local administration permits more effective coordination of social assistance with other public and private services in the community, and that it can also permit experimentation and variety, is one of the arguments most widely cited by proponents of decentralization. But here too there are grounds for skepticism. It is hard to see why similar advantages could not be achieved by means of community-based agencies administered by the province.[7] The 'flexibility' that local administration could permit would also sit uneasily alongside the need, recognized by most advocates of an expanded municipal role, to maintain adequate service standards; these standards would still have to be enforced by the provinces.

The preoccupations with property and economic growth that are usually at the centre of municipal politics also do not bode well for effective 'social planning' under municipal direction. One way of addressing this problem, of course, is to consolidate community-level health and social services under elected 'special purpose' bodies that are independent of municipal government. This was the approach taken in establishing Quebec's CLSCs; analogous bodies have been created in New Zealand. In both of these cases, however, voter turnout in local authority elections has been low and elected boards have had little ability to challenge local administrators or senior governments in establishing program priorities (Manga and Muckle 1987; Sancton 1988).

The most compelling reservation about municipal control is financial. Where municipalities continued to administer assistance in recent years, they endured a staggering increase in costs; there is not yet any hard evidence that municipal services are additionally burdened by a growing underclass, although such a development is distinctly possible in the wake of recent cuts in Canada's compensatory income security arrangements and increases in the national poverty rate. Even without this additional weight, however, Canadian municipalities are far from being able to finance their existing services from their own revenues (see the chapter by Siegel). Not only is the property tax inadequate to meet municipal fiscal needs, but the political and economic costs of raising it have also made it an undesirable tool for financing social security. It is worth noting that in Ontario, the one province that is likely to continue to assign an important social security role to local governments, the province mollified municipal resistance to a degree by reducing the burden that education costs represented for the property tax base.

As an alternative, one might envisage paying for a larger municipal social security role by increasing already substantial provincial conditional grants. But extending these grants in Canada has been associated historically with a rapid decline in municipal discretion, not with an expansion of it: 'This situation would undercut one of the main arguments for increasing the local government role: as a democratically-elected body, local governments are responsible to the local taxpayers. Their role in health and social services would become similar to other government-sponsored agencies and susceptible to political and bureaucratic influence from the provinces' (Manga and Muckle 1987: 72).

Provincial grants could, alternatively, be made unconditional to maximize municipal autonomy. But the use of unconditional grants raises a problem of accountability: funds raised by provincial governments, elected by provincial voters, would be dispensed with little provincial oversight by another jurisdiction; it is hard to imagine that any province would agree to such an arrangement. Because of municipalities' fiscal dependence on more senior governments, finally, the contemporary problem of municipal finance cannot be separated from the fiscal pressures now being experienced by governments everywhere, which are being squeezed between rising social need and diminishing fiscal capacity. Municipalities are in no way isolated from the constraints that are eroding the welfare states constructed painstakingly by nation-states throughout the Western world during the twentieth century.

Career Opportunities in Income Security and Social Services

As readers of this chapter will know, most programs of this type are now delivered by provincial governments in most jurisdictions. Ontario is the main exception this pattern; but in some other provinces, a few social services remain in municipal hands.

Either way, there are many employment opportunities in this area across the country. A degree in social work is the standard requirement for many kinds of employment in the social services field. Many employees in these services completed a bachelor's degree in the subject (a BSW), while others will hold a master's degree (an MSW), having done their first degree in another discipline, such as political science. As a profession, social work can be both rewarding and demanding. People are often attracted to the field by a desire to make a difference in the lives of needy clients; on the other hand, the interpersonal aspect of this kind of work often requires patience and sensitivity. Social workers must be able to juggle the imperatives, sometimes seemingly in contradiction, of addressing client needs while at the same time applying the rules that are prescribed by the statutes and regulations that govern social service programs.

Social services employment does offer opportunities to persons educated in other fields as well. Most larger service administrations employ social researchers (who might have some graduate training in political science or sociology), financial administrators (trained in accountancy), psychologists (usually with a master's degree in clinical psychology), and so forth.

Notes

1. *Social security* includes government-administered or government-financed benefits that are designed to meet basic human needs; these benefits are delivered either in the form of cash (income security) or in kind (social services). Several in-kind benefits—education, health, and housing—are treated elsewhere in this volume and are therefore excluded from discussion in this chapter.
2. *Relief* can include benefits either of a cash or of an in-kind variety. Modern-day relief is called *social assistance*. Cash benefits of the relief or assistance type are now commonly called *income assistance*, and in-kind benefits are termed *social services*.
3. Calculated from Statistics Canada, CANSIM, Matrix 7093.
4. The contemporary, unified, income assistance programs in these provinces are described in Health and Welfare Canada (1988).
5. The one exception to provincial administration of income assistance in Quebec is the City of Montreal, which delivers the province's income assistance program within its boundaries (see Baccigalupo 1990).
6. Calculated from Statistics Canada (1998), various tables.

7. Advocates of local control would no doubt argue that many of the services requiring coordination are already administered by the municipality, as is true of public education, for instance. But the 'special purpose' school boards that now oversee this service have escaped meaningful control by municipalities in many provinces. The same can be said of special purpose bodies that deliver many other local services. (See Magnusson 1985.)

References

Association of Municipalities of Ontario (AMO). 1997. *Bill 142: The Social Assistance Act, 1997*. (September). Toronto: AMO.

Baccigalupo, Alain. 1990. *Système politique et administratif des municipalités Québécoises: Une perspective comparative*. Montreal: Editions Agence D'ARC.

Blank, Rebecca, and Maria Hanratty. 1993. 'Responding to Need: A Comparison of Social Safety Nets in Canada and the United States'. In *Small Differences That Matter: Labor Markets and Income Maintenance in Canada and the United States*, ed. David Card and Richard Freeman. Chicago: University of Chicago Press.

Blouin, Barbara. 1992. 'Below the Bottom Line: The Unemployed and Welfare in Nova Scotia'. *Canadian Review of Social Policy* 29–30: 112–31.

Bourne, Larry S. 1993. 'Close Together and Worlds Apart: An Analysis of Changes in the Ecology of Income in Canadian Cities'. *Urban Studies* 30: 1293–1317.

Canadian Tax Foundation (CTF). 1992. *Provincial and Municipal Finances 1991*. Toronto: CTF.

Cassidy, Harry. 1945. *Public Health and Welfare Reorganization: The Postwar Problem in the Canadian Prairies*. Toronto: Ryerson Press.

Gilbert, Richard, and Don Stevenson. 1993. *Disentangling Local Government Responsibilities: International Comparisons*. Toronto: Canadian Urban Institute.

Godfrey, Stuart. 1985. *Human Rights and Social Policy in Newfoundland, 1832–1982: Search for a Just Society*. St. John's, NF: Harry Cuff.

Guest, Denis. 1980. *The Emergence of Social Security in Canada*. Vancouver: University of British Columbia Press.

Haddow, Rodney. 1993. *Poverty Reform in Canada, 1958–1978: State and Class Influences on Policy Making*. Montreal: McGill-Queen's University Press.

Health and Welfare Canada (HWC). 1988. *Inventory of Income Security Programs in Canada*. Ottawa: HWC.

Ley, David. 1994. 'Social Polarisation and Community Response: Contesting Marginality in Vancouver's Downtown Eastside'. In *The Changing Canadian Metropolis: A Public Policy Perspective*, vol. 2., ed. Frances Frisken. Toronto: Canadian Urban Institute.

McBride, Stephen, and John Shields. 1993. *Dismantling a Nation: Canada and the New World Order*. Halifax: Fernwood.

Magnusson, Warren. 1985. 'The Local State in Canada: Theoretical Perspectives'. *Canadian Public Administration* 28: 575–99.

Manga, Pran, and Muckle, Wendy. 1987. *The Role of Local Government in the Provision of Health and Social Services in Canada.* Ottawa: Canadian Council on Social Development.

Masson, Jack. 1994. *Alberta's Local Governments and Their Politics.* Edmonton: University of Alberta Press.

Milroy, Beth Moore. 1991. 'People, Urban Space and Advantage'. In *Canadian Cities in Transition*, ed. Trudi Bunting and Pierre Filion. Toronto: Oxford University Press.

Mittelstaedt, Martin. 1995. 'Harris Tells Municipalities It's Time to Be Partners'. *Globe and Mail* (23 August).

Morrisette, René, John Myles, and Garnet Picot. 1995. 'Earnings Polarization in Canada, 1969–1999'. In *Labour Market Polarization and Social Policy Reform*, ed. Keith Banting and Charles Beach. Kingston, ON: Queen's University School of Policy Studies.

Muszynski, Leon. 1995. 'Social Policy and Canadian Federalism: What Are the Pressures for Change?' In *New Trends in Canadian Federalism*, ed. François Rocher and Miriam Smith. Peterborough, ON: Broadview.

National Council of Welfare (NCW). 1987. *Welfare in Canada: The Tangled Safety Net.* Ottawa: NCW.

———. 1992. *Welfare Reform: A Report.* Ottawa: NCW.

———. 1994. *Welfare Incomes: A Report. 1993.* Ottawa: NCW.

———. 1995. *Poverty Profile 1993: A Report.* Ottawa: NCW.

———. 1998. *Profiles of Welfare: Myth and Realities.* Ottawa: NCW.

———. 1999a. *Poverty Profile 1997: A Report.* Ottawa: NCW.

———. 1999b. *Welfare Incomes: A Report. 1997 and 1998.* Ottawa: NCW.

Nova Scotia. Department of Community Services. 1997. 'New Formula for Single-Tier Social Assistance'. Press release. (11 April).

———. 1998. 'Social Assistance Program Enhanced'. Press release. (1 April).

Ontario. 1999. *Local Services Realignment: A User's Guide.* Toronto: Queen's Printer for Ontario.

Ontario. Advisory Committee to the Minister of Municipal Affairs on the Provincial-Municipal Relationship. 1991. *Report.* Toronto: Queen's Printer for Ontario.

Ontario. Ministry of Municipal Affairs and Housing. 1996. 'Panel Recommends Province Pay Full Social Service Costs'. Press release. (11 October).

Ontario. Social Assistance Review Committee. 1988. *Transitions.* Toronto: Queen's Printer for Ontario.

Peterson, Paul E. 1981. *City Limits.* Chicago: University of Chicago Press.

Rusk, James. 1995. 'Civic Leaders Face Some Tough Choices'. *Globe and Mail* (30 November).

Sancton, Andrew. 1986. *Municipal Government and Social Services: A Case Study of London, Ontario.* London, ON: Department of Political Science, University of Western Ontario.

————. 1988. 'Social Service Delivery at Relevant Government Levels'. In *Meech Lake: From Centre to Periphery*, ed. Hilda Symonds and H. Peter Oberlander. Vancouver: Faculty of Graduate Studies, University of British Columbia.

Sassen, Saskia. 1998. *Globalization and Its Discontents*. New York: New Press.

Splane, Richard. 1965. *Social Welfare in Ontario, 1791–1893: A Study of Public Welfare Administration*. Toronto: University of Toronto Press.

Statistics Canada. 1998. *Social Security Statistics. Canada and the Provinces, 1974–5 to 1998–9*. Ottawa: Statistics Canada.

Struthers, James. 1994. *The Limits of Affluence: Welfare in Ontario, 1920–1970*. Toronto: University of Toronto Press.

Tindal, C.R., and S.N. Tindal. 1990. *Local Government in Canada*. 3rd ed. Toronto: McGraw-Hill Ryerson.

Toronto. 2000. 'The Toronto Report Card on Homelessness 2000'. Accessed 23 May 2000: http://www.city.toronto.on.ca/homelessness/conclusions.htm

Union of Nova Scotia Municipalities (UNSM). 1997. 'Community Services Funding Agreement'. Press release. (11 April).

Wharf, Brian. 1990. 'Social Services'. In *Urban Policy Issues: Canadian Perspectives*, ed. Richard A. Loreto and Trevor Price. Toronto: McClelland & Stewart.

Transportation Policy in Canadian Cities

Edmund P. Fowler and Jack Layton[1]

Introduction

> Sometimes, when I am out in the city very early in the morning or very late at night, I won-
> der about the others who are up at that time as well. 'Where are you all going at this
> ungodly hour?' I ask them rhetorically and somewhat indignantly, since I expected to have
> the streets to myself. One could ask the same question at rush hour, I suppose, but then the
> answer would be more predictable and prosaic. But just as meaningful.

These musings by one of the authors suggest that at the core of any analysis of
urban transportation policy must be an understanding of why people are travelling
in the first place. Travel patterns spring from decisions that people have already made
about their work, their residence, their recreation—their lives. The corollary is that
any proposals for change in a transportation system are in effect proposals for
change in how people lead their lives.

True, individual choices about work and housing are severely constrained and
shaped in numerous ways by powerful institutions, economic realities, social inequities,
and cultural values. Nevertheless, no matter how scientific or technical transportation
policy pretends to be, it cannot be separated from our preferences in housing,
employment, and recreation, which makes transportation policy highly charged politically and at the same time connects it to other policies discussed in this book.

Urban transportation policy can be defined on several levels. First, it consists of a
philosophy or approach toward travel within the city. This philosophy might take the
form of a general value preference, such as for the car versus other means of transport (the *modal split*) or for integration of transportation policy with land use policy. Second, policy can also be thought of as the relative amount of money spent by

a municipality on transit, roads, bicycle lanes, and pedestrian access, including both capital and operating expenses. Third, policy involves where and how these funds are spent. Cities are places, after all, and funds are often directed more to one part of the city than to others; money spent on roads could be used to widen them or to modify their design to slow down traffic (*traffic calming*). Fourth, many public decisions affect a city's transportation system without being explicitly acknowledged as transportation policy: housing and land use policies, infrastructure investment, and environmental regulations, for example.

If you were to look up material on urban transportation policy on the Web or in the library, you would find documents written mostly by theoreticians, planners, and academics who count the numbers of trips made by city dwellers, analyze the times and durations of the trips, and relate all this to the mode of transport (car, transit, other) and to the destinations and reasons for those trips. The purpose of these studies is usually to find more efficient ways of moving people and goods within cities; much attention is given to how much is paid and by whom for different forms of transportation. Recently, much policy research has revolved around discouraging car use, because the automobile, as we shall see, is destructive both to our health and to the environment.

On the front lines of urban transportation policy are public works departments and the local council committees who are dealing every day with problems of congestion, transit service, and, especially, parking. Ask any local councillor what the most pressing transportation issue is in her ward and the answer will invariably be 'Parking!' The problem of *parking* is something of an anomaly for transportation policy-makers, who devote many hours of work to dealing with thousands of cars that aren't moving.

We feel that both the theoreticians and the front-line decision-makers, to say nothing of powerful agencies at other levels of government, are working within a narrow definition of the urban transport problem. We propose to broaden that definition in this chapter.

For example, transportation policy analysis too often takes for granted the form of the city around which we carry ourselves. Cities have grown so large geographically that we have serious problems getting from one part of them to another. In fact, urban transportation—ranging from travel on foot or with beasts of burden to wheeled carriages, streetcars, and automobiles—has significantly redefined and reshaped the city. In so doing, it has significantly redefined us. To put it another way, how we transport ourselves and our goods, and why we do it (*trip purpose*), is embedded in our culture. As a culture, we value single-family houses on large lots. This form of housing created urban sprawl, which makes widespread use of cars and trucks almost essential. Significantly, if we decide that we should reduce our reliance on cars, we have to confront our preference for single-family houses. (See Carroll's chapter.) Later in this chapter, we will explore the symbiosis between urban travel and the nature of the city and its inhabitants, as well as the implications of this symbiosis for transportation policy.

A second way to broaden the scope of urban transportation policy is to question the assumption that movement is good in itself. 'Let's Move' was the label for one recent Ontario provincial transportation program. The Greater Vancouver Regional District's name for similar proposals made by their transportation task force in 1989 was 'Freedom to Move'. Transportation policy in Canada tends to be predicated on encouraging more travel by more people, to more places, more quickly. Not surprisingly, Canadians are spending ever greater amounts of their time, their energy, and their money getting around their cities.

This trend may provide more jobs for automobile and truck manufacturers, for road builders and oil drillers, and for transportation analysts, but for a number of years, people have been asking: Why assume that moving farther and faster is a desirable goal? Why not start with the assumption that the less travel, the better? We suggest this because, as we demonstrate later in this chapter, less travel is ecologically and economically more sensible, reduces inequalities in the community, and contributes to the well-being, safety, and quality of life of everyone living in cities, now and in the future.

Thus, our view of transportation policy is a broad one. After a brief overview of transportation policies and systems of different Canadian cities, we will examine different sets of actors—both obvious and less obvious—who make decisions about urban transportation. Using this analysis as a base, we will illustrate how the quality of the environment and the social well-being of the residents of our cities are affected by their transportation systems. Our conclusion gives some examples of promising moves toward intelligent transportation policies for Canadian cities.

Present Canadian Urban Transportation Policy

About half of our urban land is devoted to cars (Toronto, ETF 1999). Awareness of the negative effects of auto use is growing. At the same time, pressures for expanded road systems are also on the rise, as trucking continues to replace rail haul, as offices and factories move to greenfield sites with lower taxes on the urban fringe, and as subdivision after subdivision replaces farmers' fields. More complications are added by changing price structures: gas prices rise and fall, transit fares almost always rise, and now tolls are being introduced.

The most basic point to stress about urban transportation policy is that it cannot be separated from land use policy. Transportation and land use policies do vary across Canadian cities, whose built forms reflect their age and other historical factors. For example, most cities have a relatively small downtown built before the car became dominant in the 1920s. Although older cities' downtowns, such as those of Montreal and Toronto, are somewhat larger than those, for example, of Edmonton and Vancouver, their size relative to the rest of their metropolitan areas has dwindled dramatically in every case. The density of land use surrounding these older urban cores cannot support transit. Like a self-fulfilling prophecy, dozens of provincial and municipal government policies encouraging suburban sprawl have effectively written their policies on urban travel: greater reliance on the car and less on transit, cycling, and walking. Canadian urban transport policy, very briefly, is that 90 per cent of our trips around the city are made by car. All this has happened, of course, in the context of the forces described later in this chapter—the movement industries, the media, and the development industry.

The best illustration of the centrality of the automobile to Canadian urban transport is the Ontario government's decision, taken amidst unprecedented brutal cutbacks to social services and transit, to give $100 million to Hamilton-Wentworth's regional government to help build an expressway through a large and beautiful park bordering Red Hill Creek and close to downtown Hamilton. It will be the most expensive four-lane highway ever built in Canada: $227 million for eight kilometres (Friends of Red Hill Valley 1999).

Since the 1980s, transit expansion in Canadian cities has been talked about more than acted upon. In Toronto, after a long political see-saw between provincial and municipal politicians, one out of four proposed new subway lines is being built along a suburban arterial road. In British Columbia, TransLink (the regional transportation authority), the province, and the City of Vancouver are planning to extend rapid transit westward in the south-central part of the city, along Broadway to the University of British Columbia.

A glance at current official planning documents, however, reveals an unwillingness to directly challenge our dependence on cars and, rather, a tendency to restrict recommendations to indirect measures such as increasing development densities (in fact, not an insignificant initiative if vigorously implemented), tinkering with street alignments, and promoting telecommuting.

Saskatchewan provides no funding for urban transit. Ontario used to fund 75 per cent of transit's capital costs, sometimes more, and used to advance as much as 50 per cent of operating cost for some municipalities. Now Ontario has gone the way of Saskatchewan. Quebec has the best record: in its nine largest cities, it subsidizes the operating costs of municipal transit with dedicated gas taxes, vehicle registration fees, or both, and contributes almost half of the low-priced monthly pass on the Montreal Urban Community's transit system. Smaller transit systems in Quebec are subsidized directly by the province (Michael Canzi, personal communication, 9 August 2000; James 2000). Nonetheless, hundreds of miles of arterial roads continue to be built to support development on the fringes of Canadian cities. In fact, many transit systems have tried to service lower-density development and, in the process, seriously threatened their own solvency (Kitchen 1990). For many years, Canadian transit has been caught in a downward spiral of decreasing ridership, greater deficits, decreasing service, and increasing fares. In the closing years of the twentieth century, ridership does seem to be increasing somewhat (see Figure 7.1).

The existing road infrastructure is in itself a powerful disincentive to change. This infrastructure represents billions of dollars invested in one form of transport, a policy not easily reversed. Roads themselves beget more cars. The phenomenon is common: build more lanes, or more highways, and cars appear out of nowhere to clog

Figure 7.1: Annual Transit Passenger Rides Per Capita, 1950–1998

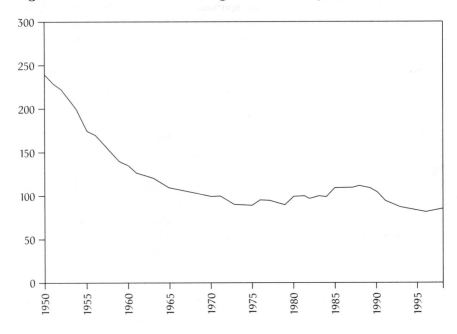

Source: Canadian Urban Transit Association.
Graph prepared with the help of Alix Cook and Don Ogner.

them; take away that road space, and the cars mysteriously disappear (Fowler 1991; Jacobs 1961; Friends of Red Hill Valley 1999).

Canadian cities' current transportation policies are put in perspective in Table 7.1, which compares transit and car use in Canada with three other cities: Phoenix, Vienna, and Tokyo. Land use patterns are also given. The figures suggest that there are much broader options for urban travel than those found within Canada. For example, Vienna, with double the residential density of Toronto, has much more ridership on transit vehicles that travel slightly less far. Before we consider some of these options, we turn to who is responsible for current policies in Canada and to those policies' implications for our health and well-being.

How Is Transportation Policy Made?

There are many players in the transportation policy game. The issues are becoming more complex. As an aid to understanding what moves our policies about movement in cities, we present here an outline of the forces behind and the components of the urban transportation policy process.

Transport policy in urban Canada has not always been about highways. What is timeless, though, is the link between transportation policy, politics, and money. After the era of ships and canals, transportation policy was synonymous with railroad building. The technology was rail and the big business was moving raw materials from sea to sea. Several fortunes and a nation were built on these transportation policies. In those days, the policy process was fairly easy to understand. Over half the Canadian federal cabinet in the 1880s consisted of presidents and chairmen of railroad companies (Myers 1972). Little wonder that the national dream and the National Policy were built with the spike, the rail, and the locomotive.

Half a century later, new sets of rails reached from central cities out to the new 'streetcar suburbs' (Warner 1962). Streetcar builders and turn-of-the-century developers of suburban housing were often one and the same firm. In this heyday of the tram, homes were built close together on streets that ran perpendicular to the streetcar routes a delightful twenty-minute ride out of the city. City politics had a lot to do with where the next streetcar line would be permitted to go. Today, it's the location of the new highway (and the sewer line) that are the focal points of development debates at city and suburban councils.

Fortunes are still being built on transportation policy. Canada's third highest paid executive is the CEO of an auto parts manufacturer, Frank Stronach of Magna Corp., whose 1998 annual salary and benefits exceeded $26 million ('50 Best-Paid CEOs' 1999). Car makers are among the largest economic entities on the planet, larger than most national governments, and certainly transnational in their operations; but it would be rare to find an auto executive in a federal cabinet or on a city council (for a couple of exceptions, see later in this chapter).

So, if there is no longer a cabal of transportation profiteers and politicians meeting in the back rooms to decide how we are going to get around our cities, how does policy get made? One simplistic explanation of the process is that policy is made in accordance with the wishes of the public, who 'vote' with their feet on the accelerators every time they clamber behind their wheels. No doubt consumer power could be a real force in shaping policy if consumers had free choices and had full information on which to decide. But it is not accurate to say that city dwellers are actually choosing their own transportation policy by using cars at every opportunity. Planning, advertising, and development processes are major factors in shaping transportation plans and systems along with individuals' choices.

We can identify almost a dozen different sets of players in the transportation decision-making game. To put those players in context and to understand their relationships with each other, it helps to see their links with two key forces at work in the contemporary city.[2] These forces often work in tandem; they are deeply rooted common interests that influence urban transportation policy like background gravitational fields:

- the corporate impetus to market expansion based on profitability, and
- the community impetus to create, protect, and enhance the quality and health of neighbourhood and city life.

Table 7.1: Urban Travel and Sustainable Development: The Canadian Experience Summary of Major Canadian Cities and Selected International Comparisons, 1991

	Canadian Cities								International Cities[a]		
	Toronto City	Toronto GTA[b]	Montreal MUC[b]	Montreal GMA[b]	Vancouver GVRD[b]	Calgary	Ottawa RMOC[b]	Winnipeg	Phoenix	Vienna	Tokyo
Population	2,276,000	4,235,530	1,775,871	3,127,242	1,542,744	710,677	678,147	616,790	1,509,052	1,531,346	11,597,211
Urban form											
Size of urbanized area (km²)	630	1536	496	3509	1200	530	359	459			
Residential density (people/km²)	3613	2758	3580	891	1286	1341	1889	1344	850	7210	10,460
Employment density (jobs/km²)	2305	1571	2286	430		770	1066		400	3840	6630
Central area characteristics											
Parking availability (spaces/1000 central area jobs)	210	210	79	79		620	301		1033	190	66
Proportion of population (%)	6.7	3.6	2.9	1.7		1.2	0.83		0.5	1.3	1.3
Proportion of jobs (%)	31	17	30	23		22	22		4	15	27
Transportation systems											
Automobile ownership (vehicles/1000 people)	493	463	369	413	444	669	482	509	499	311	156
Road extent (m/person)	2.6	2.7	2.7					4.3	10.4	1.7	1.9

Transit ridership (annual rides/person)	186	128	225	154	94	68	133	87	9	313	472
Transit service (annual vehicle km/person)	82	62	75	56	58	50	71	42	7	69	94
Environmental performance											
Gasoline use (MJ/person)	25,139	27,324	19,595	26,221					74,510	10,074	8488
Carbon dioxide (annual tonnes/person)	1.7	1.9							5.1	0.7	0.6

Courtesy of Richard Gilbert; IBI Group.

Source: Statistics Canada and data provided by local planning staff/reports. Blanks indicate that comparable data were not available.

Notes: [a]These are 1980 figures, drawn from Peter Newman and Jeffrey Kenworthy, *Cities and Automobile Dependence: An International Sourcebook.* Brookfield, VT: Gower, 1989.

[b]GTA = Greater Toronto Area; MUC = Montreal Urban Community; GMA = Greater Montreal Area; GVRD = Greater Vancouver Regional District; RMOC = Regional Municipality of Ottawa-Carleton

Each force has many components, and there can even be conflict or competition between different sectors, actors, or elements within these main driving forces. This conflict is often expressed clearly in the political sphere. Still, keeping the two thrusts in mind as we review the *dramatis personae* can be helpful in understanding the outcomes of Canadian urban transport policy.

The Movement Industries

One key element of the contemporary capitalist economy is an inexorable pressure to move—farther, faster, in a wider variety of situations. Movement makes money. Here is a short list of activities and participants in the movement business:

- gasoline and oil sales (the carbon industry, perhaps the world's largest)
- car manufacturing and sales
- tire and other auto-parts sales
- road-building industries and suppliers (asphalt, gravel, concrete, machinery)
- workers who build cars and roads
- repair shops, carwashes
- auto insurance companies
- doctors treating accident injuries, mortuaries
- moving services: taxis, transportation companies, haulers, truckers

Many of the players listed above shape transportation policy, either directly or through their lobbying associations, such as the Canadian Automobile Association or the Canadian Oil Producers' Association.

The automobile manufacturers and their associated businesses are motivated by the corporate impetus and are central to the economies of several Canadian regions, especially southern Ontario. Their formidable political power has often been apparent at the national and provincial levels. Huge government loans and grants for factories flow regularly to the auto industry. International trade agreements affecting car and auto parts manufacturing preoccupy whole departments of government. Some individuals in the industry become openly involved in politics: Frank Stronach, CEO of Magna, was a Liberal candidate for the House of Commons; Jimmy Pattison, a one-time car dealer and now a multimillionaire businessman, is an active Tory fundraiser and shaped key parts of Vancouver's downtown as head of the World's Fair organizing committee in the 1980s; Al Palladini, an icon in the world of car salesmanship in the suburbs of Toronto ('Canada's Auto Marketeer of the Year', 1994), became the Minister of Transportation in Ontario's Conservative government in 1995. He initiated his term of office with a comment that the province needs public transportation because not everyone can afford a car. Palladini clearly cannot comprehend the fact that some people who can afford a car *choose* not to buy one.

Land Developers and the Property Industry

Land development companies are also grounded in the corporate impetus and are another important influence on transportation decisions. So are their associate industries: construction companies, building materials suppliers, architects, and engineers. The post-war process of suburban development created many fortunes, such as Bramalea Developments (chaired by former Ontario premier Bill Davis), but none of it could have happened without a transportation policy to build roads that gave cornfields and pastures their development potential. Lorimer puts the issue succinctly:

> Transportation programmes amount to decisions about which vacant land is going to be developed, which built-up areas are going to be redeveloped, and who is going to be making money from the growth and development of the city. The property industry greatly benefits from new transportation facilities. (Lorimer 1972: 177)

North York's 'Yorkdale Development' was built by the Trizec Corporation, under the control of the Reichmann financial empire. Trizec was able to convince government in the late 1960s to design the Spadina Expressway (now called the Allen Road) with an elaborate interchange leading directly into its development. Later, the same developer argued that the shopping centre could be expanded only if a new subway was routed past its doors with a special entrance. This required the subway to be built under a precious ravine system rather than under a major artery, which would have brought many more riders to the line. It has been plagued by low ridership ever since.

Such decisions are made in part because the property industry has always been a heavy supporter of political candidates willing to vote for roads and subways that provide better access to developers' land holdings (Lorimer 1979). These campaign donations are often not public and can increase substantially the chances of electing a council adopting a pro-development transportation policy. An analysis of contributions to June Rowlands' successful campaign for Toronto's mayoralty in 1988 showed that out of the total of $200,000, almost $100,000 came from corporations that included 'some of the biggest developers in the city'. Also, 'out of a sample group of 250 of the mayor's 322 personal donors, 70% are linked with Toronto's big-business community' (Carder and Norwich 1992).

The Media

Another set of influential actors is in the media. Studies of the role of the media in local politics in Canada are few (Black 1982). Those that have been conducted note a distinct pro-growth bias (the corporate impetus) in editorials, headline patterns, and photographs (Lorimer 1972). The real estate section of most daily papers is a mainstay of the advertising department. The auto section of the daily paper and its associated promotions are another source of media profits, so the temptation to bias is inherent. Often, the media are controlled by firms that themselves have major strategic land holdings that are in turn dependent on transportation infrastructure. In Toronto, all four major dailies are associated with firms that are significant landholders in the core and could be negatively affected if local councils opposed growth plans. This fact is never mentioned in editorials so that the reader might be informed of a conflict of interest. The *Toronto Star*, in particular, has regularly railed against efforts to block the expansion of the Toronto Island airport and has attacked community groups wanting to prevent widening of the Gardiner Expressway or of roads through ravine lands. The *Star* rarely mentions its land holdings and those of its partners, which lie in the centre of these policy controversies. With no alternative source of information, citizens are often left with a distorted view of the real issues.

Most Canadians watch three or four hours of television a day. In the process, they are exposed to dozens of car ads. The omnipresent new-car image is surrounded by sensuality: forests and natural landscapes, carefully orchestrated music and other auditory stimuli, colour, and feelings—sexuality, freedom, and even love for Nature. Of course, everyone knows that the reality is precisely the opposite in each case— smelly smog, intrusive noises, blackened asphalt, and bumper-to-bumper traffic— but fantasy is the most effective marketing ploy. It is clear that the public's fantasies about the car help drive transportation policy and that advertisers working for car manufacturers must be part of our understanding of that policy's context.

Sometimes the media reflect the community impetus, when small neighbourhood or alternative papers provide contrasting perspectives, or when big papers print feel-good stories about local neighbourhoods in the city. The small publications rarely have the real estate or automaker ads sufficient to achieve significant circulation. And if they did, could they carry the same critical message? In all, the media have a pivotal role in manufacturing our consent to problematic transportation policies.

Planners and Experts

In the past, road engineers held sway. Now the field of expertise is broader and urban planners and transportation experts are becoming influential. Urban planning is still a young profession, but it has brought new perspectives to transportation policy, especially the notion that transportation should be considered integral to all urban system planning. This is a remarkably sensible objective in principle, but the land on which the planners place their zoning designations and for which they recommend services is usually privately owned. Thus, planners and their political masters, the councillors, end up reacting to initiatives by developers (see Leo's chapter in this volume), and transportation policy is subordinated to those initiatives. Planners put the development proposals into professional language for their employers. This doesn't mean that planners are neutral servants of rapacious developers, but it does mean they are usually (not always) responding to these political forces like other government officials. Planners are a heterogeneous group, most of whom are committed to remaining in the public service; however, some municipal planners and transportation experts end up leaving the civic service and working—at much higher salaries or consultants' fees—for land developers. Some of them, psychologically, seem to have a foot in both camps.

Many communities who have raised concerns about transportation issues and who have been able to convince their local council to delay, modify, or cancel these projects find that the promoters take their case to a provincial appeal board. These hearings are structured in such a way that gives inordinate weight to the testimony of 'experts'. Community residents are deemed not to be experts at all, even though they often know more than anyone else about their own neighbourhood and have often gone to extraordinary lengths to inform themselves on the technical issues. In these hearings, the community's views are too often discounted.

The Public Transit Sector

In contrast to the private-sector orientation of automobile-centred transport, most mass transit systems are run by provincial and local governments. Usually, they are administered by a special board or agency. Sometimes a municipal council keeps tighter control of the operations by insisting that the transit system be handled by a civic department reporting directly to city council. In either case, a team of transit planners, maintenance workers, fare collectors, and executives spend their working days, full-time, developing and implementing transit policy.

Multidisciplinary planning teams and comprehensive official plan processes are gradually bringing transit into the development decisions of councils. In the 1960s and 1970s, community impetus against urban freeways strengthened the image of transit as an antidote to the ravages of the car on neighbourhoods, especially in Canada's downtowns. However, in a study of urban public transport in Canada, 'transit staff interviewed in every city complained about urban sprawl as the biggest obstacle to providing good transit service. Yet, in most places, transit planners and operators have little formal power to influence the land use planning and development process' (Vanderwagen 1995: 9).

One group of players that is bringing pro-transit pressure to bear is the bus and subway-car manufacturers. Heavily subsidized by government and bolstered by government contracts to supply equipment, these firms have become increasingly concentrated, with a small number now dominating the industry. Canadian companies, such as Quebec's Bombardier, have become thriving businesses, serving worldwide markets. Naturally, governments are keen to see jobs created as equipment rolls off the assembly lines.

Another pro-transit force is the Canadian Urban Transit Association (CUTA), funded by transit systems across Canada. It collects statistics on these systems and acts as an advocate for public transit. CUTA has been actively lobbying the federal government to make transit passes tax-exempt. Also sprinkled here and there are flashes of involvement by groups of transit riders; recently, workplace programs stimulated by employers and unions and 'school-based sustainable transportation initiatives' have been developed in a number of cities (Toronto, ETF 1999).

Environmentalists and Community Groups

The community impetus in transport politics rises in the localities where people live and thus where the cars' impact is creating unsafe conditions, especially for children, or is causing a significant problem, such as noise. Driving home from work is common and considered a necessity, but once there, drivers want to minimize the impact of the car on their neighbourhood. This is not entirely hypocritical. The contradiction simply illustrates what happens when we try to separate one part of our life (work and the trip to work) from another (home life). In fact, local neighbourhoods in large cities, especially rich neighbourhoods, have been able to put in mazes and speed bumps to protect themselves from rush-hour traffic.

There are transit riders and pro-transit groups who can cause councillors to squirm in their seats when they face a fare-hike vote—sometimes so much so that a fare increase will be delayed or reduced. However, the going for the rider is tough. It took ten years of lobbying and protesting to establish a monthly pass system for major transit systems in Quebec. A decade was also required for high school students in Toronto to wrestle a reduced-rate Metropass from a succession of reluctant councils ('How many of these students vote, anyway?' was the all-too-common aside). Two years after the victory, when the students were not looking, council jacked the fare back up to pennies shy of the adult fare.

In general, transit users are left out of decision-making processes. So-called 'public participation programs' tend to exclude those who would be most likely to use a service if it were provided: low-income families or children, who are almost always dependent on public transport.

Municipal, Provincial, and Federal Governments

'Most municipal councillors tend to be drawn from middle class professional backgrounds and have little experience with or understanding of the lives of those constituents who use public transit' (Frisken and Bell 1994: 103). The result is politicians who are predisposed to respond more favourably, even enthusiastically, to pro-road arguments than to pro-transit plans.

On the other hand, local politicians have much less influence on transportation planning than one might expect. In the Vancouver area, all transit planning and funding is coordinated by a regional organization called TransLink. In the past, local politicians' preferences about transportation policy have been routinely ignored (Oberlander and Smith 1993). In Ontario, after the former Metro Toronto Council agonized over how many new subway lines it could afford (because of provincial government cutbacks), it was ordered by Premier Bob Rae to build four lines instead of the two chosen by council. Then the newly elected Tories told Metro in 1995 that it could only build one—not much autonomy here. The real merits of subway lines become submerged in provincial election politics.

Provincial governments have an overwhelming influence on transportation policy in cities and towns across the country (Frisken 1994b). Much of this influence is invisible because it is indirect. Road building is heavily subsidized by provincial governments. Although some provinces also subsidize transit, a close examination of most provincial budgets will show that investments in road construction and reconstruction, even at a lower rate of subsidy, are greater in dollar value than they are for transit.

Federal intervention seems to move through cycles. When the asphalt version of the national railway policy—the Trans-Canada Highway—was proposed, it was used as a way to introduce significant highway construction within major cities as well as between them: Montreal's Highway 40 and Decarie Expressway, Toronto's Highway 401, Vancouver's Highway 1 through Burnaby and North Vancouver, and dozens of others. This allowed the federal government to intervene in shaping urban transportation infrastructure more dramatically than it had since the height of the railway age. After considerable and lengthy pressure by the Federation of Canadian Municipalities, Jean Chrétien's Liberals introduced a national urban infrastructure program that offered federal dollars for local projects, many of them transportation-related. Federal forays into these policy areas are usually aimed at enhancing the popularity of incumbent governments; in addition, there is a reluctance to interfere in what are essentially provincial matters (see the chapters by Carroll and by Andrew and Morrison).

In the past, both federal and provincial governments have had a significant impact on transportation policy by subsidizing urban sprawl indirectly. For example, the federal agency Canada Mortgage and Housing Corporation, by underwriting mortgages only for single-family suburban homes in the 1940s, 1950s, and 1960s, spread out development and its attendant problems of car-centred transportation (Fowler 1992).

Summary

This brief sketch of the forces and players that drive urban transportation policy produces a complex but disturbing picture. The car seems to have become central to our culture, shaping urban planning as much as planning shapes car use. With a new car manufactured every second of every day worldwide, a rate that is rising, the impulse to pave and sprawl is more powerful than ever. So too are the forces that drive this process, which is accompanied by the downward spiral of many cities' transit systems.

The negative effects of this transportation infrastructure are outlined in the next section. In the final section, we will explore imaginative alternatives, some just on the drawing board, others already in place.

The Effects of Transportation Policy

The purpose of this section is to sketch links between urban transportation in Canada and our personal experiences of city life. Since close to 90 per cent of all urban travel is presently made by cars, it is not surprising that most of our examples dwell on that mode of travel. It is worth noting, however, that the total amount of travel in a city, by any mode, is directly related to its dependence on the automobile (Newman and Kenworthy 1989). The more cars there are, the farther everyone has to travel. The central theme of this section is to demonstrate that reliance on the car for urban travel is harming the environment, our personal health, the vitality of our local economies, our sense of community, our political intelligence, our children, and whatever attempts we make to create a just and equitable society.

The widespread use of the car for urban transport has totally transformed both our natural and our built environments. This transformation is so familiar to us by now (most of us have grown up in an automobile-centred city or suburb) that its visible as well as its invisible dimensions are not noticed. But sensible thinking about transportation policy requires us to be aware not only of the transformation but also of its penetration into our personal lives (Vanderwagen 1995).

Pollution

Most of us have learned that the air we breathe—the air we *have* to breathe—is filled with poisonous particulates and gases from the internal combustion engine. Canadian cities' air pollution, which is considerable (Toronto, Department of Public Health 1993), can be largely traced to cars and trucks, with trucks accounting for a larger proportion than their numbers would imply, partly because of their diesel engines (McAndrew 1999; Toronto, Department of Public Health 1993; Zuckerman 1991). 'Between 400 and 1200 people die annually in Toronto from . . . problems aggravated by smog' (McAndrew 1999). The amount of research on this topic has exploded over recent years, and one can infer from US studies that 10,000 to 15,000 deaths probably occur every year in Canadian cities from vehicular pollution (Freund and Martin 1993; Ostro 1993; Stieb et al. 1995). This figure does not include many other sicknesses and deaths with pollution from cars as the significant contributing factor (Burnet et al. 1995; Toronto, Department of Public Health 1993). Our personal health is worse, in other words, because of auto-centred transport. On the other hand, the contribution of some pollutants from car exhaust to urban air has decreased significantly in the last fifteen years (Furmanczyk 1994) particularly because of enlightened policy on auto emissions. This shows that we are capable of turning things around if we put our heads together.

Cars kill us directly, too, of course. Over 3,000 drivers, passengers, pedestrians, and cyclists are victims every year (Transport Canada 1998), and these victims tend to be children, older people, and the poor (see later in this chapter). By contrast, between 1988 and 1997, only three people were killed while riding Canadian urban-transit buses (Transport Canada 2000).

Chronic sickness and death from air pollution are insidious, because it is hard to place blame. It makes the relationship easy to ignore (Freund and Martin 1993). It is even easier, however, to ignore other effects of the car that are just as dangerous. An excellent example is the emission of carbon dioxide by cars, trucks, and buses in cities. This emission, which accounts for one quarter of CO_2 output by the human species, is changing the composition of the earth's atmosphere so that our weather is growing hotter every year (Toronto, ETF 1999; Zuckerman 1991). The so-called greenhouse effect—directly related to our urban transport systems—is creating a vast array of economic problems, from crop damage to catastrophically severe weather, not to mention species dislocation and even extinction. Global warming is creating a rise in the level of the oceans and threatening to inundate not only many of the cities producing the CO_2 but also many island nations and coastal communities around the world (Fowler 1992). This logic, understandably, is not persuasive to Calgary commuters getting into their cars at 8:00 a.m. when it's −30°C. They may never have heard of those islands; the effects of commuting by car spread to places too remote from the daily experience of the commuters. This phenomenon is a real barrier to framing a constructive transportation policy that depends on tangible political support from the local citizenry.

Fortunately, or unfortunately, there are many examples of the car's impact on the natural environment closer to home, among them the pollution and safety considerations just mentioned. Another example is soil. The vast majority of living organisms of the planet, probably over 90 per cent, are in the first foot of soil (Suzuki and Dressel 1999; Tompkins and Bird 1989). Once we pave over this mass of microbes, the soil can no longer serve the natural functions on which we as a species have relied for millennia—food production, hydrological cycles, and water absorption during rainstorms (Hough 1984; Spirn 1984). Land close to—and under—Vancouver, Toronto, Hamilton, and Montreal, not surprisingly, has the most fertile soil in Canada; and we have buried vast portions of it under shopping malls, suburbs, golf courses, and twelve-lane expressways and interchanges (some large interchanges take up several hundred hectares). Legislation in British Columbia has moved towards stricter controls on 'developing' this prime agricultural land (Kluckner 1991), but thousands of hectares have already been lost and the effectiveness of any controls will depend on the political will of incumbent governments. Through their transportation and land use policies, provinces and cities have already seriously compromised Canadians' ability to be self-sufficient in their food supply.

Urban Infrastructure

Outside their front doors, inhabitants of Canadian cities are faced daily with an enormous infrastructure devoted to servicing automobiles and trucks: anywhere from 35 per cent to 65 per cent of urban land is either streets or parking facilities (Fowler 1992); there are repair shops, gas stations, and dealers; auto graveyards are often not far from factories; and one can find an unbelievable variety of retail outlets designed specifically to serve the consumer-driver, such as shopping malls and drive-through windows. The automobile is not just 'the defining technology of our built environment', as architect Peter Calthorpe says (1991: 45), but 'the principal material for the built environment' of the Canadian city (Freund and Martin 1993: 111). Because all these car-related land uses reflect an awesome capital investment, they present a huge barrier to alternative systems of transport.

Still, the infrastructure of other transportation modes is also evident. In the nineteenth century, cities across the continent were competing to attract railroads because these were considered, not unrealistically, central to economic growth, if not to survival (Gutstein 1983; Magnusson 1983). Municipalities literally gave away land to attract the rail companies to lay tracks through their cities. As a result, most Canadian cities' downtowns contain huge tracts of immensely valuable land acquired in this manner by Canadian National and Canadian Pacific railways. As railroading became less profitable, CN, and CP's development arm, Marathon Realty, transformed this land into office high-rises and other mega-projects (Gutstein 1975; Nader 1975).

With more than half of all our urban land used by the transportation system, the true functions of city life—authentic, face-to-face contact with people on our street or around the corner, for a myriad of commercial, intellectual, cultural, and social purposes—are relegated to the other half.

Perhaps the most remarkable thing about this massive infrastructure is that we don't notice it. We consider it completely normal. Before we can develop sensible policies, we need to ask ourselves just how normal it is.

Financial Waste

Car-centred urban transport is expensive—in fact, wasteful. If thousands of people get sick from automobile-induced air pollution and have to be treated by the health system (Bates and Sizto 1987; Burnet et al. 1995); if our food has to be imported from California because we have paved over our good local land (Kluckner 1991; Lowe 1994); if millions of cubic metres of topsoil are polluted by metal and mineral particulates from tires, brake linings, car-battery production, and diesel fumes (Freund and Martin 1993); and if crops we do grow are stunted and disease-prone because of cars' and trucks' air pollution (Renner 1988), then we are wasting billions of dollars by choosing cars to move us around our spread-out cities. Sadly, this is precisely what is happening (Fowler 1992; Laird 1995).

The actual data respecting these effects have been computed by a broad range of analysts (Fowler 1992; Lowe 1994; Vojnovic 1995), and automobile-centred transport emerges as collective economic foolishness for everyone except car manufacturers, the oil industry, and some land developers. Personally, we are spending 15 per cent to 30 per cent of our incomes on our cars, and the proportions keep rising (Litman 1999; Stillich 1995). The total costs are subsidized by our taxes—in Ontario by as much as 59 per cent (Komanoff 1995; Laird 1995; MacMillan 1993; Zuckerman 1991). The total costs of the car have been computed by Komanoff (1995) for the United States as $725 billion a year.

Social and Political Costs

The astonishing economic and environmental impact of our transport system on Canadian cities needs to be put into a social and political context. In other words, this system has worked its way into other parts of our lives, a fact which students of public policy must take into account.

Consider that highways, multi-level parking lots, streets, and bridges need to be constructed by large institutions—municipal corporations and private contractors—who hire teams of experts to design and build this transportation infrastructure. Most city dwellers have grown up believing that we are incapable of understanding the technical requirements of our system and the complex modelling behind what gets built and where. This is a false belief, of course: we ourselves are paying for the infrastructure, and because it pervades every aspect of our lives, we are superbly qualified to give an opinion on what gets built.

The technology of transportation infrastructure—transit as well as roads—is authoritarian. Its political message is 'The experts know what is needed; please do not interfere'. Numerous disastrous public works projects based on questionable reasoning and analyses by experts indicate that this is a deceptive and at times duplicitous message (Fowler 1992; Franklin 1990; Lupo, Colcord, and Fowler 1971), but it continues to be broadcast. It bespeaks an authoritarianism that, in fact, constitutes the decision-making pattern for much of our urban built environment. Alternative transportation systems, such as walking and bicycling, have a far more democratic face.

There is another, more homely link between the quality of our politics and urban transportation. The many expressway controversies of the 1960s and 1970s illustrate the incompatibility between highways and local, well-knit communities that fought against them (Leo 1977; Lupo et al. 1971).

In fact, there is a direct relationship between traffic and neighbourhood vitality. One classic study, by Donald Appleyard in San Francisco, showed that, other things being equal, the more traffic on a city street, the less vibrant its social life and the more confined residents felt in their living quarters (1981; see Figure 7.2). Jane Jacobs observed a similar relationship: road widenings and sidewalk narrowings cut down or eliminate casual but essential encounters among street users (1961). These encounters are essential because, although they 'may not be significant in themselves, they provide a context for solutions when problems do arise, such as increases in vandalism or burglaries, proposals for a development in the neighbourhood, or a misfortune suffered by a local resident' (Fowler 1994: 2).

We believe that the present distrust of government and the erosion of the public sector can be traced to an erosion of the healthy street-level contact that underlies any sense of basic competence in collective public action. An authentic politics must be based on face-to-face local relationships on our street. Such relationships are being systematically erased by reliance on the car, which demands the use of streets solely as thoroughfares (or parking lots), not as public meeting places. This kind of street use is a powerful incentive to turn our backs on real civic management and to rely instead on the vicarious politics of electronic media and of symbolism.

A healthy social and political life includes everyone by definition. But the car has isolated many kinds of people in our society. Particularly vulnerable to automobile dominance are children: 'Cars are the single largest killers of Canadian school children (cancer is second)' (Columbo 1992). In Britain, which has fewer cars per person than Canada, 80 per cent of children aged 7 and 8 were allowed to walk to school on their own in 1971. By 1990, the same figure was 9 per cent (Barber 1995). A similar trend has been noted in Canada (Toronto, ETF 1999). The outcome of this trend is that 'the victim is being removed from the street' (Appleyard 1981; Barber 1995). This means that children do not grow up having a knowledge of, or a sense of responsibility for, their neighbourhood. They have no opportunity to feel the self-confidence of making their own way through the city.

It is worth stressing that children are a permanent and central part of a community. They may grow up, but there will always be children. Because their experiences of street life and mobility inform their choices about public involvement and transportation as adults, we are perpetuating an anemic commitment to civic responsibility as well as dependence on the car. It will seem normal, not a collective dysfunction.

Figure 7.2: San Francisco: Home Territory on Three Streets with Light, Moderate, and Heavy Traffic

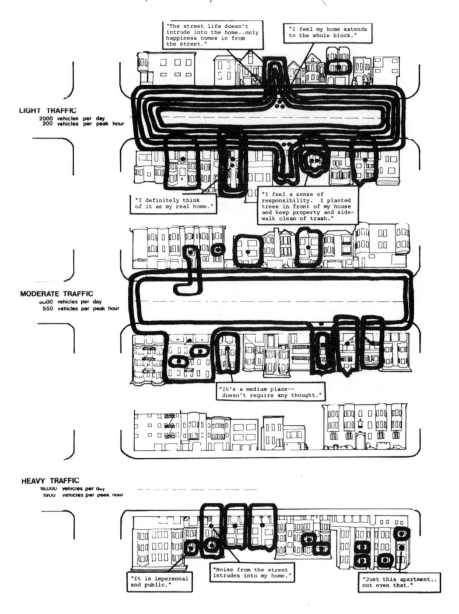

Source: Donald Appleyard. 1981. *Livable Streets.* Berkeley, CA: University of California Press, 23. Used by permission.

Note: Lines show the areas residents indicated as their 'home territory'.

Automobile-centred transport harms other population groups. It is not too much to say that to spend money on cars is to hurt the poor and to help the rich, in very real ways. Research has shown that a car-dominated city makes it harder for the poor to find jobs: not only do fewer poor people own cars, but public transit in such cities is typically so bad that jobs in distant suburbs are geographically out of reach, even though most jobs are being created there. The exaggerated physical mobility required by sprawl becomes a prerequisite for economic and social mobility (Freund and Martin 1993; Klodawsky and Spencer 1988).

Inequalities are made worse because owning a car is so expensive; the personal vehicle has been made almost a necessity by land use, but it takes two to three times as much of a poor person's income as of a rich person's (Litman 1999).

Car exhaust kills a much larger proportion of the poor, who tend to live in areas more polluted by automobile emissions. Cars also kill more pedestrians, especially children, by a factor of three (Freund and Martin 1993; Lerner 1997). Similar figures have been compiled for women and for the disabled.

Where public transit is provided, it is most frequently designed radially—like the spokes of a wheel—to maximize high-speed access from suburbs to a down-town core of offices and white-collar employment (Frisken 1994a). This pattern accentuates transportation problems not only for the poor but also for many non-poor women, who have different travel needs from men (Overton 1995). Gerda Wekerle has made this clear: 'The journey to work for women . . . is often more time consuming, more costly and more complicated than men's. Women frequently use public transportation for shopping and household errands, and women workers combine these trips with the journey to work to save precious time' (Wekerle 1980: 205).

The crisis of the welfare state can be traced, in part, to billions of dollars spent on public goods like transportation that are accessible to all only in theory. The net effect of such expenditures more than offsets the programs that 'give' money directly to the poor.

One further note: we have been unabashedly critical of car-centred transport. Can a case be made for the car? Not in cities, we feel. Besides, it is meaningless to talk about 'the car' separate from its supporting infrastructure of roads and other facilities that take up half of the urban land in Canada. As we have suggested, individuals who insist on their right to drive may not be aware of how this urban form has influenced our definitions of alternative ways of living as well as getting around the city.

Bright Lights and New Directions

We have described a tangled web of causes and effects, but the message has been clear: urban travel is dominated by the car and the situation is dangerous to our well-being. We have also stressed that our mode of transport is intimately related to our habits of life and our cultural values.

In particular, we have underlined the symbiosis between land use and urban travel. This symbiosis has important implications not only for substantive policy, but also for policy formation and policy change. Urban development since World War II has been large-scale: office towers, expressways and stadiums, shopping malls, suburban subdivisions, and high-rise condominiums. This form of building has produced not so much cities as urban smears with segregated uses that require an individual to make substantial trips just to shop, work, and sleep. It is clear as well that these smears have been planned and built for us by big institutions such as developers and 'local' governments whose jurisdictions include millions of people. These institutions, in turn, are following the logic of an economic system consisted of a placeless capital and technology that have become international in scope. In a sense, we are justified in feeling that this transport-intensive development has been forced on us by these institutions and their economic logic—that they are real policy-makers. But we have played our own part in welcoming the development into our towns and cities. It is important to be aware that both global and local choices created the contemporary city's transportation problems.

The complex interconnectedness between land use and transportation, between local and global decisions, between culture and modes of travel, could engender a sense of hopelessness. In fact, however, some of the most significant transportation initiatives have come from community groups, advocacy organizations, and individuals' choices about how they live, where they work, how much they consume, and what role neighbours play in their lives. In a few cases, professionals and politicians have picked up the ball from creative grassroots thinking and worked in partnership with local groups to achieve remarkable results.

In this section we highlight what governments and individuals have been doing to rethink and re-form urban transportation.

Sprawl

The Greater Vancouver Regional District (GVRD) has made a concerted effort to control sprawl. All of the municipalities in the GVRD were asked to identify the lands in their communities that they wanted to preserve as some sort of open space. Anything left over became the only land where development could occur. Green Zones included ecologically important lands; lands with renewable resources, such as agricultural areas; outdoor recreational lands; and lands that sustain community health, especially watersheds important to drinking water quality. The Green Zone covers two-thirds of the GVRD land base. Communities were then asked to define the density and type of development they wanted in the remaining lands, but it was made clear that any low-density development areas would not receive high-intensity public-transit investment. Some communities still opted for low-density development (see Fowler and Hartmann's chapter), but most chose medium- and higher-density development in order to secure some transit investment.

Key to the Vancouver solution is its new sustainable transportation governance structure. A new regional transportation authority, TransLink, was created to realize the vision with the power to introduce tolls, charges for car licenses, and other techniques to raise funds for the transit investments. Most important, the provincial government turned over a percentage of the gasoline tax that it was collecting from gas pumps in the GVRD. With this planning base and funding foundation, a new vision of transportation and a livable region seem possible.

The momentum of the past is considerable, and politics often intervenes; suburbanites tend to be adamantly opposed to intensification, for example, no matter how environmentally correct it is (Fowler 1996). Nevertheless, policy initiatives such as those in the GVRD give reason for hope (see also Leo's chapter).

Regulating the Car and Its Movement

Outright banning of automobiles is one of the least imaginative policy alternatives. There are many other possibilities. For instance, to counter the growing tendency of parents to drive their children to school, creative communities have formed *walking school buses*, whereby organized volunteer parents follow a route to school picking up children on the way. Each walking bus eliminates hundreds of auto trips per year and brings people and children together, creating safer neighbourhoods. Car travel does exactly the opposite.

Another initiative is traffic calming. Thirty years ago, angry because three of their children had been killed by cars within a year, a neighbourhood in Delft, Holland, organized an impromptu, late-night street reconstruction, taking away curbs and replacing pavement with trees. Cars could still get through, but only at walking speed (Egan 1995). Many older city neighbourhoods across Canada today have one-way mazes, speed bumps (or speed platforms), planter boxes in the middle of intersections, four-way stop signs, and very low speed limits.

As often happens with innovations, the traffic calming phenomenon is in danger of becoming a cliché, as minor adjustments to traffic flow or isolated steps to slow a lane or two are wrapped in the 'calming' cloak. In fact, the concept was founded on a vision of city life that challenged the conventional view of cities, which sees them primarily as money-making machines. Phil Day, a senior planner in Brisbane, elaborates:

> Traffic calming involves a fundamental re-thinking of metropolitan planning and organization, and a revived emphasis upon quality rather than the quantity of life. Some may even see the ultimate goal as the calming of society itself—abandoning the frenetic pursuit of ever more development and its generation of increasing inequalities, and breaking the habit of the ever increasing consumption of the finite resources of a fragile planet. (Engwicht 1993: 118)

European ideas such as closing sections of the central city, once anathema, are now receiving serious consideration. Montreal's Tour de l'Isle mass bicycle ride sees huge sections of the city taken over by throngs of cyclists who literally tour the whole island. It's possible to stand in one place for three hours and watch a continuous river of cyclists, twelve riders wide, of all ages, sizes, and abilities. A charitable Ride for the

Heart in Toronto gives freedom of the expressway to cyclists and roller bladers for a Sunday as the infamous Don Valley Parkway is closed in both directions, much to the delight of both bike riders and the breathing population. Still, the concept of complete closures of streets runs into the brick wall of commercial opposition, with retailers fearing economic strangulation—a groundless worry, to judge by the experiences of European cities. In the Brazilian city of Curitiba, after initially opposing a downtown pedestrian mall, merchants starting clamouring for its extension because business had improved so significantly (Hawken, Lovins, and Lovins 1999). In the spring of 2000, the publication of a report by Toronto's Medical Officer of Health, which indicated that there were 1,000 preventable premature deaths annually as a result of smog, brought serious consideration by city council and the media of the heretical ideas of banning cars from the city, or downtown parts of it, and of free transit on smog days.

Arterial roads are a more difficult problem, because they are more likely to serve through traffic than local streets are. There have been some successes. Toronto's Bay Street 'urban clearway', which limited one of the two lanes in each direction to buses, taxis, and bikes, was so successful that the Commissioner of Works now boasts that the road handles just as many cars as it did when all four lanes were devoted to cars. The predicted traffic chaos never materialized. Elsewhere, Sherbrooke, Quebec, has carved out two-way bicycle lanes from their road system in strategic locations without widening the road at all. Ottawa has established buses-only lanes on Rideau Street.

In Toronto, High Occupancy Vehicle (HOV) Lanes have been introduced on some of the inner suburbs' arterial roads: a lane is reserved for transit vehicles, taxis, and private cars with three or more occupants. While violations are high, HOVs are moving more people in cars more efficiently, and transit vehicles cover the distance in less time (Metro Transportation 1995).

At least some of these street restructurings are not merely regulating the car: they are, in effect, redefining the street, from a movement corridor to an urban place. The idea of roads as the exclusive preserve of the car is being challenged. Stopping is allowed. Interacting is encouraged, as sidewalks become places. If we are going to honour the city as a place, then we have to pay attention to how each place can be a part of its users, and vice versa. Movement within and through the area needs to harmonize with the intricate blend of activities that characterize vibrant city life. This implies a very different approach to transportation policy, one that goes far beyond regulating car use, as Day noted.

Another way of discouraging cars is to make the price of parking reflect its true costs. Because most North American workers' free parking takes more space than their work area, policies are being enacted in places such as California to charge employees fair market value for their parking space 'and pay every[one] a commuting allowance of equal after-tax value. Workers—a third of whose household driving miles are for commuting—could then use that sum to pay for parking, or find access to work by any cheaper method—living nearby, walking, biking, ridesharing, vanpooling, public transit, or telecommuting' (Hawken, Lovins, and Lovins 1999: 41–2). As mentioned earlier, drivers in Quebec's largest cities are now 'paying a new tax on either gasoline, parking, or their driver's license in 1996 in order to better finance the transit system' (Canadian Urban Transit Association 1995: 1).

One other method of car regulation should be mentioned: toll roads and other ways of charging motorists for their use of streets and highways are under consideration in Alberta and British Columbia. In Ontario, the toll expressway Highway 407 is already open across the northern edge of Metro Toronto. Charging for road use is a complex issue, because everything depends on the pricing mechanism, which can interfere with accountability and democratic government. In New York and Chicago, quasi-public corporations with expropriation powers have used tolls not just to maintain highways and bridges, but to build massive new ones that destroyed thousands of houses in stable and healthy neighbourhoods (Fowler 1992; Thompson 1996). These agencies are impervious to community input; they represent the kind of 'flexible' organs of metropolitan governance we can do without (Fairlie 1994). Thus, Canadians could choose to work with private consortiums, subsidized by taxpayers, that build new highways with tolls (this is the case in Ontario, Nova Scotia, and California). Another option would be publicly controlled congestion taxes on all roads, using electronic devices in each car, and sending revenues to alternative modes of transport.

Public Transit

Car owners might feel that it is unfair to subsidize transit out of their pockets, as some of the proposals in the previous section suggest. This puts the spotlight on what is normally considered to be the basic problem of transit: its expanding costs and requirements for subsidy, a problem being addressed in the United Kingdom at this moment (Solomon 1995). This fixation on only the economics of transit ignores not only land use, but also the subsidization of cars, which is indirect and mostly invisible, unlike transit subsidies. Furthermore, transit riders pay up front for their rides. Fares cover as little as one-third of the cost of the ride in the United States, 53 per cent in Montreal, and 84 per cent in Toronto. The shortfall is publicly and clearly covered by sources other than transit authorities.

The costs of cars are difficult to pin down, but estimates of government subsidies for car users (over and above what they already pay in gas taxes, etc.) vary from $300 billion a year in the United States, or 35 per cent of total costs of the car (Komanoff 1995), to over 85 per cent (Zuckerman 1991). These estimates do not include items such as income tax lost through deduction of car expenses for business purposes or the cost of defense establishments in the Middle East to protect the West's sources of oil.

Isolating transit costs from motor vehicle costs is not as silly as isolating both forms of transportation from land use policy. Transit systems' financial woes stem mostly from their desperate attempts to service spread-out development spawned by the auto. Transit needs a certain population density to make money—about 3,000 persons/km^2 for surface routes and 6,000 persons/km^2 for subways. Thus, an immediate moratorium on low-density development on the outskirts of cities, whose densities average 2,000 to 2,500 persons/km^2, and a requirement that all new development involve intensification of existing built-up areas would be the best transit policy a city could adopt, without spending a single dollar. This has been the GVRD's strategy. Until the physical context—the shape of the city—is changed, public transit may never lure drivers from their cars, no matter how cheap and accessible the service. Here is an area of real choice for decision-makers, however, one that transcends the narrow focus on finances. By redefining the problem, a different set of forces and actors are implicated—and perhaps a different power structure (Rochefort and Cobb 1994).

Sea changes are at work in even the most car-addicted communities. Surrounding Toronto's core are the so-called 905 communities, known by their telephone exchange and decidedly suburban.[3] Still, at meetings of the regional round table known as the Greater Toronto Services Board, mayors, councillors, and regional chairs of communities with miles of sprawling subdivisions have increasingly commented that 'more roads will not solve our problems'. Mississauga's mayor, worried about how the city's 'planning policies may be contributing to sprawl', is suggesting light rapid transit as a solution (Funston 2000).

One should be cautious about making comparisons with Europe, whose urban areas are already more compact than ours, but several nations there have improved transit ridership by coordinating fares, routes, and timetables. In an era when affluent West Germany's car ownership of 503 per 1,000 inhabitants surpassed Toronto's (463) and Vancouver's (444), making transit cheaper and seamless produced a remarkable ridership increase of 13 per cent between 1988 and 1993. Other countries—the Netherlands, Switzerland, Austria, and France—have achieved similar increases. At the same time, lowering subsidies and privatizing public transport in Norway and Great Britain has produced dramatic decreases in ridership (Pucher and Kurth 1995).

Canadian cities are undertaking a few initiatives. For example, Montreal's Transit Revival program in 1992 started servicing areas which up to then had had very little service, and ridership began to rise. Calgary and Edmonton achieved a coup when they secured an agreement from their provincial government in late 1999 to receive a share of the gasoline taxes raised in their cities for use in financing public transit. New facilities can now be planned knowing that a secure funding base is in place.

In the context of many other chapters in this book that document the financial straits of Canadian municipalities, it is worth noting that these initiatives supporting transit (and regulating the car) are economically beneficial, because as we've noted, the car culture is ruining our local economies. Consider that 85 cents on every dollar spent by local residents on gasoline leaves the regional economy, much of it leaving the country as well. In contrast, out of every dollar that buys a fare on public transport, an estimated 80 cents goes towards transit workers' wages; those 80 cents then circulate in the local economy, generating more than $3.80 in goods and services in the region (Zielinski 1995–96).

Canadian cities have much to learn from elsewhere. Probably the finest public transportation system in the world can be found, not in Canada, not in Europe, but in Curitiba, Brazil, where 28 per cent of bus users have cars, yet prefer the bus, which—in its articulated version—carries up to 270 passengers and comes by once a minute during rush hours. This means that express bus lanes have a capacity of

20,000 travelers per hour, half that of a full-fledged subway, for a tiny fraction of the cost. Other features of this system include a highly efficient bus stop infrastructure; service provision by ten private bus companies paid not per passenger, but per route kilometre; and operating costs financed entirely by fares—unheard of in the world of public transit (Hawken, Lovins, and Lovins 1999).

Bicycles

One of the most sensible ways of getting around the city is not a new idea at all, but it is certainly an idea whose time has come. Bicycles were treated for years as the vehicles of the eccentric. Recently, however, there has been a huge growth in cycling, especially in utilitarian bike riding just to get to work, school, shopping, or visiting. The Toronto Cycling Committee recently released a comprehensive survey showing that up to 3,000,000 bicycle trips are taken every week, not only in summer, but in spring and fall as well. This compares to 7,000,000 transit rides. In all Canadian cities, cycling is growing, and facilities are beginning to be built with a vengeance. Whole master plans are unfolding for interconnected bike paths and routes. Ottawa and Edmonton are particularly notable for their cycling facilities, so much so that tourists now rely on bikes to see the sights. The famous post-and-ring bike rack is sprouting up more quickly than weeds despite its meagre origins—it was designed on the back of a napkin in a pub by a small group of 'velo-lutionaries'.

Only a few years ago, it would have been impossible to imagine a network of towns and cities joining with a provincial government to create an 800-kilometre bicycle trail for ecotourism, commuting, and fitness. Yet the first phases of such a trail have been opened in Quebec, and its immediate popularity is accelerating the project's completion.

Some Canadian towns have initiated 'free bike' programs, using unreturned, reconditioned stolen bikes in cooperation with local police and community groups. In Jasper, Alberta, for instance, the White Bike Program 'works on the honour system. Bikes are initially put in bike stands around town and the users are asked to return them to a bike stand when they are finished' (Environment Network News 1998: 21). Even the bike-theft capital of North America, Toronto, with its annual criminal harvest of 11,000 stolen bikes, is contemplating a free bike program. European experience suggests that when bikes are free, fewer are stolen.

Access through Proximity

Some have argued that exploding telecommunications and computer technologies will allow more people to work at home and decrease the need for urban travel (Irwin 1994). Frisken contends, however, that only a relatively small and privileged group of highly skilled workers will fit that scenario; most of us—especially women and the unskilled—will probably need to make yet more trips 'to adapt to economic and technological change' (Blais 1994; Frisken 1994a). There is general agreement that we shall have to travel farther because computer-based business technology is a central force in the decentralization of enterprises and in continuing sprawl.

Nevertheless, access through proximity is an important principle. At the start of this chapter, we invited you to consider why people are traveling around the city so much in the first place. At the risk of being obvious, we might say that it is to get to work, to shop for food, to visit friends, or to go to a show. Rather than taking urban sprawl—and its living habits—for granted and looking for more efficient ways to travel across that sprawl, we could plan to have access to work, food, and friends by gathering them around us: working at home, buying groceries at the corner or even growing vegetables, and making friends in the neighborhood (Freund and Martin 1993).

Many have made such choices, consciously, in where they choose to live or in how they live where they are (Elgin 1981; Elgin and LeDrew 1997). We thus disagree with David Foot in this volume, who argues that travel behaviour is not susceptible to change; however, that change cannot be imposed from above—it must come from below. Obviously, new living patterns could be supported, rather than frustrated, by urban development that combines higher densities and small-scale, mixed land use. (See Leo's discussion of the new urbanism in this volume.) Solving many of our transportation problems involves land use and lifestyle changes that already are undeniably attractive to many Canadians.

It bears mentioning that these changes will have other policy benefits as well: more efficient use of infrastructure (see Andrew and Morrison's chapter in this volume), stronger communities (Fowler 1987), and a cleaner environment (see Price's chapter in this volume).

Conclusions

The next time you take a trip through a city (we realize that some of our readers live in rural areas), think about the reasons for your trip and mode of transport. These reasons reflect your own personal preferences, your gender and socio-economic status, and a transportation infrastructure built by government officials, probably without your input. Urban transportation policies are part of the whole equation, but, like your personal choices, they are embedded in cultural conditioning that it is difficult to be aware of. We have expressed our own strong opinions about urban travel and urban life, with which you may well disagree. We stress, however, that whatever you believe, there will always be an interplay between your individual choices and collective policy.

In fact, any unilateral, blanket transportation policy for a city is by definition unintelligent. It is instructive here to recall Jane Jacobs's mistrust of broad planning policies (1961). Her position is that urban vitality sprouts of its own accord if unhindered by zoning, by concessions to and subsidies for moneyed interests, and by mega-projects. Thus, a decision made from above to ban cars or to intensify is relatively meaningless. In her mind, 'attrition of the automobile' needs to be place-specific: when an area's diversity and vitality is threatened by cars, that's when cars must be discouraged. A fitting conclusion: sensible transportation policy comes from coordinating the specific—places and individuals—with the general—principles of access and sustainability. This change must come from individuals, but from individuals who are working together in local communities to create the livable city of our dreams.

Notes

1. We have benefited from advice, information, knowledge, and wisdom given freely to us as we prepared this chapter by Don Ogner; Richard Gilbert; Brendon Hemily and Michael Canzi of the Canadian Urban Transit Association; Tom Samuels; Perry Gladstone; David Yap; Tom Furmanczyk; Paul Morton; and Franca Ursitti. We take full responsibility for any errors of fact or interpretation.
2. A complete overview of political forces in cities can be found in Layton (1990).
3. A second exchange has been added to the 905 area, but the original label will probably stick.

References

'50 Best-Paid CEOs'. 1999. *Report on Business Magazine* 6(July): 125.

Appleyard, Donald. 1981. *Livable Streets*. Berkeley: University of California Press.

Barber, John. 1995. 'Mom's Taxi Could Be a Death Trap'. *The Globe and Mail* (8 March).

Bates, D.V., and R. Sizto. 1987. 'Air Pollution and Hospital Admissions in Southern Ontario: The Acid Summer Haze Effect'. *Environmental Research* 43: 317–31.

Black, Edwin R. 1982. *Politics and the News: The Political Functions of the Mass Media*. Toronto: Butterworths.

Blais, Pamela. 1994. 'Cities in the Information Age'. *The Intensification Report* 11: 13–16.

Burnet, Richard T., Robert Dales, Daniel Kravski, Renaud Vincent, Tom Dann, and Jeffrey R. Brook. 1995. 'Associations between Ambient Particulate Sulfate and Admission to Ontario Hospitals for Cardiac and Respiratory Diseases'. *American Journal of Epidemiology* 142: 15–22.

Calthorpe, Peter. 1991. 'The Post-Suburban Metropolis'. *Whole Earth Review* 73: 44–51.

Canadian Urban Transit Association. 1995. *Forum* (5 June).

Carder, Chris, and Marni Norwich. 1992. 'Donor List May Be Required before Vote'. *The Globe and Mail* (26 August).

Columbo, John Robert, ed. 1992. *The Canadian Almanac 1993*. Toronto: Macmillan.

Egan, Daniel. 1995. 'Calming Traffic, Exciting People'. In *Beyond the Car: Essays on the Auto Culture*, ed. Sue Zielinski and Gordon Laird. Toronto: Steel Rail Publishing/Transportation Options.

Elgin, Duane. 1981. *Voluntary Simplicity: Toward a Way of Life that is Outwardly Simple, Inwardly Rich*. New York: William Morrow.

Elgin, Duane, and Coleen LeDrew. 1997. 'Global Paradigm Report: Tracking the Shift Underway'. *YES! A Journal of Positive Futures* 6(Winter): 19–25.

Engwicht, David. 1993. *Reclaiming Our Cities and Towns: Better Living with Less Traffic*. Philadelphia, PA: New Society.

Environment Network News. 1998. 'Take a White Bike'. *Alternatives* 24(1): 21.

Fairlie, Simon. 1994. 'The Theory behind Road Tolls: New Clothes for the Road Lobby'. *The Ecologist* 24: 213–19.

Fowler, Edmund P. 1987. 'Street Management and City Design'. *Social Forces* 66: 365–89.

————. 1991. 'The Mystery of the Disappearing Car'. *Alternatives* 18(1): 16.

————. 1992. *Building Cities That Work*. Montreal: McGill-Queen's University Press.

————. 1994. 'Reflections on Building Cities That Work'. *Blueprint for Social Justice* 47(8): 1–6.

————. 1996. 'Intensification of the People or by the People?' *Alternatives* 22(2): 12–13.

Franklin, Ursula. 1990. *The Real World of Technology*. Toronto: CBC Enterprises.

Freund, Peter, and George Martin. 1993. *The Ecology of the Automobile*. Montreal: Black Rose.

Friends of Red Hill Valley. 1999. 'Our Local Share of the Cost of the Red Hill Free Way'. FRHV HomePage. Accessed 31 January 2000: http:/www.freenet.hamilton. on.ca/link/forhv/costrise.html

Frisken, Frances. 1994a. 'The Challenge for Public Transit in the Telecommunications Age'. *The Intensification Report* 11: 4–6.

————. 1994b. 'Provincial Transit Policy Making for the Toronto, Montreal, and Vancouver Regions'. In *The Changing Canadian Metropolis: A Public Policy Perspective*, ed. Frances Frisken. Toronto: Canadian Urban Institute.

Frisken, Frances, and David V.J. Bell, eds. 1994. *Human Society and the Natural World*. Toronto: York University.

Funston, Mike. 2000. 'Mississauga Seeks Sprawl Solutions'. *The Toronto Star* (15 June).

Furmanczyk, Tom. 1994. *National Urban Air Quality Trends, 1981–90*. Ottawa: Environment Canada.

Greater Vancouver Regional District (GVRD). Policy and Planning Department. 1999. *Greater Vancouver Regional Greenway Vision*. (July). Vancouver: GVRD.

Gutstein, Donald. 1975. *Vancouver Ltd*. Toronto: Lorimer.

————. 1983. 'Vancouver'. In *City Politics in Canada*. ed. Warren Magnusson and Andrew Sancton. Toronto: University of Toronto Press.

Hawken, Paul, Amory Lovins, and L. Hunter Lovins. 1999. *Natural Capitalism: Creating the Next Industrial Revolution*. Boston: Little Brown.

Hough, Michael. 1984. *City Form and Natural Process: Towards a New Urban Vernacular*. New York: Van Nostrand Reinhold.

Irwin, Neal. 1994. 'Telecommunications and Urban Form'. *The Intensification Report* 11: 9–16.

Jacobs, Jane. 1961. *The Death and Life of Great American Cities*. New York: Random House.

James, Royson. 2000. 'Time for TTC Budget Chief to Get Along'. *The Toronto Star* (10 March).

Kitchen, Harry. 1990. 'Transportation'. In *Urban Policy Issues: Canadian Perspectives*, ed. Richard A. Loreto and Trevor Price. Toronto: McClelland & Stewart.

Klodawsky, Fran, and Aron Spencer. 1988. 'New Families, New Housing Needs, New Environments: The Case of Single-Parent Families'. In *Life Spaces: Gender, Household, Employment*, ed. Caroline Andrew and Beth Moore Milroy. Vancouver: University of British Columbia Press.

Kluckner, Michael. 1991. *Paving Paradise: Is British Columbia Losing Its Heritage?* Vancouver: Whitecap.

Komanoff, Charles. 1995. 'Car Economics Made Easy: A New York Case Study'. In *Beyond the Car: Essays on the Auto Culture*, ed. Sue Zielinski and Gordon Laird. Toronto: Steel Rail Publishing/Transportation Options.

Laird, Gordon. 1995. 'Manufacturing Value: The Modern Auto Corporation'. In *Beyond the Car: Essays on the Auto Culture*, ed. Sue Zielinski and Gordon Laird. Toronto: Steel Rail Publishing/Transportation Options.

Layton, Jack. 1990. 'City Politics in Canada'. In *Canadian Politics in the 1990s*, 3rd ed., ed. Glen Williams and Michael Whittington. Scarborough, ON: Nelson.

Leo, Christopher. 1977. *The Politics of Urban Development: Canadian Urban Expressway Disputes*. Toronto: Institute of Public Administration.

Lerner, Steve. 1997. *Eco-Pioneers: Practical Visionaries Solving Today's Environmental Problems*. Cambridge, MA: MIT Press.

Litman, Todd. 1999. *The Costs of Automobile Dependency and the Benefits of Balanced Transportation*. Victoria, BC: Victoria Transport Policy Institute.

Lorimer, James. 1972. *A Citizen's Guide to City Politics*. Toronto: James, Lewis and Samuel.

———. 1979. *The Developers*. Toronto: Lorimer.

Lowe, Marcia. 1994. 'Reinventing Transport'. In Worldwatch Institute, *State of the World 1995*. New York: Norton.

Lupo, Alan, Frank Colcord, and Edmund P. Fowler. 1971. *Rites of Way: The Politics of Transportation in the U.S. City*. Boston: Little Brown.

McAndrew, Brian. 1999. 'Toronto Gets D Grade on Anti-Smog Action'. *The Toronto Star* (9 June).

MacMillan, Neale. 1993. 'File on Cars'. *Canadian Forum* 71(April): 48.

Magnusson, Warren. 1983. 'Toronto'. In *City Politics in Canada*, ed. Warren Magnusson and Andrew Sancton. Toronto: University of Toronto Press.

Metro Transportation. 1995. 'Review of High Occupancy Vehicle Lane Operation and Policy'. Toronto: Municipality of Metropolitan Toronto.

Myers, Gustavus. 1972. *A History of Canadian Wealth*. Toronto: J. Lewis & Samuel.

Nader, George A. 1975. *Cities of Canada: Theoretical, Historical and Planning Perspectives*. Toronto: Macmillan.

Newman, Peter, and Jeffrey Kenworthy. 1989. *Cities and Automobile Dependence: An International Sourcebook*. Brookfield, VT: Gower.

Oberlander, H. Peter, and Patrick J. Smith. 1993. 'Governing Metropolitan Vancouver: Regional Intergovernmental Relations in British Columbia'. In *Metropolitan Governance: American/Canadian Intergovernmental Perspectives*, ed. Donald N. Rothblatt and Andrew Sancton. Kingston, ON: Institute of Intergovernmental Relations.

Ostro, Bart. 1993. 'The Association of Air Pollution and Mortality: Examining the Case for Inference'. *Archives of Environmental Health* 48: 336–42.

Overton, Karen. 1995. 'Auto-Dependence: A Driving Force for Gender Inequality'. *Urban Ecology* 1(1): 16–23.

Pucher, John, and Stefan Kurth. 1995. 'Making Transit Irresistible: Lessons from Europe'. *Transportation Quarterly* 49: 117–28.

Raad, Tamim, and Jeff Kenworthy. 1998. 'The U.S. and Us'. *Alternatives* 24(1): 14–22.

Renner, Michael. 1988. *Rethinking the Role of the Automobile*. Washington, DC: Worldwatch Institute.

Rochefort, David A., and Roger W. Cobb, eds. 1994. *The Politics of Problem Definition: Shaping the Policy Agenda*. Lawrence, KS: University Press of Kansas.

Solomon, Lawrence. 1995. 'Coming Soon to a Subway Near You'. *Next City* 1(1): 32–43, 69–72.

Spirn, Anne Whiston. 1984. *The Granite Garden: Urban Nature and Human Design*. New York: Harper/Basic.

Stieb, David L., David Pengally, Nina Arron, S. Martin Taylor, and Mark E. Raizenne. 1995. 'Health Effects of Air Pollution in Toronto: Expert Panel Findings for the Canadian Smog Advisory Program'. *Canadian Respiratory Journal* 2(3): 1–6.

Stillich, Udo. 1995. *The Liveable Toronto Area*. Toronto: Transportation Options.

Suzuki, David, and Holly Dressel. 1999. *From Naked Ape to Superspecies: A Personal Perspective on Humanity and the Global Eco-Crisis*. Toronto: Stoddart.

Thompson, Shannon. 1996. 'Road Pricing Takes Its Toll'. *TransMission* 3(2): 15–17.

Tompkins, Peter, and Christopher Bird. 1989. *Secrets of the Soil*. New York: Harper and Row.

Toronto. Department of Public Health. 1993. *The Healthy City Report*. Toronto: City of Toronto.

Toronto. Environmental Task Force (ETF). 1999. *Sustainable Transportation Workgroup Final Report*. Toronto: City of Toronto.

Transport Canada. 1998. *Canadian Motor Vehicle Traffic Collisions Statistics*. (November). Ottawa: Government of Canada, TP 3322.

———. 2000. 'Victims of Collisions Involving Buses'. *Traffic Accident Information Data Base* (5 January). Ottawa: Transport Canada.

Vanderwagen, Joell. 1995. 'Coming Down to Earth'. In *Beyond the Car: Essays on the Auto Culture*, ed. Sue Zielinski and Gordon Laird. Toronto: Steel Rail Publishing/Transportation Options.

Vojnovic, Igor. 1995. 'Pathways to Sustainability'. *The Intensification Report* 15: 3–10.

Warner, Sam Bass, Jr. 1962. *Streetcar Suburbs: The Process of Growth in Boston, 1870–1900*. Cambridge, MA: Harvard University Press.

Wekerle, Gerda. 1980. 'Women in the Urban Environment'. *Signs* 5: 188–214.

Zielinski, Sue. 1995–96. 'Insights on Infrastructure'. *TransMission* 3(2): 18.

Zuckerman, Wolfgang. 1991. *End of the Road: The World Car Crisis and How We Can Solve It*. Post Mills, VT: Chelsea Green.

CHAPTER 8

Sustainable Cities

Trevor Price

Introduction

The approach taken in this chapter goes beyond merely analyzing environmental activities within Canadian cities to examine what might be called the 'footprint' of major Canadian cities on the total biosphere across the entire globe. The concept of the city footprint focuses on the entirety of the resources consumed within the city and the impact of waste products discharged from the city. This would encompass such items as energy drawn from thousands of miles away, timber and agricultural products from all over the world, and food products from the world's oceans. Waste discharges include greenhouse gases from automobiles and toxic contaminants discharged into the air, soil, groundwater, and surface water. From this perspective, a city of a few thousand hectares can have a footprint covering many hundreds of thousands of hectares, penetrating land, water, and air.

Clearly, urban growth is changing the face of the earth. Currently, half the world's population lives in cities. In Canada, approximately 65 per cent of the total population live in 35 census metropolitan areas, up from 55 per cent in 1971 (Statistics Canada 1994). The source of most of the world's environmental degradation is found in activities taking place within the world's major cities. However, it would be quite unrealistic to expect the governments of cities to be able to reorder the life and the organization of city functions to minimize environmental impact. As discussed in other chapters, cities on their own lack the financial resources, the legislative powers, and even the scientific know-how to create sustainable cities that could greatly minimize their footprints.

This chapter will discuss the importance of various levels of government and of international organizations such as the United Nations. All these organizations play some role in establishing standards and rules that influence the conduct of cities. The behaviour of these various organizations may either act as a beacon toward higher levels of performance or as a hindrance to improvement because of lack of financial resources and mandate. Cities are pushed to neglect environmental priorities because they seek to amplify their economic base for the sake of jobs and increased taxes, even if it means sacrificing environmental quality.

Government Organization, the Global Context, and the Environment

Although cities create an enormous footprint that affects the biosphere in a major way, the setting in which cities operate is influenced by a highly complex interaction that starts at the level of international organization, through the federal government, to the provinces, and ultimately to the operating level of the city. It is difficult for cities as independent actors to play a major initiating role in this increasingly complex setting. They find themselves at the terminal position where they react to goals that have been agreed upon at the global level, then interpreted at a national level, and finally implemented through consensual agreements between the federal government and the provinces (see Fowler and Hartmann's chapter).

This description simplifies considerably the complexity of interactions both within the global community and within the Canadian federal state. This complexity can be illustrated by the ebb and flow of world opinion in the last twenty years, as major environmental crises and world conferences heightened public interest only to see it wane when other issues and problems grabbed the national agenda (see Fowler and Siegel's chapter).

World interest in environmental matters reached a high point in 1987 when the World Commission on Environment and Development reported to the United Nations. This report (commonly called the Bruntland Report) caught the imagination of much of the world community. It argued that economic development was possible for both developed and developing countries while still protecting the environment. This came to be known as *sustainable development*. In Canada, the Mulroney government reacted positively to the message of the commission and developed the 'Green Plan'. This plan required all matters involving major economic developments to be subjected to environmental assessment, although matters of provincial jurisdiction would have to be dealt with at that level. The recurrent problem of federalism has meant that unilateral initiatives of the federal government are politically difficult and that the implementation of most international commitments can only be undertaken after long, and often tortuous, discussions with the provinces. Nevertheless, governments at all levels in Canada have used the concept of sustainability to justify policies affecting growth, although it is not certain that all users of this term share a common interpretation of the concept.

The recession of the early 1990s and the consequent problems of unemployment, along with the fiscal difficulties of governments at all levels, caused a significant decline in public interest in sustainable development across the country. This decline in interest was followed by the development of green plans for most major cities and regions across Canada (for one example, see Fowler and Hartmann's chapter). However, the early 1990s was a time of increasing taxes, diminished purchasing power, and increasing government debt. The resources to pursue environmental initiatives were perceived to be in short supply, and after a few token programs, environmental budgets were slashed at nearly all levels of government. As the twenty-first century opens and the economy improves, it is apparent that the neglect of the past ten years has had an adverse impact on the environment and, consequently, on public health. The result is that governments at all levels are beginning to take new interest in and loosen the purse strings for environmental projects.

The 1990s saw a series of international conferences that attempted to implement various elements of the World Commission Report. Among the most important were the Rio Conference on Biodiversity and Climate Change in 1992, the Habitat 2 Conference in Istanbul in 1996, the Kyoto Conference on Climate Change in 1997, a conference on population in Cairo in 1998, and a follow-up meeting in Buenos Aires on climate change. Canada played a leading role in all these conferences and promised to play its part in meeting established goals.

However, since the Chrétien Liberal government was elected in 1993, its chief priority has been balancing the budget, which it has done largely by cutting transfer payments to the provinces. The provinces were also faced with serious deficiencies in revenue and consequently cut their grants to municipalities at the same time as they downloaded more responsibilities to municipal governments. This occurred at a time when governments at the local level were facing a near crisis in worn out and inadequate infrastructure. As Siegel's chapter on finance shows, municipalities faced a severe financial squeeze at a time when major capital expenditure on items such as better sewage treatment, better roads, improvements to green space and natural areas, low-income housing, and improved mass transit were all needed; the result was all too often cuts to the services or a substantial increase in user fees. (See also Andrew and Morrison's chapter on infrastructure.)

The remainder of this chapter will deal separately with each of the principal environmental topics related to the city. This is done for purely analytical reasons, because it will be obvious that all of these issues are closely related in the sense that action or inaction in a particular area can have repercussions on all the other concerns. The ecosystem approach demands that the environmental implications of each city service be assessed for its impact on all others; this is why a green plan is essential. In addition, comprehensive environmental guidelines have been developed for the benefit of cities wishing to create an environmental overview for all their activities. The issues to be discussed are

- Air: climate change, acid rain, smog, ozone depletion, toxic fallout
- Water: supply, quality, pricing, exports, wetlands, conservation
- Waste Management: waste disposal, recycling and reuse, hazardous wastes, resource management
- Land Use: urban sprawl, food lands, transportation issues, infrastructure costs, nature reserves

- Energy: sources, conservation, planning and building, sustainable sources, pollution impact

The conclusion will discuss some potential strategies and problems that have hindered the implementation of a holistic environmental approach toward government policy-making in general.

Air Pollution: Its Causes and Consequences

Ever since the Industrial Revolution, highly industrialized and advanced economies have developed a high standard of living and a way of life based upon the consumption of vast amounts of energy. This energy is largely derived from the burning of fossil fuels, such as coal, petroleum, and wood. In more recent times, electricity from nuclear power has been widely used, giving the impression of non-polluting energy; in fact, it has produced many other problems, including the threat of catastrophic accidents, the disposal of radioactive wastes, and the spread of nuclear weaponry to a number of states not known for political stability.

Fossil fuels used in industrial, transportation, and residential situations give rise to all kinds of gases, which have begun to have an adverse effect on the environment. Greenhouse gases produced from burning fossil fuels in coal-fired power stations, most forms of transportation, and domestic heating have created a blanket retaining more of the sun's heat and raising the average temperature of the globe. Some gases, such as sulphur and nitrogen oxides, contribute toward acid rain, which damages buildings, crops, forests, lakes, and fish. Fluorocarbons used in refrigeration and air conditioning cause thinning of the ozone layer, which exposes us to excessive ultraviolet rays from the sun, resulting in skin cancer and crop damage. Small quantities of toxic substances are leaked from incinerators and industrial activities and may be carried great distances by the atmosphere. Substances such as PCBs and dioxins have been found in remote areas such as the Canadian Arctic. All of the above effects travel long distances across the globe and impact on the whole of the world community.

The quality of air has been found to be harmful to health in such places as Greater Vancouver, the Windsor–Quebec corridor, and parts of Atlantic Canada (see Fowler and Layton's chapter). There are many sources of air pollution, but the main ones are transportation and fossil fuel–burning power stations. One of the worst consequences of this kind of air pollution is photochemical smog, which occurs mainly in the summer months when sunlight interacts with petroleum products to produce ground-level ozone and smog, which in turn can have an adverse impact on people with respiratory problems.

Canada's Approach to Climate Change

The House of Commons Standing Committee on the Environment and Sustainable Development met on 22 October 1998 to hear testimony from experts regarding climate change. Brian Emmett, Commissioner of Environment and Sustainable Development, Office of the Auditor General of Canada, stated that 'we took as our starting point the federal government's own assessment of the consequences of climate change, which indicate they will be potentially severe for Canada. According to the government's own projections, every region of the country and every sector will be affected, especially agriculture, forestry, and fisheries' (Proceedings of House of Commons Standing Committee on Environment and Sustainable Development, 22 October 1998, http://www.parl.gc.ca/infocomduc/36/1/ensu/meetings/evidence/ensuev76-e.htm, accessed 30 January 2001).

The health of Canadians may be seriously affected. The government has therefore concluded that the problem is real and serious and warrants immediate action. The commissioner went on to say that of nineteen management principles to be applied, only three had been implemented. He suggested that the objective of meeting the target of reducing greenhouse gas emissions in the year 2000 to the same level as that of 1990 would fall short by 11 per cent. He argued that Canada's problem is not a lack of ideas about what should be done, but a lack of agreement on a broad national portfolio of practical measures designed to achieve a specific target (Proceedings of House of Commons Standing Committee on Environment and Sustainable Development, 22 October 1998, http://www.parl.gc.ca/infocomduc/36/1/ensu/meetings/evidence/ensuev76-e.htm, accessed 30 January 2001).

Robert Hornung of the Pembina Institute for Appropriate Developments was equally harsh in his criticism of the approach taken by the federal government. He argued that

the failure to meet Canada's climate change commitments was primarily the result of poor planning and ineffective management [as well as] the lack of political will and leadership to address the issue.

Federal leadership is critical, frankly, because if the federal government fails to demonstrate that it's willing to take action on this issue, it's unlikely that provinces are going to follow or that industry will take initiative. Frankly, even individual Canadians aren't likely to act without some strong signal from the federal government. (Proceedings of House of Commons Standing Committee on Environment and Sustainable Development, 22 October 1998, http://www.parl.gc.ca/infocomduc/36/1/ensu/meetings/evidence/ensuev76-e.htm, accessed 30 January 2001)

Hornung was critical of the approach that Canada took to reach its targets. Canada's approach of focusing on education, voluntary compliance by industry, and the trading of emissions with developing countries meant that it would not have to take direct action against such sources of emission as industry and motor vehicles.

Motor vehicles are a major source of carbon monoxide, nitrous oxides, and sulphur oxides (see Fowler and Layton's chapter). Motor vehicle emissions have been reduced significantly since 1970 by the introduction of greater fuel efficiency and better emission controls; however, the number of vehicles in Canada increases by approximately 6 per cent per year, and the distance traveled on average has also risen. Carbon emissions have levelled off but have not been rolled back as Canada promised at Kyoto.

Since the 1970s, when OPEC first put the squeeze on Western economies by controlling the total production of petroleum, there has been little support for the early initiatives by such governments as Ontario to discourage the driving of motor vehicles and to encourage mass transit. OPEC failed to stay united, and the price of oil in real terms actually fell in the 1980s and 1990s. Governments at all levels, dealing with revenue shortages, failed either to support existing mass transit or to initiate new programs. The automobile became by far the most popular method of travel for work and recreation, even in cities such as Toronto that had fairly highly developed transit systems. The relatively low cost of gasoline encouraged the public to move away from economical vehicles toward larger and heavier vehicles such as the sports utility vehicle (SUV), which now constitutes a significant percentage of the Canadian market.

In spite of recent increases, fuel prices seem likely to stay fairly low in Canada compared to other countries. The number of vehicles is constantly expanding, especially in the developing countries, such as China. This means that OPEC is likely to keep the price of oil on the world market much higher than the prevailing price in 1999. If the price of oil increases to the level that it reached in the late fall of 2000, it is possible that the market might do what it did in the 1970s, when it motivated governments to encourage mass transit and restrict the use of automobiles.

The Federation of Canadian Municipalities (FCM) has attempted to give leadership along the whole spectrum of environmental improvements and has encouraged the federal government to bring about closer intergovernmental cooperation and create a common front of policy innovations. This would move cities toward the ideal of sustainability. For example, the FCM has established the '20 per cent club' of cities, which aims for a target of 20 per cent reduction in greenhouse gases produced by municipal government operations by the year 2005. The federal government's 2000 mini-budget provided substantial funding for this FCM initiative.

In general, however, there has not been a strong federal presence in urban matters since the Trudeau government wound up the Ministry of State for Urban Affairs in 1979. In the crucial field of transportation, Canada has slid backwards by allowing the rail system and urban transit to falter. Automobile and truck traffic have increased enormously in the last twenty years, resulting in high levels of air pollution and greenhouse gas emissions and in continuing problems of acid rain (see Fowler and Layton's chapter).

It has been fashionable to argue that Canadians cannot do much to clean up our air so long as we receive large amounts of cross-border pollution from the United States, particularly from coal-burning power stations located mainly in the American Midwest. Although Ontario has reduced substantially the emissions of sulphur dioxide from nickel smelting and coal-burning power stations, our record in greenhouse gas emissions has been relatively poor. The breakdown of many nuclear-powered generators has caused Ontario to expand its coal-burning power stations and thus to increase the quantity of greenhouse gases, giving Canada a relatively weak bargaining position with the United States, which can rightfully demand that we clean up our own backyard first before pointing at anyone else's deficiencies.

A recent report by the Suzuki Foundation criticized the view held by many political and business leaders that implementation of measures to reduce greenhouse gas emissions significantly would be a major drain on the economy. The Suzuki Foundation takes a completely contrary view, arguing that moving to curb greenhouse gas emissions would in fact stimulate the Canadian economy and that exploitation of new technologies would place Canada in the vanguard of innovation and bring in many millions of dollars from the export of technologies and expertise (MacKinnon 2000).

The Suzuki Foundation envisages the gains being made by a combination of factors, including such measures as more energy-efficient buildings and the transformation of automobiles to burn fuel efficiently or to use hydrogen as a major fuel, leaving only water as exhaust. The report also called for much greater use of public transit and a switch to generating electricity from wind, solar, and hydro power (MacKinnon 2000).

The report predicts that implementation of the recommended program could reduce the 1995 discharge of 600 million tons of gases to 300 million tons by the year 2030. Although this program would cost many billions of dollars, the cost would be offset by the savings accruing from greater energy efficiency and the avoidance of the incalculable cost associated with global warming. Suzuki said, 'It's imperative that rich countries like Canada do take the lead and show that it's possible. Countries that do tackle this gain an economic advantage' (MacKinnon 2000).

The most difficult and important issue is determining the best technological path. Part of the problem is the development of a strong political consensus in the face of substantial public opinion, which still questions the seriousness of environmental problems. There is still a vocal minority opinion that questions the impact of climate change and even whether this impact will be entirely negative (Fitz-Gerard 2000). In the rush to balance the budget, cut taxes, and spend more on health and education, the environment has moved down very low on the list of government priorities.

The Management of Water

During the rise of industrial cities in the nineteenth century, the problem of a pure water supply was one of the dominant concerns of public health and resulted in major capital investments by the newly developing cities. Piping in fresh water and removing sewage made living conditions tolerable in the developed countries (see Hancock's chapter). Today, the problem of water remains a key issue for millions of people.

Canada does not have a significant problem with water supply because of our abundance of fresh water. However, we have some difficulty maintaining water quality because a good deal of our water supply from rivers, underground water, and the Great Lakes has been contaminated. Much needs to be done to prevent further pollution, as demonstrated by the tragic deaths caused by the water supply in Walkerton, Ontario, in 2000.

Another issue, which will unquestionably confront us into the twenty-first century, is whether or not we should export fresh water in bulk to other countries, either by tanker or by a system of diversionary canals. Parts of the United States are likely to face water shortages, and there is a fear among environmentalists in this country that Canada will be pressured under the North American Free Trade Agreement (NAFTA) to export water.

Water Conservation

Although Canada is fortunate in having an abundant supply of fresh water, the problems of distributing water and treating wastewater are significant, because they constitute a major part of our infrastructure expenditure (see Andrew and Morrison's chapter). Canadians have not suffered from serious water shortages, but there have been problems for those communities that do not have a nearby supply of surface water. Underground water in many places has been either depleted or contaminated, and expensive schemes to bring water a great distance have had to be contemplated, thus increasing infrastructure costs by millions of dollars.

Canadians are among the most prodigious users of water in the world, and much of this use could be considered wasteful and needlessly costly. One of the reasons for this level of use is that water has been relatively inexpensive; the fact that some supply agencies charge a flat rate regardless of consumption has encouraged this waste. In most places, water is now metered, and it is a widespread practice to add a surcharge for sewer usage as a percentage of the water bill. These practices have significantly increased the cost of water and encouraged more frugal use of this resource.

In addition to action on the part of individuals, municipalities can do much to conserve water by modernizing the distribution system to correct the current situation, which allows 15 per cent to 50 per cent of water to be lost through leaking pipes in an infrastructure that often dates back 100 years. In other countries, purified water is used only for human consumption and wastewater is used for watering lawns, golf courses, and so forth. Industries that are heavy users of water could be encouraged to recycle water and not to discharge it back to the source untreated.

The problem of climate change is closely connected to that of water supply. Rainfall in many parts of the world seems to be changing substantially, a change that is attributed to global warming. In the spring of 2000, the Great Lakes experienced their lowest water levels in thirty years, which had significant consequences not only for shipping and recreation, but also for the protection of environmental habitat such as wetlands and forests, which can act as a buffer against problems of drought and flooding. The wider effect of the lakes' water levels underlines the fact that the problem of water quality and supply must be looked at from an ecosystem perspective, which unfortunately has not been the way water management has been regarded in parts of Canada. For example, the government of Ontario has substantially cut transfer payments to conservation authorities, which were initially established to manage water.

One method of controlling water flows, which would also improve wildlife habitat, would be the massive acquisition of marginal farmlands and the return of these farmlands to their original forest or wetlands usage. In order to bring this about, the government would need to resume its grants to conservation authorities for the acquisition of lands. Voluntary contributions from donors, while useful, cannot achieve the scale of conversion to natural habitat that is required.

Water Quality

This section examines actions that have been taken to manage more efficiently the use of water and to manage the formidable task of restoring water to a safe level of water quality; it looks first at measures aimed at preventing further contamination of water supplies and second at measures aimed at cleaning up sites badly contaminated by past pollution.

The federal Department of the Environment has confirmed that the state of Canada's drinking water is relatively good. At the same time, it has been recognized that some of the bodies of water from which we extract water for industry, agriculture, and domestic consumption contain many pollutants. Among the most prominent of these are the Great Lakes and the Detroit and St Lawrence rivers. For example, over 350 chemical contaminants have been identified in the Great Lakes. The perilous state of the beluga whales—whose corpses are treated as toxic waste—demonstrates the amount of contamination that has accumulated in the lower reaches of the St Lawrence River. The fact that the Great Lakes–St Lawrence system provides water to many major cities makes this a serious problem.

The federal government and the provinces of Ontario and Quebec have signed agreements to cooperate on the cleanup of these waters. The United States and Canada have cooperated for many years in cleaning up boundary waters through such arrangements as the Great Lakes Water Quality Agreement. The initial stages of the implementation of this agreement resulted in a program of massive construction of sewage treatment facilities on both sides of the Great Lakes and in a significant improvement in water quality. A further renewal of the agreement focused on cleaning up the sources of toxic contamination, which are less visible and more intractable because the sources of contamination are many and difficult to identify. On both sides of the lakes, areas of concern were identified and proposed for remediation. In some cases, these areas of concern were entirely in Canadian or American waters, but some, such as the Detroit River, were of bilateral concern. Collingwood Harbour on Georgian Bay has been certified as clean. Hamilton Harbour has made recognizable progress. However, the Detroit River has been the subject of years of dialogue, while little has been done to improve its conditions and residents have been advised not to eat fish caught in the river.

Although most city authorities claim that water supplied by their purification plants is fit to drink, the sale of bottled water and water filters continues to rise, indicating a lack of trust in the quality of water supplied by local authorities in most sections of the country.

Sewage treatment attempts to remove all kinds of pollutants from water discharged from homes and industrial plants before it is discharged back into watercourses. There are three generally recognized levels of wastewater treatment:

- Primary Treatment: removes insoluble matter
- Secondary Treatment: removes biological impurities from primary-treated water
- Tertiary Treatment: removes remaining nutrient content and chemical contaminants after secondary treatment

Some parts of the country do not have tertiary treatment; toxins are therefore still being discharged into surface waters. On the west and east coasts, Victoria and Halifax have only recently begun to construct sewage treatment facilities. These cities relied upon the natural ebb and flow of the tides to carry pollutants into the ocean; it was felt that the vast size of the oceans would dilute the pollution. Complaints from American cities such as Seattle, situated on the opposite shoreline from Vancouver, and a reaction against the revolting conditions of the harbour have created the will to remedy the situation.

Sewage treatment removes contaminants from water and returns the water to its original source. However, many contaminants are difficult to remove even with the most advanced water treatment. Also, much contamination, particularly in large bodies of water, originates from non-point sources such as rainfall and runoff, which are not subject to treatment. *Non-point pollution* refers to pollution emanating not from a specific location, such as effluent from a factory, but from a more generalized source, such as salt on roads or fertilizer, pesticides, herbicides, and manure from farmers' fields or residences. This pollution is much more difficult to control than that from point sources because it comes from so many different sources and cannot easily be collected in one location for treatment.

Atmospheric circulation carries a large variety of substances great distances and then deposits them in rainfall or in runoff from the land. The paving of large areas and the channelling of runoff waters speed the return of water, much of which may be contaminated by its contact with industry, landfills, agriculture, streets, and parking lots. In most cities, it is too expensive to separate runoff completely from sewage. The result is that most runoff is not treated and returns to surface waters with its load of contaminants.

The state of Canada's environment suggests that the focus on water quality should shift from what comes out of people's taps toward what goes into the sources of raw water. Substances that are difficult to remove from the aquatic environment need to be controlled to protect both the ecosystem and human health. The difficulty of this task can be assessed by the history of attempts at pollution control and the slow progress of remediation programs.

In the 1980s, the Ontario government introduced a far-reaching plan to assess the sources of toxic wastes emanating from all sectors. The next step was to implement programs to detect which substances were reaching sewers illegally and to establish targets for the various polluters to develop technology and measures in order to prevent the flow of toxic effluents into the environment. The program achieved some success in that much more became known about the sources of toxic materials, and accidental spills and deliberate discharges were significantly reduced. However, some environmental groups, such as the Canadian Environmental Law Association, feel that the Harris government in Ontario has weakened environmental regulation through cuts in the budget of the Ministry of Energy and Environment; this is widely seen as one of the reasons for the Walkerton, Ontario, tragedy. There has been much reliance on voluntary cooperation from industry and mines, supplemented by a few high-profile prosecutions of the more obvious cases. There is a fear that the daily lapses in monitoring discharges from thousands of sources are not being watched by inspection and that the environment is receiving a steady flow of toxins of which we are little aware because the scientific studies are not being done.

The subject of water quality is closely connected to emissions into the air. Power plants, incinerators, and other industries discharge toxic substances, such as furans and dioxins, into the air, which are deposited by precipitation into the Great Lakes. In the lakes, these substances combine with other discharges to create toxic soup. Through bioaccumulation, this toxic soup ascends the food chain and ends up in the larger fish species, which have large quantities of metals and chemicals that make them unfit for human consumption. The signs of ill health in aquatic species are an early warning sign for humans. Although testing demonstrates that the toxins in the drinking water are low (in parts per million/billion), scientific knowledge of the long-term impact may only be known many years in the future.

Waste Management

Cities have always been responsible for disposing of the waste products of household consumption and industrial activities. This was not so difficult when consumption was on a modest scale and most consumer goods were of organic origin. Our modern economy, based on the continuing and massive consumption of new products and on the discarding of the old, produces huge quantities of solid waste. A good deal of the material, including paints, garden products, and cleaning materials, are not easily broken down by the natural processes by which organic materials are soon reduced to their basic elements.

Canadians are among the largest producers of solid waste in the world. Surveys done for Environment Canada in 1995 showed that approximately 18 million tonnes of solid waste were created in 1992, or 63.7 kg per person per year. About half of this came from residential sources. Building wastes bring the figure to almost 29.5 million tonnes (103.0 kg per person) (Environment Canada 1996). This large amount of waste represents the huge footprint cast by our cities on the biosphere. Waste products could constitute a source of raw materials and energy savings if a more complete process of reuse and recycling existed.

Since the 1980s, this country has attempted to strengthen its performance both in improving disposal methods and in attempting to recycle and reuse more of the products from the waste stream. Blue box programs now exist in most major Canadian cities whereby newspaper, cardboard, steel and aluminum cans, glass, some plastics, and spent oil are separated at the site of collection for recycling. One of the more serious difficulties in recycling some materials, such as glass and newsprint, is that markets for the product have sometimes not provided sufficient profits to cover the cost of separation and collection.

Composting garden waste, grass clippings, and leaves is also encouraged either by home composting or by community-based composting efforts. This has resulted in the diversion of significant amounts of waste from landfill sites. One of the major benefits of composting is that it can be used to restore degraded soils within our cities as a base for green areas, including former dump sites, old industrial sites that blighted inner city neighbourhoods, land along freeways that is being disturbed, and land being restored for organic gardening that would be capable of providing a good proportion of city food supplies. Unfortunately, many old sites have highly contaminated soils, which means that before compost can be added, the soils must be removed or subjected to an expensive cleaning process.

The main methods currently used for disposing of municipal solid waste are sanitary landfill sites and incineration. In Canada, landfill sites predominate, but in many parts of the country, such as the area around Toronto, acceptable space is rapidly being exhausted and other solutions, such as incineration or the shipping of garbage either to the United States or to northern Ontario, are being considered or employed. Among environmentalists, the disposal of garbage in landfill sites or through incineration is not a desirable option. The aim of policy, according to this viewpoint, is to maximize the reuse of scarce resources and limit the energy needed to bring these resources to the urban centres in question. By doing this, the footprint of the city on the ecosystem will be minimized to a more sustainable level. Halifax's new system is a good example of how much can be done (see Fowler and Hartmann's chapter).

Incineration has been touted as a method of recovering energy from waste, but in order to incinerate many materials without creating air pollution, it is necessary to burn waste at extremely high temperatures, which requires a great deal of energy. Incineration is expensive because it requires complex technologies to remove pollutants such as sulphur dioxide, nitrous oxide, heavy metals, and particulate matter. This equipment still leaves the problem of carbon dioxide and possibly of highly toxic furans and dioxins. Without scrupulous maintenance, incinerators can be a source of hazardous air pollution to the surrounding communities and even to locations thousands of miles away. Incinerators in the United States have created surplus landfill capacity, inviting the export of Canadian solid waste in competition with our own landfill sites, which therefore do not always operate at optimum capacity.

Environment Canada views the solid waste problem as a difficult and expensive one from both an ecosystem and an economic perspective:

> From an ecosystem perspective waste material constitutes a waste of energy and resources in itself. Much of the material that enters a landfill or incinerator represents a resource that has not been fully used and might have been reduced at source, reused, or recycled, thus lessening the need to extract and process new resources.

> From an economic standpoint, dealing with solid waste is expensive: annual disposal costs, including collection, transportation, and landfill or incineration, are estimated at more than $3 billion, borne almost entirely by municipalities. This sum does not include environmental or social costs or the costs represented by lost resources. (Environment Canada 1996)

Another serious problem, already referred to and common to all parts of the country, is the contamination of large and strategic land areas that were the subject of careless dumping in the past. These consist of former dumpsites and old industrial and mining locations. This land often occupies important locations that could be redeveloped for urban uses such as new industry, residential development, or recreational sites. One example is the tar pits in Sydney, Cape Breton, the result of large pools of waste from the manufacture of coke. The cost of cleanup and of compensation for adjacent properties often runs into millions of dollars. At the present time, there is no inventory of such sites in Canada, nor is there a mechanism like the Superfund in the United States to deal with them.

The revival or creation of inner-city forests would do much to improve microclimates, to clean urban air, and to offer places of relief and relaxation in urban areas, which have been dominated by concrete and asphalt. The urban garden movement has caught on to some degree in this country, but not as much as in some European countries or even in countries of the developing world. With many people reluctant to purchase supermarket fruits and vegetables grown with herbicides and pesticides, there is a movement among some Canadians to grow their own food organically, without using synthetic fertilizers, herbicides, or pesticides. In many Canadian municipalities, it is now possible to obtain compost in quantity from the municipality at no or at token cost.

The federal government and industry have cooperated to reduce packaging, which constitutes a large proportion of paper and plastic waste. Industry is also recycling packaging for further use instead of sending it to the landfill. The ultimate solution to waste generation is to develop industries that are based upon extracting raw materials and energy from solid waste. An example of this is the city of Kalundborg in Denmark, where an industrial complex based upon using both energy and materials from solid waste sources has repaid its original investment many times (Worldwatch Institute 1999).

Land Use Planning

Land use planning is one of the most important functions undertaken by municipalities (see Leo's chapter). Planning policies have been developed to achieve many objectives, including enhancement of the city environment; however, they have fallen short of creating cities that use an ecosystem approach that respects the natural environment and is based upon conservation of energy and resources, one that at the same time produces economic well-being, social security, and quality of life for all its residents.

The challenge of creating sustainable cities using planning guidelines can be difficult because it must take into account rapidly changing demographic trends (see Foot's chapter), the nature of the workforce, new technologies of communication and transportation, and both political pressures from within the city and external influences extending now to the whole globe. Although Canadian cities have long been regarded as more compact and more tightly integrated politically than American cities, it has become apparent in the last twenty years that Canadian cities have begun to sprawl, often leaving behind a decaying and less viable core area (see chapters by Leo and Sancton; Goldberg and Mercer 1985).

Sprawling cities impose a heavy cost in terms of land, infrastructure, and traffic congestion (see Fowler and Layton's chapter). Such suburbs require the use of a car for every activity from commuting to work, recreation, shopping, and social interaction. Some cities have begun to create multiple centres where work, recreation, and shopping are more integrated with residential development; however, Canadians prefer detached single-family dwellings standing on their own separate lots. The physical diversity that Jane Jacobs (1961) has promoted is not present in many urban areas. As well, these building styles often ignore energy conservation, preservation of natural features, and the facilitation of public transit.

Table 8.1 sets out some guidelines for sustainable urban development prepared by the Organization for Sustainable Development. Canadians have finally discovered that their pattern of scattered development is imposing high costs at the same time that transfer payments from other levels of government have dwindled under the pressure for fiscal responsibility. The costs include the loss of prime farmland and high infrastructure costs for roads, sewers, and drainage. In addition, there are higher expenses for such human services as policing, fire protection, education (school busing), and recreational facilities (Fowler 1992). In Europe, a great effort is being made to recover and review *brown land*—land that is being underutilized in the inner city—rather than building on greenfields on the outskirts of cities. Municipalities in Canada find themselves under a heavy burden of rising costs, but the more efficient use of existing facilities and a pattern of more dense and diverse urban development could do much to bring down urban costs and at the same time lay the foundations for sustainable cities.

Conclusion: Can We Create Sustainable Cities?

Cities can create a sustainable environment, although all the tools necessary to accomplish this are not fully under their control. After the Brundtland Report and the Rio Conference, Canada produced many documents and reports promising a new era of sustainable development to meet targets that had been established by the international gatherings. However, the same politicians who made such enlightened promises were also the people who cut environmental budgets and placed environmental concerns at the bottom of the priority list.

The political climate of the country changed radically in the mid-1990s. Paul Martin, as Minister of Finance in the Chrétien Liberal government, was determined to eliminate the deficit at the national level, and most provincial governments had a similar objective. Ontario and Alberta elected neo-conservative governments that embarked on programs of severe cuts in most sectors and also promised to lighten government regulation to produce a climate friendlier to business. Much of the environmental work was thrown back on the municipal sector, but with considerably fewer provincial subsidies than had existed in the previous decades.

It is too early to say that we have developed a consensus on global actions toward the environment. All we can do is take note of certain events, actions, and changing attitudes. We can tell that heightened public interest in the environment in the past has influenced political leaders to take a new interest in the subject.

Table 8.1: Themes for Sustainable Development: Building and Planning

- Promote the use of building materials that maximize standards of safety, durability, and environmental performance.
- Encourage a full consideration of the needs of the proposed uses of new buildings early in the design process.
- Encourage stimulating architecture that makes a positive contribution to the townscape.
- Protect important aspects of the local heritage, including landmark buildings, so as to maintain local identity.
- Use the planning system to integrate different land sites in order to minimize the need to travel and ensure good access to public transport.
- Protect green spaces from development.
- Promote design that minimizes the risk of crime.
- Provide opportunities for people to participate throughout the planning/design process.

Source: Organization for Sustainable Development, http://www.sustainability.holdorg. uk/info/policyguidelines/buildings, accessed 12 February 1998.

Between 1999 and the midpoint of 2000, a remarkable series of international conferences took place that were largely devoted to fostering economic cooperation, with an agenda ostensibly controlled by the economic elites. There was a World Bank meeting in Washington, a World Trade Organization conference in Seattle, an Organization of American States conference in Windsor, Ontario, and finally, in June 2000, a conference of the World Petroleum Producers in Calgary. While it has been the practice of non-governmental organizations to hold counter-conferences with the idea of influencing the main conference proposals, in the case of the four listed meetings, direct action in the streets occurred to demonstrate dissatisfaction with the perceived policy directions. The demonstrators made it clear that they feel past policies have ignored the environment, social inequality, the plight of the poor in all societies, and the rights of workers and women.

To bring the focus back to Canada, we may ask: How have we been influenced in resurrecting the environment as an issue and, particularly, its applicability to sustainable cities? In the three conferences where government leaders from Canada were present, it was strongly affirmed by Canadian representatives that future policies should take into consideration the demands of the protestors.

It is fortuitous that at the same time as the above general debates are occurring, there have been a number of environmental crises developing that have placed governments on the defensive. These include events as varied as the contaminated water at Walkerton, continued smog alerts in large cities, a series of deadly traffic accidents on Highway 401 in Ontario, and a rapid rise in gasoline and natural gas prices heralding potential shortages of petroleum products.

Putting all these circumstances together reminds one of the situation of the early 1970s, when environmentalism became a central focus of public debate. One element that seems lacking in our political system, compared to others, is a political party that can lend saliency to the debate at the level of both the federal and provincial governments, such as an effective and popular Green Party. At present the main opposition is the Canadian Alliance (Reform) Party, which is even more free-market in its orientation than the incumbent Liberals. Until our electoral system is reformed toward proportional representation, there is little chance that the Green Party can elect members except, possibly, at the provincial level in British Columbia.

One representative report is the Environmental Scan prepared for the Canadian Council of Ministers of the Environment, which lays out a comprehensive plan to reach sustainability. It presents a three-pronged approach that emphasizes that economic growth must be achieved, but only because such growth is an essential accompaniment to the achievement of the other two goals: the achievement of an ecological balance with the natural world and remediation of the social deficits. Within the orbit of the national program, which has been forgotten by most political leaders, there are also several green plans drawn up by cities and regions (see Fowler and Hartmann's chapter). These await only the necessary funding and political will. The one imponderable is the ticking time bomb of an environmental disaster, whether it be climate change, the health effects of pollution, or the destruction of more species. It is difficult to predict how much shock treatment is necessary to shake the political elites from their complacency and lethargy.

References

Environment Canada. 1996. *State of Canada's Environment*. Ottawa: Supply and Services Canada.

Fitz-Gerard, Sean. 2000. 'Thaw Creates Longing for "Jamaica of the North"'. *National Post* (24 February).

Fowler, Edmund P. 1992. *Building Cities That Work*. Montreal: McGill-Queen's University Press.

Goldberg, Michael A., and John Mercer. 1985. *The Myth of the North American City: Continentalism Challenged*. Vancouver: University of British Columbia Press.

Jacobs, Jane. 1961. *The Death and Life of Great American Cities*. New York: Random House.

MacKinnon, Mark. 2000. 'Halve Greenhouse Gases Soon, Easily, Suzuki Says'. *The Globe and Mail* (18 April).

Statistics Canada. 1994. *Human Activity and the Environment*. Ottawa.

Worldwatch Institute. 1999. *State of the World: A Worldwatch Institute Report on Progress toward a Sustainable Society*. New York: Norton.

CHAPTER 9

City Environmental Policy: Connecting the Dots

Edmund P. Fowler and Franz Hartmann[1]

Introduction

In the previous chapter, national and international issues in environmental policy, especially as they relate to cities, were outlined by Trevor Price. Our purpose is to link these issues to the ground level, to particular cities and places. Abstract principles notwithstanding, whether or not we fit gracefully into the biosphere is still expressed—and often determined—locally, even personally. Every day—in fact, every minute—social workers, teachers, garbage workers, the police, and many other municipal employees are making decisions that affect the biosphere, both positively and negatively. We first give the reader an idea of how one municipal authority is defining and implementing environmental policy. Then we examine the process of governance itself as an appropriate agent for real change, especially when urban sprawl is constantly pre-empting any kind of long-term political culture as a basis for intelligent policy decisions. Finally, we give some specific examples of small-scale initiatives that illustrate how much can be done by small groups working together, both within and outside of government. Throughout, the interconnections between other policies analyzed in this book and environmental policy will be stressed.

By way of introduction, it is worth stressing Price's point that the 'environmental crisis' has not gone away. Twice in recent history—the early 1970s and the late 1980s—concern about humans' pollution of the biosphere became serious and widespread only to be engulfed as a public issue by depressions and wars, as Price pointedly remarks. Our assaults on our natural environment (and on each other) have continued to intensify, despite occasional successes such as the phase-out of leaded gas and a rapid drop in the production of CFCs. Global warming and catastrophic weather have grown worse; the ozone layers at both poles are still deteriorating; more and more people are dying from the effects of air pollution; the quality and quantity of water, both in lakes and aquifers, continue to decline; and the loss of fertile soil to chemicals and to erosion has, if anything, accelerated—much of the topsoil in North America's Midwest is now gone (Jackson 1980).

Confronted with such facts, our eyes tend to glaze over. What can one person do, anyway? Our argument is that there is much one person can do, because environmental issues are woven into every policy issue in this book, as well as into our daily lives. In a real sense, then, it does not matter where we start. Unfortunately, we usually analyze problems by separating them into parts. The chapters of this book are a good example. There are separate treatments of urban infrastructure, tax policy, parks and recreation, housing, and so forth. Each of these policy areas has its own bureaucratic structures, budgets, and academic experts. Yet each of these policies is related to the other and, especially, to environmental policy.

Consider housing as an example. We have been building it in a particular way. Most new housing these days (and since World War II) comes as spread-out suburbs that require the use of cars as well as trucks to deliver people, goods, and services over longer distances than in more compact downtowns. Over 50 per cent of our cities' air pollution (plus much of the water and soil pollution) can be traced to cars and trucks, so urban sprawl is clearly a major cause of damage to the environment— and therefore to us. Public health officials tell us that thousands more people are being admitted to hospital and even dying because of this air pollution (see the chapters by Hancock, Price, and Fowler and Layton).

As Price has already remarked, these sprawling suburbs aggravate cities' financial problems as well, since the lower densities make dwellings more expensive to service with electricity, sidewalks, education, police and fire protection, sewers, transit, and roads.

In addition, there are interesting social consequences of suburban development. The need for a car and greater housing expenses mean that such housing is out of the financial reach of many people, exacerbating Canada's social inequities. Moreover, large tracts of homogeneous land use, such as suburban housing developments and large shopping malls, have been found to suffer from greater crime rates relative to the total number of users (residents, shoppers, workers) of an area (Fowler 1987).

This suburban development has an important cultural impact on us. Very few older buildings or unmanipulated natural landscapes remain, so that it is no longer possible for us to experience the amazing variety of ways humans can relate to their environment (both natural and built). In fact, much new development is homogeneous and ignores the uniqueness of individual places, making it increasingly difficult to be aware of one's physical environment. Urban infrastructure—highways, bridges, new buildings, public transportation facilities—is already overwhelmingly in place, supporting all this kind of development. We are so used to it, and it so influences how we look at the world, that this infrastructure has become a cultural fact.

Thus, the way we build our housing connects to most of the other policy issues covered in this book. This fact has important implications for environmental policy analysis. What follows is an examination of Toronto's environmental plan, which makes a point of stressing the relevance of many other policies to environmental policy and which tries to specify what can be done by a government to achieve more sustainable patterns of living in its jurisdiction.

The Toronto Environmental Plan

On 12 April 2000, Toronto City Council adopted an environmental plan. Entitled 'Clean, Green and Healthy: A Plan for an Environmentally Sustainable Toronto', the plan was a culmination of two years of work and contained sixty-six policy recommendations that were designed to benefit simultaneously the environmental, economic, and social health of the new mega-city.

Before outlining some of the key themes and recommendations of Toronto's environmental plan, and in order to understand better the genesis of the plan's recommendations, let us first examine the political context within which the plan was developed.

On 1 January 1998, the former Metropolitan Toronto and the seven municipalities were forceably amalgamated by the provincial government into the new City of Toronto, often called the mega-city. The aftermath of the first mega-city election, which saw a reduction of elected officials from 106 to 57, not only shifted the political balance to the right, it also shifted political power from the downtown core to the generally more conservative suburbs. The new mayor, former North York mayor Mel Lastman, came to power on a Tory-style agenda featuring a tax freeze. And he could count on a majority of councillors—mostly from the suburbs—to support his neo-liberal agenda.

Economically, Toronto was on the road to 'recovery' after the deep recession of the early 1990s: unemployment levels were falling and a local GDP that was increasingly reliant on global markets was rising (Gertler 2000). However, the growing prosperity was unequally shared, for levels of homelessness were rising dramatically (Toronto 2000) and disparities of income were level or increasing (Bourne 2000; see also Haddow's chapter). In short, after years of wanting to be a world-class or global city, Toronto had joined the ranks of cities like New York and Los Angeles by becoming a place attracting significant amounts of international capital that spawned a combination of extreme wealth alongside growing levels of poverty.

The new governance structure of the mega-city, the economic recovery that concentrated wealth and entrenched the growing underclass, and a new council dominated by fiscal conservatives completed the neo-liberal sweep of the political system, which had already transformed both the federal and provincial levels.

Within this political economic context, the Toronto environmental movement and other allies struggled to keep environmental issues from falling off the public policy radar screen. After a decade of growing success,[2] environmental advocates found themselves in a new political terrain that left little room for any environmental initiatives that could not be presented as 'good for business'.

Fortunately, the agenda of the new mayor and other power brokers on city council focused on a tax freeze that did not include a wholesale dismantling of the many positive environmental gains that had been made at the Metro or municipal levels.

One of the main reasons for this is that the Transition Team, set up by the Provincial Tory Government to create a temporary governance structure for the new mega-city, acknowledged the many and difficult environmental issues facing the new city. Indeed, the Transition Team's key environmental recommendation was to set up an Environmental Task Force that would report to the new city council on how best to deal with the pressing environmental issues facing the new city.

Even though there was a recognition that environmental issues were important enough to warrant a special task force, this did not translate into an automatic acceptance by the new council of a green agenda. The neo-liberal dominance meant that any environmental initiative that hoped to move forward had to be packaged in a way that, at minimum, did not appear to contradict the fundamental tenet of neo-liberalism: the market is supreme and governments are there to facilitate private-sector capital accumulation, not to impede it through regulation. In other words, whereas in the past, environmentalists could develop political support for initiatives simply by making a case for environmental protection, the new reality required making a 'business' case if the initiative was to go beyond being an interesting idea.

In March 1998, the Environmental Task Force (ETF) was established by city council. Membership included city councillors, senior city staff, representatives from other levels or branches of government, union representatives, environmentalists, businesspeople, and influential citizen members. Jack Layton, long-time Toronto city councillor and environmental advocate, was appointed as Task Force chair, and four city staff were assigned to help fulfill the ETF's mandate.

From its beginnings, the ETF's deliberations reflected two important tensions: the more traditional environmentalists wanted the Task Force to act as a vehicle for entrenching the best environmental protection initiatives from the former municipalities throughout the new mega-city; however, other members saw environmental protection as intimately tied to economic prosperity and social health. Some members believed that if the Task Force promoted this 'sustainability' approach, it would help overcome the suspicion—or at best apathy—non-environmentalists had toward environmental protection by advocating policies that integrated environmental, social equity, and economic concerns.[3]

Over the next two years, this tension permeated all the work of the Task Force. In the early summer of 1998, the Task Force instigated a process of developing 'Quick Start' environmental initiatives, which had the intent of generalizing particular environmental practices from one or more old municipalities across the new mega-city and of introducing new, non-contentious environmental protection policies. Various multi-stakeholder working groups were established to develop a short list of Quick Starts to improve the quality of the city's air, land, water, and green space. By mid-fall, more than fifty Quick Starts had been identified and city staff had begun the process of implementing them.

While traditional environmental protection was being promoted through the Quick Starts, economic and social sustainability became a key concept driving the Task Force as it developed options for a new governance structure to deal with environmental issues. An increasing number of Task Force members accepted that the only way to ensure that environmental issues were taken into account effectively within the new city was to infuse an environmental ethic throughout all decision-making processes. The only way to ensure this, in turn, was through a sustainability approach that necessitated considering—simultaneously—environmental, economic, and social equity issues in all decisions.

As mentioned above, the sustainability approach is potentially compatible with the neo-liberal ideology, because both sets of ideas accept the fact that environmental initiatives can be economically practical. For some, however, this compatibility is not acceptable. In fact, many activists (sometimes called 'red-green') have also called for the integration of environmental and economic issues, but they have done this by arguing that sustainability can only be achieved through the transformation of existing economic relations (Hartmann 1999). In sum, the sustainability approach paradoxically seems to allow both reinforcement and transformation of our economic system. An example is given later in this chapter of how this paradox can be explained.

After months of consultation with city staff, with councillors, and with the public, the Task Force recommended a governance structure that supported the sustainability approach. The key institutional recommendation was for the establishment of a 'Sustainability Roundtable', to be made up of city councillors, senior staff, citizen members, and an equal number of representatives from the environmental, business, and social equity sectors. The primary mandate of the new Roundtable would be to recommend to city council actions that will promote sustainability throughout the city government. City council adopted the Task Force's new governance structure in December 1999, and the Roundtable met for the first time in the summer of 2000.[4] The idea of the new governance structure is to subject every possible decision, taken by every City agency and committee, to sustainability criteria.

Not surprisingly, sustainability also became an important principle in shaping the entire Environmental Plan, not just the portion about governance. In some ways, the city's first-ever Environmental Plan is as much a sustainability plan as an environmental plan. The first part of the plan contains more conventional recommendations aimed at improving the health of the city's air, land, and water (see Price's chapter). The latter part of the plan contains a number of recommendations that promote sustainability in the transportation, energy use, and economic development sectors and thus operationalizes some of the more general points made by Price in the previous chapter.

How a city organizes the transportation of goods and people has a huge impact on the natural environment: a car-dependent urban form leads to much higher levels of resource use, air pollution, and contaminated lands than does a transit-dependent urban form. And as an increasing number of North American cities facing traffic congestion are realizing, the transportation infrastructure plays an important role in determining the economic health of the city.

The Environmental Plan's recommendations dealing with transportation effectively argue that the City of Toronto can reap huge environmental and economic benefits by simultaneously developing a transportation system premised on minimizing the movement of goods and people; relying more on public transit, walking, and cycling; and relying less on cars. Air and water quality will improve, and Toronto will become a better place to do business thanks to less congestion and increased mobility (see Fowler and Layton's chapter).

This sustainability approach also underlies the recommendations dealing with the City's energy use policies. As the plan states, 'energy use is a vital part of our urban lives. . . . We use energy to heat and light our homes and offices, operate our factories, power our vehicles, and run our appliances' (Toronto, ETF 2000: 57). Every part of the current energy-use cycle has an adverse effect on the environment. For example, the mining of fossil fuels such as coal devastates local ecosystems. The burning of coal to make electricity causes smog and acid rain and contributes to global climate change (see Price's chapter). Therefore, the Environmental Plan recommends that the City 'adopt, as a long range goal, the development of a Sustainable Energy Infrastructure for Toronto that supports the efficient production, transmission and use of energy from renewable resources' (Toronto, ETF 2000: 58).

Key ingredients of this sustainable energy infrastructure are energy-efficient buildings; district heating and cooling systems that use energy efficiently; renewable or green power production, such as windpower and photovoltaics; and co-generation facilities, which serve users with different energy needs (say, higher or lower temperatures) from the same energy source.

The environmental benefits of a sustainable energy approach will lead to improved local air quality, less acid rain, and a reduction in Toronto's greenhouse gas production. The economic benefits of a sustainable energy approach are numerous. For example, reducing energy use through energy retrofit projects in municipal buildings saves the City money in reduced energy bills. It also means that municipal tax dollars will be directed to creating local construction retrofit jobs as opposed to purchasing fossil fuels from outside the region. In addition, spending municipal tax dollars on green power could bring about a transformation in the energy market away from fossil fuels. Having the biggest energy consumer in the Greater Toronto Area, the City of Toronto, demand clean and green power would be an important factor in spurring the development of new green power sources, such as co-generation, wind power, and photovoltaics. This, in turn, would help lower the cost of renewable or green power, making it financially more viable for other consumers to switch away from fossil fuels and to get energy from various independent suppliers. In this way, the high concentration of energy capital in a few hands would be attenuated. This fact illustrates the paradox referred to above: sustainable practices can transform economic relations without necessarily getting rid of the market system (Korten 1999).

This potential of the Environmental Plan to transform the market is found in many of its recommendations. Through its capacities both to develop policy and to purchase goods and services, the City of Toronto fundamentally affects the local economy and how the economy harms or helps the natural environment. This relationship is most explicitly addressed in the recommendations dealing with economic development. The Environmental Plan recommends that the City use both its policy-making and its spending powers to promote environmentally sustainable urban development, energy efficiency in the industrial sector, the development of green industry, local food production, and recycling of construction and renovation waste. Most of these recommendations focus on actions the City can take to assist local economic actors making money from business practices that are less environmentally destructive.

For example, the plan calls on the City to promote urban development premised on 'reurbanisation of the City to increase the population and employment opportunities and set aggressive targets in the Official Plan; pursue a strategy of "strategic reinvestment" that encourages compact urban growth and directs growth to those areas of the City where infrastructure capacity already exists' (Toronto, ETF 2000: 66). Thus, by using the Official Plan to guide private-sector development, the City might help create an urban form and urban economy that, over time, becomes less destructive to the natural environment (see the section in Price's chapter on land use planning).

In summary, the City of Toronto's Environmental Plan not only assumes that all our day-to-day actions have an impact on the natural environment, it also sets out a number of actions that chart a course toward an urban form and economy premised on sustaining economic, environmental, and social health simultaneously.

In the midst of a city council dominated by people caught up in a neo-liberal agenda of tax cuts and economic growth at any cost, in the midst of increasing disparity of wealth among Torontonians, and in the midst of a worsening of environmental conditions in Toronto, the Environmental Plan suggests an alternative: a particular type of economic growth that is both financially frugal and also sensitive to environmental and social concerns. By adopting the Environmental Plan, city council has accepted, at least in principle, the existence of another path that, if followed, will lead to a much healthier, happier, environmentally benign, and vibrant economic future for Torontonians. The Toronto plan also shows how many tools local governments have at their disposal to make a difference in environmental policy (Paehlke 1994).

Why Governments Don't Have Sensible Environmental Policies

The Toronto Environmental Plan does us a great service in showing just how pervasive environmental issues are, as well as in suggesting tangible steps governments can take to make urban development ecologically more sensible.

It is important to remember, however, that in the past—and today—government policies are still financing ecologically damaging development, whether it involves subsidizing oil and gas exploration, building more roads, or allowing unsustainable suburban subdivisions to spread farther and farther from the city core. Governments, in other words, are part of the problem, as Price makes clear in his chapter.

There are many reasons for our governments' failure to deal firmly with the ecological crisis, a failure that goes deeper than how good or bad their 'policies' are and that is not even related to the mix in government of those who are genuinely concerned about the environment, those who are opportunistic in handling the issue, and those who simply see sustainability as an extremely low priority.

One reason has to do with scale. Ecological damage always occurs in specific places. As mentioned in the introductory chapter, large governments (many of which are 'local') by definition have difficulty dealing with such places. Provincial and federal governments are responsible for policies that have contributed mightily to the uncontrolled spread of suburbs (Fowler 1992); we are not as sanguine as Price about the potential of higher-level agencies for grappling effectively with the ecological crisis. Most governments are simply too big to be intimately acquainted with environmental degradation—and indeed with other problems—in each neighbourhood, or even in each industrial subdivision or retail district. Some government employees, such as inspectors, teachers, police, and social workers—sometimes called 'street-level bureaucrats' (Lipsky 1976)—can become quite knowledgeable about specific localities; but street-level bureaucrats don't really talk to each other, and their specific knowledge is difficult to translate into effective policy for the entire government. General principles can inform a policy, of course, as we shall see below, but policies are useless without supportive local action. Smaller governments could help us deal more effectively with our environmental crisis.

However, smaller governments are doing much damage as well. Throughout this book, for instance, evidence is presented that sprawl, with its attendant dependence on the car, can be blamed for bad air, dirty water, and disappearing farmlands—a serious threat to our species' health. It is probably the number one environmental problem, if such a phrase is meaningful. Yet municipalities of all sizes on the fringes of Canada's larger cities are perpetuating urban sprawl. Leo's chapter in this volume gives some specific examples of this process.

Herein lies a second reason why governments are part of the environmental problem. The process of urban sprawl is responsible for the absence of defined political communities with a history of public concern and intelligent discourse about sensible development policies. Subdivisions are being authorized so fast and municipal boundaries are so permeable that no local or regional authority on the fringes of cities has the political self-consciousness to take responsibility for truly sustainable growth. And provinces not only lack the political will to impose policies to stop sprawl, they also subsidize it in numerous ways (Fowler 1992; GTA Task Force 1996). A number of Chambers of Commerce and other business groups across the United States and Canada are realizing that sprawl is actually bad for business (Leo 1998). Aside from its enormous economic costs, often borne by the taxpayer (Blais 1995), it also seems to make city regions less competitive.

One rare attempt to curb sprawl through consistent policy is the Regional Growth Management (RGM) Plan of Portland, Oregon. This plan seems to have been responsible for increasing the density of Portland proper, which is a plus; however, sprawl has certainly continued in the Portland region (Jackson 2000; Leo 1998). Many other proposals have been put forward elsewhere advocating regional tax incentives and disincentives, as well as zoning restrictions that prohibit further spread of subdivisions or require certain minimum densities (GTA Task Force 1996). Zoning, though, is place-specific; it must be implemented by people who know the locality. Thus, the principle of higher-density development could be adopted as a general policy, but its application depends on a fortuitous confluence of political forces that have long-standing identity with an allegiance to a particular region—as was the case in Portland.

In the Greater Vancouver Regional District (GVRD), a concerted, participatory effort by member municipalities produced the Liveable Region Strategic Plan in 1995, which represented (amazingly) something of a consensus among Vancouver's suburbs on a process to concentrate development in certain centres and to keep other lands forever free from development (Raad and Kenworthy 1998; Smith 1998; Fowler and Layton's chapter in this volume).

As promising as this sounds, one of the largest suburbs, Surrey, withdrew its commitment to the plan in August 1997 (Simpson 1997). Raad and Kenworthy argue that the original consensus was superficial 'because the regional authorities lack any effective legal mechanisms to ensure plan implementation' (1998: 20). In fact, the viability of the whole project was undermined by provincial unwillingness to fund the public transit needed to support the land use policies. The political process at both local and provincial levels, then, works against the carrying out of perfectly sensible, rational general principles (see the introduction to this book). The proof of the pudding is that decades of pronouncements and even policies against urban sprawl have produced few tangible results.

An excellent example of how sprawl's political fragmentation sabotages rational environmental planning is the present controversy over suburban development of the Oak Ridges Moraine, a 160-kilometre-long pile of gravelly hills north of Toronto marked by lakes and woodlands and the source of sixty-five rivers and streams flowing into Lake Ontario. Those who wish to protect the moraine stress that it crosses the boundaries of five regional governments as well as twenty-six local municipalities, all with land use planning functions. A commission to control development across the entire area is now being proposed—evidence that small-scale local structures may not be able by themselves to protect the integrity of this natural feature (Moloney 2000). The women and men who staff these local structures, nevertheless, know what is going on at the ground level, which is a necessary condition for the formulation of sensible regional environmental policy. However, it is not a sufficient condition, because many small governments – especially suburban governments—suffer from tunnel vision or feel that they benefit from new subdivision development, as suggested earlier.

The third reason that governments have difficulty coping with human destructiveness to the rest of Nature relates to what has been elsewhere called the 'policy mindset' (Fowler 1996). Leaving aside the fact that policies are often meant to be purely symbolic and thus ineffectual, policies that mediate our (inescapable) connection to the rest of the biosphere are plagued by our habit of taking a solution set that works in one place at one time and applying it everywhere (Jones and Bachelor 1993). Sometimes this works, but sometimes it doesn't.

To illustrate this point, consider what is called the 'new urbanism' (see Leo's chapter in this book). This is a movement made up of architects and builders who acknowledge the social and environmental stupidity of large, homogeneous residential subdivisions, which require suburbanites to travel many miles by car to get to work or to shop at huge shopping malls. Taking their cue from older, more compact central-city neighbourhoods or small towns with mixed land use (so that work and shopping are often within walking or cycling distance), the new urbanists are building new suburban developments that have higher densities, houses that are designed for people who work at home, and a mixture of dwellings and commercial uses, and they are putting in place restrictions on car use, including narrower streets and pedestrian zones. The problem is that these new enclaves are still suburbs whose survival is tied to post-war sprawl's infrastructure of arterial roads and expressways and to its distribution system of consumer goods and municipal services. The new urbanist developments, in other words, are plopped down onto some pasture, far from the downtown context that produced the real thing. The complex web of social and economic relationships that makes a dense, physically diverse city neighbourhood work, that connects it to other such neighbourhoods, and that renders these neighbourhoods ecologically sensible is absent. So the new urbanism is a generalized policy solution—one size fits all—applied to particular places.

In fact, *environmental policy* is itself a problematic term. We carry around in our heads a model that sees the environment as something surrounding us yet separate from us, in a way that allows us to damage it, restore it, care for it. In this model, *environmental policy* makes a certain amount of sense. We forget, however, that our relation to that environment is considerably more intimate: like all species, we can and do modify it, but we also eat it, drink it, breathe it, and absorb it through our skin and through our senses. And the environment eats us as well. We are of this planet.

This symbiosis extends to our built environment. It is instructive to ponder the many different ways in which our behaviour and movements are determined by the places we ourselves have constructed. At an obvious level, office space is not used for taking a shower (with the exception of some cyclist-friendly offices) or having Christmas dinner (usually!). Less obviously, there are parts of the city and suburbs that we feel uncomfortable in, without necessarily knowing why. Subconsciously, we tend not to notice, for example, that we have built cities where it is unlikely for workers to go home for lunch, which is commonplace in Europe (Nelson 1980). Because it, too, is like the air we breathe, the built environment has many effects that go unnoticed (Fowler 1992).

Thus, even though, to many of us, it is clear that humans have been behaving badly and trashing the environment (and therefore ourselves), our preferences, biases, values, and personalities have already been at least partially shaped by those surroundings, whether human-made or 'natural'. Any policy we formulate will be similarly shaped. This fact should partially explain the behaviour of individual suburban governments that continue to build sprawl. It should also persuade us to be modest about what we plan for, because we do not exercise independent judgement.

Nevertheless, we must act. The above considerations suggest that environmental policy-making should be an interactive process in every sense of the term—with give and take among *all* those involved and with constant awareness of different kinds of feedback from the biosphere. Nothing should be taken for granted, especially the outcome. In other words, environmental policy-making should involve a process different from our usual procedures, which tend to treat goals and objectives and outcomes as a given and to see the real problem as how to get there. Not surprisingly, many environmental plans are now talking about 'moving targets': modifying expectations and rules while the policy is being implemented.

Once we acknowledge the intimacy of our link with the biosphere (the rest of which does not seem to have to make environmental policy), then our own policy-making can become more creative by clarifying our general intentions and then by experimenting on a small scale with what seem to be good ideas. Those who are impatient with this incremental approach should be reminded that evolution, while incremental, is also profoundly radical, whereas revolutions tend to replace one kind of tyrant with another. In this vein, rather than trying to buck the authority of immense public works departments staffed with traditionally trained engineers, urban planners and politicians often design smaller projects that show just what can be done. Many books on greening the city have appeared, and it is remarkable how many of them are full of examples of this seemingly piecemeal approach; but as we shall see, it is anything but piecemeal. (For further reading, a short bibliography is provided at the end of the chapter.)

Piecemeal but Holistic

One of the simplest and clearest places to start is with flat-roof planting, one of the TEP's Quick Starts. If you were to fly over most Canadian downtowns, you would see many thousands of square metres of asphalt and rubber flat roofing. By contrast, in Switzerland and in some cities in Germany, all new flat roofs are required to be constructed so as to sustain soil and greenery. In some cases, only perfunctory landscaping is added, but on many other buildings, urban agriculture has taken root, so to speak. Not only is food produced, but the buildings are warmer in winter and cooler in summer; and the presence of more foliage adds importantly to the quality of life outside the buildings—less noise and cleaner air, for instance (Roseland 1998).

Flat roofs with planters are a perfect example of how practical environmental policy in cities can be, because such roofs have so many kinds of benefits, from the ambience of the neighbourhood to savings on energy costs and the growth of our own food.

Food production is so alien to our image of cities that one might be forgiven for being startled at the suggestion that for most of urban history, city dwellers have grown their own food. Jacobs (1969) argues that, contrary to the usual hypothesis, humans domesticated plants and animals first in towns (which grew up around trading activities), not in the countryside, on the basis of archaeological evidence from a Turkish settlement of several thousand inhabitants that existed over 9,000 years ago. According to Stokes, 'in ancient times, urban Greeks planted quick-growing seeds of lettuce, wheat, and barley in earthenware containers. The Romans often had windowsill and balcony gardens' (1981: 77). Mumford (1938) reports that towns and cities in medieval Europe were filled with gardens and that livestock—especially pigs—roamed the streets around their owners' houses. Even more to the point, contemporary Hong Kong grows 45 per cent of its own vegetables. Almost a third of

Nairobi's inhabitants grow their own food, producing on average about 30 kilograms of vegetables and legumes each year (Freeman 1991). And many thousands of Western Europeans and North Americans grow food in big cities, in backyards, front yards, window boxes, and community gardens (Stokes 1981).

From the point of view of urban environmental policy, it is important to note that most—though not all—of this prodigious amount of food is consumed by the growers. In other words, urban agriculture is not included in conventional measures of economic activity. Indeed, a number of dedicated people have found that farming in cities is only marginally viable as a commercial enterprise (Baker 2000). However, this fact only underscores its significance for sustainable cities. Here is why: Industrial agriculture, by replacing labour with petrochemicals and by externalizing the excessive ecological costs of its operations, can market produce, meat, and fish at unrealistically low prices (Hawken, Lovins, and Lovins 1999). The direct environmental benefits of urban food production lie, in part, in the elimination of those costs, which are almost invisible to the average city dweller but which cause great damage to the biosphere in general and to human health in particular: thousands of tons of pesticides and herbicides that permeate our water and soil; extensive pollution from thousands of diesel engines transporting our food from California, Mexico, and Florida; and the loss of millions of tons of topsoil due to unsustainable industrial farming methods.

Indirect environmental benefits involve the consciousness arising from direct and visceral contact with the soil and from participation in the mystery of vegetative growth, which includes a deeper understanding of the cycles and rhythms of one's own bioregion. Also, there are dozens of community gardens and public gardening plots in every Canadian city, all of which knit together the social fabric of neighbourhoods in powerful ways that are out of reach of conventional social policy (Stokes 1981). If Hong Kong can do it, Canadian cities surely can. And climate is not a barrier: John and Nancy Todd have grown abundant vegetables and raised fish year-round in greenhouses with almost no auxiliary heat in Prince Edward Island, where winter temperatures frequently drop below –20°C (Todd and Todd 1994).

Canadian cities are in desperate need of managing their garbage more sensibly; as Price shows in his chapter, our huge amounts of urban waste are also a threat to our health. Here, the individual example of Halifax is inspiring. A few years ago, Nova Scotia enacted a general law requiring all municipalities to eliminate organic waste from their horribly smelly landfill sites within three years, using whatever methods were necessary. Interestingly, this law was the brainchild of the newly elected premier, John Savage, who had been medical officer of health for Dartmouth, Halifax's twin city across the harbour. A task force in Halifax got to work and produced a system with four collections: all organic waste, fibre (paper and cardboard), recyclable containers (plastic, aluminum, and glass), and unsorted garbage (for which a user fee is charged). The organic waste is composted, the fibre and containers recycled, and the unsorted garbage is sent to a sorting plant, where it is divided into twelve categories. The sorting plant is free of unpleasant odours, because the organic waste has already been removed. Some of the sorted waste is able to be sold, while the rest is sent to landfill—but not before it has gone through an aerobic composter, which reduces it to something resembling fluff (Jack Layton, personal communication, 22 May 2000). This is a maritime province, but the seagulls are gone from the landfill sites, which now receive less than 40 per cent of Halifax's curbside garbage.

Edmonton, where a facility opened early in 2000, is composting and recycling 70 per cent of that city's residential waste, although the cost per tonne is nearly double that of Toronto's waste program. Perhaps, however, both citizens and city officials are no longer using up-front cost as the only measure of success in dealing with garbage (Henton 2000).

This is a good example of how government policy can be really effective; but note that it is piecemeal, in that it involves just one policy area. A more holistic approach is to take a small territory of the city and make it more sustainable on many different dimensions. This makes sense, because waste, food production, sewerage, energy use, and public health are all intertwined, as we have noted.

The City of Vancouver is planning the development of 36 hectares of downtown land (23 hectares of this is city-owned) so that it will meet a variety of sustainability guidelines. The Southeast False Creek (SEFC) development will be mainly residential, with buildings ranging from 50 to 275 feet in height—in other words, a fair bit of high-rise. Simply by building downtown close to mass-transit stops, the plan ensures that inhabitants of SEFC will have a lighter ecological footprint (see Price's chapter). The guidelines also propose that 25 per cent of roof area carry plant life, that 25 per cent of sewage be treated within the neighbourhood, that 12.5 per cent of the residents' produce be grown on site, and that the buildings use less than half the non-renewable energy of other Vancouver high-rises and offices (Alexander 2000; Holland and Smith n.d.) Actually, energy use could be much lower: an apartment house in Mississauga has been constructed that has achieved a 65 per cent reduction in energy use at the same capital cost, using a sophisticated building envelope and air-handling systems, as well as using its own gas-powered turbine for all its energy needs (Jack Layton, personal communication, 22 May 2000).

When we combine these examples with real action on the environmental plan described earlier, it sounds as if progress is being made toward more sane urban development; but as we pointed out at the beginning of the chapter, things are not that great overall. Canada's greenhouse emissions continue to rise, as do many other indicators of pollution. Suburban development is still spreading uneconomically out from Montreal, Toronto, Calgary, and Vancouver.

Whatever policies we make, they will only be a reaction to a situation that has already gone wrong. Not just our environmental problems but also our whole definition of what constitutes an environmental problem are deeply embedded in cultural practices and beliefs that shape not only daily choices about work, food, child-rearing, housing, and recreation, but also our acceptance of myths about the high economic costs of living sensibly on the Earth or of decommissioning oversized corporations and governments.

Recognizing this truth, many of the people thinking seriously about greening cities are not just public policy-makers. They are people of all kinds who are rethinking our culture's conditioning about work, styles of life, and attitudes toward Nature. They are acting out their philosophy in their own lives by cutting down on the amount of regular paid work they do and living more simply (Dominguez and Robin 1992; Elgin 1981; Nozick 1992), growing their own food, retrofitting their dwellings and making them more energy-efficient—even building their own houses.

Actually, a remarkable number of Canadians are involved in a housing movement that results in many changes in their lives, a movement called *cohousing*. This concept of shelter, developed thirty years ago in Scandinavia, has several features: First, it is small, usually including from five to forty families. Second, it is a single development, designed collectively by those families. Third, the cluster of dwellings always includes common space that is multi-functional: a communal kitchen and dining room, meeting rooms, guest rooms, communal washing machines, a workshop, perhaps a community garden or a practice room for teenage rock bands, or a daycare facility. Fourth, there are private dwellings with their own kitchens, living rooms, and bedrooms. Fifth, there are explicit attempts to make the project even more ecologically benign through low use of energy and water, minimal waste, and compact design (Fromm 1992; McCamant and Durrett 1988; *Network News*). Finally, in Europe, cohousing usually includes affordable units, often subsidized by governments. Many cohousing projects in North America attempt to do this, but most of our governments seem too short-sighted to help them out. Still, it is important to note that when the people themselves design sustainable housing, they include the concept of social equity.

People who join together to create cohousing are, in a sense, making public policy, but at an extremely local level. They are making decisions on waste management, housing, social services, parks and recreation, energy, land use, and even finance and safety issues. Of course, at such a small scale, these policy areas blend together so seamlessly that it's difficult to see where one leaves off and the other begins. Community gardens, for instance, have been known to increase the safety of neighbourhoods (Fowler 1996). Cohousing illustrates at a micro-scale the way housing is part of all the other policy chapters in this book. Essentially, it is a very intelligent form of environmental policy, paying attention not only to buildings, but to spaces between buildings, which in North America are dominated by the car (Alexander, Ishikawa, and Silverstein 1977; Gehl 1987).

Sensible urban environmental policy ultimately revolves around the intelligent use and creation of diverse places, calling for redefinitions of what we mean by both *policy* and *policy-making*. To be effective, though, as we hope to have shown, this policy-making needs to be local:

> No one understands how, or even if, sustainable development can be achieved; however, there is a growing consensus that it must be accomplished at the local level if it is ever to be achieved on a global basis. (ICLEI 1996, cited in Roseland 1998: 15)

Notes

1. The authors would like to thank Lauren Baker, Mary Lou Morgan, Perry Gladstone, Paul Morton, Marcia Nozick, Jim Love, Nathan Edelson, Andalee Adamali, and Mike Naylor for their help and advice. Responsibility for errors in fact and interpretation remain with the authors.
2. See Hartmann (1999) for a brief history of the Toronto environmental movement.
3. Sustainability is, of course, closely related to the sustainable development approach made popular by the Report of the World Commission on Environment and Development (1987), known as the Brundtland Report. Since then, the federal and provincial governments have partially embraced this concept through the creation of the National Roundtable on the Environment and Economy and the Ontario Roundtable on the Environment and Economy.
4. In many ways, the new Sustainability Roundtable will continue the work of the Environmental Task Force, which formally ended with the adoption of the Environmental Plan in April 2000.

Bibliography on Green Cities

Aberley, Doug, ed. 1994. *Futures by Design: The Practice of Ecological Planning.* Gabriola Island, BC: New Society.

Engwicht, David. 1987. *Reclaiming Our Cities and Towns: Better Living with Less Traffic.* Gabriola Island, BC: New Society.

Girardet, Herbert. 1992. *The Gaia Atlas of Cities: New Directions for Sustainable Living.* New York: Doubleday.

Gordon, David. 1990. *Green Cities: Ecologically Sound Approaches to Urban Space.* Montreal: Black Rose.

Hough, Michael. 1995. *Cities and Natural Process: Towards a New Urban Vernacular.* London: Routledge.

Nicholson-Lord, David. 1987. *The Greening of the Cities.* London: Routledge and Kegan Paul.

Register, Richard. 1987. *Ecocity Berkeley: Building Cities for a Healthy Future.* Berkeley, CA: North Atlantic Books.

Roelofs, Joan. 1996. *Greening Cities: Building Just and Sustainable Communities.* New York: Bootstrap.

Roseland, Mark. 1998. *Toward Sustainable Communities: Resources for Citizens and Their Governments.* Gabriola Island, BC: New Society.

Spirn, Anne Whiston. 1984. *The Granite Garden: Urban Nature and Human Design.* New York: Basic Books.

Todd, Nancy Jack, and John Todd. 1994. *From Eco-Cities to Living Machines: Principles of Ecological Design.* Berkeley, CA: North Atlantic Books.

Walter, Bob, Lois Arkin, and Richard Crenshaw, eds. 1992. *Sustainable Cities: Concepts and Strategies for Eco-City Development.* Los Angeles: EHM Eco-Home Media.

References

Alexander, Christopher, Sara Ishikawa, and Murray Silverstein. 1977. *A Pattern Language: Towns, Buildings, Construction*. New York: Oxford University Press.

Alexander, Don. 2000. 'The Best So Far'. *Alternatives* 26(3): 10–15.

Baker, Lauren. 2000. 'Warehouse Rooftops Support Urban Agriculture'. *In Business* (March/April): 16–18.

Blais, Pamela. 1995. *The Economics of Urban Form*. Toronto: Background Paper for the Greater Toronto Area Task Force.

Bourne, Larry. 2000. *People and Places: A Portrait of the Evolving Character of the Greater Toronto Area*. Report to the Neptis Foundation, Portrait of a Region Project. Toronto: Department of Geography, University of Toronto.

Dominguez, Joe, and Vicki Robin. 1992. *Your Money or Your Life: Transforming Your Relationship with Money and Achieving Financial Independence*. New York: Viking.

Elgin, Duane. 1981. *Voluntary Simplicity: Toward a Way of Life that is Outwardly Simple, Inwardly Rich*. New York: William Morrow.

Fowler, Edmund P. 1987. 'Street Management and City Design'. *Social Forces* 66: 365–89.

———. 1992. *Building Cities That Work*. Montreal: McGill-Queen's University Press.

———. 1996. 'The Link between Politics, Policies, and Healthy City Form'. In *Local Places in the Age of the Global City*, ed. Roger Keil, Gerda Wekerle, and David V.J. Bell. Montreal: Black Rose.

Freeman, Donald B. 1991. *A City of Farmers: Informal Urban Agriculture in the Open Spaces of Nairobi, Kenya*. Montreal: McGill-Queen's University Press.

Fromm, Dorit. 1992. *Collaborative Communities: Cohousing, Central Living, and Other New Forms of Housing*. New York: Van Nostrand Reinhold.

Gehl, Jan. 1987. *Life between Buildings: Using Public Space*. New York: Van Nostrand Reinhold.

Gertler, Meric. 2000. *A Region in Transition: The Changing Structure of Toronto's Regional Economy*. Portrait of a Region Project. Toronto: Planning Department, University of Toronto.

Greater Toronto Area (GTA) Task Force. 1996. *Greater Toronto: Report of the GTA Task Force*. Toronto: Queen's Printer.

Hartmann, Franz. 1999. 'Nature in the City: Urban Ecological Politics in Toronto'. Ph.D. diss., York University, Toronto.

Hawken, Paul, Amory Lovins, and L. Hunter Lovins. 1999. *Natural Capitalism: Creating the Next Industrial Revolution*. Boston: Little Brown.

Henton, Darcy. 2000. 'Mayor Doubtful about Alberta Facility'. *The Toronto Star* (24 October).

Holland, Mark, and Ian Smith. n.d. *Urban Sustainable Development*. Vancouver: City of Vancouver Planning Department.

International Council for Local Environmental Initiatives (ICLEI). 1996. *The Local Agenda 21 Planning Guide*. Toronto: ICLEI; Ottawa: International Development Research Centre.

Jackson, K. 2000. 'The Hype That Was Portland'. *Auto-Free Times* (17, Winter/Spring): 7.

Jackson, Wes. 1980. *New Roots for Agriculture*. Lincoln, NB: University of Nebraska Press.

Jacobs, Jane. 1969. *The Economy of Cities*. New York: Random House.

Jones, Bryan D., and Lynn W. Bachelor. 1993. *The Sustaining Hand: Leadership and Corporate Power*. 2nd ed. Lawrence: University Press of Kansas.

Korten, David. 1999. *The Post-Corporate World: Life after Capitalism*. West Hartford, CT: Kumarian.

Leo, Christopher with Mary Ann Beavis, Andrew Carver, and Robyne Turner. 1998. 'Is Urban Sprawl Back on the Political Agenda?' *Urban Affairs Review* 34: 179–211.

Lipsky, Michael. 1976. 'Toward a Theory of Street-Level Bureaucracy'. In *Theoretical Perspectives on Urban Politics*, ed. Willis Hawley and Michael Lipsey. Englewood Cliffs, NJ: Prentice-Hall.

McCamant, Kathryn, and Charles Durrett. 1988. *Cohousing: A Contemporary Approach to Housing Ourselves*. Berkeley, CA: Ten Speed Press.

Moloney, Paul. 2000. 'Commission Urged for the Moraine'. *The Toronto Star* (2 June).

Mumford, Lewis. 1938. *The Culture of Cities*. New York: Harcourt Brace Jovanovich.

Nelson, Ruben F.W. 1980. *The Illusions of Urban Man*. 2nd ed. Ottawa: Square One Management.

Network News. Available: The Cohousing Network, 1460 Quince Ave. #102, Boulder, CO 80304.

Nozick, Marcia. 1992. *No Place Like Home: Building Sustainable Communities*. Ottawa: Canadian Council on Social Development.

Paehlke, Robert. 1994. 'Possibilities for and Limitations on Environmental Protection in the Changing Canadian Metropolis'. In *The Changing Canadian Metropolis: A Public Policy Perspective*, ed. Frances Frisken. Toronto: Canadian Urban Institute.

Raad, Tamim, and Jeff Kenworthy. 1998. 'The U.S. and Us'. *Alternatives* 24(1): 14–22.

Roseland, Mark. 1998. *Toward Sustainable Communities: Resources for Citizens and Their Governments*. Gabriola Island, BC: New Society.

Simpson, Scott. 1997. 'Surrey Shelves Commitment to Regional Plan'. *Vancouver Sun* (2 August).

Smith, Patrick J. 1998. 'More than One Way towards Economic Development: Public Participation and Policy-Making in the Vancouver Region'. In *Citizen Engagement: Lessons in Participation from Local Government*, ed. K.A. Graham and S.D. Phillips. Toronto: Institute of Public Administration in Canada.

Stokes, Bruce. 1981. *Helping Ourselves: Local Solutions to Global Problems*. New York: Norton.

Todd, Nancy Jack, and John Todd. 1994. *From Eco-Cities to Living Machines: Principles of Ecological Design*. Berkeley, CA: North Atlantic Books.

Toronto. 2000. *The Toronto Report Card on Homelessness: 2000*. Toronto: City of Toronto.

Toronto. Environmental Task Force (ETF). 2000. *Clean, Green, and Healthy: A Plan for an Environmentally Sustainable Toronto*. Toronto: City of Toronto.

World Commission on Environment and Development. 1987. *Our Common Future*. New York: Oxford University Press.

CHAPTER 10

Public Policy on Recreation and Leisure in Urban Canada

Bryan J.A. Smale and Donald G. Reid

Introduction

Perhaps the most interesting conundrum of public-policy development with respect to leisure in Canadian municipalities has been the general lack of policy with, nonetheless, a common adherence to a basic principle of public delivery of leisure services. That common principle is 'equal opportunity'. In fact, so widely accepted is this basic principle that most authorities and policy analysts focus on *how* equal opportunity is achieved and how well, and not on *if* it is an appropriate cornerstone for policy (Harper and Balmer 1989). Over the years, 'equality' of provision had been the premise upon which equal opportunity has been based, but with changing political, social, and economic forces in urban areas, it has given way to the related notion of 'equity'. *Equal* provision means equal in terms of quantity or quality, whereas *equity*—or equitable provision—refers to fairness or justice (Crompton and Lamb 1986). This distinction will be explained more fully later. The shift in how equal opportunity is implemented in public policy has been an inevitable outcome of the historical development of public recreation, its infrastructure and profession in Canadian cities and towns, and the various forces brought to bear on local service delivery. Where it may be going in the future is the subject of this chapter.[1]

History of Urban Parks and Recreation Development in Canada

When one thinks of public recreation today, such things as neighbourhood parks, arenas, and swimming pools will likely come immediately to mind. But public recreation extends well beyond these more visible properties. Generally speaking, public recreation has evolved into three principal areas of responsibility. First, there are the *facilities and open space*, which may include such things as pools, arenas, community centres, sports fields and courts, parks, and trails. Very often, libraries, theatres, galleries, museums, and even golf courses and cemeteries may also be part of the mix of facilities operated by public recreation departments. Second, public recreation agencies develop and provide various *programs and services* geared toward many different demographic cross-sections of the community. Among program offerings, there are those focusing on the fine and performing arts, continuing education, health and fitness, hobbies and personal-interest activities, and sports. Minor league sports for youth are undoubtedly the most familiar and heavily participated-in programs supported by the municipality. Typical services provided include those facilitating access and participation in community programs by individuals with special needs (e.g., persons with physical or mental disabilities), services geared toward older adults, and specific services such as English as a second language and volunteer services providing for a variety of needs across the community. Finally, public recreation agencies organize and promote *special events*, including annual festivals, cultural and ethnic celebrations, sports tournaments, and events celebrating community pride and development.

In each of these areas of responsibility, the development of public recreation agencies in Canadian communities has been remarkably similar. Indeed, most municipal parks and recreation departments in urban Canada now boast an infrastructure reflecting almost all the aforementioned facilities, programs, and services. Although their overall development has been slow and evolutionary, it cannot be said that much change has occurred in the basic structure of public recreation throughout much of Canada for many, many years. Indeed, the current state of public recreation in Canada—a focus on infrastructure and an adherence to direct delivery—is revealed in its evolution.

The early history of Canadian public involvement in leisure and recreation was in the area of open space and park development. Some claim that a public garden in St John's, Newfoundland, created in 1583, was the first site (Wright 1983). In 1837, the Nova Scotia Horticultural Society developed a garden 'for the production, sale and viewing of plant materials' (Wright 1983: 55), which was open to the public one day per week. Whether these gardens can truly be defined as public parks, given that the public was not always free to use them, is debatable. It was not until the period following 1883, when Manitoba and Ontario passed their Public Parks Acts, that public recreation and open space really began to develop as a part of the everyday mandate of local government (Wright 1984).

The period between 1880 and 1914 saw a dramatic increase in open spaces and parks in Canadian cities. These parks were initially located on the properties of federal buildings and on old military parade grounds, and their advocates described them as important and integral components of the urban landscape. The parks were portrayed as the 'lungs' of the city, providing refuges from the built environment, places for exercise and 'psychic restoration' (Wright 1984: 3) that contributed to the quality of life in increasingly crowded cities. The public mandate for urban parks mimicked National Park policy in many ways, in that parks were designated as places for the benefit and enjoyment of all people in the community.

Parkland development in urban areas was the sole visible expression of leisure and recreation provision in Canada until the early 1890s. At that time, the National Council of Women was formed; it campaigned for the creation of places for children, where they could play and thereby foster the development of their health, strength, and moral character, ultimately becoming productive members of the community. Arguing from a social welfare perspective, the National Council of Women asserted that such places should be available to all children in the community. Eventually, the responsibility for developing and maintaining these play spaces—the early playgrounds—became part of the public mandate (McFarland 1970). It was in these playgrounds that the first organized programs were provided.

Park development slowed in Canadian cities following World War I (Searle and Brayley 1999). It was not until the depression of the 1930s that significant development of parks picked up again; parks and public gardens provided a focus for job creation as Canada struggled to draw itself out of this economic malaise (Carver 1975). Ironically, the onset of World War II provided another opportunity for an element of the recreation movement to find its way onto the scene. Concern about the fitness level of the troops saw the introduction of the Physical Fitness Act in the Canadian Parliament, and the Act drew attention to the general level of health and fitness among the population as well as the troops. The experience of the war caused many Canadians to decide that life needed to be more than just work and personal diligence. The Parks and Recreation Association of Canada was created at the end of World War II to maintain this fitness-conscious attitude among the general public during peacetime, and the responsibility for providing programs and facilities for the community's residents increasingly fell to the still-fledgling recreation agencies within municipal governments.

The late 1950s and early 1960s saw the proliferation of the built infrastructure. Ice hockey arenas and community halls were fast becoming a mainstay in most large and middle-sized municipalities in Canada. Even many rural communities with populations no greater than 1,500 created these types of facilities. Also at this time, the 'community school' emerged as a concept that saw the schools as having the potential to serve as public facilities outside of those times when they were devoted to formal education.

The grand scale of facility development prompted the recognition of the need for leadership training in order to maximize the use and potential of these many facilities and parks. The development of leadership training was the major thrust of the 1960s and initiated the emergence of the recreation profession. The size of the capital expenditure that municipalities were now putting into the recreation infrastructure demanded well-trained professional staff and policy-makers.

The 1970s and early 1980s saw the municipal recreation infrastructure continue to grow in sophistication and size. Today, as a consequence, in almost every large city across Canada, the size of the municipal budget devoted to recreation is on the order of such basic areas as transportation and protection (see Siegel's chapter). The infrastructure, by this point, had broadened and now included swimming pools, performance centres, and library systems along with the parks and arenas from years past.

The recreation movement has experienced growth and development both in capital expenditure and in operation budget since its crude beginnings. In fact, the municipal recreation movement has been defined historically by infrastructure and direct program delivery, as we have seen. However, these developments are simply the physical manifestations of two intentions: to provide opportunities in the community for people to experience leisure in diverse and personal ways and to enhance the quality of their lives and the quality of life for the community as a whole. In an effort to ensure that everyone in the community did benefit from such development, the distribution of facilities and programs has been driven by the basic principle of 'equal opportunity'. However, the way in which equal opportunity has been defined in practice has slowly evolved as municipal recreation agencies felt the effects of social, political, and economic change.

Today, with increased stress on the ability of the public sector to maintain the infrastructure, the debate focuses on whether or not that infrastructure is, in fact, effectively meeting these basic goals. This debate is accentuated by the realization that the growth in infrastructure and financing characteristic of the past is unlikely to continue as we move into the twenty-first century. A process of redefining the public expression of leisure and recreation has begun to develop through policy creation, ironically not at the local level, but at the federal and provincial levels.

The National Recreation Policy Statement

During the early and mid-1980s, the provincial ministers responsible for leisure and recreation met on an annual basis to consider issues of mutual interest; essentially, they were interested in how they might increase and consolidate their mandates, which had expanded with the social gains of the 1960s and 1970s. During that period, leisure, it was thought, was on the way to becoming as important to society as work. In fact, the prevailing conventional wisdom suggested that the developed world was steadily moving toward a 'leisure society'. It was generally felt that increased technology would reduce the need for labour input in the production process, with workers taking this increased productivity in leisure dividends (Schor 1991a, 1991b; O'Hara 1993). Hindsight suggests, however, that sufficient preparatory groundwork had not been undertaken by society to encourage this social transformation. Instead, society opted, at least until now, to take the gains from technologically enhanced productivity in material wealth and consumer goods. Although it is true that we can produce more with less labour because of the technological revolution, we have not transformed the reduction of labour into meaningful leisure. As a result, there are a growing number of individuals in society who are unemployed and have more free time but not more leisure, while the majority of people today are working at least as much as, if not more than, in earlier years. Society, it would seem, has chosen or unthinkingly wandered into a 'work-spend-work' cycle of existence without concern for questions about quality of life or for a changed social organizational strategy that encourages leisure (Reid 1995).

Notwithstanding this unrealized leisure potential, the provincial and territorial ministers responsible for leisure and recreation met in Edmonton in 1974 and produced the beginnings of a policy statement that was meant to guide the development of leisure in society into the modern era. The ministers released a statement at the conclusion of these meetings:

> *Be it therefore resolved* that this Conference recognizes the fact that recreation is a social service in the same way that health and education are considered as social services and that recreation's purpose should be: (a) to assist individual and community development; (b) to improve the quality of life; and (c) to enhance social functioning. Such recognition will indicate the constitutional responsibility of the Provinces and Territories in recreation services. (Fitness Canada 1987: 6)

The group of ministers continued to meet annually, and on 23 September 1987, they produced an expanded version of this statement at the conclusion of their Quebec meetings (Fitness Canada 1987). The policy statement presented by the ministers is quick to point out that the primary responsibility for one's leisure and recreation on a day-to-day basis falls to the individual and the local community. They state,

> Municipal governments are the closest to the people; they are likely to respond more flexibly, more quickly and more effectively to the needs of the community in matters of recreation. For this reason the municipality is the primary public supplier of direct recreation services. Therefore, in its policy on recreation, each provincial/territorial government must outline the role it intends to assign to its municipalities. (Fitness Canada 1987: 9)

In promoting the general philosophy of the provincial/territorial role of government as one of coordinator of inter- and intraprovincial activity and facilitator of municipal action, the policy statement lays out six duties of the municipal government:

1. establish a designated municipal recreation authority to serve as the focus for the provision of community recreation opportunities;
2. be continually aware of all relevant community resources and recreation opportunities and ensure that this information is readily available to the public;
3. provide incentives and services to these programmes, as required, to ensure effective development relevant to the needs identified;
4. undertake a regular assessment to determine community needs or interests not being met through existing community programmes;
5. make every effort to respond to recreation needs or interests through the development of initiatives by:

(a) existing community groups, organisations or agencies;
(b) the establishment of community associations, etc.;
(c) the private and commercial sector or, if none of the above are [sic] feasible;
(d) direct involvement of the municipal authority;
6. co-ordinate the development and best use of community resources through the establishment of an appropriate mechanism that can stimulate joint planning, information exchange, and programme evaluation, among all groups and agencies currently providing recreation opportunities. A community recreation 'council', 'board' or 'commission' is one mechanism that can be used to good effect. (Fitness Canada 1987: 10)

Many of the provinces created their own leisure and recreation policies, such as Ontario's *Community Recreation Policy Statement* (Ontario, Ministry of Tourism and Recreation 1987), to emphasize further the principles contained and enunciated in the national statement. The Ontario statement sets out the responsibilities of the municipality as envisioned by the national document. It clearly designates the municipal role as the direct service provider of last resort. The municipality's primary function is to encourage and facilitate recreation responses to the leisure needs of the public through the development and growth of local voluntary and private-sector venues before it provides direct service to the public itself.

This primary function, however, is not in keeping with how the municipal role has developed over the years. Municipalities have been directly providing activities and programs to individual citizens and not acting as facilitators of the voluntary and private sectors. In fact, municipal departments often compete with these community groups for market share rather than encouraging and fostering their development, so that what the senior government policies encourage and how these policies are implemented may not coincide. This apparent contradiction is in large part due to the increased sense of professional expertise held by those individuals responsible for leisure service delivery and to the overwhelming infrastructure with which they have been charged to 'deliver' those services to the community's residents.

Complicating the picture today is the added pressure on all levels of government because of the apparent change in public attitude toward government and the fiscal concerns produced by large public debt. (The breadth and nature of these concerns are described in greater detail in chapters by Siegel, Haddow, and Hancock.) These and other forces will profoundly influence the future development of the municipal recreation service.

Current Forces Affecting Municipal Recreation Services

As alluded to in the previous section, municipal governments are being officially guided by a series of senior government policies that were created during a time period during which a unique set of opportunities and constraints were being faced. The present social environment is in such rapid change that it is difficult, if not impossible, to create policy with a sufficiently long shelf life to meet these changing conditions. The questions of whether or not it is possible to establish meaningful recreation policy and what it must emphasize to be effective need to be answered.

Consequently, it is of fundamental importance as a prerequisite to policy development to reconsider how leisure is conceived and how a municipal recreation agency expects to provide for the leisure needs of the community. The traditional focus on developing the infrastructure and on training a recreation profession responsible for it has created a system based on direct delivery, a system that treats leisure as a commodity rather than as a means of personal expression and of meeting basic human needs. An inherent problem in this approach is defining *need* and determining how need may be most effectively satisfied through alternative strategic policies. Typically, recreation agencies have confused the *demand* for recreation (e.g., participation rates in various programs) with real expressions of need within the community (e.g., lack of access to meaningful leisure opportunities). Ultimately, how public leisure policy may change and develop is very much dependent on those forces in effect today.

Critical to the development or evaluation of any set of public policies are the prevailing social conditions that demand attention and that have an impact on local government's ability to implement policy in everyday practice. Perhaps the primary change driving or affecting public policy today is the apparent shift to a more liberal perspective by all political parties at both the provincial and the federal levels. *Liberal* in this paper follows on the concept of *liberal-democratic* as described by Macpherson (1977). He provides two ways of looking at the term *liberal*: 'the democracy of a capitalist market society (no matter how modified that society appears to be by the rise of the welfare state), or . . . a society striving to ensure all its members are equally free to realise their capabilities. . . . Liberal can mean freedom of the stronger to put down the weaker by following market rules; or it can mean equal effective freedom of all to use and develop their capacities' (Macpherson 1977: 1). The most telling characteristic of this shift is the single-minded fixation on privatizing government services. Murdock summarizes the consequences of this liberal movement on the public enterprise:

> At the most obvious level, it involves the transfer of public assets to private enterprise so that facilities and services that were previously paid for out of taxation and open to all become commodities that are only available to those who can pay the prices asked. But there are also more subtle dimensions of privatization that are reshaping institutions still formally in the public sector. They are under increasing pressure to demonstrate their efficiency and 'value for money' by adopting managerial practices and philosophies developed by private enterprise. They come to be evaluated, and to judge themselves, by the same criteria as commercial companies. They increasingly see their role as competing for consumers in a competitive marketplace rather than meeting the needs of citizens. Measures on quantity are eagerly developed—how many users are attracted to spend time with the services, how quickly are they processed. Qualities that cannot be easily calibrated disappear from managerial rhetoric. The commitment to contribute to the common good is displaced by the

injection of square demands of clients—individually and in aggregate—with the pressures generated by an increasingly privatized operating environment. (Murdock 1994: 241)

It is legitimate to ask if the policy developed by the provincial and territorial ministers responsible for leisure and recreation outlined earlier can act as the guiding principle it was meant to be in a climate that produced this extreme shift to a classic liberal perspective. In other words, in what way can public policy ensure that equal opportunity to leisure will be maintained in Canadian cities and towns within such a climate? Even the more socially oriented governments have either privatized or drastically cut back public services, including recreation. At best, the need to privatize may be rationalized as a promotion of the ministers' policy of facilitating development of the volunteer and private sector. At worst, it may be an abandonment of those in society who need the help of government service in order to support an acceptable quality of life through their leisure experiences.

Much of the pressure for change can be attributed to the adoption of a liberal (sometimes called *neo-conservative*) ideology and the globalization of the economy and to the complex relationships that these two factors have created. Whatever the reasons for this apparent shift to a classic liberal perspective, the mere fact there is a shift in attitude has profound effects not only on how municipal governments and departments deliver their services to the public, but also on what services are to be delivered at all. Traditionally, government engagement in recreation service provision has rested on two factors: The first is market failure; that is, if the market is unable to provide service to those in need of that service, government therefore provides it. The second factor is a concern about service as a public good. The government needs to ensure that the service is accessible to the public without any of the restrictions that the market may impose because of the determined social value of that service. This notion of social value and the public good is inextricably tied to the principle of equal opportunity. We may be witness to a retraction of these basic social tenets today.

The rationale for regarding leisure services as a public good can be highlighted by contrasting them with the characteristics of private goods. Private goods are divisible, in that 'they come in units small enough to be afforded by individual buyers. Furthermore, private goods are subject to the exclusion principle, in that those who are willing and able to pay the equilibrium price get the product, but those who are unable or unwilling to pay are excluded from the benefits provided by the product' (McConnell, Brue, and Pope 1990: 194–5). Municipal recreation service has been founded on the ideal that what it provides must not fall victim to this exclusion principle. The service is seen to be sufficiently in the public interest that it must be provided by the state so that everyone in society can participate—in other words, equal opportunity. Additionally, some recreation 'products', such as parks, are not divisible and therefore are not subject to market processes. Finally, a primary characteristic of a public good is that 'the demand for the product expressed in the marketplace therefore will not generate sufficient revenue to cover costs of production, even though collective benefits of the good may match or exceed these economic costs'

(McConnell, Brue, and Pope 1990: 431). Hence, leisure services are regarded as a public good because it can be argued that they ought not be subject to the 'exclusion principle', they are generally not divisible, and the collective benefits generated by them are deemed greater than the real costs to provide them.

A more problematic outcome of the recent political shift than the fundamental economic response suggested above is the change in the ideological principles that guide government policy in the future. For example, what has been considered as a public good is now being questioned, as the emerging value system seems to be more concerned with privatization than with notions of the public good. In fact, privatization itself may be interpreted as a public good in today's ideological world, which places an emphasis on the profitability rather than the accessibility of leisure opportunities. If the service can be provided through the marketplace, then it may very well end up there without great concern for its value as a public good. Consequently, even though the service may become 'successful', it would likely only serve a certain segment of the population and hence would no longer be available to the entire community. Therefore, the principle of equal opportunity is compromised.

Beyond the issues imposed by this ideological shift to classic liberalism are the problems faced by the municipal recreation practice as a result of dramatic changes in the demographic structure of the population. There is considerable evidence that Canadian society is aging (see, for example, Perreault 1990 and Foot's chapter). For the last fifty years, much of municipal recreation practice has been devoted to infrastructure development heavily dependent on capital expenditures. Most municipal recreation departments' budgets are devoted to maintaining a large infrastructure of sports and community facilities that are typically dominated by programs devoted to youth. In a society with an aging population, many of these facilities may no longer be in such great demand. Indeed, it is unclear whether an older population will maintain its interest in a facility-based recreation service or divert its attention to other pursuits that are less service-dependent. Nevertheless, few if any municipal recreation agencies in Canada are seriously examining their existing infrastructure or planning for this inevitable future, apparently believing that the status quo will be maintained. Further complicating the situation is that most of these facilities are, on average, at mid-life and have life expectancies of twenty to twenty-five years; so change, even if it involves decommissioning, will be gradual and must be anticipated.

These major political and social changes are occurring in a time period of severe budget constraint. Municipal recreation agencies are being asked to increase revenue in order to offset reductions in the public purse. This results in pressure to increase user fees at a time when individuals and families are feeling increasing financial pressure. It has recently been reported that Canadians are poorer today than a decade ago (Jorgensen 1995)—the continually rising standard of living familiar to Canadians halted in the 1980s. The combination of increased user fees and lower discretionary incomes may now be pricing many citizens out of the municipal recreation service. Increasingly, the municipal recreation facilities and programs may be catering to the middle class while forcing out those less able to pay. Indeed, recent organized protests over the harmonization of user fees and charges in the city of Toronto certainly are evidence that the public is concerned about losing access to public leisure services as the city struggles with amalgamation. Given the broader economic concerns expressed earlier and the reduction in what is being considered germane to the public good, the provision of municipal recreation may now be facing a squeeze from both ends. On the one hand, politicians and the public are demanding that municipal recreation services become more self-financing, while at the same time, increasing numbers of individuals in society have less available income for such services. The ability of the municipal recreation agency to meet the principle of equal opportunity to leisure for everyone in the community is increasingly being compromised. The direction that municipal recreation services must take to overcome these emerging problems is undoubtedly the major policy and program issue facing the practice as it plans for the future.

The Practice of Recreation

Both the recreation profession and municipal officials have responded to changes in the social and political environment in a variety of ways. Some of the responses have been deliberate attempts to address the new pressures and some have been evolutionary, in that the profession has slowly adapted in an effort to accommodate these new forces. The most notable deliberate response in the 1990s is described in the document *The Benefits of Parks and Recreation*, produced by the Parks and Recreation Federation of Ontario in cooperation with the Ontario Ministry of Tourism and Recreation (Parks and Recreation Federation of Ontario 1992). This document, widely accepted by recreation professionals and now distributed nationally by the Canadian Parks and Recreation Association (CP/RA), catalogues the various benefits of recreation to individuals and communities within four domains, described as personal, social, economic, and environmental. Essentially, the document was devised primarily for promotional reasons, so that recreation practitioners could use it in promoting their mandate to municipal councillors and society at large. It describes the benefits of recreation to the individual and society within each of the four domains by reviewing both the popular and academic literature, by conducting interviews with experts on the subject, and then by summarizing this information into several statements of principle.

The difficulty with the document, however, is that while it describes the benefits to society reasonably well in general terms, it does not connect these benefits to the larger social context. In other words, it describes *what* the benefits may be for the constituents of the recreation agency, but it does not answer the question of *why* municipal governments should be concerned with supplying these benefits. Even though the document was updated in 1997 and now places greater emphasis on the outcomes associated with the now forty-four statements of the benefits of recreation, it has wrapped these outcomes within a structure based on eight primary marketing messages, two of which are ominously tied directly to the economic rather than the social well-being of the community (CP/RA 1997).

The process of connecting the benefits of recreation to problems and issues with which municipalities and their officials are concerned is an important but, as yet, uncompleted step. Completion of this step would not only publicize the potential benefits of public recreation to society, but also demonstrate how public recreation may contribute to the solution of social problems with which municipalities are grappling. Indeed, it could answer the basic question of why it is vital for municipalities to be engaged in the development and delivery of recreation services. For example, in the Karen Walk neighbourhood of the city of Waterloo, Ontario, residents came together in an effort to solve some local safety problems, and their solutions emerged from within planned leisure contexts (Reid and van Dreunen 1996). Until such connections are made, the document on the benefits of recreation really can only be considered as a marketing instrument designed to justify the status quo and not to rationalize the existing leisure service agency to address the new issues of postmodern society and ultimately to better meet the leisure needs of the community.

With the increased fiscal pressures placed on society, municipal recreation departments are being asked by their political masters to generate more revenue for their services. A more evolutionary response to these pressures has been the overwhelming adoption by public leisure service agencies of business practices, and especially of marketing approaches, used in the private sector. One of the most visible responses to the fiscal pressures has been the introduction of user fees (or the raising of existing ones) to replace lost dollars from tax sources (see Siegel's chapter) and the increasing involvement in promoting special events, such as sports tournaments and festivals, to attract tourism revenues and fuel local economic development. Indeed, in cities such as Burlington, Ontario, and Saskatoon, Saskatchewan, pricing strategies and the imposition of fees based on cost-recovery principles are central components of the administrative policies in the municipal recreation departments. These responses have had both subtle and not-so-subtle consequences.

The most obvious impact of the imposition of and subsequent increases in pricing of user fees is the limitation these fees place on certain groups in society. The poor, often made up of such groups as senior citizens and single-parent families, are among these groups. When emphasis is placed on financial viability rather than on protecting the public good, important services that have been operating at a loss and may ultimately be deemed incapable of breaking even are in serious jeopardy of being eliminated. With economic factors being the primary consideration, those services that cost the least to implement or that generate the greatest revenues receive priority and those that are less cost-effective are sacrificed irrespective of the need they fulfill. In the case of special events, the revenues generated from tourism have become the greater goal despite the original intent of such events to instill a sense of community.

In the meantime, user fees are serving as a means to delay the ultimate decisions of which services to retain and which to eliminate. Unfortunately, this strategy has meant that recreation departments are moving increasingly toward a business model of service delivery, in which the bottom line is of primary concern. This is not surprising given the historical development of a recreation infrastructure based in facilities and services and managed by a profession trained in direct delivery as opposed to community development and facilitation. However, this shift toward a business model has also meant the loss of a vision based in the social goals of the common good and, in particular, equal opportunity. The recreation profession has become more focused on the maintenance of the infrastructure and less attentive to determining need and providing the opportunities to meet that need. Understandably, the recreation profession has been quick to respond to the new economic realities but has failed to attend to emerging social concerns.

The challenge, then, is to consider what type of approach may be best suited to deal with the forces that are changing the face of public recreation. Beyond the reaffirmation of leisure as a public good and the commitment to equal opportunity in leisure-service provision, public recreation departments must consider which system will be most effective operating under the current constraints in a postmodern society.

Possible Operational Systems

An early indication of the dramatic changes in what provincial and local governments will do and how they will do it was revealed in the recent reduction in transfer payments to the provinces by the federal government. Balanced budgets and cost-cutting may have become the driving forces on federal and provincial agendas well into the twenty-first century, but it will nevertheless fall to municipal governments to implement many of the service reductions as a means of cutting costs. The challenge for municipal governments, including recreation services, will be to develop ways and means of undertaking these cuts while minimizing the loss of service to the public. Partnerships with the private and voluntary sectors are likely to be absolutely necessary in order to deliver a complete service package to local residents. This redefines community recreation as a holistic system made up of many agencies, departments, and enterprises, rather than looking at it from a single-agency perspective. In this view, the private and voluntary sectors may become the growth area in leisure provision in the future, with the municipal agency's role becoming more specialized, focusing on certain population groups and program areas. This move to developing partnerships in the community also may be timely given the recent downloading by the provinces to the municipal governments of social service delivery. Local governments will need to rationalize their already tight budgets, and those programs that can demonstrate viable linkages to social services will fare better in this environment than those that cannot.

A number of authors have provided frameworks for recreation policy development within the municipal and local government structure. Beckers (1989) provides six model options for the creation and delivery of municipal recreation service. His typology—based on the perspectives offered by Bramham, Henry, Mommas, and van der Poel (1989)—is made up of the following six models:

(a)   the *minimalist model*, which, as the term implies, demands the least leisure service provision possible on the part of local government as leisure service becomes primarily the responsibility of the commercial or volunteer sector;

(b)   the *welfare model*, which focuses on a local government that operates under a traditional social welfare policy and provides specialised leisure services to counteract gaps in provision by the commercial sector (typically associated with disadvantaged groups or those least able to pay);

(c)   the *entrepreneurial model*, which suggests that local government should engage in the provision of leisure activities and programs that generate profits, which in turn can be used to subsidize activities that are traditionally not self-supporting but are socially desirable;

(d)   the *therapeutic model*, which regards local government's provision of leisure services as primarily a tool for community development for special populations such as individuals with disabilities;

(e)   the *economic model*, which sees recreation activity on the part of local government as a vehicle for attracting outside investment and industry into the community, thereby producing economic benefits to the community as a whole; and

(f)   the *cultural model*, which views leisure as an integral part of an autonomous cultural policy, such that leisure experiences, provided by the public sector, are expressions of the prevailing societal and community culture.

Which of the models described by Beckers (1989) is embraced by local recreation agencies depends very much on the prevailing political attitude within the community and on what role leisure is intended to play. He notes that while some models may reflect the basic *principle* of leisure service provision by the public sector (e.g., the welfare model), others reflect the current *practice*. Indeed, the model adopted mirrors the overriding policy direction of local government. For example, municipal councils that view the local government role in leisure provision to be minimalist are likely to fit the classical definition of *liberal* in the sense of feeling that it is the prerogative of the market to supply such goods. From the opposite end of the spectrum, those municipalities that take more of the social-democratic perspective are likely to be in favour of the welfare model, which demands an active role of local government in the provision of leisure services. In reality, more than one orientation to service delivery may be embraced by the local recreation agency because not all the various programs and facilities it provides can logically operate within one model. For example, although a municipal golf course may fit nicely within an entrepreneurial model because of its revenue-generation capability, the local parks and trails are more closely tied to the cultural model, where the belief in the benefits of open space to the community is more firmly grounded.

The approach taken by Henry (1988) in his typology is to offer models of leisure service provision that are grounded more in the ideologies of local government. Henry begins with five 'idealised' types or models of local government and describes what economic and political preconditions must exist for each model to emerge. Then he speculates how the public leisure service agency might operate within each type, arguing that the agency's policy direction necessarily operates within these political ideologies and may evolve in a variety of ways:

(a) The *contract management model* puts local government in the position of being the provider of last resort, in that only those services regarded as essential are delivered to the public by government. Individuals take responsibility for their own physical and mental well-being and pursue their interests through the marketplace. Consequently, the role of the public leisure service agency is to determine what are the leisure needs of the community and directly provide only those that cannot or will not be provided by the commercial or voluntary sectors (e.g., urban parks).

(b) The *financial stringency model* is local government's practical response to increasingly strained economic conditions rather than an ideological view of government's enabling role. Without the political commitment to leisure as a community good (and consequently a 'need'), public leisure agencies have difficulty justifying expenditures on the provision of services in the face of increasing economic pressures. The model is similar to Beckers' (1989) minimalist model, in which government reduces service provision to the lowest expenditure possible.

(c) The *Keynesian model* views the local government's role as a manager of the equilibrium between supply and demand, where increased investment in local goods and services is made to stimulate the demand for these and other services in order to redistribute the resultant wealth such that those individuals most in need are provided for. The role of leisure services is to identify the needs of the community and to expand resources in those areas, thereby bringing about greater community well-being. In this model, a community's latent needs for leisure services are increasingly determined by expert assessment—especially in financially constrained times—rather than through community self-determination.

(d) The *post-industrial model*, like the Keynesian model, invests in the local economy and redistributes resources to reduce inequalities, but it differs in that government's intervention is aimed specifically at facilitating change to an information and service economy. In this model, leisure services emphasize a shift away from central delivery of services toward facilitating citizen involvement in the creation and implementation of recreation activity in the local area (i.e., greater self-determination and emphasis on the needs of disadvantaged groups).

(e) The *municipal socialist model* has local government actively intervening in community economic development to serve the interests of the community as a whole, typically with a focus on countering the social problems produced by the market, such as high rates of unemployment and social unrest. Consequently, heavy investment in social services such as education, housing, and leisure is seen as essential in maintaining a healthy, educated community and, ultimately, in restoring the local economy. Leisure services would expand into areas typically held by the commercial sector in order to use the profits to subsidize needed programs and services provided for the community good.

Both Beckers' and Henry's models explain fairly well the theoretical options for service creation and delivery that are available to the municipal government in this time of shrinking budgets and ideological shifts to classic liberalism. It is likely, however, that the configuration of service structure, at the end of the day, will be constructed out of pragmatic motivations that were originally influenced by political ideology and explained by theoretical frameworks. So what then are the likely scenarios for the future provision of recreation service here in Canada?

At least two possible proactive courses of action are available to municipal governments and the recreation practice. Each model combines many of the elements that are found in different models described in the two typologies presented above; however, the combination of elements in these two models better fits the pressures being experienced by present-day society.

(There is, of course, a third, less viable alternative that would be essentially a scaled-down version of the status quo. In this case, municipal recreation agencies would simply continue on their current path of reducing services and shutting down facilities and programs as economic circumstances demand. The remaining services would cater to an increasingly narrow segment of the population but would undoubtedly be financially viable and may even contribute to the wealth of the local economy.)

The first possible proactive approach is the *market model,* whose main feature is the downsizing of the present repertoire of services and which focuses on the facilitation role suggested by the ministers' policy statement of 1987. The second approach embraces the *community development model* and views the role of leisure to be a proactive means to self-development and self-definition rather than an end in itself.

The Market Model

The market model is influenced by the present political climate and stresses the importance and appropriateness of providing services primarily through the market mechanism. The implementation of this approach focuses on downsizing and the retraction of direct service provision by the municipal government in favour of encouraging voluntary and private-sector development.

In this model, the role of municipal government and the recreation profession is, first, to assist these agencies to develop and grow where possible and, second, to provide subsidies to individuals who are unable to buy services through the market (Balmer and Reid 1986). Furthermore, the municipal recreation profession will continue to produce and maintain facilities that are similarly subject to market failure, just as in the private sector, and that are unable to be provided by the marketplace. These are likely to include parks and capital-intensive enterprises such as arenas, swimming pools, libraries, and performance halls. However, if the municipality ceases to be a competitor in the marketplace, some of these facilities, such as swimming pools, might become profitable and attractive to the private sector. Business could charge market prices that would make privatization possible if municipal subsidization of individuals and groups deemed to be excluded from the use of these facilities due to financial constraints was given priority in a public leisure policy.

Such a policy of subsidization is not as dramatic a shift as might first be thought. At this time, many public recreation facilities are being provided to individuals and groups in need at reduced rates in order to facilitate or encourage participation. Consequently, municipal government is paying the cost of capital construction and operation of those facilities as well as subsidizing certain individuals and groups to use them.

Under the market scenario, the municipal government would not own the facility but would simply assist designated groups to purchase services at the market price through a policy of subsidization. The municipality would accomplish its goals without owning and maintaining the infrastructure or the program apparatus. The municipality benefits because it is no longer necessary to invest large sums of money in infrastructure and programming but simply to subsidize those who are excluded from participating due to lack of finances.

An intermediate position in this scenario could be for municipal governments to accept the role of constructing high-cost facilities and to contract out the operation of those facilities to the private and voluntary sectors. The municipality would incur the capital cost of construction but not the ongoing operation costs associated with it. It is often not the capital cost of facility construction that is of critical concern; rather, it is the ongoing operating costs that represent the greatest burden to the municipal budget.

The Town of Ingersoll, Ontario, for example, recently privatized its recreation function by contracting out the operation to a private recreation company. In this case, the municipality continued to own the facilities and paid the private company to provide programs to the public and to maintain the facilities; however, capital expenditures were still the responsibility of the municipality. This contract included all the publicly owned recreation facilities in the corporation, including a major recreation complex, all the parks, and an arena. There was an escape clause that allowed the municipality to withdraw from the contract by providing thirty days' notice if it determined that the company was not living up to the contract. The company's annual revenue consisted of a lump-sum payment from the municipality plus fees and charges to operate the facilities and programs. Each year, the municipality received an audited financial statement and had the right to undertake two unannounced inspections. If the company wished to increase any of the fees and charges, it first had to negotiate an agreement with the municipal council. Such negotiations occurred twice during the tenure of the agreement, which was signed in 1994. Reallocation of time from one activity to another also needed the approval of council. This prevented, for example, the reduction of time allocated to minor sports, which was provided for at less than cost, in favour of adult activities that could generate higher fees and, hence, more profit for the company. The company was obliged to offer to citizens on welfare one activity per family member at reduced or no cost.

The contract was not renewed by the municipality at the end of the five-year period, and the entire recreation function has been assumed again by the local government. The company that originally undertook the contract went bankrupt during the life of the contract and a second company assumed it. The instability of the private sector may be, in part, one reason for the decision of the municipality not to continue with the public/private partnership; however, a wide range of concerns about this model re-emerge following such experiments.

Among the more serious concerns identified by Scott (1996) are (1) that decision-making processes are decentralized to those parties not directly committed to the principles underlying the provision of such services; (2) that a policy with a mandate of contracting out specific services places the public sector in a weak negotiating position, thereby reducing its ability to guarantee desired levels of provision; (3) that the question of accountability for service quality becomes increasingly blurred; and (4) that the fundamentally different cultures driving the public and the private sectors bring into conflict potentially unresolvable priorities (e.g., equal opportunity versus the profit motive). Ironically, the most compelling question that public recreation agencies have generally failed to address when entering contractual agreements has been whether the arrangements effectively serve the public and not just the agency's financial efficiency.

On a much larger scale, the uncertain future of such collaborations between the public and private sectors was underlined in Quebec City and Winnipeg, where public monies were marshalled to help build new arenas in the failed efforts of 1995 and 1996 to keep the National Hockey League's Québec Nordiques and Winnipeg Jets in their respective cities. The political debate surrounding the use of public monies to support a private venture—even if the city benefits by having a significant addition to its recreation infrastructure—polarized opinion dramatically. In the final analysis, even if the local communities had made a municipal expenditure of this magnitude, there was no guarantee that long-term commitment to stay in the city would necessarily have been made by either franchise. Indeed, the fates of NHL teams in Edmonton, Calgary, and Ottawa can all be considered in this regard, with the concession and subsequent withdrawal of federal tax incentives to the Ottawa-based team in 1999 reflecting the volatility of the debate.

The concern with the market approach, however, is that it may become quite easy for municipal governments to eliminate subsidization when the municipal budget needs to be squeezed again. In times of cost-cutting, it is usually the poor who are marginalized in society because of their lack of a political voice. Given the recent shift to the political right and this shift's resultant effect on public policy, there is every reason to be concerned that this will occur under this scenario.

An unresolved issue under the market model is the determination of 'need'. In this model, need continues to be determined by recreation professionals through the market rather than by all the people themselves, and consequently, there is little self-determination despite the apparent role of 'facilitator' taken on by the recreation agency. Marketing strategies employed by the agency would likely still flourish because recreation professionals would define which services would be subsidized and at what levels. Unfortunately, these determinations are based on demand rather than on need, as explained earlier, and are driven by the marketplace rather than by a sense of the public good and equal opportunity.

The Community Development Model

The second approach to the postmodern delivery of leisure services at the municipal level is the community development model. Although on the surface, some of its characteristics might appear to be somewhat similar to the market model, there are some fundamental differences. The basic distinguishing characteristic of the community development model is its orientation toward leisure as a means to a higher goal. The market model turns recreation into an end in itself. This orientation is indicated by the method by which it is evaluated, which is normally through the number of participants and/or the revenues each program generates. Basing the evaluation of the provision of recreation service essentially on the return on investment defines recreation activity simply as a commodity to be purchased and consumed rather than something that leads to a higher human or social goal. Indeed, the marketing approach to recreation typically uses such economic criteria to evaluate effective service delivery, thereby rendering recreation untenable as a means to the greater societal good.

The community development model would change this fundamental notion of municipal recreation as an end to one that views it as a means to a larger goal. Most notably, the goal of municipal recreation would become the enhancement of individual and community functioning and growth. This is the goal arising out of the fundamental principle of the ministers' 1987 statement. The primary focus of the municipal recreation agency would be to assist individuals to develop not only meaningful lives embracing all components and aspects of modern society, but also a strong sense of community. The creation of such meaningful lives would involve a shift from primarily work venues more toward the inclusion of non-work venues, of which leisure is a part, as work becomes more fragmented, as well as a more unrealizable possibility for many, in the postmodern era. Society will need to pay more attention to the increasing numbers of people who are being marginalized from work, which has been the traditional means in defining life satisfaction. New approaches to creating a central life-focus beyond work will need to be developed in the postmodern world, and these approaches would become the primary goal of the municipal recreation department operating under the community development model. In addition, an expanded definition of recreation would be required that included all meaningful non-work activity rather than the limited repertoire of sports, social, and cultural activities that it now embraces.

Professional skills, methods, and strategies for this focus would also be different. This orientation would embrace community development as an approach to *social* development, rather than purely as an approach to economic development, which has been the focus of many of the early community development strategies. The role of the recreation professional will be as a facilitator, centring on creating opportunities for individuals to construct meaningful lives. Hence, leisure needs will be self-determined by the community, and the recreation professional will assist the community in meeting those needs by enabling access to services and facilities, by subsidizing community-based projects, or perhaps by simply providing advice and expertise. Rather than relying on a central agency to determine where gaps in provision may be, the community defines its own needs, thereby giving all individuals, especially those in marginalized groups, the same opportunities to fulfill their needs and, ultimately, to contribute to the community good.

Several examples of the community development model are currently in place in municipalities across Canada. In Saanich, British Columbia, the Community Services Section, which is responsible for leisure services, regards its role as one that 'assist[s] the community to identify and address its needs through citizen and community involvement' (Hutchison and Campbell 1996: 21). To realize this vision, the Section's staff serve as facilitators working directly with community groups to assist them in organizing programs and events that bring the residents together and develop a strong sense of community. Similar initiatives are in place in communities such as Mississauga and Waterloo in Ontario and Richmond in British Columbia. However, even though many such examples exist, a widely recognized set of principles and strategies for the community development model is not in place, which has likely hindered the wide adoption of this model as the prevailing vision of municipal recreation.

With the abdication of this broader function by local government, there is a need for some group in the community to address issues of individual and social development in order to re-balance the present fixation on economic matters in the community. By focusing on these issues, the municipal recreation agency could be that group and could fill a unique and important niche in the postmodern world.

Conclusions

Municipal recreation services are at a crossroads. Governments at all levels are looking to reduce their budgets and to shed some of their functions to the private and voluntary sectors. Municipal recreation departments need to respond to this shift in public policy while minimizing the impact on individuals within their communities. This chapter has presented two of the ways in which this may occur.

We believe that the community development model is the best strategy by which to plan the future development of municipal recreation services. This model views leisure as a means that society can use to assist people to construct a more advanced quality of life as we move into the postmodern world. Its major focus is to reaffirm individual and social goals and then to use leisure and recreation as partial means in attaining these goals. Leisure would no longer be treated as a commodity to be consumed, but rather used as a method of personal and social development. By embracing the community development model, the public recreation agency becomes a facilitator of and advocate for leisure as a public good. The community development model is concerned far more with equity in the provision of leisure services, programs, and facilities than with equality, because equity emerges from principles of fairness and need, rather than from arbitrary standards and demand. Such a perspective helps to ensure that the basic tenet of equal opportunity is extended to all members of the community and not just to those who are able to afford it. Consequently, groups that may have been marginalized by the marketplace, such as the poor, the elderly, or those with disabilities, are enabled as fully participating members of the community striving to enhance the quality of their lives through leisure. Municipal recreation and leisure service provision will be significantly different in the future. The challenge to recreation professionals and policy-makers alike is to avoid the maintenance of the status quo—as successful as some policies have been—and to reconstruct a service that changes with the times.

Career Opportunities in Public Recreation Services

Municipal recreation agencies are increasingly recognized as a human and/or social service, and given the diverse nature of programs and services that these agencies deliver to the public, a variety of areas of training, such as recreation and leisure studies, planning, education, social work, and many of the social sciences, are well suited for preparing individuals for the recreation profession. Nevertheless, an understanding of the subtle but important distinctions between recreation and leisure (as well as play, sport, culture, heritage, and so on), their relationship to health and well-being, and how the relationship can be facilitated within the community is best served by some exposure to the discipline of leisure studies. Several universities in Canada now offer such degree programs, with emphases on recreation management and administration, therapeutic recreation, community development, and outdoor recreation and parks. These programs can be accessed by students in other, complementary, programs of study.

The two dominant operational systems described in this paper—the market model and the community development model—are typically the focus not only of university programs, but also of many municipal recreation agencies, where some blending of both models frequently occurs in the provision of services to the public. Consequently, an emphasis on one or both models of service and program delivery will prepare an individual quite well to work within the public sector. Furthermore, because of the increasingly recognized connection of leisure to other domains of life, preparation in the field of recreation and leisure studies also prepares individuals for most other human service areas.

Notes

1. The terms *leisure* and *recreation* are distinguished in the academic literature, with *leisure* regarded as a higher-order goal, such as a personal state of mind or the free time during which the individual has the freedom to engage in pursuits of personal meaning and fulfillment. *Recreation* is generally regarded as the specific activities and opportunities undertaken during one's free time. Nevertheless, *leisure* and *recreation* are used interchangeably in the chapter, as is commonly the practice in most Canadian municipal departments. Arguably, this lack of distinction between the terms has contributed to the debate over the direction of policy in the urban context.

References

Balmer, Ken R., and Donald G. Reid. 1986. 'Privatizing Responsibility for Parks and Recreation Purposes'. *Recreation Canada* 12(5): 37–43.
Beckers, Theo. 1989. 'Integrating Leisure Policies in Advanced Societies: The Squaring of the Circle'. *Cities for the Future: The Role of Leisure and Tourism in the Process of Revitalization.* Post-Congressbook, Recreatie Reeks Nr. 7. The Hague: Stiching Recreate.
Bramham, Peter, Ian Henry, Hans Mommas, and Hugo van der Poel, eds. 1989. *Leisure and Urban Processes: Critical Studies of Leisure Policy in Western European Cities.* London: Routledge.
Canadian Parks/Recreation Association (CP/RA). 1997. *Benefits of Parks and Recreation Catalogue.* Ottawa: CP/RA.
Carver, Humphrey. 1975. *Compassionate Landscape.* Toronto: University of Toronto Press.
Crompton, John L., and Charles W. Lamb, Jr. 1986. *Marketing Government and Social Services.* New York: John Wiley.
Fitness Canada. *National Recreation Statement.* 1987. Ottawa: Fitness Canada.
Harper, Jack A., and Ken R. Balmer. 1989. 'The Perceived Benefits of Leisure Services: An Exploratory Investigation'. *Loisir et société/Society and Leisure* 12: 171–88.
Henry, Ian. 1988. 'Alternative Futures for the Public Leisure Service'. In *The Future of Leisure Services,* ed. John Benington and Judy White. Essex: Longman.
Hutchison, Peggy, and Julie Campbell. 1996. 'Community Development: Promising Practices in Recreation and Leisure'. *Parks and Recreation Canada* 20: 20–3.
Jorgensen, B. 1995. 'Why You're Poorer Today'. *The Financial Post* (3–5 June).
McConnell, Campbell R., Stanley L. Brue, and W.H. Pope. 1990. *Microeconomics.* Toronto: McGraw-Hill Ryerson.
McFarland, Elsie Marie. 1970. *The Development of Public Recreation in Canada.* Ottawa: Canadian Parks/Recreation Association.
Macpherson, C.B. 1977. *The Life and Times of Liberal Democracy.* Oxford: Oxford University Press.
Murdock, Graham. 1994. 'New Times/Hard Times: Leisure, Participation and the Common Good'. *Leisure Studies* 13: 239–48.
O'Hara, Bruce. 1993. *Working Harder Isn't Working: How We Can Save the Environment, the Economy, and Our Sanity by Working Less and Enjoying Life More.* Vancouver: New Star.
Ontario. Ministry of Tourism and Recreation. 1987. *A Community Recreation Policy Statement.* Toronto: The Ministry.
Parks and Recreation Federation of Ontario. 1992. *The Benefits of Parks and Recreation.* Toronto: Parks and Recreation Federation of Ontario.
Perreault, J. 1990. *Population Projections for Canada, Provinces and Territories: 1989–2011.* Catalogue 91-520 Occasional. Ottawa: Statistics Canada.

Reid, Donald G. 1995. *Work and Leisure in the 21st Century: From Production to Citizenship.* Toronto: Wall and Emerson.

Reid, Donald G., and Elizabeth van Dreunen. 1996. 'Leisure as a Social Transformation Mechanism in Community Development Practice'. *Journal of Applied Recreation Research* 21: 45–65.

Schor, Juliet B. 1991a. *The Overworked American: The Unexpected Decline of Leisure.* New York: Basic Books.

———. 1991b. 'Workers of the World Unwind'. *Technological Review* 94(8): 25–32.

Scott, Graham. 1996. 'The Use of Contracting in the Public Sector'. *Australian Journal of Public Administration* 55(3): 97–104.

Searle, Mark S., and Russell E. Brayley. 1999. *Leisure Services in Canada: An Introduction.* 2nd ed. State College, PA: Venture.

Wright, J.R. 1983. *Urban Parks in Ontario. Part I: Origins to 1860.* Ottawa: University of Ottawa.

———. 1984. *Urban Parks in Ontario. Part II: The Public Park Movement 1860–1914.* Ottawa: University of Ottawa.

Culture, Heritage, and the Arts

Donna Cardinal

Introduction

For most of the past fifty years of the welfare state in Canada, culture and the arts have been relatively uncontested aspects of public policy—when they have received public policy attention at all. At the turn of the twenty-first century, governments at all levels in Canada (and in Europe and Australia) are wrestling with appropriate policy and program responses to rapidly changing, radically diverse societies (Baeker 2000). Previously accepted assumptions underlying the allocation of public resources are now challenged by persons and groups not heretofore considered in the decision-making processes. Municipalities especially, but also the provincial and national levels of government, have looked to publicly debated policies on culture as a way of grounding their decision-making about arts, culture, and heritage. As a consequence, there is a surge in cultural policy-making activity at the local level in Canada.

In this chapter, I will look at the arts and heritage policies of four Canadian municipalities and examine a recent policy process undertaken in each of these communities. We will see that policies in support of arts, culture, and heritage in Vancouver, Edmonton, Toronto, and Halifax differ, although some common threads can be perceived. So too do their approaches to policy-making differ. Differences in policies and policy-making are generally attributed to the distinctiveness of each municipality and their unique historical evolutions. Another explanation may be the relative newness of municipal cultural policy-making as a field of study and practice and the fairly recent emergence of culture onto the public policy agenda at the municipal level. Current initiatives to link municipal culture directors for exchange of information and expertise (Watson 2000) may have a normative effect on municipal approaches to cultural policy and cultural policy-making over time. Such a result may or may not be desirable.

The terms *arts* and *heritage* seem to be used quite consistently across municipalities and provinces, the former to encompass visual, performing, literary, and multimedia symbolic expressions, the latter to encompass museums, archives, historical associations, and those important aspects of the built environment that remind us of our history. Uses of the term *culture*, however, vary across municipalities and among observers. Sometimes *culture* is used synonymously with *arts*; sometimes it includes or exclusively denotes ethnically defined groups and expressions; and sometimes the term encompasses arts, heritage preservation, ethnocultural expressions, libraries, and cultural industries. With the exception that this chapter does not address libraries or cultural industries, it is this broader meaning that I will assign to the word.

Culture and Public Policy in Canada

Cultural activity in Canada is older than the nation (Tippett 1990). Culture as an area of policy activity for governments is more recent. The Constitution Act of 1867 did not assign culture to any jurisdiction; indeed, it did not name culture as a responsibility of governments. Gradually, though, the federal, then provincial, and eventually municipal governments in Canada gave attention to culture as an area of policy activity that might advance various social, economic, and political goals.

Culture emerged onto the federal policy agenda in the late 1920s with the debate over ownership of the airways, a debate that has resurfaced with each advance in broadcast technology. The response of the federal government of the day was to become a standard one for all levels of government confronting cultural policy issues: the establishment of a somewhat arm's-length commission to sound the depth of public preferences and to make recommendations to the government for its consideration. The Royal Commission on Radio, established in 1928 and chaired by Sir John Aird, was the first at the federal level. The best known was the Massey Commission, established in 1949; its principal recommendation, enacted in 1957, was the establishment of the Canada Council for the Arts.

Culture emerged onto the policy agenda in the provinces mid-century. In 1946, Alberta was the first province to create a unit within the administration to support cultural development. In 1948, Saskatchewan established the first arm's-length provincial entity to fund cultural development activity, the Saskatchewan Arts Board. These early steps set the path in each case: Saskatchewan has maintained its Arts Board while adding culture to the responsibilities of the provincial administration; Alberta has maintained culture as a direct governmental responsibility while adding a (ministerially controlled) funding foundation. Ontario created the first provincial arts funding council, the Ontario Arts Council, in 1963. Subsequently, most provinces have created some form of governmental, advisory, or arm's-length body to guide cultural development and allocate cultural funding.

Culture emerged onto the municipal policy agenda more recently. In 1976, the Federation of Canadian Municipalities (FCM) passed a resolution that deemed 'this area of national concern too important to be left solely to provincial and federal governments' and called upon them to 'consult with municipalities on capital and operating expenditures in cultural matters within their jurisdictions, and allocate additional transfers or access to other tax sources that will enable municipal governments to accept their proper responsibilities in this area' (Bailey 1978, cover verso). The resolution also urged upon its member municipalities 'the goal of achieving a minimal annual expenditure [on grant support to cultural institutions] of $1 per capita within the next three years' and proposed that they request 'that provincial support reach $2 per capita and federal support $3 per capita in the same period'. Other clauses in the resolution called for member municipalities to 'bring forth plans for capital and operating development in the cultural sector [and] establish administrative departments to deal with the planning, administration, and operation of cultural activities' (Bailey 1978, cover verso).

Throughout the following decade, repeated calls were heard for municipalities to increase their involvement in the areas of culture, heritage, and the arts. In 1978 and again in 1987, the Canadian Conference of the Arts (CCA), a national arts advocacy organization, made municipalities the focus of its annual conference. Both the Federal Cultural Policy Review Committee (1982) and the Bovey Committee on Financing the Arts in Canada to the Year 2000 (Task Force on the Funding of the Arts in Canada 1986) identified the municipal level as being of increasing importance in the overall picture of public support to culture. In 1984, Statistics Canada began making available cultural statistics for the municipal level, and in 1987, Judith and Tom Hendry initiated a project called Arts and the Cities/Les Arts et la Ville that was designed to collect and make available information about cultural activity from cities across Canada.

After fifteen years of heightened attention to the potential role municipalities might play in cultural development, most municipalities responding to an FCM survey indicated that they had developed policy and support mechanisms to assist arts, culture, and heritage in their communities (FCM 1990). Sixty-four per cent had a council committee, community advisory body, or similar group to provide advice or to deal with programs and funding for arts, culture, and heritage; 79 per cent provided direct cash grants to arts, culture, or heritage groups; 63 per cent provided free or reduced rentals for arts, culture, or heritage groups; 49 per cent had developed procedures, bylaws, or regulations on heritage preservation; and 44 per cent directly operated cultural or heritage facilities, such as a cultural centre, an art gallery, or a historic site. One in three municipalities provided some form of tax relief for arts, culture, or heritage activities; nearly one-third had developed a written cultural plan or set of policies in support of arts, culture, and heritage; and one-quarter had developed procedures, bylaws, or regulations that dealt specifically with arts and culture (FCM 1990). We can conclude that culture was very much on the policy agenda of Canadian municipalities by the early 1990s.

Municipal Cultural Expenditures

Expenditure patterns reflected the growing attention being given to culture at the local level. The same FCM research mentioned above found that across the 168 municipalities responding to the survey, overall per capita expenditures for 1990 were $7.93, with 56 municipalities reporting per capita expenditures over $10, fifteen of these over $20. Those reporting the highest per capita expenditures usually operated major facilities such as museums, cultural centres, or historic sites (FCM 1990), expenditures not included in the 1976 target figures for grant support. Statistics Canada data on municipal cultural expenditures (including libraries, which account for approximately two-thirds of municipal cultural expenditures) indicate that spending increased each year from the mid-1980s through the mid-1990s, with the overall level of increase for the first half of that decade being 15 per cent (Verma 1999). Municipalities were the only level of government showing an increase in support to culture during that time. Federal and provincial/territorial levels of government slowed their support and then decreased it beginning in the mid-1990s (Verma 1998). Statistics Canada figures indicate that municipal expenditure on culture continued to rise for 1994/95 (by 1 per cent), the tenth consecutive year of increases (Statistics Canada 1996) before dropping 0.5 per cent in 1995/96 to $48 per capita (Statistics Canada 1997). A decade of increases raised the municipal share of expenditures on culture by all governments to 24 per cent in 1995/96 (Statistics Canada 1997).

Cultural Plans

The first cultural policies put in place in most municipalities are those authorizing financial support to community cultural organizations and guiding the allocation of that support. Usually, these policies create grant programs and outline criteria for the distribution of the grants; they also often specify who will allocate, or recommend allocations of, these grants. Some of the large municipalities have opted for arm's-length funding arrangements similar to the arts funding councils that exist at the provincial and federal levels. (See the discussion of Toronto and Edmonton later in this chapter.) Vancouver and Halifax, however, have maintained an in-house system of recommending on grant allocations, with final approval by the elected politicians.

In addition to providing operating funds, municipalities might assist, through a variety of mechanisms, in the provision of operating space. A civic government may own and operate cultural facilities; may institute programs of grants to offset rent; may develop grant programs for the construction, renovation, or planning of spaces; may establish policies for forgiveness of taxes on properties used by cultural groups; and may use the municipality's development bylaws and procedures to leverage provision of arts-specific spaces in commercial developments. Toronto and Vancouver practise all of these forms of support; Edmonton and Halifax practise fewer forms of support in the provision of operating space.

Many of the major urban municipalities now have policies to support the creation and placement of art in public places. None of the cities studied in this chapter has a comprehensive cultural plan, and none was under development. However, all have an assortment of policies to guide various aspects of cultural development.

Heritage Conservation

Policies, programs, and practices enabling heritage conservation seem to be well-developed, thoroughly integrated into municipal operations, and fairly consistent across the four municipalities studied. Perhaps this is accounted for by the presence of enabling provincial legislation in every case, by the tangible nature of the heritage being conserved, and by the close ties to planning, with its status as a recognized profession. All four cities have citizen advisory boards involved in the process of designation and have professional staff who review applications for development permits, provide advice to land-owners, and undertake public education. A heritage register in each city identifies buildings of heritage value.

Dedicated Staff
At the time of the FCM's resolution in 1976 and for a decade thereafter, persistent calls were heard for municipalities to hire professionally qualified staff in positions dedicated to arts, culture, and heritage responsibilities. Now, most urban municipalities have dedicated staff positions and qualified professionals filling them. Some municipalities have culture specialists in a number of portfolios, including planning, heritage conservation, economic development, tourism, and leisure and recreation. The new City of Toronto has 125 full-time equivalent positions in the post-amalgamation Culture Division.

Vancouver

Heritage Conservation
The Heritage Register completed in Vancouver's centennial year in 1986 lists over 2,200 buildings, landscapes, monuments, and archeological sites dating from the pre-1940 era. Recently, post-1940s buildings were inventoried for the Recent Landmarks Program, and City staff are now giving attention to identifying and cataloguing heritage interiors. Since 1971, 175 Vancouver properties have been municipally designated and 200 provincially designated.

The City's stated long-term goal is to 'protect through voluntary designation as many resources on the heritage inventory as possible' (City of Vancouver, Planning Department 1992). The City may initiate designation of buildings of 'extraordinary merit', in which case it will address the question of compensation to the owner. Generally, however, the City relies on relaxations of various bylaws to provide incentives to land-owners to conserve and designate the registered buildings. These relaxations may be with respect to parking, building height, floor-space ratio, changes of use, and/or density. They are provided only in exchange for designation of the building.

Vancouver's heritage density bonus and density transfer program are the most liberal and flexible in North America (Robert Lemon, personal interview, 24 August 1995). Because decisions about heritage conservation are integrated into planning, the full weight of the civic administrative machinery and processes are available to support the goal of heritage conservation. In 2000, Vancouver amended the city's building code to permit more flexibility for designated buildings, and it is piloting tax incentives as an additional policy mechanism for encouraging heritage preservation and designation (Yardley McNeill, personal interview, 5 April 2000).

Arts Development

Vancouver's first grant to an arts organization was in 1893, when the City Band requested a grant for its summer concert series. Now Vancouver invests close to $6.5 million annually in over 120 local non-profit arts organizations through its cultural grants programs. Project and operating grants are allocated by city council on recommendation from the staff of the Office of Cultural Affairs.[1] Vancouver provides use of three municipally owned theatres in lieu of a grant to designated arts organizations and also makes grants to groups that perform occasionally in the civic theatres. Incentive grants encourage arts groups to undertake staff training, organizational development, and training in cultural diversity. Capital grants assist in facility purchase, construction, renovation, or expansion. Vancouver provides free advertising space in bus shelters.

An incremental approach to cultural policy has been successful in Vancouver. Council responds well to very specific policies, action plans, and programs that address clearly identifiable, measurable needs (Burke Taylor, personal interview, 24 August 1995). When a concern for acknowledging and responding to cultural diversity was recognized, a Cross Cultural Initiatives Program and the MAATSEN Equity Training Program were developed, and the Office of Cultural Affairs began to communicate its programs and services more effectively to specific cultural communities. When a concern was recognized regarding the lack of and ad hoc placement of art in public places, three programs were developed and submitted for city council approval, including one that requires major new private developments to allocate $0.95 per foot to public art. When a concern was identified regarding the lack of funding available to individual artists (Vancouver's charter prohibits support to individuals), city council approved the creation of the Vancouver Arts Endowment, subject to developing the ways and means. When concern was raised regarding the lack of financial stability in arts organizations, the municipality responded to overtures from the Vancouver Foundation, becoming a participant (along with senior levels of government and the private sector) in the Vancouver Arts Stabilization Program.

An amenity bonusing program similar to the heritage bonusing program has been applied effectively to the City's goal of 'ensur[ing] the existence of adequate facilities for the participation, creation and presentation of the arts in Vancouver' (City of Vancouver, Office of Cultural Affairs 1998). Organizations such as the Canadian Craft Museum, the Greater Vancouver Alliance for Arts and Culture, and the Vancouver Community Arts Council have benefited. In the mid-1990s, in response to community-identified needs for a mid-size concert and production hall and a smaller, flexible studio theatre, the municipality secured from a developer, through the rezoning process, a waterfront site and a $7.5 million capital contribution toward construction of such a facility. Describing the project, the Director of the Office of Cultural Affairs observed that 'this City has been very conscious of the ability of land use economics to advance public interest goals' (Burke Taylor, personal interview, 24 August 1995). Other facility needs have been met through the capital budgeting process, the provision of city-owned land, direct capital grants for facilities (now a separate line in the capital budget), and the heritage density bonusing program.

Because Vancouver's land costs continue to escalate, policy action encouraging affordable artist live/work studios is one area of arts facility development that continues to be problematic.[2] The City recently initiated a bonusing program for affordable housing; the first such bonus secured was an artist live/work studio. The City makes this studio available as a City of Vancouver Artist Residency Award; a second award was added in 1999.

Vancouver Arts Initiative

Vancouver was one of several Canadian cities to undertake a public consultation regarding culture during the 1990s. The Vancouver Arts Initiative task force appointed by city council consisted of the mayor, two councillors, and twelve citizens who were artists, arts administrators, business representatives, and interested persons. Its mandate was fourfold: to look at the state of the arts in Vancouver; to develop strategy to address current federal, provincial, and regional funding imbalances; to undertake a review of the public perception of the arts in the city; and to recommend ways to improve community awareness of and participation in the arts.

The task force consulted directly with 150 organization representatives, individual artists, and other citizens, as well as inviting written responses from 600 persons and hosting public meetings. Its report, entitled *Toward the Creative City* (Vancouver Arts Initiative 1993), contained twenty-three recommendations. City council referred the report to the administration for review by an interdepartmental group. The review supported adoption of several of the recommendations that could be implemented within existing resources, advised further study on others in order to 'fully inform Council on the feasibility and resource implications of the specific initiatives' (City of Vancouver 1993), and recommended priorities for immediate staff action. These priorities focused staff resources on the recommendations dealing with accessibility/equity, arts and youth, the relationship between arts organizations/ artists and civic government departments, facility priorities, overtures to other funding jurisdictions, and the creation of a Vancouver Arts Endowment as a means to provide funding to individual artists.

Although the city council's intention had been to create a task-specific group to address matters requiring policy attention, the participants offered 'more than concrete solutions to today's challenges. They also shared their broader vision for the future of the arts in Vancouver. What emerged was a vision of Vancouver's potential as a creative city: a city where the arts are valued as highly as the natural beauty that surrounds it' (Vancouver Arts Initiative 1993: 2).

The timing of the Vancouver Arts Initiative was such that this broader vision and the concrete recommendations giving it substance found their way almost immediately into Vancouver's first comprehensive plan since the 1930s. CityPlan was itself a widely consultative process, one that had as its focus the future of the entire city. Commissioned in 1992, CityPlan was adopted by city council as a draft document in 1995 'as a broad vision for the city, to guide policy decisions, corporate priorities, budgets and capital plans' (n.p.). The creative city emerges as a clear theme in *CityPlan: Directions for Vancouver*: 'Vancouverites want art and culture to contribute more to their city's identity, their neighbourhoods' character, and their own learning and self-expression' (City of Vancouver 1995: 24). Subsets of this theme emphasize broadening art and culture activity at the neighbourhood level, respect for the diverse cultural heritage of the city, and joint programming among civic departments, the School Board, the Parks Board, and the Library Board. Protecting heritage structures is seen as an aspect of maintaining and enhancing the distinctive character of a neighbourhood in a city form based around neighbourhood centres. Here we see the justifications offered for arts and heritage at the city level being reprised at an intra-city level: cultural tourism, city image, quality of life, participation, respect for differences, and social cohesion.

By the end of the 1990s, Vancouver had turned its attention to two pressing matters. One was the disproportionate share of the bill for cultural amenities and activities being carried by the City itself, even though the benefits accrued equally to the surrounding twenty-one municipalities. The other was the disproportionate share of the total public investment in culture in Vancouver being paid for by the municipality in comparison with the investments by the two senior levels of government. A steering committee for a regional cultural plan was at work from 1997 through 1999 commissioning studies and formulating strategies to address these two imbalances.

Edmonton

Edmonton was another of Canada's urban municipalities that initiated a cultural policy process during the 1990s. A number of cultural policy issues were percolating in Edmonton at that time. Dissatisfaction was increasing over the City's process for allocating arts and cultural grants and over the lack of increases in the grants budget (Mahon 2000). Detailed guidelines for art in public places were being developed to supplement the 'per cent for art' policy (a requirement that a fixed percentage of construction cost be devoted to art), which had been the centre of successive controversies since it was approved in 1992. Changes in provincial legislation opened up a complex discussion on forgiveness of municipal taxes to non-profit organizations, including cultural organizations, prompting a review of the variety of lease-subsidy arrangements practised by the municipality. A provincial government review of the distribution of lottery revenues was recommending that a percentage of lottery revenues flow to each local community on a per capita basis for distribution by local lottery boards to community priorities, including arts and culture. An arts district was proposed in the downtown plan review, an arts housing survey was undertaken, a heritage master plan was about to be published, and the general municipal plan was scheduled for revision.

Edmonton Task Force on Investment in the Arts

With increasing conviction and determination, the professional arts community in Edmonton had called for a separate, arm's-length funding body. An autonomous funding council for the arts was the principal recommendation of *Building Creative Capital* (Mayor's Task Force on Investment in the Arts 1994), the report of the 1995

Mayor's Task Force on Investment in the Arts. The mandate of the task force was fivefold: to review existing research relating to the role of the arts in Edmonton's community and economy, to examine the role of all levels of government in relation to the arts, to recommend funding strategies to develop the arts in Edmonton, to evaluate different models for funding and promoting the arts, and to address specific policy issues identified in previous studies on the arts in Edmonton.

The task force, anticipating the usual referral to the civic administration, recommended to city council the composition of a transition planning team and showed council how the operating budget of the proposed arts council might be assembled from existing municipal resources. The planning team reported back to city council that it agreed that the proposed arts council would best be structured as a non-profit organization under the Societies Act of Alberta, governed by a board of directors; the team also suggested mechanisms for city council representation. With office space pledged by a business partner, staff positions available to be seconded from Parks and Recreation, names of persons willing to sit on an interim board, and surplus municipal budget funds identified to cover the balance of a first year's operations, city council agreed to a one-year pilot project.

During that first year, the Edmonton Arts Council left granting responsibilities with the Parks, Recreation and Cultural Advisory Board and applied its personnel and financial resources to non-granting priorities. These included some of the strategies recommended by the task force: increasing the profile, recognition, and awareness of the arts as a vital component of the economy and community; increasing the investment base for the arts through partnerships with business and all levels of government; developing recommendations to city council regarding the future of municipal funding for the arts; providing support services for Edmonton's arts and cultural community; and establishing a long-term business plan and a fully defined structure for the Edmonton Arts Council in consultation with the arts community (Edmonton Arts Council 1995). Although the city council to which the Edmonton Arts Council reported at the end of the pilot year was a substantially altered one—six of the twelve councillors and the mayor were replaced in the November 1995 municipal elections—the Edmonton Arts Council was confirmed as the channel for delivering municipal funding support to the arts. The single-mindedness of the Mayor's Task Force in focusing on and pressing for an arts council and the endorsement by the community of this model resulted in the creation of a new structure for support of the arts in Edmonton. As it turned out, the Edmonton Arts Council has been able to achieve in its first three years many of the goals formulated for it by the task force.

Arts Development

Under an agreement with the City, the Arts Council appoints peer juries, which recommend allocations to festivals ($887,000 in 2000) and arts organizations ($767,000 in 2000). In the first three years, city council has endorsed the Arts Council's recommendations without modification. Discussions are underway to have the City assign grant funds to the Arts Council for disbursement directly to recipient organizations.

When this happens, Edmonton will be one of only a few municipal jurisdictions to distribute arts funding through an autonomous, arm's-length body. (Toronto is another; see later in this chapter.) The Arts Council has been effective in its first few years in raising the profile of the arts in Edmonton and of Edmonton arts and artists beyond the city. It formed partnerships with private- and public-sector organizations to create affordable live/work spaces for artists, to delineate and promote an arts district, and to establish a same-day rush ticket outlet downtown. Most important, the Arts Council has managed to increase the funds available to the arts in Edmonton and to begin several new grant programs. These increases have been realized partly through an increase in the annual municipal budget allocation, partly through having grant funds transferred to the Arts Council at the start of the year and invested until distributed and partly through partnering with the Edmonton Community Foundation to create the Edmonton Artists' Trust Fund, an endowment from which interest earnings are allocated annually as awards to individual artists. And although it is a seemingly small matter, the arts community has also been pleased that the Arts Council was able to effect a change in name from 'Grant in Aid' to 'Community Investment'.

Heritage Conservation

The Register of Historic Resources in Edmonton was completed in 1993 and identifies 437 of Edmonton's most significant buildings. Buildings and bridges listed in the Register are all considered worthy of designation and preservation; to date, eight have been designated by municipal bylaws. Provincial legislation requires municipalities to compensate owners of designated Municipal Historic Resources if the designation results in a loss in property value (Alberta 1992, Section 24). Compensation is to be 'in the form of a tax cancellation or rebate of property taxes, or a payment to the builder's owner equal to the value of the amount of taxes payable on a building, transfer of land use density, relaxation of parking, loading and amenity requirements, land transfers or any other means' (Edmonton 1989, Section 1, Item 1.2).

Although the capacity—and requirement—to compensate owners is envied by some other municipalities, the Edmonton approach has limitations. The tax policy is not as effective in instances in which an owner is exempt from paying property taxes, as with schools, churches, and municipally owned heritage resources. Also, the compensation approach means that designation and preservation cost money, which the City must budget on an annual basis. Edmonton is now investigating other means to assist owners with the ongoing cost of building rehabilitation and maintenance through such mechanisms as grant programs for residential and other properties; it is also considering new policies that provide non-monetary incentives, such as wider latitude of uses for buildings on the Register.

Toronto

The pivotal event of the 1990s in Toronto was the amalgamation of six municipalities and the regional government into a new City of Toronto. In Toronto's civic government machinery prior to the amalgamation, one searched in vain for a single locus of cultural policy-making and implementation.[3] Instead, the City of Toronto had adopted a distributed approach to cultural responsibilities. A Public Art Commission Office in the Planning and Development department was responsible for the 'per cent for art' policy—a one per cent art contribution for all major, privately owned development proposals. The Commission also oversaw the portion of the City's capital budget allocated to municipally sponsored public-art initiatives. The Protocol Office was responsible for programming Nathan Phillips Square, and the City Clerk's Office ran the Market Gallery. Parks and Recreation did cultural programming, as did the Toronto Historical Board. The City operated three theatres and the City of Toronto Book Award competition. An independent organization, the Toronto Arts Council (TAC), channelled municipal funds to local arts organizations and artists.

In the amalgamation, cultural affairs, arts services, museum services, and heritage preservation services were brought together in the Culture Division of the Department of Economic Development, Culture and Tourism. The Culture Division works in close partnership with a wide range of agencies, boards, commissions, and advisory bodies in the cultural sector. It is structured in such a way that administration, policy, and planning are centralized, while delivery of services is distributed, providing 'points of contact at the community level' and allowing programs and services to reflect the diversity and uniqueness of the former municipalities now making up the new City (Toronto n.d.: 24).

Arts Development

The TAC and the principle of arm's-length funding for arts and culture survived amalgamation. In anticipation of amalgamation, the TAC had initiated an extensive consultation with the arts and cultural sectors of the six municipalities and the Metro government. Their deliberations resulted in a statement of beliefs held in common about the future of the arts in the new City of Toronto. One of these beliefs was that there should be a central arts administrative framework that would include appropriate structures to deal with arts issues locally. The TAC recommended that funding in the new City of Toronto be administered through an arm's-length model (Toronto Arts Council 1997). This recommendation was adopted, and in 1999, the TAC assumed responsibility for allocating arts grants to eligible organizations and individuals throughout the former area municipalities. Responsibility for funding of the major arts organizations remains for the time being with the Culture Division, although discussions have begun concerning moving these groups to the Arts Council (A. Bermonte, personal interview, 6 April 2000).

Since 1974, the TAC has had a mandate to advise Toronto City Council on cultural policy matters and to make recommendations on the allocation of civic grants to the arts. The relationship between the Arts Council and the former City of Toronto was transformed from advisory to autonomous through a grants agreement executed in 1994 that provided for the Arts Council to receive the cultural grants allotment from the City annually and to distribute it directly to the recipient organizations and individuals without city council ratifying the specific allocations.[4] The grants agreement between the TAC and the City of Toronto 'safeguard[s] the principle of arm's length and the process of peer panel review of grants' and defined an arm's-length arts body as one that 'operates by interposing between government and the arts themselves a body of instructed and knowledgeable people, independent of government' (Toronto 1994: 2). The document also affirms that the majority of members of the board of directors would at all times be working artists. Twenty years after the creation of the Toronto Cultural Advisory Corporation (the legal name of the entity that operates as the TAC), it had formally negotiated with the City the autonomy that it had always envisioned for itself. The arm's-length relationship has been maintained in the current partnership between the TAC and the new City of Toronto.

The grants program administered by the TAC is multi-faceted and continually evolving. Operating and project grants are available to professional and community-based non-profit organizations and collectives. Cultural Facilities Support Grants for the renovation of owned or leased premises, the purchase of an existing building, or the acquisition of land that may include construction of a building are available to small and medium-sized non-profit organizations eligible to receive operating grants from the Arts Council.

The TAC has led the way in developing programs of assistance to individual artists in response to needs identified within and by the cultural communities. Grants are made available to choreographers, composers, visual artists, and writers. Criteria, maximum grant amounts, and eligible projects vary by discipline; however, all grants to individuals are recommended by juries of peers made up of practising artists in the discipline category and appointed by the relevant discipline committee. A full program review and a needs assessment were conducted by the TAC in the summer of 1999 to ensure that TAC programs would appropriately serve the needs of its expanded client base.

Although direct grant funds from the former municipalities were transferred to the TAC, none of the resources for administration were. Nor was there any increase in funding, although the population base to be served quadrupled. As a consequence, TAC's priorities post-amalgamation were to secure the funds needed to administer its programs to an expanded client base, to increase the funds available to individual artists from all former municipalities, and to address geographic and historical funding inequities across the entire region. Some of those inequities had been brought into sharp relief several years earlier during a policy consultation undertaken by the TAC on the subject of cultural diversity.

Cultural Equity and CultureForce

The changing ethnocultural makeup of Toronto's population has been evident to the people involved with the TAC for many years, as has their awareness that the composition of the Arts Council's staff, board, committees, and juries had not been keeping pace with that change (Tom Hendry, personal interview, 9 September 1995). In 1989, the board commissioned 'a comprehensive examination of artistic communities underserved by TAC and the reasons behind this exclusion. Above all, the Council wanted to have advice on action to be taken so that the Toronto Arts Council would be—and would be seen to be—no longer part of a problem, but part of a solution' (Julian 1992: 1). The consultative process involved both internal and external reviews; that is, it involved access to decision-making meetings at all levels within the organization as well as participation in regular TAC public consultation meetings. In addition, special intra-cultural consultations were arranged to garner the views of specific cultural communities not yet served by the Toronto Arts Council. The resulting report recommended 'that Cultural Equity be achieved at the TAC through policies of inclusion and through all-inclusive funding programs, [and] through equitable representation in the decision-making process' (Julian 1992: 2). The report did not recommend that any 'dedicated' funding programs be implemented at that time.

A number of specific recommendations addressed aspects of the TAC's functioning that were seen to be hindering access to its programs by specific cultural communities. The TAC was encouraged to communicate more effectively, even to the point of 'finding the resources necessary to assist artists for whom language itself is a barrier to application and information' (Julian 1992: 27). Other recommendations exhorted the TAC to add to its committees and juries people from specific cultural communities, although the report did not call for quotas in this regard. The board of the TAC, while cautioning that current economic conditions might not permit the expansion of budgets called for, essentially endorsed all of the recommendations of the report and adopted for itself a policy and principles of cultural equity.

Moving to operationalize its cultural equity policy, the TAC initiated almost immediately a project designed to increase the mutual awareness and engagement of the TAC and specific cultural communities, beginning with Black/African, Asian, and First Nations communities. By all accounts, the project, entitled 'CultureForce', was a remarkable success.[5] Funds were made available to build up the infrastructure within each community, but without dictating how that was to happen. Instead, trust was placed in the knowledge, wisdom, and experience of those comprising each community. In addition to funds and expertise, other facets of CultureForce addressed intra- and inter-community education and networking needs. All the while, information was flowing back to the TAC—information about people, practices, strengths, and needs, and also about opportunities to make the mandate and resources of the Council known in a wider community than had been served to date. The TAC and the various communities were being demystified for each other. Individuals from specific cultural communities emerged who could be invited to sit on the board, committees, and juries of the Council, thus advancing other goals of the cultural equity policy.

CultureForce was a project of limited duration that addressed itself to artists and infrastructures in three specific cultural communities. Although it eloquently illustrated the need for the democratization of cultural policy, the pilot project did not translate into ongoing programs of involvement and integration. Nevertheless, CultureForce stands as a demonstration of what can be done in response to rapidly diversifying demographics in Canada's urban municipalities and as a call to other cities to reconsider arts and cultural policies and institutions that still favour predominately white artists and audiences of British background.

Heritage Conservation

Prior to amalgamation, the Toronto Inventory of Heritage Properties listed 5,000 buildings, structures, and sites, of which approximately 1,000 were designated by council bylaws under the Ontario Heritage Act. Toronto had a familiar array of incentives available to encourage property owners to retain and reuse buildings listed in the Inventory: designated property grants, density bonuses, parking and loading exemptions, and other incentives that could vary according to location and use. Throughout the 1980s, density bonuses and density transfers were important instruments for encouraging voluntary conservation of heritage buildings. In 1991, the City of Toronto revamped its Official Plan, disallowing density transfers. Dissatisfaction with density bonusing and transfer practices was one of a number of issues that gave impetus to revising the heritage section of the plan. Other issues were the desire to include archeological concerns, which are now in the plan for the first time; the need for an overall heritage master plan for the city; and dissatisfaction with 'façadism', the practise of keeping a façade and permitting the demolition of the rest of the building or structure. Although the Official Plan called for the development of an overall heritage master plan, no significant work had been done on it for lack of resources (Richard Stromberg, personal interview, 15 September 1995).

With amalgamation (see Sancton's chapter), heritage conservation responsibilities in Toronto were brought under the umbrella of the newly created Culture Division. In December 1998, the council of the new City of Toronto instructed the Commissioner of Economic Development, Culture and Tourism to develop an implementation strategy for the delivery of heritage services. The strategy subsequently adopted by council set in place a structure made up of successive layers of Local Architectural Conservation Advisory Committees (LACACs). Each Community Council area would have a Community LACAC Panel represented on the city's official LACAC, to be known as the Toronto Preservation Board (Toronto n.d.). Staff for the Preservation Board are to be seconded from the City.

Halifax

Earlier than Toronto, Halifax experienced a municipal amalgamation, bringing together the former Cities of Halifax and Dartmouth, the County of Halifax (with a population larger than the City of Halifax), the Town of Bedford, and the regional authority into the Halifax Regional Municipality (see Sancton's chapter). Culture was not a priority in planning for the merger (Richard Matthews, personal interview, September 1995), and discussions aimed at bringing heritage conservation and arts and cultural development under the same umbrella at the time of the amalgamation did not succeed (Daniel Norris, personal interview, 15 June 2000). However, amalgamation brought together a critical mass of people and energy from the formerly separate municipalities into a new Tourism, Culture and Heritage unit that has been able to break a long-standing log-jam in the way of municipal leadership in arts, culture, and heritage.

Heritage Conservation

Halifax passed its Heritage Property Ordinance (No. 174) in 1981, establishing an advisory committee and a heritage registry. The Halifax List of Heritage Resources consists of 24 landmarks, 11 historic sites, and approximately 360 registered properties. Only the exterior appearance of registered heritage buildings is controlled by the ordinance. The heritage resources section of the Municipal Development Plan provides for other means by which Halifax might meet its heritage objective of preserving and enhancing 'areas, sites, structures, streetscapes and conditions in Halifax which reflect the City's past historically and/or architecturally' (City of Halifax 1995: 21). These include considering the acquisition of registered properties whenever acquisition is the most appropriate means to ensure their preservation; maintaining a data bank on heritage conservation methods, costs, sources of funding, techniques, methods, and materials for use by the City and in encouraging private-sector involvement in heritage conservation; and committing the City, in the purchase or lease of space for its own use, to first consider accommodation in designated heritage structures (City of Halifax 1995: II:23).

Arts Development

Prior to the amalgamation on 1 April 1996, Halifax had provided limited funding to the arts ($51,870 in 1992, to twelve performing arts groups) as part of a program to support not-for-profit organizations offering cultural, artistic, recreational, social, or health-related programs. With the amalgamation, a larger, more comprehensive grants policy was put in place, providing $350,000 in operating grants to community organizations in culture, arts, heritage, and tourism. Through the capital portion of the program, $500,000 was allocated to Pier 21, a museum of immigration history. In addition, the City has contributed $2.9 million to a new Downtown Dartmouth Plaza, which incorporates a 350-seat theatre and an outdoor performance plaza. The new Tourism, Culture and Heritage division created within the Department of Tourism in 1998 has worked with two community groups housed in heritage buildings to further goals of heritage promotion and arts and cultural development. A program is under development that will cross-promote heritage and tourism. In the fall of 1999, Halifax published a book celebrating the many communities that make up Halifax and the families who founded them (Withrow 1999), and in the spring of 2000, it launched the first Mayor's Award for Cultural Achievement. Plans are being made to develop a policy for arts and culture as a way for the municipality to provide leadership and direction, including leadership in developing criteria and involving staff in review of grants to cultural groups. These developments go a long way toward realizing the goals of repeated community consultations that had failed to yield direct results.

Mayor's Advisory Committee to Promote the Arts

The most recent municipally sponsored public consultation on the arts and culture in Halifax was the 1992 Mayor's Advisory Committee to Promote the Arts. Its mandate was 'to develop municipal policies and mechanisms to encourage and support the creative, literary, visual and performing arts; and to advise on policies and procedures for providing civic grants to the arts' (Mayor's Advisory Committee to Promote the Arts 1993: 1). The committee's *Report and Recommendations* are brief: five pages of text, plus appendices. Its research and meeting process was equally streamlined: the committee met ten times, reviewed arts and cultural policies and levels of grants and funding in a selection of Canadian municipalities, and formulated four recommendations supported by suggestions for implementation or by examples. The principal recommendation was that the municipality increase its support to the arts to 1.5 per cent of the gross municipal operating budget by 1998/99 (from 0.7 per cent in 1992). Support for arts facilities development was urged; the municipality was called upon to encourage, foster, and implement programs in the arts, including new initiatives in partnership with existing arts organizations; and an arts advisory committee was proposed to make recommendations to city council on arts policy, programs, facilities, and funding. The advisory committee's responsibilities would include implementing aspects of the grant program.

The response of the administration at the time was non-support for the target funding levels or for any implementation role for an arts advisory committee in the grants process. The entire review was put on hold pending regional amalgamation. Subsequently, two full-scale consultations have taken place initiated by the arts community with, again, no response forthcoming from the municipal government. However, in the early actions of the Tourism, Heritage and Culture division, we see many of the directions recommended by the Mayor's Advisory Committee and subsequent community conferences.

Future Challenges

Just as the Aird Commission report provides us with a snapshot of cultural policy issues and responses as they were in 1929, so too do each of the cultural enquiries surveyed above give us a picture of recent municipal policy concerns and preferred policy responses. Some of the issues are shared across all four—and perhaps many other—municipalities. These shared issues, and the trends fuelling them, are likely to dominate municipal cultural policy agendas in the coming decade.

Regional collaboration in some form was on the agenda of all of the cities studied. (See Sancton's chapter on metropolitan and regional governance.) Indeed, amalgamations occurred in two of the four municipalities during the preparation of this chapter, and Vancouver initiated activity toward the development of a regional cultural strategic plan for the Greater Vancouver Regional District. Montreal has been a model of regional support to culture since 1980.[6]

As new modes of regional collaboration are being explored, relationships between municipalities and their provincial governments are also being redefined. Perhaps the biggest impetus for this redefinition is the reduction in transfer payments by provinces seeking to balance their budgets. With these reductions coming at the same time as reductions in provincial and federal programs of direct support to arts, culture, and heritage, the decrease in funds available to these areas could be considerable. Concurrently, new possibilities for municipal–provincial partnerships in supporting cultural activities are being explored. One example of this is the Alberta initiative to distribute lottery revenues to municipalities on a per capita basis, with allocations being made by local leaders in accordance with local priorities.

Renegotiating relationships among municipal governments in a regional arena, and between municipalities and the parent government, may be part of an emerging effort by municipalities to identify and activate new sources of funds. (See Siegel's chapter on urban finance.) Taxes levied on hotel accommodation and earmarked for cultural spending are an example of a source being used by some municipalities. Arts communities will find both allies and competitors in this push toward identifying new municipal funding sources; their innovative ideas may be welcomed now more than in the past.

Several demographic trends are also bringing cultural issues into focus on municipal policy agendas. (See Foot's chapter on urban demographics.) The most pronounced of these is the aging of the baby-boom generation, with its attendant demands for increased cultural programs and facilities. Higher levels of education are a contributor to the same demand. Another important demographic shift already having an impact on municipal policy is the increased ethnocultural diversity of our major urban centres and, especially, a highly diverse and fast-growing youth population resulting from differential birth rates for specific cultural communities. These phenomena have implications for every urban area in Canada and in many policy arenas besides culture, heritage, and the arts.

An increased attention by knowledge-based industries to quality-of-life considerations in their decisions about location and a growing recognition of the value of arts and heritage conservation to economic development and urban revitalization are helping to push cultural issues to the forefront of the municipal agenda. The value of the arts to a knowledge-based economy includes the capacity for creativity, innovation, and entrepreneurship that makes for a competitive workforce. More important, these same qualities make for a citizenry able to engage in constructive dialogue, in societal problem solving, and in building shared identity and meaning in their lives. One occasion for this was the Kitchener CulturePlan project, in which the public policy process itself provided a new political space wherein residents experienced themselves as citizens. They articulated connections among public life, public decision-making, city-building, and the arts as follows:

> The meaningfulness of public life is important to us, and underlies a yearning to be more involved in public decision making. The arts and artists generate symbols of our lives in their work, and invite us to respond. . . . We see that the arts provide an avenue for relating to our city as a collective entity and participating in its re-creation decision by decision. (Kitchener 1996: 4)

Our century of experience in public policy-making for culture in Canada has brought us to a threshold where we might make the leap in our local governance from viewing the arts and heritage as isolated elements of human activity to seeing culture as an integral part of our community life in all its dimensions. This could become the function of cultural policy at the municipal level as we enter the new century. As Franco Bianchini writes in his conclusion to *Cultural Policy and Urban Regeneration: The West European Experience*,

> Making the advancement of local democracy and citizenship rights a central priority for cultural policies in the 1990s and adopting a cultural planning perspective would involve the rethinking of many of the assumptions upon which the policy-making process was based during the last decade. To start with . . . there would have to be a change in the notion of 'quality of life' adopted by policy-makers, from that as a commodity to be marketed as an element of urban competitiveness, to quality of life determined by how residents relate to their city as a collective entity, and how they participate in its public life. (1993: 210–11)

Careers in Arts, Culture, and Heritage Administration

Career opportunities in arts, culture, and heritage administration are increasing at the municipal level. Most urban municipalities and many smaller ones now employ specialists in cultural planning, arts development, and heritage planning.

Career preparation for these positions varies. For heritage planning, possible routes include education in planning, architecture, and public administration. For arts development, the study of general arts, fine arts, education, and planning might all be appropriate. Additionally, there are close to a dozen college and university programs in arts and cultural management and administration in Canada. The college programs might be combined with a university degree as a possible route into arts management and/or cultural administration. Management experience in a producing arts organization (theatre, gallery, museum, orchestra, choir, dance company, etc.) or in the cultural industries would stand one in good stead when applying for a position in the government sector; experience in private-sector conservation and restoration would do the same for a position in a government heritage portfolio. For arts and cultural development and planning positions, salaries within government tend to be higher than those in the not-for-profit sector for positions requiring equivalent training and experience.

Notes

1. Despite the preference of arts communities in most jurisdictions to have arm's-length entities adjudicating cultural grants, the Vancouver process of grants adjudicated by staff seems to satisfy all parties. Final authority rests with the elected officials, review and recommendations are provided by staff with knowledge of the arts and the groups applying, and administrative costs are kept to a minimum. Should the municipality, through the Vancouver Arts Endowment, begin making grants to individual artists, a peer-assessment process would be put in place (Burke Taylor, personal interview, 24 August 1995).
2. In the late 1980s, bylaw relaxations were permitted in order to encourage the upgrade of industrial buildings where the production of arts was combined with

ancillary residential use. The resultant studios were primarily rental renovations in industrial and downtown historic districts. Petitioned by the development community in 1992, city council granted the same relaxations for new, purpose-built condominium developments. While a significant number have been built, the resultant live/work studios were beyond the financial means of many of the artists to whom the original initiative was targeted and caused surrounding land values to escalate (Burke Taylor, personal interview, 24 August 1995).

3. There was, briefly, a position of cultural affairs officer, established in the fall of 1991 and fulfilling one of the recommendations of *Cultural Capital*, the 1985 enquiry into the state of the arts in Toronto. However, the position was eliminated three months after it was established and was not restored.

4. This change made the City of Toronto the second municipal jurisdiction in Canada to work this way. The Calgary Region Arts Foundation has been functioning in this manner since its inception in 1976; it receives an annual allocation from Calgary City Council, which it dispenses directly to the recipient organizations from its own bank account, without any requirement to seek Council endorsement for the specific allocations.

5. For a complete description of CultureForce by its coordinator, see Fernandez (1994); for an external assessment, see Fraticelli (1994).

6. In Montreal, all support to cultural development is channelled through the Communauté urbaine de Montréal, a regional corporation covering a territory made up of twenty-nine municipalities located on the islands of Montreal, Bizard, and Dorval. The Conseil des arts de la communauté urbaine de Montréal was established as a permanent commission of the Communauté in 1980, with a mandate to harmonize, coordinate, and encourage artistic and cultural initiatives in all member municipalities. It provides general financial aid to organizations involved in dance, literature, music, theatre, and visual arts, as well as a development fund to support activities of an innovative nature. The focus of many of the Conseil programs is to heighten awareness and improve accessibility to the arts across all member municipalities and particularly to cultivate the audiences of tomorrow.

References

Alberta. 1992. 'Historical Resources Act'. *Revised Statutes of Alberta 1980*. Edmonton: Queen's Printer for Alberta.

Baeker, Greg. 2000. *Cultural Policy and Cultural Diversity in Canada*. Ottawa: Strategic Research and Analysis Directorate, Department of Canadian Heritage.

Bailey, Robert. 1978. *Rapport: The Arts, People, and Municipalities*. Toronto: Canadian Conference of the Arts

Bianchini, Franco. 1993. 'Culture, Conflict and Cities: Issues and Prospects for the 1990s'. In *Cultural Policy and Urban Regeneration: The West European Experience*, ed. Franco Bianchini and Michael Parkinson. Manchester, UK: Manchester University Press.

City of Halifax. 1995. *Municipal Development Plan for the City of Halifax. Part II (unofficial copy) Heritage Policies Only.* Halifax: City of Halifax.

City of Vancouver. 1993. 'Policy Report: Culture'. Report to City Council by the Director of Social Planning. (14 October).

———. 1995. *CityPlan: Directions for Vancouver.* Vancouver: City of Vancouver.

City of Vancouver. Office of Cultural Affairs. 1998. 'Arts Report 97'. (April).

City of Vancouver. Planning Department. 1992. 'Heritage Policies and Guidelines'. Photocopy. (June).

Edmonton. 1989. 'Municipal Policy C-450A, A Policy to Encourage the Designation and Rehabilitation of Municipal Historic Resources in Edmonton'. Edmonton: City of Edmonton.

Edmonton Arts Council. 1995. 'Goals and Objectives'. Edmonton: Edmonton Arts Council.

Federal Cultural Policy Review Committee (Canada). 1982. *Report of the Federal Cultural Policy Review Committee.* Ottawa: Information Services, Department of Communications, Government of Canada.

Federation of Canadian Municipalities (FCM). 1990. *Survey of Municipal Expenditures on Arts, Culture and Heritage.* Ottawa: FCM.

Fernandez, Sharon. 1994. *CultureForce.* Toronto: Toronto Arts Council.

Fraticelli, R. 1994. *CultureForce: An Assessment.* Toronto: Toronto Arts Council.

Julian, E.A. 1992. *Cultural Equity.* Toronto: Toronto Arts Council.

Kitchener. 1996. *CulturePLAN: A Cultural Strategic Plan for Kitchener.* Kitchener, ON: Arts and Culture Advisory Committee.

Mahon, John. 2000. 'Development of the Edmonton Arts Council: A Case Study'. Paper presented at the Canadian Cultural Research Network Colloquium 2000, 'Diversity and Culture: Beyond the Rhetoric', Edmonton, 29 May 2000.

Mayor's Advisory Committee to Promote the Arts. 1993. *Report and Recommendations.* Halifax: City of Halifax.

Mayor's Task Force on Investment in the Arts. 1994. *Building Creative Capital.* Edmonton: City of Edmonton.

Statistics Canada. 1996. 'Government Expenditures on Culture 1994–95'. *The Daily* (12 August). Ottawa: Statistics Canada.

———. 1997. 'Government Expenditures on Culture 1995–96'. *The Daily* (25 September). Ottawa: Statistics Canada.

Task Force on the Funding of the Arts in Canada. 1986. *Funding of the Arts in Canada to the Year 2000: The Report of the Task Force on Funding of the Arts.* Ottawa: Government of Canada.

Tippett, Maria. 1990. *Making Culture: English-Canadian Institutions and the Arts before the Massey Commission.* Toronto: University of Toronto Press.

Toronto. n.d. *Phase 2B Report: Economic Development, Culture and Tourism.* Toronto: City of Toronto.

———. 1994. 'Grant Agreement'. Photocopy.

Toronto Arts Council. 1997. *A Blueprint for Arts and Culture in the New Toronto: A Discussion Paper.* Toronto: Toronto Arts Council.

Vancouver Arts Initiative. 1993. *Toward the Creative City.* Vancouver: Vancouver Arts Initiative.

Verma, Norman. 1999. 'Government Committing Less to Culture'. *Focus on Culture* 11(2): 5–8.

Watson, Karen. 2000. 'Culture in the Cities'. *Blizzart* 5(1): 4, 6.

Withrow, Alfreda. 1999. *One City, Many Communities.* Halifax: Nimbus.

CHAPTER 12

Urban Development: Planning Aspirations and Political Realities

Christopher Leo[1]

Introduction

Involvement in the process of city planning often induces a feeling akin to our experience when we watch a film with excellent special effects. It all seems so real, and yet we know it is not. The words spoken in planning hearings and written in planning documents represent aspirations, often laudable ones, ones that have legal status and that are backed by administrative and political processes. But if we look around, we frequently find that there is a disconnect between the bureaucratic and legal theory of planning and the reality on the street.

In this chapter, I look at the reasons for this disconnect. I begin with an overview of the formal planning process, together with some necessary explanations of planning history and principles, and then proceed to look at the political realities that often thwart the apparent aims of planning documents and the laws and regulations that back them.

Evolution of Planning Ideas

Planning begins with a map of the city, with colours designating what kind of development will be permissible in each area. Since roughly the end of World War II, the Canadian and American orthodoxy has been that the best way of drawing these maps is to designate areas, called *zones*, as exclusively residential, commercial, industrial, or agricultural, with the different types of land use clearly separated from each other. As well, larger commercial buildings are typically separated from smaller ones, single-family homes from townhouses and apartment buildings, and so forth.

'Rational' Planning

This separation of uses has a fascinating history, which we cannot cover in detail here. In part, it is a reaction to often unsanitary and dangerous conditions in the much more mixed nineteenth-century industrial city. It was also shaped by such visionary thinkers as the British utopian social theorist Ebenezer Howard, the brilliant and controversial French architect Le Corbusier, and the celebrated American architect Frank Lloyd Wright. These influences and others have helped to produce a widespread conception, especially prevalent in Canada and the United States, that cities are most attractive and livable if they are spread out, with shopping centres and shopping strips, residential areas, and industrial parks sharply separated from each other (Fowler 1992; Levy 1997). This assumption is vigorously disputed by many planners and students of urban politics, as well as by residents and business people in many of the more mixed, older neighbourhoods that still flourish. Their position has been perhaps most cogently argued by Jane Jacobs in the classic *Death and Life of Great American Cities* (1961).

Although we cannot do justice to the critique of such commentators as Jacobs in these pages, it worth noting one point. The ideas of Howard, Le Corbusier, and Wright differed sharply from one another, but they had one important thing in common. Howard wanted to substitute compact towns for the cities he knew and wanted to intersperse them with greenery. Le Corbusier was in favour of very high-density development, presaging the office towers so familiar to us, and wanted to surround them with grass and trees. Wright wanted to spread cities far across the countryside, by building each home on a one-acre lot. These are radically different visions, but all three utopians did not like the cities they knew and, each in his own way, wished to separate the colourful, chaotic nineteenth-century city out into its component parts, to make it more 'rational' and orderly.

Jacobs and other critics of the utopians notwithstanding, the conception that separation of uses is the best course has hardened into a belief that property values will be adversely affected if mixing takes place. A proposal for a corner store or restaurant at the edge of a residential district, or an apartment complex near an area of single-family homes, will often produce a strong reaction from residents fearful of a loss of property value. In newly built areas as well, the most common expectation is that 'rational' separation of uses will prevail. As a result, modern planning has tended to replace more compact neighbourhoods of the past—in which stores, workplaces, and homes were often within walking distance of each other—with single-family residential districts, areas of multi-unit housing, shopping malls and strips, and industrial parks, all clearly separated from each other.

Counter-Trends

The regulations that mandate such patterns remain substantially unchanged despite some counter-trends that have gradually become evident in the past twenty years or so. For one thing, older-style neighbourhoods have retained a durable and growing appeal, such as the Bloor-Bathurst district and Queen Street West in Toronto, much of downtown Montreal, Corydon Village and Osborne Village in Winnipeg, Kitsilano and Fairview Slopes in Vancouver, and many others. As well, since the 1970s, with the size of family units shrinking and the cost of housing escalating, developers have repeatedly identified market opportunities for more compact forms of housing and for neighbourhoods where the proximity of stores and public facilities encourages more walking, only to be thwarted by planning regulations affecting such things as lot sizes, widths of rights-of-way (the areas reserved for streets and sidewalks), or separation of uses.

City governments in Vancouver and Toronto relaxed these strictures in a few selected neighbourhoods and produced mixed housing and retail developments, the success of which surprised even their supporters. False Creek in Vancouver is a stunningly situated waterfront development including housing, a row of shops, and a restaurant. Toronto's St Lawrence Neighbourhood is a very dense, mixed-income development of housing, shops, and community facilities, almost in the shadow of downtown office towers. Developments such as these have made it clear that support for the utopians' separation of uses is something less than unanimous.

The New Urbanism

Since the late 1980s, the cause of compact housing and mixed-use neighbourhoods has been taken up by proponents of the so-called 'new urbanism', or neo-traditional design, who advocate the development of compact neighbourhoods, with community facilities, stores, and transit within walking distance[2] (Duany, Plater-Zyberk, and Speck 2000). These proved to be so attractive to buyers that the original good intention of making them mixed-income developments was defeated by market pressures: their desirability in the eyes of buyers made them into upper-income enclaves. In addition, some neo-traditional developers have contradicted their own advocacy of more compact development by choosing locations at the urban fringe or by making ultra-generous allowances for open space.

Nevertheless, the often attractive appearance of these developments and their ready acceptance by buyers have promoted the idea that neighbourhoods with compact housing and with shopping within walking distance can be good places to live. Some of the best-known developments in this style have been new, fashionable communities in the United States, such as Kentlands in Maryland, Seaside in Florida (the location for the film *The Truman Show*), and Celebration, a development in the neo-traditional style by the Walt Disney Corporation. Such developments have also gained a foothold in a number of Canadian cities. The best-known Canadian development in this style is Cornell Village in Markham, located in the Greater Toronto Area (Immen 2000). Another is McKenzie Towne in Southeast Calgary.

In 1999, the Congress for the New Urbanism claimed that a total of 275 such developments were underway (Congress for the New Urbanism 1999). It has also become obvious that neo-traditional design principles are beginning to be applied in moderate- and lower-income developments. Indeed, the United States Department of Housing and Urban Development has adopted neo-traditional design principles for its Hope VI program for the renewal of public housing.

Bureaucratic Barriers

But bureaucratic barriers remain. A perusal of the postings on the e-mail list of the Congress for the New Urbanism produces numerous examples of the frustrations posed by conventional planning regulations. The ideas of the utopian planners also influence bankers. Prospective developers of neo-traditional projects report that financing is more readily available for conventional suburban developments than for neo-traditional designs (Congress for the New Urbanism 1999). Developers faced with such obstacles are business people, not politicians. Typically, their reaction to regulatory obstacles is to find a profitable way of working within the regulations rather than to try to get them changed.

The zoning map, therefore, began as a response to concerns about conditions in the nineteenth-century industrial city and to utopian ideals current then and in the early decades of the twentieth century. Today it remains the standard instrument of city planning. It promotes a style of development that remains, by a substantial margin, the most popular in Canada and the United States, but it also casts it in bronze and puts barriers in the way of alternatives.

The Planning Process

A typical zoning map undergoes periodic, usually incremental, changes, which may come about because a prospective developer wishes to change the designation of a piece of land she or he owns, for example to have an agricultural tract at the edge of the city rezoned for residential and commercial development. Or city council may, on the advice of professional planners, change the zoning of an area to reflect changes in its market potential. For instance, a decaying residential area near the commercial heart of the city might be rezoned commercial to reflect the fact that it is losing its desirability as a residential area but may now be a good location for an office tower.

The Official Plan

Most professional planners, and many citizens and politicians, believe that changes that take place as a city evolves are most likely to produce desirable results if they are not made piecemeal. Therefore, most provinces require municipalities to prepare an official land use plan every ten or fifteen years. The official plan sketches out what revisions city council intends to make to the zoning map over a specified period of time—say, ten or twenty years—and explains the reasons for these proposed changes as well as the objectives they are intended to pursue.

Concretely, an official plan may include economic and population growth targets and projections as to what kinds of growth are likely to take place, as well as discussions of the implications of that growth for infrastructure development, the transit system, parks, other city services, the environment, adjacent agricultural and resource areas, and so forth. The plan tries to bring these elements together in a coherent way so as to maximize the well-being of residents, promote economic growth, make wise use of resources, and protect the environment from unnecessary harm.

Usually, an official plan first becomes public knowledge as a draft plan prepared by professional planners employed by the municipality or prepared by planning consultants hired by the municipality. Minimally, this plan will be debated by city council at an open meeting. Often, this minimal exposure to public input is deemed inadequate and efforts are made to provide more opportunity for citizens to become involved in the planning process.

A citizen participation process may range from token or even manipulative to extensive. Minimally, it can take the form of a questionnaire on some key issues sent out to residents or available, together with some information brochures, at a kiosk. Such an effort may be little more than window dressing, or worse, the questions may be loaded—carefully structured so that the only 'reasonable' responses turn out to be the ones the planners, or politicians, want (Leo 1998a). A more serious effort at citizen participation may involve public hearings or a series of consultations on various elements of the plan.

At its most serious, participation would begin with a process of public education on planning alternatives, followed by the setting of planning goals with public input, and then by the drafting of a plan that, again, would be exposed to public hearings before a final draft was prepared for public debate and passage by city council. The level of seriousness about public participation varies greatly from jurisdiction to jurisdiction. In Canada, Vancouver and Toronto, for example, are far more serious about citizen participation than Winnipeg. The full-dress, multi-stage process just described is perhaps most closely approximated in Vancouver and in a number of American jurisdictions, including Oregon (Berry, Portney, and Thomson 1993; Leo 1994, 1998b).

Development Proposals

With the official plan in place, actual development is initiated by a development proposal. Occasionally, this can originate with one or more governments, generally as a response to an opportunity that private developers may not be willing or able to seize. In Vancouver, Granville Island, a defunct warehouse district near the water, was turned into an attractively off-beat commercial area by an agency of the federal government. In Winnipeg, all three levels of government formed an agency to develop The Forks, a downtown waterfront area, into a park, a market, shopping, restaurants, and other attractions. In other cases, government and private developers work together to produce a joint development venture.

Typically, however, it is a development company that assembles a piece of land and proposes a new development on it. The proposal sets out, usually in considerable detail, what will be included, what revenues the City can expect to gain from property taxes on the development once it is completed, and what will be needed to make the development feasible. The needs may range from connections to the city road, sewer, and water systems, to zoning changes, to actual alterations of the guidelines in the official plan. The proposal is taken to the city planning or development office, and a negotiation between the developer and a professional planner ensues.

Negotiations

In this negotiation, many factors must be taken into consideration, but it is protection of property values that tends to override other concerns. For developers, even more than for most people, time is money, and lost time in completing a planned development can be extremely costly. Developers are also mindful of the fact that the properties in a development, once built, must be sold or leased, as well as of the widespread belief, discussed above, that mixing uses will undermine property values. The path of least resistance to the preservation of property value is usually to stick with what is well-established and easily reconciled with zoning and building regulations. Those regulations, as I noted above, tend to privilege 'rational', land-use-separated planning over alternatives.

Planners on the city's side of the negotiation, meanwhile, will try to ensure that the new development is cost-effective, that it can be included in the city's network of infrastructure and services without incurring unnecessary costs, and, most of all, that the costs to the city of the new development or subdivision will be covered by the tax revenues it will produce. The official plan also typically mandates a concern for social considerations, protection of the environment, and, where applicable, the protection of agriculture and natural resources. However, here, as on the developer's side of the negotiation, financial concerns tend to override others. It is therefore the question of how much the development will cost compared with the revenue it is expected to produce that looms particularly large in the city negotiators' minds.

How is this calculation done? Winnipeg is as good an example as any, and what is true there will be reflected, with some variations, in most Canadian jurisdictions and in most American ones as well. When a proposal for a new subdivision is brought to Winnipeg city planners, three cost factors are taken into consideration: roads, underground municipal services (sewer and water service), and parks. If the subdivision proposal incurs extra costs in any of these areas, the developer is responsible for covering the costs. When negotiations are complete, the subdivision is deemed a winning proposition for the city if the prospective revenues outweigh these costs. Indeed, in Winnipeg, when negotiations are complete and the subdivision proposal comes before city council for approval, the reaction has repeatedly been delight that new tax assessment will be added to the city's coffers with the developer covering all the 'costs'.

Unfortunately, things are not always as they seem. In order to appreciate better how they really are, we must take our leave of planning procedure and descend into the gritty arena of political reality.

Political Realities

The picture we have looked at so far is not an altogether happy one. I have noted, for example, that the ideas that shaped the cities we know today grew out of a reaction against the often unsanitary and dangerous nineteenth-century industrial city and that the originators of these ideas shared a dislike of cities. Even on the strength of those observations, it might be reasonable to ask whether it is a good idea to allow our cities to be patterned on the ideas of people who did not like cities.

In addition, I observed that citizen participation in the process of urban development is often less than adequate—indeed, that sometimes it is manipulative, that it is used as a tool for persuading citizens that they have no realistic alternative but to accept the proposals of planners or politicians. It might be reasonable to suggest that such citizen participation could be worse than no consultation with the public at all.

Finally, I made the observation that preservation of property values often overrides other considerations, including such things as environmental considerations, social concerns, and preservation of resources.

However, these are only suggestions. We can get a better idea of the real impact of these problems upon our highest aspirations for cities by looking at the politics of the development process.

Developer Proposals Drive the Process

The first point we need to consider is implicit in what I have noted already: typically, it is not the official plan but developers' proposals that drive the actual process of development. The exceptions are such cases of government-driven developments as Granville Island and The Forks, both referred to earlier. However, in the typical case, as I have noted, it is a private developer who assembles a tract of land, puts together a proposal for its development, and takes it to the City for approval. In theory, the city government is still in control. It has drawn the zoning map, it has authority to alter or not alter it, and it has the clear and undisputed legal right to decide where development takes place and what can be developed there and to regulate the details of how it will look and how it will be constructed.

However, city governments rarely exercise this authority fully, for a number of interrelated reasons. One of them is interurban competition.

Interurban Competition

Interurban competition has always been the way North America has developed. In both Canada and the United States, the settlement of the West and the Industrial Revolution were marked by the promotion of cities as commercial entities, accompanied by vigorous competition among them for investment (Artibise 1981; Wade 1959). Within metropolitan areas, especially in the United States, a similarly growth-oriented and competitive environment was evident. From the earliest days of suburban development, much of the outward expansion of cities took the form of competition among urbanizing municipalities vying for residential, commercial, and industrial development (Binford 1985; Logan and Molotch 1987).

In the dawn of the twenty-first century, this competition has become fiercer than ever as it increasingly takes on global dimensions. Cutbacks in the size of government and deregulation in many areas where governments previously exercised control have had the effect of removing limits that once existed on many companies and freeing them to compete more vigorously. The development of transportation networks and new communications technologies has freed money, ideas, and people to move around the world as never before. Such free-trade arrangements as the North American Free Trade Agreement, the European Union, and numerous others have removed barriers to the movement of goods, investment dollars, and companies themselves to wherever they can do business in the most advantageous manner. Local business communities everywhere are keenly aware that they can do business anywhere and that they must anticipate competition from around the world (GTA Task Force 1996; Leo et al. 1998).

This has had the practical effect of reducing the bargaining power of cities in many of their dealings with developers. Often, mobile developers who are planning a development a city wants can, in effect, dictate the terms of the development and force the city to rewrite its bylaws or regulations. In Edmonton in the early 1980s, the city government had laid a series of plans for increasing the attractiveness of its moribund inner-city commercial area. Included in the plans were controls on the designs of new buildings to make the streets more attractive to pedestrians, the transformation of a major downtown street into a pedestrian mall, and restrictions on the demolition of some better-quality older buildings in order to preserve something of the character and the attractiveness of the historic cityscape. Similar measures have been successful in many cities.

However, when the Bank of Montreal decided to establish a regional headquarters in Edmonton, it chose one of the protected older buildings as its location, decided to tear it down, and also decided, for good measure, that it did not wish to adhere to the City's design controls in the construction of the new building. In short, the bank was asking the City to scrap its design controls and its measures for the protection of historic buildings. The municipal government resisted, but when bank officials dropped a suggestion that Calgary would make as good a regional headquarters as Edmonton, resistance crumbled and the City capitulated (Leo 1995).

The bank was not located near the planned pedestrian mall, so at least the City's plans for that new facility were safe, but not for long. Another developer laid plans for a new downtown mall, the Eaton Centre, straddling the planned mall, demanded cancellation of plans for the mall, and also asked for some $30 million in other concessions. Once again, the City capitulated. The developer won the concessions and built a shopping mall, and the City gave up its plans for a pedestrian mall (Leo 1995).

In the case of the bank headquarters, there was an explicit threat that the building—and attendant business—could be located in another city. In the case of the Eaton Centre, the threat was simply that the development would not go ahead, but that is really another way of saying the same thing. The developers of the Eaton Centre were the Ghermezian brothers, developers of the West Edmonton Mall and the Mall of America in suburban Minneapolis. They look for opportunities to do major developments and, in some cases, market them not just as shopping centres, but also as entertainment centres and tourist attractions. If they are not investing in one place, they can invest in another. Their mobility is similar to that of a bank. In other words, their threat not to go ahead with the Eaton Centre was essentially a threat to invest their money in another city.

Another kind of business that is usually mobile, or potentially so, is a manufacturing plant. An example is Schneider Corporation, which had a pork-processing plant in Kitchener, Ontario. The company announced in 1995 that it would spend $40 million on a Manitoba hog-processing plant at a location to be announced. It was rumoured that the company was choosing between Winnipeg and a neighbouring small town, Steinbach. In order to get the plant, and some 300 new jobs, the City of Winnipeg agreed to spend $1.7 million to acquire a property and service it, reduce its sewer rates for the largest users by 35 per cent by 2002—thereby increasing the amounts smaller users had to pay—and pay the company $750,000 in cash. Upon gaining the concessions and agreeing to locate the plant in Winnipeg, the company closed its Kitchener plant and laid off 600 workers.

In short, mobile companies often call the tune in their dealings with local governments, and, in the process, they can cancel development plans, zoning rules, building code regulations, and even the taxes that are levied to support the city's services. It is important to note that this kind of bargaining power applies only to mobile firms. Large-scale commercial operations and manufacturing plants often find themselves in this fortunate position, but firms that serve a local market, such as developers of housing and local retail establishments, are not similarly placed.

In housing and local commercial development, either there is a market or there is not one. If there is not a market, no one will want to propose a development to serve it, and if there is one, someone will likely be found to do it, even if the first applicant is turned down. In other words, lack of mobility turns the tables. Cities need mobile companies. Immobile companies need the approval of the city where they wish to do business. In practice, however, immobile companies are often able to win substantial concessions as well, for two reasons: the psychology of slow growth, and influence and corruption.

I turn first to the psychology of slow growth; next I show how rapid growth can affect planning; and finally, I look at influence and corruption. I argue that politics makes planning difficult under the best of circumstances, but difficult in different ways, depending on the rate of growth.

Growth Psychology and Planning[3]

Cities that are growing rapidly, that are magnets for development, such as Toronto and Vancouver, have problems, but they are often not the same as those of slowly growing cities (Leo and Brown 2000). I have already noted that Canadian and American cities have, from the beginning, developed in an atmosphere of avid competition for growth. This atmosphere has made perceived 'losers' of cities that are growing slowly, in terms of either population or economic expansion, and often induced a sense of inferiority in the citizens and leaders of slowly growing cities.

Winnipeg is a case in point. The city has, for a long time, been growing at less than 1 per cent a year. When economic development efforts are under discussion, the tone and the words carry a mixed message of assertiveness and self-deprecation that makes it clear that Winnipeggers do not feel happy about their home. An undercurrent of desperation is palpable in advertising campaigns on such themes as 'Winnipeg: 100 reasons to love it' or 'Love me, love my Winnipeg'. What comes through most clearly are two contradictory messages, often asserted simultaneously: (1) because Winnipeg is not Toronto or Vancouver, there must be something wrong with it; and (2) there is absolutely nothing the matter with Winnipeg.

Economic development efforts in slowly growing cities often reflect that same mood of ambivalence with a hint of desperation. Predictions of economic changes tend to take the form either of pessimistic warnings of a clouded future or of declarations that 'the big break' is just around the corner: if the Jets leave Winnipeg, $50 million a year will be lost to the economy; if the Canadian Wheat Board is abolished or relocated, 5,000 jobs will be lost; Winnipeg is about to become a major North American transportation hub, thousands of jobs will be created, and millions added to the economy. These recent examples of speculations trumpeted in the local media are just samples of what amounts to a steady stream of journalistic manic-depression. Economic development efforts are undertaken in a mood akin to that of an addicted gambler, simultaneously desperate and hopeful.

Europeans see things differently

This seems normal in North America, though it looks odd in a wider frame of reference. For example, a glance at population-growth figures for European cities allows one to draw up a list of cities that are growing at rates of less than 1 per cent a year or even declining—a list that, at the same time, is a list of some of the world's great cities, certainly not ones where residents or leaders are likely to be suffering from a sense of inferiority over their home town. Included in the European slow-growth list for 1985–95 are Vienna, Cologne, Frankfurt, and Hamburg. Declining in population over the same period were Brussels, Copenhagen, Milan, Genoa, Florence, Naples, and Rome (Leo and Brown 2000).

Canada is not Europe, however, and here the city councils of slowly growing cities tend to be desperate and are typically all too eager to make concessions to developers, even when the projects developers propose cannot be relocated. A good example of this can be found in the curious calculations that are used in deciding whether a proposal for a new subdivision will make a net contribution to the local economy and to the city coffers.

Curious calculations

I have already noted that, in the typical case of Winnipeg, three items are taken into consideration when making this calculation. If the developer is prepared to cover the costs of road connections, underground municipal services, and parks needed for the new subdivision, anticipated tax revenues are counted as a net gain.

Forgotten is the fact that new development at the city's fringe influences not just the costs of these three items but of the full range of municipal services. Once the new, allegedly no-cost subdivision is in place, the new residents rightly argue that as residents and taxpayers of Winnipeg, they deserve services comparable to those that other residents enjoy. City politicians have no valid answer when these residents ask: Why is there no conveniently located library branch and community centre? Why are police and fire response times here slower than in other subdivisions? Why do we not have a neighbourhood school? City councils and school boards have no politically realistic alternative but to spend money to meet the demands.

As one such subdivision follows another, each responding not to a rational calculation of what will be required to sustain the overall city network of services and infrastructure but rather to a limited calculation that treats each subdivision as a self-contained unit requiring only minimal services, the city gradually loses its ability to pay its bills. As the population migrates outward, responding to the reasonably priced housing that results from unrealistically priced development, downtown residential neighbourhoods become depopulated, serviceable downtown schools are closed while new ones are built in the suburbs, subdivisions too thinly populated to support public transit nevertheless get subsidized bus service, downtown streets and sewers deteriorate while new roads are built to serve the latest subdivisions, and so forth.

An example of the practical result of this downward spiral can be found in a meticulous 1998 survey of the state of Winnipeg's infrastructure, which documented a massive disparity between the amount needed to maintain existing infrastructure and the amount actually being spent. Regional streets, for example, were found to be $10.2 million per year short of the required amount. Even more drastic was the situation of residential streets, which were found to have benefited from an average annual budgeted expenditure of $2.5 million, compared with a requirement of $30 million—a disparity of $27.5 million each year (Winnipeg 1998). In 2000, the total deficit in the maintenance budget for residential streets alone—not including regional streets, back lanes, or sidewalks—was $200 million.

To be sure, development patterns characterized by thinly scattered suburban subdivisions and decaying inner-city neighbourhoods are typical in rapidly growing cities as well, and recent studies suggest that they are, in the long run, unsustainable, or at least dangerously cost-ineffective, in any urban area (Blais 1995; 'The Costs of Sprawl' 1996; GTA Task Force 1996). Even the wealthiest and most rapidly growing metropolitan areas have experienced inner-city deterioration in the face of uncontrolled suburban and exurban development. The South Bronx in New York City turned first into an urban jungle and then into something resembling a post-war saturation-bombing victim while Queens and Long Island expanded. Most of downtown Detroit became an unoccupied wasteland ringed by older neighbourhoods and prosperous suburbs.[4]

Although problems may well develop in growth magnets, they are guaranteed to overwhelm slowly growing cities that persist in these development practices. Why are rapidly growing cities better placed? A rapidly growing city can mask the costliness of sprawl development, at least for a while: a subdivision located beyond the fringe of existing development may not incur an immediate financial penalty if growth potential is strong enough to assure, within the foreseeable future, that in-fill development will help to pay for the needed infrastructure. Downtown decay may not occasion immediate alarm when there are proposals for commercial developments to replace decaying downtown residential districts.

In a city that is growing slowly, however, the piper demands immediate payment when council calls the scattered-development tune. Here there are no heavy pressures for new development, with assurances of growing tax revenues, to cover up mistakes. But thanks to the obsessive belief in rapid growth as the cure for all ills, these realities are ignored. The conviction that growth is unconditionally desirable, that it must be pursued at all costs, and that any other risk is preferable to that of lost growth has taken precedence over other considerations.

More interurban competition

In Winnipeg, the uncontrolled deterioration of infrastructure and services and the costs of trying to keep things patched together have driven residential property taxes to tax-revolt levels, and now interurban competition is an issue not only between Winnipeg and other, comparable cities across Canada and around the world, but also within Winnipeg's own orbit. For some time, residents of the metropolitan area have been voting with their feet and accepting the property-tax reductions they can achieve by moving beyond the boundaries of the city. Businesses are beginning to follow.

Indeed, the problem is now largely out of the hands of city council. With exurban migration underway, city council has lost much of the control it once might have exercised over new development. Developers now have alternatives: if the City is not sufficiently generous in dealing with residential subdivision proposals or commercial developments, it is becoming increasingly easy for them to find a parcel of land for a similar development in an adjacent municipality. Thus, a tax base that was already inadequate to cover mounting costs before exurban migration began is now slowly eroding. Planning the growth of the city is no longer an option, at least for city council and its officials. Only a higher authority, or a city with expanded boundaries, could implement a meaningful plan now.

Planning under Conditions of Rapid Growth

Rapidly growing cities such as Vancouver and Toronto are less subject to interurban competition than Winnipeg and other more slowly growing centres. When Logan and Molotch argue that 'cities, regions and states do not compete to please people; they compete to please capital' (1987: 42), they characterize the situation of Winnipeg, Edmonton, and other slowly growing centres correctly. However, if we applied this quotation to Vancouver, we would be overstating the case.

In Vancouver, attitudes toward development are influenced by a strong public attachment to the city's spectacular natural setting, with the ocean or ocean inlets never far away and mountain vistas in the background. And the realities of the City's position in negotiating with developers are shaped by the fact that Vancouver is a magnet for investment. When office towers sprouting in the financial district began to overshadow the waterfront, to cut off public access to it, and to block off sunlight—which, in Vancouver, is precious because it is rare—city council found the political will to act.

The City implemented a system of review procedures and controls (Leo 1994) that opened the smallest imaginable details of new developments to a process of public discussion and decision-making. The following are a few samples from a much more detailed list of design guidelines:

- Creation and preservation of attractive and usable public open space.
- Preservation of historic buildings wherever possible, and also of viable communities, including communities located downtown, partly in their own interest and partly to ensure that the downtown remains a lively and interesting place. The guidelines call for the viability of these communities to be supported, both by ensuring that needed facilities such as daycare centres, recreation centres, and low-income housing are provided and by making their surroundings attractive and livable for an increasingly diverse population.
- Protection of views of mountains, water, landmark buildings, and art works.
- Maintenance of access to sunlight and protection from weather and from undue noise; preservation of mature trees; and development of water sources, such as fountains.
- Energy conservation.
- Avoidance of 'impersonal façades', such as street-level bank lobbies at the base of overpowering office towers.

These and many other details of any new development are fair game in discussions with a panel of experts, such as architects and engineers, and in a process of public input. In practice, these discussions become negotiating sessions, usually with give and take on all sides, but certainly with the developer obligated to make serious concessions to the public and the city government. It is clear that the discretionary zoning system imposes significant constraints on developers and has a real impact on the appearance of the developments that result, thus giving a serious measure of influence, independent of developers, to citizens, citizens' groups, and the local government (Leo 1994).

Although this may mean that planning in a growth magnet comes closer to representing real community control over the future, it by no means guarantees such control. In the first place, many communities are growth magnets, but very few take anything approaching full advantage of the bargaining power they potentially possess. Secondly, they are subject to competitive pressures from neighbouring municipalities, as Winnipeg is, though their attractiveness to developers often affords them a degree of protection from those pressures. Finally, they are highly subject to the problems I turn to now, which grow out of the use of influence and the presence of corruption in the process of development approvals.

Influence and Corruption

When we refer to public decision-making as 'democratic', we mean that the public plays a serious role in the process. Periodic municipal elections, often supplemented by a variety of measures to secure public input into particular government decisions, are signs that local government is democratic. One of the less edifying realities of democratic government, however, is that such signs do not guarantee that the voice of the public actually carries the day.

The reasons for this are well known to most people who have observed politics or participated in it. City councillors require money to wage election campaigns and often they become beholden to those who supply the funds. Even between elections, influence is wielded, especially in cities that are highly attractive to developers and where the stakes are high. In line with a well-known dictum of municipal government—'If you can eat it or drink it, it ain't graft'—it is not unusual for councillors in major cities to be treated to $100 lunches or to receive a case of premium rye at Christmas time.

In addition, powerful people—business people, members of affluent professional associations, public servants, and union leaders—frequently enjoy direct access to municipal politicians. Ordinary voters in larger cities are rarely able to pick up the telephone and talk to the mayor or to the head of a city department, but for developers, such calls are routine. Finally, even the ballot itself is usually a more effective instrument for members of the local elite than for ordinary citizens. Members of the elite often know each other personally and will have a much better idea than an ordinary newspaper reader of the policies likely to be supported by various candidates. In practice, their ballots will count for more because it is very likely to be a more effective instrument for the promotion of their own interests.

What are the practical consequences of this state of affairs for city planning? The short answer is that they will vary from time to time and place to place and that they do not eliminate the possibility of meaningful planning, but they do make it much harder to achieve. Two examples will indicate something of the range of obstacles to planning posed by political influence and corruption.

Big-city machinations

The first story, which was told in the *Globe and Mail* (Ferguson and King 1988a, 1988b) after a ten-month investigation in the late 1980s, deals with land development in what is now known as the Greater Toronto Area, specifically in the area north of Toronto. This area is part of a wide ring of suburban communities around Toronto that are the primary focus of growth in the region.

The investigation concluded that the provincial government adopted a hands-off stance toward a lack of urban planning that allowed private developers to control the growth of communities in the area and that the 'role of citizens in the planning of their communities has been trivialized to the point where it is ignored by many municipal councils' (Ferguson and King 1988b). Specifically, the investigation found that 'a small group of powerful developers . . . have a near monopoly on developable land in the . . . area [north of Toronto] and are a factor in rising house prices' (Ferguson and King 1988b).

The *Globe and Mail* documented a 'loan' of $80,000, which was not repaid, from a developer to a company owned by an official in the region; it was followed by approval of an industrial development proposal that had been filed by the company that gave the 'loan'. There were also stories of a cheque for $4,000 from a developer to a 'senior municipal official' and at least two cases of envelopes containing several thousand dollars in cash delivered on behalf of a developer to a councillor.

Although such stories are rarely told in as much detail as this one was,[5] this story comes as no surprise to anyone familiar with the conventions of growth politics in major metropolitan areas. The development of rapidly growing cities is a high-risk, high-profit business that, to put it mildly, frequently fails to bring out the best in participants. Good intentions, democratic values, and even well-organized, honest political associations and individuals may prove a poor match for the temptations and machinations of such a business.

Country wiles

A second story details circumstances very different from those in the Greater Toronto Area. It is based on attendance at two sessions of a Manitoba Municipal Board panel and on a study of the proposed official plan of the Springfield Municipality, an agricultural area and bedroom community immediately east of Winnipeg. The municipal board is a provincially appointed supervisory, appeal, and dispute-settlement body dealing with a variety of matters related to land use planning, taxation, and municipal finance.

The municipality's proposed new official municipal plan outlines physical features of the municipality, sets goals for the development of the area, establishes zoning categories, and outlines where various types of anticipated development will be permitted (Rural Municipality of Springfield 1998). The plan defines four land forms in the municipality:

- two high-potential agricultural areas,
- an area near a provincial park that is the prime source of groundwater for the municipality, and
- an area that is defined as having lower agricultural potential.

In defining objectives for development of the municipality, which are the result of a public consultation process, the plan stresses the high priority placed on the preservation of agricultural viability and natural resources and the prevention of proliferation of residential development.

A substantial scholarly literature cites a variety of ways that residential development in farming areas damages the viability of agriculture: complaints from residents about smells, heavy machinery on roads, and other perceived nuisances resulting from agriculture; residential activities that interfere with farming operations, such as commuter traffic and harassment of farm animals by pets; and escalation of land prices that inflate the cost of farming.[6]

The proposed Springfield official plan itself states that the growth potential of livestock husbandry has already been limited by past residential development (Rural Municipality of Springfield 1998). To this point in the plan, therefore, an analysis of land forms has indicated the location of good agricultural areas and important water resources, and statements of objectives have stressed the determination to preserve these assets in the face of urbanization.

However, when we turn to the part of the plan in which proposed zoning categories are set out, it appears that we are reading a different plan. Most of the residential development is in the larger of the two prime agricultural areas and in the area where the major resource of groundwater is located. All the residential development on top of the prime water resource relies on septic tanks for sewage disposal, which invariably poses a greater risk to groundwater than does a community sewage system. There is a cluster of residential development planned as well in the community of Anola, which is located in the low-potential agricultural area and would therefore seem to be the natural area for urban development if harm to agriculture were to be minimized, but that community can only accommodate a limited amount of development because it has not been provided with the water and sewerage services needed for higher concentrations of development. Nor are there any plans for providing Anola with services, even though the plan states that there is a demand for residential development there.

Meanwhile, two urban communities in the middle of the prime agricultural area, Oakbank and Dugald, have been provided with the services required for higher concentrations of urban development, one of them recently. In short, everything possible is done to encourage urban development in those areas that the plan claims a determination to protect, and almost nothing is done to encourage development in the area that the plan designates as unsuitable for other purposes: a good line of talk, but no action to back it up.

Attendance at two hearings of the municipal board panel (17 May 2000 and 24 May 2000) provided insights into the sources of this exercise in appearing to plan without actually doing so. From a variety of statements that were made, it became clear that numerous residents of the municipality had been able to improve their fortunes by subdividing farmland in the past in order to sell it for residential development and that others wished to do so now. When witnesses at the hearing called attention to the gap in the plan between objectives and proposed outcomes,[7] the argument was repeatedly made that because some had been allowed to subdivide their land, it was not fair to restrict others from doing so.

In short, the municipality was meeting its legal obligations by providing something that resembled a plan, but political pressures from constituents in a community small enough to allow almost anyone to have a personal relationship with her or his representative on council prevented the municipality from adhering to the principles stated in the plan. In a community as small as this one, it is not necessary to imagine cases of rye or thousands of dollars changing hands in order to understand what is happening. In the absence of clear provincial planning guidelines, pressures on council are too immediate and too personal to permit genuine planning.

The situation in Springfield is very different from that in the Greater Toronto Area, but the outcome is the same: it is those who stand to gain from development who largely determine the way the community will develop. The political realities of the planning process defeat aspirations to sound urban planning.

What's Wrong with This Picture?

What is to be done? What are the alternatives to a planning process that reflects the politics of privilege rather than either planning principles or wide public participation? There is no question that the planning process can work differently and have different outcomes, but there are bound to be objections to any of the alternatives. I end this chapter with a brief outline of some possibilities, together with commentary.

Scrap the Plan

When we see outcomes such as those in Toronto and Springfield outlined earlier, we may well ask why anyone bothers. In the case of Springfield, for example, we saw a careful presentation of the factors that determine the environmental and economic suitability of locations for residential development followed by a development plan that paid no apparent attention to suitability and, instead, limited itself to a response to the pressures from prospective sellers. In such a case, there is good reason to suspect that if Springfield abolished its zoning system and dismissed the planners, nothing significant would change.

This is not a fanciful notion. In the United States, a number of jurisdictions have or had no zoning. Houston, Texas, was such a case, much celebrated by advocates of this approach, and the question of whether zoning is appropriate remains controversial there (Feagin 1988; Siegan 1972; Thomas and Murray 1991). In the absence of zoning, property values can be protected privately by a provision written into each land title that limits the future uses to which the land may be put. The initial buyer and future buyers of a property must sign on to these restrictions as a condition of the sale. In a residential area, for example, the title to each house and the piece of land on which it is built would contain provisions that obligate the buyer and future owners never to sell the land to a developer of multi-family housing, commercial buildings, manufacturing plants, and so forth. From the viewpoint of the buyer and her neighbours, the property enjoys the same kind of protection that it would gain from a zoning restriction.

A substantial literature sets out the advantages and disadvantages of a non-zoning system of property development. This is not the place for a review of the literature. Suffice it to say that this system would achieve protection of the rights of property owners but would remove environmental and social protection that the zoning system purports to deliver. As we have seen from the contrasting cases of Vancouver on the one hand and Greater Toronto and Springfield on the other, such a claim is considerably more plausible in some jurisdictions than in others.

Many people would not be satisfied to 'solve' the problem of toothless plans by abolishing planning, but there is an irony here. The existence of the Houston model probably mutes the criticism that some advocates of planning would otherwise aim at such plans as the one in Springfield. Fear of the Houston alternative might well motivate some to settle for a less meaningful plan than they would accept in the absence of that alternative, on the reasoning that any plan, however inadequate, is better than none at all. In one of those ironies that is such a common feature of democratic politics, planning advocates, in practice, may become unwilling allies of those who want a toothless plan, a plan that will provide a cover for a largely unregulated pursuit of private interests.

Greater Centralization of Power

It may seem paradoxical, but one way of making planning more genuinely responsive to the problems of the local community may be to relocate more of the responsibility for planning to a higher level of government. This is true for a couple of different reasons. In the subsection entitled 'More Interurban Competition', we noted that cities surrounded by other municipalities that are becoming urbanized are subject to competition for new development.

This competition is not on a level playing field. The urbanizing municipality's property-tax payers, typically, are responsible only for a relatively minimal set of services: roads, possibly sewerage and water service (unless they have septic tanks and wells), education, a low level of policing (low, at least, in the early stages of urbanization), possibly some parks, and not a great deal else.

Major cities inevitably have a range of responsibilities that urbanizing municipalities stand a good chance of avoiding, such as social services, much more intensive policing, community centres and recreation programs to serve the needs of low-income neighbourhoods, language instruction for immigrants, roads that must accommodate regional traffic and through traffic as well as the traffic generated in the immediate area, and so forth.

Residents of urbanizing municipalities beyond the edge of the city are typically in a position to enjoy the benefits of living near a major city—big-city jobs, ethnic and gourmet restaurants, major league sports, nightclubs, symphony and chamber music, theatre, and more—but typically they are not sharing in the property taxes that city residents have to pay to enjoy these facilities. I argued earlier that competition from fringe municipalities is one of the factors that prevents cities from exercising control over their development—that prevents good planning. Cities suffering from such competition know that if they do not give developers what they want, they may move their project to the low-tax jurisdiction next door.

Provincial governments anxious to keep clear of these problems typically instruct municipalities to solve them by negotiation, but that is usually no solution at all. Once a situation has been set up in which fringe municipalities enjoy inherent cost advantages, it is unreasonable to expect the local politicians involved to come to terms. If the reeves and mayors do not take advantage of their competitive position, or if they agree to help pay for the costs of city services, they are not serving the best interests of their constituents. If the big-city politicians agree to accept the state of affairs desired by their neighbours, it is their constituents who are ill-served. This problem is not likely to be brought under control without provincial intervention.

A second reason for centralization is well-illustrated by the Springfield situation. It is asking a great deal of politicians in small communities to face down their neighbours and tell them that they have to make sacrifices in the interest of the greater good. If the province expects such municipalities to make rational plans and enforce them, it is only reasonable to suggest that the province give them the authority to do so and accept responsibility for the results.

Centralization of power is, in fact, a feasible alternative. In Europe, it is common for the national governments to exercise substantial control over city planning and major development decisions (Leo 1997). Canadians and Americans would be unwilling to accept European levels of national imposition upon local planning, but there are North American models as well. In a growing number of American jurisdictions, the problems of sprawl development are beginning to be addressed seriously. In most jurisdictions, the starting point for achieving this control is a public participation process at the state level, in which citizens from around the state become involved in the setting of goals for urban growth, including such things as improvement in water and air quality, increases in average density of development, provision of affordable housing, and clear definition of the boundaries between urban and agricultural land.

In Oregon, where this system has been in place the longest and where it has been quite successful, state legislation requires local governments to meet state goals in their official development plans, and a state-appointed board has the power to rule on whether the plans meet the objectives. This allows local municipalities a great deal of latitude in how they apply the principles, but it seeks to remove the possibility of influence being used as a means of overriding the principles (Leo 1998b).

Such a system would actually be easier to implement in Canada than in the United States. The long-standing American tradition of 'home rule'[8] places a large question mark over how far states can go in dictating to localities. In Canada, by contrast, provinces have a clear, constitutional responsibility for municipal government, and it is almost routine for provincial governments unilaterally and fundamentally to rewrite the rules of local government. Already, such bodies as the Manitoba Municipal Board have the authority to reject local planning measures. What would be needed would be a provincially supervised public participation process to set goals, legislation mandating them, and, for a change, a little bit of provincial political will to practice what they preach instead of letting local municipalities carry the freight.

An Aroused Public

That is the problem in a nutshell: It is a great deal easier to agree on the desirability of attractive, viable cities than it is to decide who carries the freight. However, there may be a glimmer of hope. Oregon has shown that it is possible to bring planning principles to bear on growth without inhibiting growth, and a rapidly growing list of other American jurisdictions are following suit, or at least trying to (DeGrove with Miness 1992; Leo et al. 1998; Nelson 2000). These efforts won national-level support from US Vice President Al Gore, and in the 1998 US federal election, more than 200 voter initiatives called for limitation of suburban expansion and a substantial number of them succeeded.

I argued that an important part of the reason for the politics that seeks to circumvent planning is a determination to increase the rate of economic growth at whatever cost. There is early evidence that this determination may be losing ground to other political tendencies. A recent study of Los Angeles found that the political consensus for growth has eroded severely over the past fifteen years and argues that similar conditions prevail in other cities (Purcell 2000). Whether or not good planning hurts growth—and findings from Oregon would suggest that it does not (Leo 1998b)—a diminution in the political support for it would certainly have the effect of removing one of the barriers to planning.

In that case, there may be a growing role for research on alternatives to utopian planning and on the political problem of turning plans into realities, as well, of course, as a great deal of scope for political action. It seems a goal worth pursuing.

In Canada, we have an old habit of preening ourselves on the superiority of our cities over American ones, and we can probably afford that luxury for a while longer. However, if provincial governments continue to refuse to mandate some planning measures to gain control of urban growth, we may yet find the United States has stolen our 'urban liveability' crown.

Notes

1. Many thanks to Edmund P. Fowler for inspiration, Nathan Edelson for some critical help in getting this project underway, Susan Mulligan for research assistance, and Heather Mathieson, with help from Susan Ronquillo and Lynne Schultz, for interlibrary loan services that are absolutely second to none anywhere. The University of Winnipeg, as always, has provided a congenial workplace as well as material and moral support, and the Social Science and Humanities Research Council of Canada has made research funds available. However, no blame is due any of them. I accept full responsibility for miscalculations, botches, or gaffes.
2. The Web address of the Congress for the New Urbanism (CNU) is http://www.cnu.org/
3. This section draws on Leo and Brown (2000).
4. Canadian commentators—when they pay any attention at all to the problem of inner-city decay—are fond of observing that American cities are in worse shape than Canadian ones. Although that is true, it is also true, in such cities as Winnipeg and Edmonton, that the American pattern of almost boundless fringe expansion combined with inner-city abandonment and decay is well underway. It is not possible to say with certainty how widespread this pattern is in Canada or how serious the decay is in cities other than Winnipeg because Canadian commentators have generally taken little interest in the subject.
5. A number of similar stories, told in less detail, may be found in Lightbody (1993: 204–7).
6. Some of this literature is reviewed in Leo et al. (1998).

7. I was present at the hearing as a witness, invited to testify as an expert, and one of several of those present who pointed to the gap.

8. For more information on 'home rule', see Judd and Swanstrom (1998: 97–98).

References

Artibise, Alan F.J. 1981. *Prairie Urban Development, 1870–1930*. Ottawa: Canadian Historical Association.

Berry, Jeffrey M., Kent E. Portney, and Ken Thomson. 1993. *The Rebirth of Urban Democracy*. Washington, DC: Brookings Institution.

Binford, Henry C. 1985. *The First Suburbs: Residential Communities on the Boston Periphery, 1815–1860*. Chicago: University of Chicago Press.

Blais, Pamela. 1995. 'The Economics of Urban Form'. Toronto: Greater Toronto Area Task Force, background paper.

Congress for the New Urbanism. 1999. *Financing the New Urbanism*. San Francisco: Congress for the New Urbanism.

'The Costs of Sprawl: Does Growth Management Pay?' 1996. *CUPR Report* 7(3). Accessed 20 February 1997: http://policy.rutgers.edu/cupr/CUPReport73/sprawl.htm

DeGrove, John M., with Deborah Miness. 1992. *The New Frontier for Land Policy: Planning and Growth Management in the States*. Cambridge, MA: Lincoln Institute of Land Policy.

Duany, Andres, Elizabeth Plater-Zyberk, and Jeff Speck. 2000. *Suburban Nation: The Rise of Sprawl and the Decline of the American Dream*. New York: North Point Press.

Feagin, Joe R. 1988. *Free Enterprise City: Houston in Political and Economic Perspective*. New Brunswick, NJ: Rutgers University Press.

Ferguson, Jock, and Dawn King. 1988a. 'Hidden Money Fuelling Regional Growth'. *Globe and Mail* (2 November).

———. 1988b. 'Ontario Blamed for Planning Chaos'. *Globe and Mail* (3 November).

Fowler, Edmund D. 1992. *Building Cities That Work*. Montreal: McGill-Queens University Press.

Greater Toronto Area (GTA) Task Force. 1996. *Report*. Toronto: Queen's Printer for Ontario.

Immen, Wallace. 2000. 'Front Porches, Sidewalks, Buses (Sort Of): It's the New Urbanism'. *Globe and Mail*. (24 April).

Jacobs, Jane. 1961. *The Death and Life of Great American Cities*. New York: Vintage.

Judd, Dennis R., and Todd Swanstrom. 1998. *City Politics: Private Power and Public Policy*. New York: Longman.

Leo, Christopher. 1994. 'The Urban Economy and the Power of the Local State'. In *The Changing Canadian Metropolis: A Public Policy Perspective*, vol. 2, ed. Frances Frisken. Berkeley, CA: Institute of Governmental Studies.

———. 1995. 'Global Change and Local Politics: Economic Decline and the Local Regime in Edmonton'. *Journal of Urban Affairs* 17: 277–99.

————. 1997. 'City Politics in an Era of Globalization'. In *Reconstructing Urban Regime Theory: Regulating Local Government in a Global Economy*, ed. Mickey Lauria. Thousand Oaks, CA: Sage.

————. 1998a. 'The North American Growth Fixation and the Inner City: Roads of Excess'. *World Transport Policy and Practice* 4(2): 24–9.

————. 1998b. 'Regional Growth Management Regime: The Case of Portland, Oregon'. *Journal of Urban Affairs* 20: 363–94.

Leo, Christopher, with Mary Ann Beavis, Andrew Carver, and Robyne Turner. 1998. 'Is Urban Sprawl Back on the Political Agenda? Local Growth Control, Regional Growth Management and Politics'. *Urban Affairs Review* 34: 179–212.

Leo, Christopher, and Wilson Brown. 2000. 'Slow Growth and Urban Development Policy'. *Journal of Urban Affairs* 22: 193–213.

Levy, John M. 1997. *Contemporary Urban Planning*. 4th ed. Upper Saddle River, NJ: Prentice-Hall.

Lightbody, James. 1993. 'Cities: "The Dilemmas Are on Our Doorsteps"'. In *Corruption, Character, and Conduct: Essays on Canadian Government Ethics*, ed. John W. Langford and Allan Tupper. Toronto: Oxford University Press.

Logan, John R., and Harvey L. Molotch. 1987. *Urban Fortunes: The Political Economy of Place*. Berkeley: University of California Press.

Nelson, Arthur C. 2000. 'Effects of Urban Containment on Housing Prices and Landowner Behaviour'. *Land Lines* (May): 1–3.

Purcell, Mark. 2000. 'The Decline of the Political Consensus for Urban Growth: Evidence from Los Angeles'. *Journal of Urban Affairs* 22: 85–100.

Rural Municipality of Springfield. 1998. *Development Plan* (By-Law 98-22). Oakbank, MB: Ruraland Consulting Ltd. (June).

Siegan, Bernard H. 1972. *Land Use without Zoning*. Lexington, MA: Lexington Books.

Thomas, Robert D., and Richard W. Murray. 1991. *Progrowth Politics: Change and Governance in Houston*. Berkeley, CA: IGS Press, Institute of Government Studies, University of California at Berkeley.

Wade, Richard C. 1959. *The Urban Frontier: The Rise of Western Cities, 1790–1830*. Cambridge, MA: Harvard University Press.

Winnipeg. 1998. *Strategic Infrastructure Reinvestment Policy: Report and Recommendations*. Winnipeg: City of Winnipeg.

Infrastructure

Caroline Andrew and Jeff Morrison

Introduction

The policy issues that are important to raise in relation to urban infrastructure are also interesting in themselves and relate to the broader issues of urban public policy. We have much to learn from debates about urban infrastructure that will allow us to better understand the nature of our cities and how to plan and build cities that relate positively to what we as a society wish to be.

The first point to be made—obvious, perhaps, but nonetheless necessary—is how important infrastructure is to our cities. Indeed, as Artibise has stated, 'it is no exaggeration to state that public works make towns and cities possible'. He goes on to emphasize that 'the planning, design, construction, operation, maintenance, and administration of public works are central to any story of Canadian urban development' (1988: 313; see also Fowler and Hartmann's chapter). *Infrastructure* includes the whole network of physical services that permits the existence, growth, and development of our cities. The term certainly includes water and sewage systems, roads and sidewalks, parks and recreational facilities, public buildings, power systems, and information networks. These are the physical bases on which urban centres are built and without which urban centres could not function. We are following, in this respect, the distinction made by Amborski and Slack (1987) between *physical overhead capital* and *social overhead capital*. In this chapter, we are principally interested in physical overhead capital, those areas of municipal infrastructure to which we have referred. Social overhead capital, on the other hand, includes educational and health facilities that, although situated in urban areas, are largely the responsibility of provincial governments.

Policy Debates: The Role of Infrastructure

The importance of infrastructure still does not address the question of the major urban policy issues that it raises. Indeed, questions relating to infrastructure have been part of a number of policy debates. One such debate concerns local government capacity for decision-making. For Teaford (1984), the improvements in the public services of American cities in the late nineteenth century represent an 'unheralded triumph'—'unheralded' because this improvement in infrastructure was little appreciated then, or even now, but a 'triumph' because North American urban residents enjoyed the highest standard of public services in the world. Teaford's argument is that this success was not understood to be a success at the time because it was the result of a political system that operated by compromise, an approach that was neither admired nor appreciated by any of the major political actors of the time. The political system worked by maintaining a balance among business elites, neighbourhood interests, and urban professionals, but none of these groups felt that compromise was noble, or even acceptable, as an objective to be aimed for. For Teaford, the system was successful, and this can be seen by looking at the improvements in infrastructure. In the final analysis, material results should be the criteria for judging the system; 'and yet American municipal government left as a legacy such achievements as Central Park, the New Croton Aqueduct, and the Brooklyn Bridge, monuments of public enterprise that offered new pleasures and conveniences for millions of urban citizens' (Teaford 1984: 313).

Infrastructure expenditures also feature prominently in the Canadian literature on local government's decision-making capacity and on the municipal 'boosterism' of the nineteenth century. The emphasis here has been on identifying the class interests of local elites and on illustrating the combination of private and public strategies that were pursued in Canadian municipalities. Artibise has described, in the case of the Prairie cities, the actions—'such as city incorporations, massive boundary extensions, huge public works programs, deficit financing, and land value taxation policies' (1982: 122)—of the community elites. Moreover, these elites were particularly interested in municipal government:

> Strong beliefs in the virtues of rapid growth, material progress, and social conformity were combined with an equally strong belief in the special role of local government. The boosters shared the view that the active encouragement of growth and business enterprise was the prime concern of municipal corporations. Local government was purely functional; it was a tool serving personal and community prosperity. (Artibise 1982: 127)

Johnson's (1982) study of Guelph shows a similar strategy by business elites; one particularly clear example of infrastructure expenditure by the municipal government was the investments made in trying to ensure that Guelph would be an important railroad centre. Linteau's study of Maisonneuve (now part of Montreal) also focuses on the link between the political influence of business elites and expenditures on infrastructure:

In one respect, however, Maisonneuve was unique—its leaders conceived and implemented an impressive beautification program for which there are no Canadian equivalents. This program, which included a combination of features such as the erection of imposing buildings, boulevard and path development, and zoning, was undertaken in 1910 and was carried out during the next few years. In contrast to the haphazard city-building process in other centres—the product of thousands of individual decisions—the shaping of the urban landscape of Maisonneuve was generally the result of conscious decisions made by a small, influential elite. (Linteau 1982: 304)

The analysis of the political significance of infrastructure expenditure is therefore well established in the Canadian urban history literature. The advancement of class interests through spending on infrastructure has been one of the major themes of these studies of municipal boosterism. The implications for the study of local government capacity are that local decisions did influence the form of urban development and that these decisions can be understood in terms of the social forces animating local government structures.

There has also been a major debate about whether or not investing in infrastructure makes sense from an economic point of view. The debate has been vigorous, and the results of the debates are mixed: the returns on infrastructure investment are neither as high, nor as low, as the various protagonists have argued. Perhaps because of the inconclusive nature of these debates, but perhaps also because of the complexities involved in translating economic debates into the political arena, there have been a variety of positions taken in the political arena. Throughout the 1990s, a large number of governments made drastic cuts in public spending without any particular concern for protecting infrastructure expenditures, but there have also been examples of governments arguing that infrastructure spending is one of the keys to economic recovery.

The argument that infrastructure spending is vital for economic recovery is sometimes linked to another policy discussion related to infrastructure investment, that related to the restructuring of the Canadian economy in the face of globalization and global restructuring. Certain analysts see the forces of globalization as leading to a revitalized role for local economies, and in such a scenario, infrastructure expenditures are a key tool in the hands of localities to advance their economic interests. Other economic policies may be less feasible to implement locally, but infrastructure spending can easily be decided upon at the local level and can enhance the locational advantages of that particular community. This theme informs debates about a wide variety of infrastructure expenditures: quality-of-life considerations can argue for spending on recreational facilities in the same way as spending on roads can be argued as an incentive to the location of industries.

Another policy debate has used infrastructure as a reflection of our values. Examining the choices made by different societies about what collective goods they wish to have is a way of understanding what these societies value. Several studies that compare Canada to the United States have made use of examples of public infrastructure to support the argument that Canada is more collectivist and/or more public-oriented than the United States. Both Horowitz (1966) and Grant (1965) evoke the example of Ontario Hydro as an illustration of a commitment to collective goods. Mercer (1991), for his part, uses public transportation as one of his examples to assert 'that Canadian cities are more public in their nature and US ones more private' (63) and that 'the public city is more attuned to Canadian values, ideologies, and to current practices' (64).

This school of interpretation has been criticized by Armstrong and Nelles (1986) for overestimating the importance of ideology and underestimating more pragmatic factors such as technology, geography, and economic structure. In the same vein, the boosterism studies referred to earlier, although emphasizing the importance of ideological factors, do raise the question of whether decisions such as those in the area of infrastructure can be taken to represent the values and interests of the population as a whole or whether they are more appropriately seen as reflecting class, or elite, interests. The thrust of these studies would be to say that what is important is not so much that Canadians give more weight to collective values but that Canadian local elites had opportunities to use the state to promote their own interests. The acceptance of these strategies by the population may be the result of greater support for public goods, but it may simply reflect greater deference to local elites. Nevertheless, the idea that decisions about collective goods reflect our values is an important contribution and one to which we shall return at the end of this chapter.

This brief survey of debates that bear on infrastructure investments has introduced a number of important themes for our analysis: the political and economic strategies that underlie local infrastructure decisions, the impact of political structures on infrastructure decisions, and infrastructure as a reflection of community values. In order to pursue this question of the multiplicity of policy debates raised by decisions about infrastructure spending, we can look more closely at the example of the 1994–98 Canada Infrastructure Works Program. It illustrates eloquently Fraser's (1989) analysis of 'the politics of need interpretation'. Fraser argues that often the most critical phase of political struggle is not around who can influence decisions, but around who can influence the definition of needs. Once there is an understood sense that certain needs exist, solutions are found. The solutions will make sense in terms of the way the needs were defined and in terms of the interpretation given to the needs (Rochefort and Cobb 1994).

The federal infrastructure program therefore came into being in 1994 because there was an understanding that there was a need for spending on infrastructure. The most widely accepted view was that Canadian urban infrastructure—particularly the water and sewage systems and the roads and bridges—was in poor condition and that the costs of replacement were such that federal government involvement was necessary. This definition of reality underlined the financial constraints of both municipal and provincial governments and therefore the importance of the federal government's saving Canadian urban areas from the collapse of their infrastructure systems. At the same time, this view argued for giving priority to what might be considered 'basic' infrastructure: water and sewers, roads, and bridges.

The very existence of the federal program suggests that this interpretation was the dominant one. As well as being strongly held by the proponents of the program, the Federation of Canadian Municipalities, it was also widely supported in media coverage of the program. At the same time, there were also other interpretations of infrastructure needs that coexisted or competed with the dominant understanding. As Fraser argues, different groups of social actors struggle to impose their view of reality.

For instance, there is another way of looking at the question about what might be the 'priority' areas for infrastructure expenditures. There is a body of literature that suggests that the chief factor for location decisions, at least in the case of the high-technology sector, is quality-of-life considerations. This could be used to argue that recreational expenditures take priority. The criticism of federal funds being used for building facilities for the Cirque du Soleil in Montreal or for the Saddledome in Calgary would, according to this view, be misplaced; creating cities with first-class recreational facilities is an economic priority.

Pursuing this argument, there are other interpretations of need that would reduce still further the priority given to expenditures on 'basic' infrastructure. For instance, at an earlier point in time, the federal government had resisted pressure to help fund municipal water and sewer expenditures on the grounds that more efficient use of water resources would result if municipalities were forced to cost and charge for water use more intelligently (Andrew 1994). In a similar vein, the position that road expenditures should be seen as having 'priority' can be challenged by those who question the dominance of the private automobile in our cities (see Fowler and Layton's chapter for further discussion of the implications of different transportation choices).

An even more 'oppositional' discourse in terms of the federal infrastructure program was the feminist criticism of the program that argued, both in terms of the jobs created and in terms of the infrastructure being built, that this was a program that benefited men. Construction jobs are heavily male, and several of the high profile projects—the Saddledome in Calgary, the Coliseum in Edmonton—were argued to be predominantly of interest to men. This discourse was marginal to the policy debate about the infrastructure program, but it could be argued that it influenced the initial presentation of the program in the Liberal Party's election platform in that the infrastructure program appeared in close proximity to proposals for federal support for child care, a program clearly seen to be of interest to women.

One could further argue, based on Foot's chapter on urban demographics and on the policy implications of those demographics, that the debate over the need for federal infrastructure expenditures should have taken the aging of the population more into account. Foot argues that population aging is gradually moving 'the nation and its communities away from sports and toward more culture' and further, that 'more of the recreational budget should be directed to local cultural facilities, such as theatres, museums, and music halls'. Victoria, BC, with the highest senior dependency ratio of all the Canadian Census Metropolitan Areas (CMAs), received federal money for a theatre renovation project and the construction of a new Conservatory of Music building, while Calgary, with the lowest senior dependency ratio, not only got federal money for the Saddledome, but also got considerable federal money for its light rapid transit system, a policy option that Foot argues is more consistent with that city's younger population. One could argue on the basis of these examples that local decisions did reflect existing demographic realities; but if the federal program had been drawn up in ways to genuinely consider demographic trends, would not federal allocation to different kinds of infrastructure have been more directed?

All these policy debates about the need for expenditures on infrastructure revolve around two central dimensions: who should pay for infrastructure, and what should get built? Material from the 1994–98 Canada Infrastructure Works Program will be used to reflect on these two questions.

Who Should Pay?

Two central dimensions can be seen in relation to the question of who pays for urban infrastructure: the public–private dimension and the question of the intergovernmental divisions of costs. The question of the public–private division of costs is a central theme for Armstrong and Nelles (1986). They have analyzed the complex organizational and regulatory equilibrium of public and private interests that established itself in Canadian cities in the early part of the twentieth century. Recently, there has been considerable attention given to the possibility of increasing the role of the private sector in the financing and management of local infrastructure. This can be seen, for instance, in the 2000 federal mini-budget, in which the federal government re-established an infrastructure program. Indeed, references to the private sector appear throughout the budget's section on the infrastructure program. Calls for privatization correspond to fiscal constraints at all levels of government and also to the strength of the ideological shift in favour of the market. Up to the present, the municipal level has moved relatively slowly toward the privatization of infrastructure spending, but this is clearly one of the lines of development for the near future.

The public–private division of responsibilities is also raised by the question of user fees for infrastructure. Siegel's and Smale and Reid's chapters discuss this issue, highlighting the arguments both for and against the introduction of user fees. As Siegel argues, there are political problems attached to the policy choice of user fees, even though there is now considerable provincial government pressure for their increased use at the municipal level.

The intergovernmental division of costs for local infrastructure has been the subject of vigorous debates during the past twenty years in Canada. These debates have been stimulated by the lobbying efforts of the Federation of Canadian Municipalities (FCM), whose campaign paid off in the form of the 1994 federal government program Canada Infrastructure Works and in the recently announced Phase III program. These most recent efforts by local governments stem from earlier experiences, and therefore we begin by looking at this earlier period.

The history of the twentieth century is the history of municipal efforts to get other levels of government to pay for municipal services. Municipalities have in general been willing, even anxious, to hand over responsibilities to these other governments in return for not having to spend municipal dollars on the services involved. Infrastructure expenditures have been one of the areas for which provincial and federal support have been actively sought. The expansive city-building strategies of the municipal elites of the nineteenth century described in the studies of 'boosterism' are much less apparent in the twentieth century; the 'decline of municipal autonomy' (Taylor 1984) becomes the dominant trend.

In the area of infrastructure, as Dupré (1968) has outlined for Ontario, it was primarily the provincial government that played an increasingly important role in the early twentieth century. The expansion of the private automobile and the resulting demands for road expenditures at the local level, for example, led to provincial grants for municipal governments to cover a part of their expenditures. It was provincial decisions about what should be provincial and what should be local that were decisive; local decision-making merely tried to influence provincial decisions.

By the 1960s, the question of pollution was increasingly on the political agenda. In 1960, the federal government established the Sewage Treatment Loans Program through which loans were given to municipal governments. By the mid-1960s, provincial governments, led by Ontario, were beginning to play a role in this area, and the provincial participation proved to be a crucial determinant of the use made of the federal program. By the end of the 1960s, provincial government participation existed in all the provinces, which allowed for some form of support being provided for municipal activity in the area of sewage treatment.

In addition to this growing provincial support, usually in the form of conditional grants, municipal governments also tried to get assistance from the federal government for local infrastructure expenditures. One of the most successful arguments made to the federal government was that encouraging municipal infrastructure projects was one of the best ways to stimulate the economy and create jobs. Municipal governments could argue that there were always infrastructure projects that were ready to be started and that, with financial support, the projects could be started rapidly.

The first federal government assistance program for municipal infrastructure was launched in the depression years and was explicitly a job creation program. This vision of federal objectives has remained very important in explaining federal government activity and has remained associated with an emphasis on support for building new infrastructure. The first federal program was implemented through the Municipal Improvements Assistance Act and was in existence from 1938 to 1940. Another federal program, similar in objectives, was the Municipal Development and Loan program, in operation from 1963 to 1966.

Federal assistance was also provided, through a variety of programs, by the Central Mortgage and Housing Corporation (CMHC) during the 1960s and 1970s. Once again, job creation was an objective, but so too, as was noted above, were the reduction of pollution, the adequate supply of serviced land, and the revitalization of centre-city neighbourhoods. However, by the 1980s, the federal government was phasing out its urban-oriented activities in the area of housing, and all forms of federal assistance for municipal infrastructure came to an end.

With the elimination of federal assistance programs in the 1980s, the fact that levels of financial support from the provincial governments either were not increasing or were decreasing made municipal governments increasingly anxious about the financing of urban infrastructure. For example, Amborski and Slack (1987) note that the provincial road subsidy allocations in Ontario decreased 18.2 per cent from 1975 to 1983.

The FCM reacted to this negative intergovernmental context by building up an information base upon which it would be able to base action plans (Andrew and Morrison 1995). A task force was created, and in 1985, *Municipal Infrastructure in Canada: Physical Condition and Funding Adequacy* (FCM 1985) was published. This was the basic document that the FCM used to lobby the federal government. It insisted that financial assistance was absolutely necessary if urban infrastructure was to remain viable. As we argued earlier, this was to become the dominant interpretation of the need for a federal program.

The FCM recommendations found some favour with the federal Liberal Party but very little with the Conservative Party. The Conservative government rejected the FCM recommendations, arguing that financial, constitutional, and policy reasons mitigated against federal support for municipal infrastructure spending.

The FCM continued to lobby the federal government and to build up support for the program proposal. Provincial governments agreed to support the recommendation for a federal government program of assistance for local infrastructure. At the same time, the federal Liberal Party continued to include the idea of financial assistance to municipalities for infrastructure in its electoral platform. Infrastructure was an important part of the Liberal election platform of 1993, and with the victory of the federal Liberals, the promise of a federal program of assistance for urban infrastructure became reality. The federal government acted rapidly to set up Canada Infrastructure Works.

This brief description of recent municipal efforts underlines the importance of the debates over the intergovernmental division of costs for municipal infrastructure. Canadian municipal governments, certainly as expressed by their associations, feel strongly that someone else should be sharing in the financing of infrastructure. Despite cutbacks in many areas, provincial governments still provide some funding for infrastructure, in part, at least, because of the high political visibility of these expenditures. This provincial financial role, as Sancton argues, gives the provincial government substantial control over infrastructure decisions taken by municipal governments: 'Provincial policies for the subsidization of housing, sewage treatment, water supply systems, public transit and other urban services effectively determine many large-scale strategic land-use decisions which, formally at least, remain the responsibility of municipal government' (Sancton 1991: 466).

It is difficult to quantify provincial involvement, because it can take a variety of forms, from regulatory control to financial incentives to provincialization of a service. To illustrate this, one can take examples from the area of public transportation. Some provincial governments have insisted that municipalities provide specialized transportation for people with disabilities. In this case, the provincial role is one of regulation of municipal activities, with no financial implications. In other cases, provincial governments give grants to municipal public transportation systems. Finally, one can think of examples (the GO train system in the Toronto metropolitan region, for instance) of provincial governments developing and operating (until recent years, in the case of the GO system) a service that is clearly part of the local public transportation system. Each of these examples has different implications for the way local and provincial government expenditures would reflect the real involvement of the levels of government in the substantive policies those expenditures represent.

The trend over the past forty years has been for an increasing provincial role in the major areas of infrastructure, but in the 1980s and 1990s, provincial governments became increasingly hesitant to increase their financial support to municipal activities (Andrew 1995). Siegel's chapter discusses this declining importance of provincial transfers and the resulting fiscal strategies by municipal governments.

This provincial picture was certainly one of the reasons behind the FCM's efforts to convince the federal government to establish a new program of financial support for municipal infrastructure. In contrast to the provincial governments, the federal government has not played a constant role in this area but, rather, has intervened on an intermittent basis, primarily for job creation objectives.

During the 1980s, the federal government resisted the lobbying efforts of the FCM and the need for federal money for local infrastructure, and it was primarily because of the preoccupation with job creation that the program proposal was included in the Liberal Party's election strategy of 1993. Once again, urban infrastructure was being seen by the federal government as a way to create jobs (and perhaps win elections) rather than as a way to create cities. Provincial governments were willing to accept the federal program because they recognized the need for investment in urban infrastructure and because they were unwilling to increase their own levels of financial support.

What Should Get Built?

One way of looking at the question of what kind of urban infrastructure is currently being built is to look at the results of the last federal infrastructure program. One of the reasons for choosing to do so is that information exists for all the projects accepted and we can therefore look across Canada at all the projects put forward by municipal governments.

But can we really argue that these projects represent municipal priorities for infrastructure expenditures? After all, the projects were to be incremental (i.e., not already budgeted for in the municipality's 1994 capital budget), and it could therefore be argued that, by definition, they do not represent priority infrastructure, but rather supplementary projects. And even if some of the provinces—most notably Newfoundland, but also Manitoba and New Brunswick (Andrew and Morrison 1995)—did not fully conform to the incrementality criteria, clearly the vast majority of the projects financed by the Canada Infrastructure Works program were projects that were additional to the infrastructure projects already being undertaken by municipal governments.

There is another difficulty in analyzing the results of the program as a reflection of municipal priorities, and that is the provincial role in the determination of eligible categories of projects. For example, British Columbia determined from the outset that 85 per cent of program funds would go to water, sewer, and transportation projects. This meant that BC municipalities were restricted in their choice of projects and suggests that the resulting very high allocation of water and sewer projects does not necessarily represent municipal desires but rather provincial objectives. In some other provinces, provincial projects were also funded.

However, despite these problems, we would argue that the results of the infrastructure program can be used as a rough measure of municipal choices. Municipal governments generally had to contribute one-third of the costs, and this meant that they were unlikely to put forward projects that were very far from their immediate priorities. In practice, municipalities seem to have played an important role in the choice of projects (Andrew and Morrison 1995), and the choices can therefore be seen to reflect the priorities of local elites.

An illustration of the importance of the municipal role can be seen by comparing two municipalities from the same province that made broadly different uses of the program. One such comparison is between Scarborough and North York (see Table 13.1). As of June 1995, Scarborough had five projects approved, four of which were basic services related to roads, water, and sewage and only one of which was on the recreational and cultural side (accounting for 26.8 per cent of the total approved costs). In contrast, North York had twenty-nine projects approved, twenty-two of which were more related to recreational and cultural facilities and public buildings (accounting for 62.3 per cent of the total approved costs). North York's choices were clearly a stronger reflection of the value being given to the quality of life as seen by urban residents.

Certain differences can be pointed out between North York and Scarborough that may help to contextualize these differing choices. However, in order to really understand these choices, it would be necessary to do detailed case studies using interviews. Nonetheless, some figures from the 1991 census, as analyzed by Siemiatycki and Isin (1997), support interesting differences. North York had a high proportion of immigrants much earlier on than did Scarborough, although by 1991, the figures were almost identical (13.62 per cent of British ethnic origin responses in North York and 19.41 per cent in Scarborough). The most numerous groups were different in the two places: the three largest ethnic-origin populations in North York were Italian, Jewish, and Chinese, and in Scarborough they were Chinese, Black, and East Indian (Siemiatycki and Isin 1997).

In Canada-wide categories of projects, Table 13.2 gives the breakdown for all projects approved up to June 1996. In terms of approved costs, the major categories are water and sewer projects (32.4 per cent of approved costs), road and bridges projects (28.5 per cent), and cultural and recreational facilities (12.0 per cent).

This table underestimates the priority attached to water and sewer projects by municipalities, because the 6.3 per cent of costs that went to educational facilities were largely undertaken by universities, colleges, and school boards. As Table 13.2

Table 13.1: Projects Approved in Scarborough and North York

Project	Approved cost ($ 000)
Scarborough	
Basic services	
(4 projects) Extension of Progress Avenue	12,000
Rehabilitation of water mains	1,500
Rehabilitation of sewers	500
Enhancement of water-quality facility	2,416
Urban amenities Replacement of Birchmount Pool	6000
(1 project)	
North York	
Basic services Construction of sub-trunk water mains	429
(7 projects) Repairs to water mains	816
Construction of water mains	2,039
Construction of water mains	1,694
Construction of water mains	3,011
Construction of water mains	3,456
Installation of sub-trunk water mains	510
Urban amenities Expansion of tennis-club building	150
(22 projects) Construction of community centre	1,150
Construction of recreation centre	2,400
Upgrading of community pool facility	650
Upgrading of outdoor pool facility	700
Construction of outdoor rink enclosure	2,800
Reconstruction of tennis courts	230
Upgrading of fire station building	100
Installation of street lights	332
Reconstruction of arena roof	178
Reconstruction of arena roof	327
Construction of indoor pool	3,450
Upgrading of community centre	44
Construction of community centre	2,600
Installation of new fire station	702
Installation of stadium lights	100
Installation of arena ceilings	350
Installation of library air conditioner	180
Installation of new library lights	544
Installation of library air conditioner	65
Installation of new playground equipment	1,100
Installation of energy-efficient lighting	100

Source: Municipalities of Scarborough and North York.

indicates, municipalities in British Columbia, Nova Scotia, Prince Edward Island, Newfoundland, and New Brunswick gave clear priority to water and sewer projects (in the case of British Columbia, as was indicated earlier, this was built into the provincial requirement of the program). In Alberta, Saskatchewan, and Quebec, over 35 per cent of the expenditures went to road and bridge projects, whereas Manitoba and Ontario had perhaps the most diversified allocation of projects.

Looking at individual projects or at projects approved in individual municipalities allows a chance to get a better picture of the political strategies behind different choices. Detailing the above comparison between Scarborough and North York, Table 13.1 lists the projects approved in the first few years in the two municipalities. North York definitely favoured the upgrading of facilities: community centres, recreation sites (including tennis courts, rinks, pools, arenas, stadium lights, and playgrounds), and libraries. Most of these projects can be seen as enhancing the quality of life, particularly as relating to opportunities for recreational and leisure-time activities. On the other hand, Scarborough clearly gave its priority to the upgrading of basic services: roads, water, and sewage. Across Canada, more projects appear to have followed the Scarborough model than the North York model, although the major urban municipalities appear to have had more projects relating to urban amenities.

These differing strategies can also be illustrated by a comparison between Calgary and Lethbridge. Lethbridge had eight projects approved, six of which related to basic services. The two projects that related to recreation expenditures were among the three projects with the lowest total cost. Calgary had fifty-one projects approved, with an almost equal split in number between basic services (twenty-five projects) and urban amenities (twenty-six projects). However, in terms of the overall project costs, the urban amenities projects dominated. Of the fifty-one projects, eight had costs in excess of $3 million, and six of these eight fell into the category of urban amenities. One could argue that Calgary was more successfully following the 'boosterism' tradition of marketing the city in terms of the quality of life.

Conclusion

It is interesting to note that relatively few of these projects relate explicitly to economic development and particularly to the development of an information-based economy for competing globally in the twenty-first century. There are few exceptions, such as the funding for the Ottawa-Carleton Research Institute, which exists to facilitate greater cooperation between industry, government, and universities to develop high-technology activities in the region and which was able to expand its information system across the Ottawa-Carleton region. There are a few other projects that relate to the encouragement of tourism and international trade, such as the Quebec City Convention Centre and the Metropolitan Toronto International Trade Centre, but these are rare.

In general, the infrastructure being built relates much more to basic services in Canadian municipalities that it does to competing globally in the information economy. Our argument in this chapter suggests a number of explanations for these

Table 13.2: Canada Infrastructure Works: Phase I
Approved Projects by Infrastructure Class and Province (thousands of dollars)

Province/Territory	Water & Sewer		Roads & Bridges		Municipal Buildings		Other Buildings		Community Cultural & Recreational Facilities		Education Facilities		Other Engineering & Equipment		Total Eligible Costs
British Columbia	490,820	71.5%	72,270	10.5%	37,280	5.4%	5,644	0.8%	60,197	8.8%	1,800	0.3%	18,097	2.6%	686,108
Alberta	158,860	28.2%	242,031	42.9%	31,922	5.7%	20,995	3.7%	93,636	16.6%	596	0.1%	16,165	2.9%	564,205
Saskatchewan	71,526	23.3%	111,793	36.4%	6,689	2.2%	42,215	13.7%	28,505	9.3%	28,874	9.4%	17,689	5.8%	307,291
Manitoba	54,186	21.6%	63,046	25.1%	2,814	1.1%	16,602	6.6%	50,253	20.0%	10,175	4.1%	53,743	21.4%	250,818
Ontario	425,427	18.0%	635,164	26.9%	214,782	9.1%	307,660	13.0%	332,839	14.1%	323,790	13.7%	121,093	5.1%	2,360,755
Quebec	649,162	33.2%	710,508	36.4%	108,267	5.5%	102,683	5.3%	183,901	9.4%	36,506	1.9%	162,480	8.3%	1,953,507
New Brunswick	94,325	57.4%	19,135	11.6%	3,684	2.2%	1,355	0.8%	16,194	9.8%	4,798	2.9%	24,961	15.2%	164,452
Nova Scotia	125,666	57.2%	26,240	11.9%	7,398	3.4%	4,650	2.1%	21,959	10.0%	24,383	11.1%	9,403	4.3%	219,700
Prince Edward Island	28,653	68.3%	5,342	12.7%	1,328	3.2%	413	1.0%	1,860	4.4%	225	0.5%	4,158	9.9%	41,978
Newfoundland	76,094	51.5%	29,518	20.0%	585	0.4%	21,241	14.4%	9,898	6.7%	–		10,304	7.0%	147,640
Northwest Territories	120	0.9%	1,640	11.9%	2,872	20.9%	2,944	21.4%	3,677	26.8%	427	3.1%	2,049	14.9%	13,729
Yukon Territory	2,330	28.3%	2,533	30.8%	595	7.2%	110	1.3%	2,127	25.9%	–		532	6.5%	8,227
First Nations	29,915	32.9%	22,656	24.9%	7,251	8.0%	791	0.9%	11,705	12.9%	414	0.5%	18,258	20.1%	90,990
Totals	2,207,085	32.4%	1,941,875	28.5%	425,467	6.2%	527,303	7.7%	816,750	12.0%	431,988	6.3%	458,930	6.7%	6,809,402

Note: Percentages may not add up to 100% due to rounding.

Source: Correspondence to authors from Canada Infrastructure Works.

results. The 'politics of need' interpretation suggests that the federal government fundamentally felt that there was a need for job creation (and for intergovernmental harmony) and that this definition of need was primary. In addition, the definition of municipal needs that was most widely accepted was that of basic infrastructure: water and sewage, roads and bridges. This bears witness to the successful lobbying strategy of the FCM, which succeeded in arguing that there was a national need for investment in local infrastructure. The major policy issue became the intergovernmental division of costs: not what should be built, but who should pay for what was to be built. The question of content (what should be built) was left to those traditionally responsible for local infrastructure (municipal and provincial governments), while the question of intergovernmental financing was seen as the central policy issue. Although questions of private-sector involvement in infrastructure expenditures were peripherally mentioned in connection with the program, they were not central either to the creation or to the actual use of the program. However, the question of the public–private division of costs will undoubtedly become a more important public policy issue in the years to come, harkening back to the debates of the early twentieth century. (See the introductory chapter and Smale and Reid's chapter.) This is already in evidence with the expected involvement of the private sector in the 2000 infrastructure program. The results of the federal infrastructure program do give some support for the themes we mentioned earlier: the impact of particular economic and political strategies on infrastructure expenditures, the impact of political structure, the study of infrastructure as a reflection of collective values. Even our very brief comparisons indicate that different municipalities pursued different infrastructure strategies. Scarborough's orientation to basic services and North York's to urban amenities could be explained in a variety of ways. Is it a question of different populations, of pressures from different municipal associations, of different municipal elites, or of different values? We would need to do more detailed case studies to attempt to answer these questions, but we can see that there were differences in use. Some municipalities gave higher priority to quality-of-life issues, whereas others were more preoccupied with upgrading basic services.

In conclusion, it seems appropriate to end as we began, with reference to Teaford's conception of an 'unheralded triumph'. Canadian cities would not exist and could not function without the high quality of infrastructure that exists. The totally pragmatic, not to say unprincipled, efforts of Canadian municipalities to get other levels of government to pay for municipal services may not make for dramatic reading, but if we follow Teaford, the criteria for evaluation should be the projects built and the resulting quality of infrastructure in our cities.

References

Amborski, David, and Enid Slack. 1987. 'Federal, Provincial and Municipal Cooperation: Past, Present and Future'. In *The Proceedings of the First Canadian Conference on Urban Infrastructure*, ed. Daniel Smith and Gary Hinke. Toronto: Sodanell.

Andrew, Caroline. 1994. 'Federal Urban Activity: Intergovernmental Relations in an Age of Restraint'. In *The Changing Canadian Metropolis: A Public Policy Perspective*, ed. Frances Frisken. Toronto: Canadian Urban Institute.

————. 1995. 'Provincial–Municipal Relations; or Hyper-Fractionalized Quasi-Subordination Revisited'. In *Canadian Metropolitics: Governing Our Cities*, ed. James Lightbody. Toronto: Copp Clark.

Andrew, Caroline, and Jeff Morrison. 1995. 'Canada Infrastructure Works: Between "Picks and Shovels" and the Information Highway'. In *How Ottawa Spends, 1995–96: Mid-Life Crises*, ed. Susan D. Philipps. Ottawa: Carleton University Press.

Armstrong, Christopher, and H.V. Nelles. 1986. *Monopoly's Moment: The Organization and Regulation of Canadian Utilities, 1830–1930*. Toronto: University of Toronto Press.

Artibise, Alan F.J. 1982. 'In Pursuit of Growth: Municipal Boosterism and Urban Development in the Canadian Prairie West, 1871–1913'. In *Shaping the Urban Landscape: Aspects of the Canadian City-Building Process*, ed. Gilbert A. Stelter and Alan F.J. Artibise. Ottawa: Carleton University Press.

————. 1988. 'Building Cities'. In *Building Canada: A History of Public Works*, ed. Norman R. Ball. Toronto: University of Toronto Press.

Dupré, J. Stefan. 1968. *Intergovernmental Finance in Ontario: A Provincial–Municipal Perspective*. Toronto: Ontario Commission on Taxation, Government of Ontario.

Federation of Canadian Municipalities (FCM). 1985. *Municipal Infrastructure in Canada: Physical Condition and Funding Adequacy*. Ottawa: FCM.

Fraser, Nancy. 1989. 'Talking about Needs: Interpretive Contests as Political Conflicts in Welfare State Societies'. *Ethics* 99: 291–313.

Grant, George. 1965. *Lament for a Nation: The Defeat of Canadian Nationalism*. Toronto: McClelland & Stewart.

Horowitz, Gad. 1966. 'Conservatism, Liberalism and Socialism in Canada'. *Canadian Journal of Economics and Political Science* 32(2): 143–71.

Johnson, Leo. 1982. 'Ideology and Political Economy in Urban Growth: Guelph, 1827–1927'. In *Shaping the Urban Landscape: Aspects of the Canadian City-Building Process*, ed. Gilbert A. Stelter and Alan F.J. Artibise. Ottawa: Carleton University Press.

Linteau, Paul-André. 1982. 'The Development and Beautification of an Industrial City: Maisonneuve, 1883–1918'. In *Shaping the Urban Landscape: Aspects of the Canadian City-Building Process*, ed. Gilbert A. Stelter and Alan F.J. Artibise. Ottawa: Carleton University Press.

Mercer, John. 1991. 'The Canadian City in Continental Context'. In *Canadian Cities in Transition: The Twenty-First Century*, ed. Trudi Bunting and Pierre Filion. Toronto: Oxford University Press.

Rochefort, David A., and Roger W. Cobb. 1994. *The Politics of Problem Definition: Shaping the Policy Agenda*. Lawrence, KS: University Press of Kansas.

Sancton, Andrew. 1991. 'The Municipal Role in the Governance of Canadian Cities'. In *Canadian Cities in Transition: The Twenty-First Century*, ed. Trudi Bunting and Pierre Filion. Toronto: Oxford University Press.

Siemiatycki, Myer, and Engin Isin. 1997. 'Immigration, Diversity and Urban Citizenship in Toronto'. *Canadian Journal of Regional Science* 20: 73–102.

Taylor, John. 1984. 'Urban Autonomy in Canada: Its Evolution and Decline'. In *The Canadian City: Essays in Urban and Social History*, rev. ed., ed. Gilbert Stelter and Alan F.J. Artibise. Ottawa: Carleton University Press.

Teaford, Jon. 1984. *The Unheralded Triumph: City Government in America, 1870–1900*. Baltimore, MD: Johns Hopkins University Press.

From Public Health to the Healthy City

Trevor Hancock

Introduction

Given the already low and now declining role of local governments in the provision of public health services in Canada as described in this chapter, is there any point in writing about public health in a book on urban policy? The answer is a resounding yes—if what we are concerned with is the health of the public, rather than just public health services. For although local government may not have much influence over the latter, it has considerable influence over the former. This is because local government policies in many sectors influence the determinants of the health of the population; this realization forms the basis for the Healthy Cities/Communities approach that has gained prominence in the past fifteen years. *Influence our daily behaviours.*

Public health has been defined as 'the science and art of preventing disease, prolonging life and promoting health through the organised efforts of society' (HMSO 1988, cited in Ashton 1990: 387). For our purposes, *public health* is a government (hence, *public*) service that is concerned with the health of the population as a whole rather than the health of individuals and with the prevention of disease rather than its treatment. It is based on the utilitarian ethic of 'the greatest good (in this case, health) for the greatest number'. A summary of the main components of local public health services is provided in Box 14.1.

This chapter does not attempt a comprehensive overview of public health services at the urban level in Canada. Rather, it seeks to provide both a sense of where public health has come from and where it might be going, as well as a general overview of public health services and issues related to those services at the local level.[1] It is concerned hardly at all with the health *care* system; it treats the public health system in some detail but then stresses the many ways in which local governments affect the health of their communities well beyond the mere provision of public health services, important though they are. The task of creating healthier communities is becoming an important role for local government, and indeed for local governance, for which it has significant implications. This is not really a new role at all, but the

Box 14.1: Public Health Services

Public health services are provided by public health inspectors, public health nurses, public health physicians, health educators, dental hygienists, community nutritionists, and other public health professionals. At the local level, the Public Health Department these days is usually part of a Regional Health Authority, although it may be part of a municipal Board of Health or even a department of city government. Provincial and federal health departments also have public health programs, particularly in the area of communicable-disease control, environmental health, and food and drug safety.

Local public health departments provide services in the areas of health protection, health promotion, and disease prevention. Although described below as essentially different activities, in practice there is considerable overlap among the three approaches.

- _Health protection_ uses the police powers of the state to require, regulate, and enforce measures to protect the health and safety of the public and, if necessary, to punish transgressors. Health protection programs include environmental hygiene (safeguarding our food and water supplies, protecting us from air pollution, ensuring proper handling of wastes and sewage, etc.). A second key program area is communicable-disease control, which, in addition to inspection of restaurants and other food premises, includes the investigation of outbreaks of communicable disease — identifying sources, tracing contacts, and, where necessary, requiring treatment and control of cases (e.g., tuberculosis, cholera, typhoid, and other serious threats to life and health).
- _Health promotion_ involves trying to ensure that our environmental, social, economic, living, and working conditions are health-enhancing. This includes advocacy for public policies in non-health sectors to be more 'healthy' (healthy public policy); community development, to strengthen the capacity of communities and individuals to take actions to improve their own health conditions; and health education in schools, homes, and community settings, to help people develop the skills they need to make healthy choices and lead healthy lives.
- _Disease prevention_ has a somewhat more clinical orientation and includes maternal and child health services, immunization of school children, preventive dentistry, nutrition counselling, mental health counselling, preventive and supportive services for seniors, and similar services.

revival of an historically significant role for local government that we have tended to overlook. Thus, it is important to begin with that history.

The History of Public Health

People have been concerned about the health of the public—and about the healthfulness of cities—for hundreds, indeed thousands of years. Two and a half thousand years ago, Hippocrates—the 'father of medicine'—wrote in *Airs, Waters, Places* about the ideal setting for a town or dwelling place so as to ensure the health of its inhabitants. The Chinese, the Egyptians, the Indus Valley civilization, the Greeks, the Romans, and many others in history have concerned themselves with public health, often creating great public works to ensure clean water, to remove sewage, and so on. The boards of health in Renaissance Italy developed codes of practice and regulations covering many aspects of life so as to ensure the health of the inhabitants; they also developed sophisticated (for those days) information and communication systems to monitor death and disease and to share that information among themselves in order to detect and control epidemics (Cipolla 1976). Thus, urban public health is an old and well-established tradition.

Our modern approach to public health has its roots in the early part of the nineteenth century, in response to the appalling conditions in the rapidly growing cities of early industrial Britain. (See Winslow [1923] for a good review of the history of public health in the nineteenth and early twentieth centuries.) So appalling were the conditions (see Box 14.2) that the British government established a Commission on Health in Towns in 1843, while public-minded citizens and health leaders established the Health in Towns Association in 1844. As a result, significant steps were taken to understand and control many of the major causes of death and disease in the towns and cities of Britain, as well as in many other countries in Europe, in Canada, and in the United States. Indeed, so much progress had been made that in 1875 Sir Benjamin Ward Richardson, a leading figure in public health in Britain, was able to describe 'Hygeia', his vision of an ideally healthy city (Cassedy 1962; Richardson 1875). For those interested in modern urban public health, his vision makes interesting reading; many of the things it describes are still on the agenda of public health and urban planning today.

From the 1870s to the 1930s, public health was still the major means of improving the health of the population. Through public works and urban planning, family hygiene and immunization, health education and food control, public health measures continued to have significant impact. (See Hancock [1997a] for a brief overview of the history of urban public health from the 1840s to the 1930s in the context of the Healthy Cities/Communities movement.) It was not until the 1930s, with the advent of the sulpha drugs and penicillin, that the medical model—with its emphasis on the diagnosis and treatment of individuals with powerful medical and surgical therapies—began to dominate.

Particularly since World War II, the medical model has come to assume overwhelming importance in the health arena, consuming between 7 per cent and 10 per

Box 14.2: Nineteenth-Century Manchester: A Sick City

In 1845, Frederick Engels described Manchester's River Irk as

> a narrow, coal-black, foul-smelling stream . . . in dry weather, a long string of the
> most disgusting, blackish-green slime pools are left standing . . . from the depths of
> which bubbles of miasmatic gas constantly arise and give forth a stench unen-
> durable even on the bridge forty or fifty feet above the surface of the stream.
> (Girouard 1985: 262, 264)

Hippolyte Taine wrote of his visit to Manchester in 1859:

> Earth and air seem impregnated with fog and soot. The factories extend their flanks
> of fouler brick one after another, bare, with shutterless windows, like economical
> and colossal prisons. . . . Through half-open windows we could see wretched rooms
> at ground level, or often below the damp earth's surface. Masses of livid children,
> dirty and flabby of flesh, crowd each threshold and breathe the vile air of the street,
> less vile than that within. (Girouard 1985: 257–8)

cent of the GNP of Western industrialized countries (and a full 14 per cent in the
United States) and becoming a major factor in social and economic policy. Today, the
medical model is the only model that most people know about; we have forgotten
the public health approach. But as Parfit noted in her history of the health of Oxford
between 1770 and 1974,

> many would be surprised to learn that the greatest contribution to the health of the nation
> over the past 150 years was made not by doctors or hospitals but by local government. Our
> lack of appreciation of the role of our cities in establishing the health of the nation is
> largely due to the fact that so little has been written about it. (1986: flyleaf)

Local government's contribution came from its work to create healthy living and
working conditions for its citizens. The improvement in these conditions was based
on and was part of a larger picture, namely, the rapid economic and social development that accompanied industrialization and urbanization in Europe and North
America in the nineteenth century. Improved nutrition, improved hygiene and sanitation, smaller family size, and improved education were the principal factors that
led to improved health, whereas specific biomedical measures, such as immunization and antibiotics, played a comparatively minor role (McKeown 1979). Such
large-scale environmental, social, economic, and political factors are likely to continue to be the major determinants of health in the twenty-first century (Hancock
and Garrett 1995).

Municipal Public Health in Canada

Some of the earliest public health measures that were undertaken in Canada were in response to the spread of epidemics of cholera, typhoid, smallpox, and other infectious diseases as waves of immigrants came to Canada from Europe. Quarantine stations were set up at Grosse Île, Quebec, in 1832 to try to protect Canada from the first epidemic of cholera, and the earliest municipal health boards were set up in response to that epidemic (Bilson 1984; 'Canada's Amazing Health History' 1984). For example, one of the first acts of the newly incorporated City of Toronto in 1834 was to establish a Board of Health.

These early Boards of Health often came and went with each succeeding epidemic. It was 1884 before Ontario enacted its Public Health Act, resulting in the permanent establishment of Boards of Health. Initially, Boards of Health were much concerned with issues of environmental sanitation, the construction of sewers, the provision of clean water, and similar public health works. Indeed, public works departments and other municipal departments were often established in part out of a concern with public health. In Toronto, for example, research by Severs (1989) found that ten out of sixteen city services that were studied grew out of a concern for the health of the public, including public works, buildings, housing and welfare departments, and, to a lesser extent, the fire, police, parks, and planning departments (Severs 1989). In particular, there was a strong link historically between public health and urban planning in Canada. (See Box 14.3.)

In the early part of the twentieth century, as environmental conditions were brought under control and as effective vaccines became available, attention switched to issues such as the pasteurization of milk, food inspection and control, immunization, maternal and child health, and family hygiene. The period during and after the first world war was also a period of great social reform, and public health leaders, such as Dr Charles Hastings in Toronto, were equally concerned with issues of housing, poverty, and working conditions (see MacDougall [1990] for a detailed history of public health in Toronto).

But although local governments in Canada have played an important role in public health, their role in health care has been more constrained. As Manga and Muckle point out, 'local governments in Canada have neither a long history of involvement in health and social services, as in Europe, nor an extensive legal obligation to provide for the poor as do local governments in the U.S.' (1987: 9).

Hospitals were established by voluntary groups or religious organizations in local communities, although they were supported in some communities by local government. But in the twentieth century, some municipalities also became involved in insuring medical services and hospital care; at the time of World War I, 107 municipalities, 14 towns, and 19 villages in Saskatchewan had contracted for physician services (Manga and Muckle 1987), and by 1942, 88 rural municipalities, chiefly in Saskatchewan, Alberta, and Manitoba, were operating municipal care plans (Shah 1998).

But with the advent of a national program of hospital insurance in 1958 and then universal medical insurance in Canada in 1968, Ministries of Health became, in effect, ministries of medical insurance and medical care. The role that some munic-

Box 14.3: Public Health and Urban Planning

The connection between public health and urban planning is particularly clear in Canada. In 1912, the Government of Canada established a Commission on Conservation, prompted by a concern that resources would soon run out. The concept of conservation the Commission used was a broad one, as illustrated by Dr Charles Hodgetts, Chief Medical Officer of Health for the Province of Ontario and Secretary to the Commission's Public Health Advisory Committee:

⁜ [There are] two important factors in the question of national conservation, the physical and the vital. The former relates to the protecting of our land, our forests, our minerals, our waters, and our sunlight, our fresh air; the latter, to the prevention of diseases, to health and to the prolongation of life. In housing and town planning we are dealing with most of the former and all of the latter. (Armstrong 1959: 18)

It was Hodgetts and the Public Health Advisory Committee who brought to Canada the leading British urban planner Thomas Adams, a protegé of 'Garden City' pioneer Ebenezer Howard and first Secretary of the Letchworth Garden City Company. Working for the Commission's Public Health Committee between 1914 and 1919, Adams drafted a great deal of early planning legislation and helped organize the Civic Improvement League and the Town Planning Institute of Canada, of which he was the first president (Armstrong 1959). Thus, urban planning, public health, and the sustainable use of resources were closely linked in the early part of the twentieth century.

ipalities had played in health care was made redundant with the coming of medicare, and they once again became responsible only for public health (if for anything at all), at a time when public health itself—which is not covered by the Canada Health Act and thus not cost-shared by the federal government—was given little priority.

The 'New' Public Health

By 1971, all provinces had entered into the national health insurance program and the federal government was able to turn from its agenda of ensuring universal health insurance to considering the health of the population. Thus, in 1974, the federal government produced a document (the Lalonde Report) that was to have a revolutionary impact on public health—and, indeed, on our understanding of health and its determinants. It noted that major improvements in the health of Canadians would result primarily from changing our lifestyles and improving our environment, not from more health care. And it proposed a strategy of 'health promotion' to improve health (Health and Welfare Canada 1974).

The new paradigm of health promotion envisages health as a positive value, not merely as the absence of disease, and calls for the development of health-promoting public policies. These policies must create physical and social environments supportive of health and must strengthen communities, as well as help people to develop their personal health skills and reorient health services toward prevention and community-based care (WHO 1986). The ultimate objective is to reduce inequalities in health and to achieve 'Health for All', as a 1986 federal government policy paper suggested (Health and Welfare Canada 1986).

As a result, health promotion—the 'new' public health—has achieved considerable prominence in Canada and around the world. Strong and effective leadership by the Health Promotion Directorate of Health Canada in the mid- to late 1980s was complemented by the development of health-promotion programs in most provinces and by many local public health agencies. Many of these programs went beyond conventional lifestyle-oriented educational programming aimed at improving health habits to address the basic determinants of health through a combination of community development and intersectoral action—action *across* different policy sectors and involving the public, private, and voluntary sectors. This 'Healthy Cities' approach has been one of the major successes of the health promotion approach (Tsouros 1990).

However, in recent years, while our knowledge of the determinants of health has grown considerably (Evans, Barer, and Marmor 1994; 'Health and Wealth' 1994) and the commitment of federal and provincial governments to 'population health' is rhetorically strong (Federal, Provincial and Territorial Advisory Committee on Population Health 1994), the commitment to a broad health-promotion agenda and to actually addressing and doing something about the determinants of health has wavered (Hancock 1994b; Health Canada 1997; Sutcliffe, Deber, and Pasut 1997). (See Box 14.4 for a contemporary summary of the major determinants of health.) The commitment to health promotion, to public health, and to the Healthy Cities/Communities approach may be slipping somewhat. Only time will tell.

Urban Public Health Services Today

Because public health services are not included in the Canada Health Act, public health at the local level is funded entirely by the provinces; however, the federal government maintains some international and national public health functions and provides some limited support in community grants for health promotion. Not surprisingly, in the absence of federal cost-sharing, public health has generally suffered from underfinancing; only about 5 per cent of total health care expenditures in 1996 were devoted to public health, including federal, provincial, and local expenditure, as well as the contribution of voluntary health organizations (Shah 1998).

Provincial governments have, until recently, financed almost all public health expenditures directly; the province also provided the services in the Atlantic provinces and (except in the main cities) in Manitoba, Saskatchewan, and British Columbia. Even in those cases where municipalities have operated their own public

Box 14.4: The Determinants of Health

In the 1996 *Report on the Health of Canadians*, the Federal, Provincial and Territorial Advisory Committee on Population Health identified a comprehensive set of determinants of health, as follows:

Living and Working Conditions

- a thriving and sustainable economy, with meaningful work for all
- an adequate income for all Canadians
- reduction in the number of families living in poverty
- achieving an equitable distribution of income
- ensuring healthy working conditions
- encouraging lifelong learning
- fostering friendship and social support networks, in families and communities

Physical Environment

- foster a healthy and sustainable environment for all
- ensure suitable, adequate, and affordable housing
- create safe and well-designed communities

Personal Health Practices and Coping Skills

- foster healthy child development
- encourage healthy life-choice decisions

Health Services

- ensure appropriate and affordable health services, accessible to all
- reduce preventable illness, injury, and death

Biology and Genetic Endowment

- heredity
- gender
- development and aging

Source: Federal, Provincial and Territorial Advisory Committee on Population Health (1996).

health services, however, the province still paid the bulk of the costs. Thus, in recent years, municipalities have paid only a small part of the total cost of public health services; the municipal share of Canada's total health care budget in 1997 was 0.9 per cent (Canadian Institute for Health Information 1999). Nonetheless, this represented 0.9 per cent of almost $78 billion spent on health care in Canada that year, or $700 million—a not-inconsiderable sum.

Yet the small but significant role for local government in public health has recently been dramatically reduced. In every province except Ontario, reforms of the health care system have resulted in the establishment of some form of regional health authority. These regional authorities are responsible for managing most aspects of health care services in their region as a single system; in most cases, this includes public health services. As a consequence, even in those municipalities where there was previously a local board of health managing a municipal public health service, the role and responsibilities of the board of health have generally been reassigned to the new regional health authority.[2] (See also Sutcliffe, Deber, and Pasut [1997] for a recent brief overview of public health services in six provinces: Newfoundland, New Brunswick, Ontario, Manitoba, Saskatchewan, and Alberta.) The problem is that in places where there was a municipal public health service, this reassignment removes public health from its important links to local government and in particular to local government departments that have an important role to play in improving the living conditions and thus the health of the public.

The situation is different in Ontario, where prior to 1997, the province contributed 75 per cent of the approved budgets for thirty-six of its forty-two local health units (the exceptions were the six Boards of Health in Metropolitan Toronto, as it then was, which received 40 per cent). But as a result of downloading and restructuring, the provincial government now pays 50 per cent of the approved costs for its thirty-seven health units (including the single amalgamated health unit in the new City of Toronto) and 100 per cent of the costs of some programs, such as vaccines, AIDS prevention, speech and audiometric services, and family planning.

The Provincial Picture[3]

The Atlantic provinces

In the Atlantic provinces, public health services are now provided by regional health boards in three of the four provinces. In Newfoundland, 'the major responsibility for public health services rests with the newly appointed community health boards' (Matthews 1995), although under the Municipalities Act, municipalities have certain powers with respect to regulating water supply and sanitary services, removing buildings that pose a health risk, and making regulations pertaining to nuisances. In Prince Edward Island, regional health boards have been established and 'municipal councils in P.E.I. have very limited involvement in the management of public health services' (McEwen 1995). In Nova Scotia, 'all health and social services have been transferred from the jurisdiction of municipalities to the purview of the Provincial

Government. . . . Health services are at present being regionalized in Nova Scotia. Each of four regions will have the responsibility for the delivery of public health services. . . . The only direct involvement of municipalities in public health issues might be in the areas of recreation and water supply' (Stewart 1995). In New Brunswick, however, public health services are the responsibility of regional offices of the Ministry of Health: 'Municipal administrations have minimal involvement, if at all with the provision of such services with the possible exception of . . . matters related to land use, drinking water quality or sewage disposal' (King 1995). Sutcliffe, Deber, and Pasut note that New Brunswick is the only one of the six provinces they surveyed where public health decision-making is 'clearly centralised' (1997: 248) as part of the Ministry itself, rather than decentralized to a regional community board.

Quebec

In Quebec, public health units and municipal health services were abolished over twenty years ago, as a result of the report of the Castonguay Commission (Quebec, Commission d'enquête sur la santé et le bien-être sociale 1970). In their place, thirty-two hospital-based organizations called DSCs (départements du santé communautaire) were established. These DSCs 'receive no funding from and are not politically accountable to local governments, have hardly any public health nurses providing direct services and do not have any public health inspectors' (Hancock, Pouliot, and Duplessis 1990: 191). The Ministry of Health has no direct role in providing public health services; the public health nursing role is generally provided through CLSCs (community health centres), 'while public health inspectors work for the municipality or the provincial environment ministry' (Hancock, Pouliot, and Duplessis 1990: 191). Recent changes have led to the merging of the thirty-two hospital-based DSCs to form sixteen Regional Public Health Directorates that are linked to the Regional Health and Social Services Boards that manage the health and social services system at a regional level. These Boards are locally accountable—although not elected—and have considerable autonomy. The public health function is more caught up in bureaucracy than before, is still separate from municipalities, and still does not provide direct services. Meanwhile, the CLSCs, some of which have been merged with small hospitals or nursing homes, are struggling to maintain a health-promotion and disease-prevention role in the face of the growing demands for ambulatory and community care services that they face (Réal Lacombe, personal communication, December 1997).

Ontario

In Ontario, municipally based public health services have been the norm for over a century, with only the unorganized parts of Northern Ontario having public health services provided directly by the province. For the rest, the province is divided into thirty-seven municipally based health units, each with its own Medical Officer of Health and Board of Health. These Boards of Health may include citizen representatives and provincial appointees as well as local councillors. In recent years, however, the Boards of Health in nine regional municipalities have been replaced by Health and Social Service Committees established by regional government councils. These committees consist of regional councillors appointed solely by the municipality, but the committees are only partly accountable to local governments, as they are also accountable to the Minister of Health under provincial legislation for meeting provincial standards for a set of mandatory programs (see Box 14.5).

In 1999/2000, $337 million was budgeted for public health in Ontario out of a total Ministry of Health budget of $21.5 billion, or just over 1.5 per cent. Of this, $167 million was transferred to local public health agencies to be matched by municipal contributions, while some of the remaining funding was fully transferred for select programs funded at 100 per cent. Thus, total public health spending (provincial plus municipal) is 2.34 per cent of the provincial health budget, with municipalities contributing just under 0.8 per cent (data from the Ontario Public Health Association and the Association of Local Public Health Agencies). But at a time when there is growing interest in the integration of health services, the key public health sector continues to be somewhat isolated from the rest of the health care system. Moreover, the amalgamation of Toronto has created one large health unit to serve the 2.1 million people of the city, with implications arising from the need to merge

Box 14.5: Public Health Services

In 1983, Ontario replaced the century-old Public Health Act with the Health Protection and Promotion Act, which confirmed the municipal basis of public health while establishing a broad set of core programs that all health units are required to provide at a specified level of service (Ontario, Ministry of Health 1983). The 1983 Health Protection and Promotion Act in Ontario mandates seven sets of core programs that health units must 'provide or ensure the provision of'. These are

- community sanitation
- communicable-disease control
- preventive dentistry
- family health
- home care
- public health education
- nutrition

These services are generally delivered by the appropriate staff on a disciplinary/divisional basis. While this outline of public health services is, of course, specific to Ontario, it is generally representative of the responsibilities of provincial, regional, and municipal public health services nationally.

six quite different corporate cultures and approaches to public health. In particular, there is concern that the progressive leadership shown by the old City of Toronto Department of Public Health will be less acceptable to the new mega-city and that the community-based approach will be less feasible in such a large city.

The Western provinces

In the four Western provinces, public health services have generally been subsumed in new regional health boards, as is the case in the Atlantic provinces. In Manitoba, the province is responsible for public health services throughout the province, except for the City of Winnipeg, which is the only urban centre in Manitoba to have its own health department; however, the city's health department provides public health services only to the inner-city area of Winnipeg, with about one-third of Winnipeg's total population. There is no health board in Winnipeg; instead, public health services are part of the Community Services department, which is in turn accountable to the Commissioner of Planning and Community Services (an interesting integration) and, through the Commissioner, to city council. In Saskatchewan, 'municipalities have traditionally been required to support health services'; however, 'recently the influence of municipal councils has decreased' (Langlois 1995). The creation of thirty health districts has meant that 'over 400 boards and commissions were collapsed into these . . . districts' (Langlois 1995), although municipal council members were eligible to be elected to the district health boards at the elections held in October 1995.

In Alberta, the twenty-seven health units and health boards were disestablished on April 1, 1995, and the public health function was absorbed into the seventeen new Regional Health Authorities (RHAs). These authorities 'have assumed responsibility for resource allocation, as well as planning and delivery of health services, at the regional level within an overall provincial framework of legislation, policies and standards' (Fulton 1995). The Regional Health Authorities Act requires the RHAs to 'promote and protect the health of its population in the health region and work toward a prevention of disease and injury' (Fulton 1995)—clearly, the public health function. Moreover, RHAs have final authority in this respect, although 'while the act does not specifically legislate the involvement of municipal councils, there are clear opportunities for RHAs to enter into agreements with the municipal governments . . . [and] community health councils, once they are established, may include municipal government representation' (Fulton 1995). The former health units had been independent boards appointed by the province, except in Edmonton and Calgary, where city council appointed the Board of Health. But even in those two cities, the funding for public health was entirely from the province. In the new system, each RHA is required to have a Medical Officer of Health, but there are no provincial standards with respect to public health services. As a result, while some RHAs treat it very seriously, others treat public health rather lightly. The chief result of all this has been that there is no identifiable and distinct public health organization in Alberta now and there is no accountability to local government in Edmonton and Calgary, where previously there was.

In British Columbia, 'five municipal health departments have operated ... for many years. However, under the Ministry of Health's initiative to regionalize the health care system, newly established Regional Health Boards and Community Health Councils [are] responsible for delivering public health services. . . . [However,] many municipal councils will continue to be involved in the governance of public health services through representation on RHBs and CHCs' (Greschler n.d.). In some areas (e.g. Coast-Garibaldi), a Community Health Services Society has been created that provides public health and community care services and that coordinates, but does not own and manage, hospitals.

In short, it is apparent that the direct municipal governance of public health services in Canada, slight as it was, has all but disappeared everywhere except in Ontario, where it is cost-shared 50-50 with the province. On the other hand, since in most provinces municipal councillors are members of the new RHBs or CHCs, there is now a degree of direct local political input to the provision of health services—including public health—that was not present before. And to the extent that public health services were previously provided by the province, there is now local direction and local accountability for those services where before there was none. Moreover, while some local governments may not have direct accountability anymore for public health services, they can and should be accountable for those many aspects of the determinants of health that do lie within their jurisdiction, as will be discussed shortly.

Public Health Issues in the Twenty-First Century

In addition to the important structural and organizational changes noted above, public health has also undergone significant change in the focus of its concern in the past few decades. The most profound change in public health services from the early part of this century has been their increasing focus on non-communicable diseases. In the nineteenth century and into the early twentieth century, the major causes of death and disease were infectious diseases. The dramatic improvement in life expectancy and health status in the nineteenth and twentieth centuries resulted from the high degree of control over infectious diseases that resulted from public health measures and socio-economic development. For example, in 1921, cardiovascular disease and cancer accounted for only 26 per cent of deaths in Canada, while infectious diseases accounted for 14 per cent. By 1991, infectious disease was responsible for only 1.3 per cent of deaths, while cardiovascular disease and cancer accounted for 66 per cent (Federal, Provincial and Territorial Advisory Committee on Population Health 1994).

Underlying these and other major causes of death are a set of risk behaviours, of which the most important are smoking, diet, alcohol and drug abuse, fitness, driving habits, and other 'lifestyle' factors. These have become the target of a wide variety of public health programs, many of them educational but some of them addressed to the broader social and political issues. This latter approach—known as *health promotion*—is based on the recognition that underlying these risk behaviours are a set of risk conditions: poverty, illiteracy or low levels of education, unhealthy and unsafe living and working conditions, powerlessness, unsafe products, intensive marketing of unhealthy lifestyles, and other factors. This has prompted many public health services to pay attention to the underlying socio-political and environmental conditions of their communities, to address the public policy aspects of the determinants of health, and to work with their communities to bring a community-development approach to major health concerns. Some departments of public health have also focused on the inequalities in health that are found within communities, arguing that the best way to improve the overall health of the population is to improve the health of the least healthy, who are almost invariably the poorest members of the community. Taken together, this set of approaches is the basis of the Healthy City or Healthy Community approach discussed in the next section.

However, while the conceptual and rhetorical commitment to this broad approach to the determinants of the health of the population has been strong, Sutcliffe, Deber, and Pasut (1997) found in their survey of six of the ten provinces that, in practice, the provincially mandated core content area for public health remains focused on communicable-disease control, environmental sanitation, and health protection. Only Ontario mandates a broad range of health-promotion programs, while for the rest there was 'no evidence of mandated programs that were explicitly health focused, that addressed broader determinants of health or that used multiple strategies approaches' (Sutcliffe, Deber, and Pasut 1997: 247; i.e., health promotion, community involvement).

Moreover, Sutcliffe, Deber, and Pasut (1997) found that while nearly all provinces recognized the need for broader approaches based on population health, health promotion, and community involvement, the people they interviewed[4] also recognized that these broader approaches are not presently adopted, due to a combination of financial constraints, low morale, and lack of political will.

The authors reflected a concern that public health is being overshadowed by a focus on the reform of acute and long-term care within the health care system, that 'opportunities for reinvestments in public health were being forfeited', and that 'long-term prevention activities would receive lower priority than short-term acute care activities' (Sutcliffe, Deber, and Pasut 1997: 248). They also noted that 'for the six provinces under study, the reality is a retrenchment of public health scope during a time that should have been considered conducive to public health expansion' (248). Thus, despite Canada's international reputation for adopting a broad approach to public health, their study 'described a current role of public health that is much more circumscribed . . . [and] that despite the rhetoric of determinants of health, really represents some backtracking and risks to Canada's reputation as a world leader' (249).

If, indeed, public health is being weakened and its focus is becoming more narrow and conventional, as this survey suggests, then, paradoxically, this makes it all the more important that municipal governments themselves take up the mandate—their historical role, in fact—of creating healthier cities and communities. The more that public health becomes divorced from municipal governments, the more important the Healthy Cities/Communities approach becomes. Indeed, this may in part explain why this approach has been more widely adopted by municipal governments in Quebec—where public health has been separated from municipal government since the early 1970s—than elsewhere in Canada.

Healthy Cities/Communities

From its inception in 1986 as a World Health Organization (WHO) project for six to ten cities in Europe, the Healthy Cities movement (or Healthy Communities, as it is more commonly known in North America) has grown enormously. By mid-1997, there were several thousand cities, towns, and villages involved in the Healthy Cities/Communities movement in Europe, North America, Latin America, Asia, Africa, and Australasia; at least thirty national networks exist, some with as many as one hundred participating municipalities. In Canada, a national project was established in 1988 at the Canadian Institute of Planners, with the Canadian Public Health Association and the Federation of Canadian Municipalities acting as co-sponsors. Although Health Canada did not renew its funding in 1991, provincial governments in Quebec, British Columbia, and Ontario have established their own Healthy Community networks (in Quebec, Villes et villages en santé) with upwards of one hundred communities participating in each province. In addition, there is an active network in Manitoba that, while not funded by the provincial government, involves some twenty or thirty communities. Low levels of involvement in the Healthy Communities movement can be found in most of the other provinces and territories. (For more information on Healthy Communities/Cities, see Ashton 1992; Hancock 1993a; Hancock 1997a; Tsouros 1990; WHO 1992; or contact one of the provincial networks listed at the end of the chapter.)

The Healthy Communities approach is very simple: given that the major determinants of health are environmental, social, economic, and political in nature, the Healthy Communities approach attempts to improve the health of the community by bringing together a coalition that is both broad in its scope, encompassing as many different sectors as possible, and deep in its involvement, with participants from the wealthiest and most powerful segments of the community as well as from the poorest and least powerful segments.

In addition to this commitment to intersectoral action and community involvement, the Healthy Communities approach pays particular attention to the role of local government. As indicated at the beginning of this chapter, local governments historically have played an important role in improving the health of the community, and it is an essential tenet of the Healthy Communities movement that they can and must continue to play a central role in improving the health of the community. Thus, the Healthy Communities approach calls for both local government commitment and involvement and for the development of healthy public policy at the local level, that is, ensuring that health is on the social and political agenda of the community and that the health impacts of public policy decisions are taken into account.

The Intersectoral Approach

The broad, holistic, intersectoral approach of the Healthy Communities concept can perhaps best be illustrated by reference to the issues raised in other chapters of this book. It will quickly become clear that the process of creating healthier communities touches upon most if not all dimensions of urban policy.[5] For example:

- The concern with economic growth raises the issue, What is the purpose of economic growth? Is it simply growth for the sake of growth or, as will be argued later, is economic activity (not growth, not development) a means to an end, that end being the maximizing of human development for all, within communities that are environmentally and socially sustainable?

- Land use planning is of particular concern in the Healthy Communities movement; it was no accident that the Canadian Healthy Communities Project was housed at the Canadian Institute of Planners. The growing interest in 'new urbanism' reflects a desire to build communities that are more livable, more environmentally and socially sustainable, more healthy (see, for example, Beatley and Manning 1997; Calthorpe 1993). Land use planning has significant implications for the physical, mental, and social well-being of members of the community; several municipalities (e.g., Halton Region and York Region in Ontario, Parksville in British Columbia) have been integrating Healthy Community principles into their official plans (Hancock 1997b), and the first book on designing healthy communities has recently been published (Aicher 1998).

- Urban infrastructure has always had a significant role in the improvement of the health of cities and towns. Indeed, one can argue that the construction of sewers, the provision of clean water, the management of solid waste, the building of safe roads, the provision of public transit, and similar activities have been among the most important factors in improving the health of Canadians over the past 150 years (see Fowler and Hartmann's and Fowler and Layton's chapters in this volume). The maintenance and improvement of that infrastructure in the years ahead—and the addressing of ecosystem health concerns in the process—will continue to play an important role in creating healthy communities.

- Adequate shelter is a basic determinant of good health. Improvements in housing conditions were fundamental to improvements in health in the nineteenth century, and they remain so today. Housing standards are essentially based on concerns with health and safety. Moreover, the role of housing design in the mental and social well-being of residents is of significant concern. We have more than enough evidence that suggests that the sort of high-rise, low-income housing that was built in Europe and North America in the period following the second world war has had adverse effects on the mental and social well-being of its residents (Fowler 1992; Freeman 1984). Ensuring that housing is designed and built in a way that improves health remains an important task for urban policy-makers.

- The links between health and sustainable development, and between healthy communities and sustainable communities, have been of growing interest. It is frequently—if not invariably—the case that what is good for the natural ecosystem is good for human health, while what is bad for one is bad for the other. There is a growing literature on the links between health and sustainability at the community level (Hancock 1993b, 1994a, 1994c, 1996, 1997b; UBC Task Force on Healthy and Sustainable Communities 1994), while the notion of urban sustainability has been expanded to encompass social as well as environmental sustainability (Yiftachel and Hedgcock 1993).

- Transportation is a significant factor in the health of any community (see Fowler and Layton's chapter). The automobile is associated with accidental injury and death, air pollution, the stress of commuting, a sedentary lifestyle, and segregated-use urban sprawl that destroys a sense of community. Public transit is safer and less polluting per passenger mile, and it plays a social role; former Toronto mayor John Sewell once described Toronto's transit system as 'the great democratizer' because it is used by everyone and people literally rub shoulders with the diversity of the community on a daily basis. Good public transit is a key to the design of more environmentally and socially sustainable 'new urbanist' communities. The growing emphasis on pedestrian- and bike-friendly design also has a beneficial health effect, due to improved opportunities for exercise (as long as people and bicycles are effectively and safely segregated from cars).

- Human services and the social safety net—the 'soft' infrastructure—are vital to the health of any community. Human services such as education, health care, social services, recreation, and culture are essential means of ensuring human development and maximizing human potential, while the various forms of social assistance try to ensure that everyone's basic needs for health are met and that there is an equitable (just or fair) distribution of the community's resources for the benefit of all. In addition, support for the informal networks and associational life that constitute the social web of the community (what Putnam [1993] refers to as 'civicness') is of fundamental importance in maintaining the health of individuals and groups in the community.

- Police, fire, and emergency services have obvious implications for the health and safety of the public. The capacity to respond to emergencies effectively is an important task of local government. But policing is—or should be—much more than deterring crime and arresting wrongdoers; a safe community requires that the police participate in and support civic life and community activity as a fundamental means of preventing crime. The new commitment in many cities to community policing is entirely consistent with the Healthy Communities approach; in a number of communities, community police have become involved in a wide range of issues (such as recreational opportunities for youth and prenatal care for young women) that contribute to the health of the community.

Implications for Governance[6]

The examples noted just now have some interesting implications for the way in which we govern our society—and here it is important to draw a clear distinction between *government* and *governance*: 'Governance is the process by which we collectively solve our problems and meet our society's needs. Government is the instrument we use' (Osborne and Gaebler 1991: 24).

While it would have been preferable to say that government is *one of* the instruments we use, perhaps the main one, Osborne and Gaebler's point—and in particular their distinction between *government* and *governance*—is important. Governance involves many players other than governments; in fact, the community as a whole—at least in theory—should be involved in the process of governance. The Healthy Cities/Communities approach has a number of implications for governance, including

- the *purpose*, which should be to improve the health, well-being, and human development of the population;
- the *approach*, which should be holistic and intersectoral;
- the *level* at which governance occurs, which should be more on both the bioregional and the neighbourhood levels;
- the *style*, which needs to be collaborative and participatory;
- the *structure*, which will need to include 'cross-cutting' structures, round tables, and other mechanisms to work across traditional disciplinary and departmental lines; and
- the *democratic process*, because creating a healthy city is, in essence, an exercise in citizen participation and democracy.

Challenges for the Twenty-First Century

If local government is to have an impact on the health of the public, it should be clear that it depends less on the extent to which it manages health services and more on the extent to which it adopts a Healthy City/Community perspective and integrates a concern for health into all of its policy considerations. In the twenty-first century, these two themes—management of health care services and the commitment to creating healthier cities and communities—will be important challenges for local governments.

First, to what extent are local governments, as the locally-elected representatives of the community, willing to allow health care and public health services to be organized and managed at a community or regional level by organizations, such as Regional Health Authorities, that are for the most part unelected, locally unaccountable, and responsible primarily to the province? It seems likely that locally managed, integrated systems of health care, spanning the spectrum from public health to tertiary hospital care, will be the way of the future, providing an appropriate set of efficient and effective services responsive to local needs. In the interest of ensuring that health care is appropriate, accountable, and sensitive to local needs, perhaps local government needs to be more directly involved in managing local health services, as is the case in the Nordic countries. Or alternatively, should the special purpose bodies that run health systems be elected locally, as are school boards in many parts of the country?

Second, health care and public health services will not in themselves ensure the health of the community; that depends on the complete range of local government services—and, indeed, on the total effort of the entire community. To what extent will local government take up the challenge of the Healthy Communities approach, ensuring that its own operations take into account the health and well-being of the community?

This is the fundamental challenge that local governments face as they try to promote health, preserve the environment, and seek to ensure healthy, just, and sustainable human development in the cities, towns, and villages of the twenty-first century.

Careers in Public Health

Public health nurses constitute the largest single group of professionals in the public health field. They are usually registered nurses with additional training in public health. Those seeking management positions usually pursue a master's degree in health sciences or similar subject areas.

The second largest group are public health inspectors. Two-thirds of Canada's public health inspectors are trained at Ryerson Polytechnic University in Toronto, which has a four-year undergraduate degree program. Public health inspectors are also trained at the British Columbia Institute of Technology and at small, new programs in Cape Breton and Edmonton.

Health promotion and education staff have an undergraduate degree and often a graduate degree in health studies, health education, health promotion, or related disciplines.

Public health physicians are specialists who pursue a four-year postgraduate training culminating in Fellowship in Community Medicine.

Community nutritionists are usually nutritionists with a postgraduate degree in community nutrition.

Healthy Community Contacts in Canada

Manitoba Healthy Communities Network
Liz Hydesmith, Administrative Coordinator
265 Lanark St.
Winnipeg, MB R3N 1L3
Tel.: (204) 487-0067
Fax: (204) 487-0093
E-mail: healthy@pangea.ca
Web site: http://www.pangea.ca/~healthy

Ontario Healthy Communities Coalition
Lorna Heidenheim, Coordinator
180 Dundas St. West, Suite 1900
Toronto, ON M5G 1Z8
Tel.: (416) 408-4841 or 1-800-766-3418
Fax: (416) 408-4843
E-mail: ohcc@opc.on.ca
Web site: http://www.opc.on.ca/ohcc

Réseau Québecoise de Villes et Villages en Santé
2400 Av. D'Estimauville
Beauport, QC G1E 6Z9
Tel.: (418) 666-7000
Fax: (418) 666-2776
E-mail: vvs@esi.ulaval.ca
Web site: http://vvs.neomedia.com/

The Quebec WHO Collaborating Centre on the Development of Healthy Cities
and Towns
Michel O'Neill, Professeur titulaire et Codirecteur
Groupe de recherche et d'intervention en promotion de la santé (GRIPSUL)
Faculté des sciences infirmières
4108-J Pavillon Comtois
Université Laval
Québec, QC G1K 7P4
Tel.: (418) 656-2131 ext. 7431
Fax: (418) 656-7747
E-mail: Michel.ONeill@fsi.ulaval.ca
Web site: http://www.ulaval.ca/fsi/oms/p1En.html

Notes

1. Readers interested in more detail are referred to Shah's comprehensive text on public health in Canada (Shah 1998) and to an excellent short text on the topic of the role of local government in health and social services by Manga and Muckle (1987), although the latter has been somewhat overtaken by the rapid change in health care organization in most provinces (except Ontario) in the past few years.
2. Thus, the share of the total health care budget formerly contributed by municipalities may now be much less (except in Ontario).
3. In view of the rapid and ongoing changes in the management structure of the health care system across Canada, I wrote to the Minister of Health in each province in the summer of 1995 asking for an update on the situation in their province. The information in this section comes from their responses; quotations are from their letters, unless otherwise indicated.
4. They interviewed the Chief Medical Officer of Health in each of the six provinces, as well as the Medical Officer of Health in five of the provinces and the Public Health Association president in three of the provinces.
5. There is a growing literature on Healthy Cities/Communities that includes examples of many of the issues described in this chapter. See the References in this chapter and/or contact your provincial network.
6. This section is a very brief summary of a much more extensive paper presented at a British Council Conference on Health and the Urban Environment held in Manchester, England, in 1993 (Hancock 1994a).

References

Aicher, Joseph. 1998. *Designing Healthy Cities: Prescriptions, Principles and Practices.* Malabar, FL: Kreiger.

Armstrong, Alan. 1959. 'Thomas Adams and the Commission of Conservation'. *Plan Canada* 1(1): 14–32.

Ashton, John, ed. 1992. *Healthy Cities.* Milton Keynes, UK: Open University Press.

———. 1990. 'Public Health and Primary Care: Towards a Common Agenda'. *Public Health,* 104(6),(November):387–98.

Beatley, Timothy, and Kristy Manning. 1997. *The Ecology of Place: Planning for Environment, Economy, and Community.* Washington, DC: Island Press.

Bilson, Geoffrey. 1984. 'Cholera and Public Health in Canada'. *Canadian Journal of Public Health* 75: 352–5.

Calthorpe, Peter. 1993. *The Next American Metropolis: Ecology, Community, and the American Dream.* New York: Princeton Architectural Press.

'Canada's Amazing Health History: Let's Murder the Medical Officer'. 1984. *Canadian Journal of Public Health* 75: 344–7.

Canadian Institute for Health Information. 1999. *National Health Expenditure.* Ottawa: Canadian Institute for Health Information.

Cassedy, James. 1962. 'Hygeia: A Mid-Victorian Dream of a City of Health'. *Journal of the History of Medicine* 17: 217–28.

Cipolla, Carlo. 1976. *Public Health and the Medical Profession in the Renaissance.* Cambridge: Cambridge University Press.

Evans, Robert, Morris Barer, and Theodore Marmor. 1994. *Why Are Some People Healthy and Others Not? The Determinants of Health of Populations.* New York: A. de Gruyter.

Federal, Provincial and Territorial Advisory Committee on Population Health. 1994. *Strategies for Population Health: Investing in the Health of Canadians.* Ottawa: Health Canada.

———. 1996. *Report on the Health of Canadians.* Ottawa: Health Canada.

Fowler, Edmund P. 1992. *Building Cities That Work.* Montreal: McGill-Queen's University Press.

Freeman, Hugh, ed. 1984. *Mental Health and the Environment.* London: Churchill Livingston.

Fulton, Jane. 1995. Letter to the author. (15 September).

Girouard, Mark. 1985. *Cities and People: A Social and Architectural History.* New Haven, CT: Yale University Press.

Greschler, John. n.d. Letter to the author.

Hancock, Trevor. 1993a. 'The Evolution, Impact and Significance of the Healthy Cities/Communities Movement'. *Journal of Public Health Policy* 14(1): 5–18.

———. 1993b. 'Health, Human Development and the Community Ecosystem: Three Ecological Models'. *Health Promotion International* 8(1): 41–7.

———. 1994a. 'Creating Healthy and Sustainable Communities: The Challenge of

Governance'. In *Health and the Urban Environment*, ed. David Britt. Manchester, UK: British Council.

———. 1994b. 'Health Promotion in Canada: Did We Win the Battle but Lose the War?' In *Health Promotion in Canada: Provincial, National and International Perspectives*, ed. Ann Pedersen, Michel O'Neill, and Irving Rootman. Toronto: W.B. Saunders.

———. 1994c. 'A Healthy and Sustainable Community: The View from 2020'. In *The Ecological Public Health: From Vision to Practice*, ed. Cordia Chu and Rod Simpson. Brisbane, Australia: Faculty of Environmental Sciences, Griffith University; Toronto: Centre for Health Promotion, University of Toronto.

———. 1996. 'Planning and Creating Healthy and Sustainable Cities: The Challenge for the 21st Century'. In *Our Cities, Our Future: Policies and Action for Health and Sustainable Development*, ed. C. Price and A. Tsouros. Copenhagen: WHO Europe, Centre for Urban Health, Healthy Cities Project.

———. 1997a. 'Healthy Cities and Communities: Long Tradition, Hopeful Prospects'. *National Civic Review* 86(1): 11–21.

———. 1997b. 'Healthy, Sustainable Communities: Concept, Fledgling Practice and Implications for Governance'. In *Eco-City Dimensions: Healthy Communities, Healthy Planet*, ed. Mark Roseland. Gabriola Island, BC: New Society.

Hancock, Trevor, and Martha Garrett. 1995. 'Beyond Medicine: Health Challenges and Strategies in the 21st Century'. *Futures* 27: 935–51.

Hancock, Trevor, Bernard Pouliot, and Pierre Duplessis. 1990. 'Public Health'. In *Urban Policy Issues: Canadian Perspectives*, ed. Richard Loreto and Trevor Price. Toronto: McClelland & Stewart.

'Health and Wealth'. 1994. *Daedalus*. Special issue. 123(4).

Health and Welfare Canada. 1974. *A New Perspective on the Health of Canadians: A Working Document*. Ottawa: Office of the Canadian Minister of National Health and Welfare.

———. 1986. *Achieving Health for All: A Framework for Health Promotion*. Ottawa: Health and Welfare Canada.

Health Canada. 1997. 'Health Promotion in Canada: A Case Study'. Initial research and background documentation by Trevor Hancock and Ron Labonté. Ottawa: Health Canada.

King, Russell. 1995. Letter to the author. (22 August).

Langlois, Cathy. 1995. Letter to the author. (30 October).

McCrae, James. 1995. Letter to the author. (27 September).

MacDougall, Heather. 1990. *Activists and Advocates: Toronto's Health Department, 1883–1983*. Toronto: Dundurn.

McEwen, Walter. 1995. Letter to the author. (13 September).

McKeown, Thomas. 1979. *The Role of Medicine: Dream, Mirage or Nemesis?* Oxford, UK: Blackwell.

Manga, Pran, and Wendy Muckle. 1987. *The Role of Local Government in the Provision of Health and Social Services in Canada*. Ottawa: Canadian Council for Social Development.

Matthews, Lloyd. 1995. Letter to the author. (22 September).

Ontario. Ministry of Health. 1983. *Health Protection and Promotion Act*. Toronto: Queen's Printer.

Osborne, David, and Ted Gaebler. 1991. *Reinventing Government: How the Entrepreneurial Spirit Is Transforming the Public Sector*. Reading, MA: Addison-Wesley.

Parfit, Jessie. 1986. *The Health of a City: Oxford 1770–1974*. Oxford, UK: Amate.

Putnam, Robert. 1993. *Making Democracy Work: Civic Traditions in Modern Italy*. Princeton, NJ: Princeton University Press.

Quebec. Commission d'enquête sur la santé et le bien-être sociale. 1970. *Rapport de la commission d'enquête sur la santé et le bien-être social*. Quebec City: Gouvernement du Québec.

Richardson, Benjamin Ward. 1875. *Hygeia: A City of Health*. London: Macmillan.

Severs, A. 1989. 'Public Health as a Catalyst in the Growth of Municipal Departments in Early Toronto'. *Canadian Journal of Public Health* 80(4): 291–4.

Shah, Chandrakant. 1998. *Public Health and Preventive Medicine in Canada*. 4th ed. Toronto: C.P. Shah.

Stewart, Donald. 1995. Letter to the author. (22 September).

Sutcliffe, Penny, Raisa Deber, and George Pasut. 1997. 'Public Health in Canada: A Comparative Study of Six Provinces'. *Canadian Journal of Public Health* 87(4): 246–9.

Tsouros, Agis, ed. 1990. *The World Health Organization Healthy Cities Project: A Project Becomes a Movement: Review of Progress 1987 to 1990*. Milan: WHO Healthy Cities Project Office.

University of British Columbia (UBC) Task Force on Healthy and Sustainable Communities. 1994. 'Tools for Sustainability: Iteration and Implementation'. In *Ecological Public Health from Vision to Practice*, ed. Cordia Chu and Rod Simpson. Brisbane, Australia: Faculty of Environmental Sciences, Griffiths University; Toronto: Centre for Health Promotion, University of Toronto.

Wilson, Jim. 1995. Letter to the author. (10 October).

Winslow, C.E.A. 1923. *The Evolution and Significance of the Modern Public Health Campaign*. New Haven, CT: Yale University Press. Reprinted by *Journal of Public Health Policy*, 1983.

World Health Organization (WHO). 1986. *Ottawa Charter on Health Promotion*. Copenhagen: WHO.

———. 1992. *Twenty Steps for Developing a Healthy Cities Project*. Copenhagen: WHO Europe.

Yiftachel, Oren, and David Hedgcock. 1993. 'Urban Social Sustainability: The Planning of an Australian City'. *Cities* (May): 139–57.

Education Policies: Challenges and Controversies

Peter Woolstencroft

Introduction

Education policies have become a pivot point for political debate in the contemporary liberal democracies. In the United States, presidential candidates vie for the mantle of education leader. In Great Britain, education and training are priorities for the Labour government. Canadian national politicians, despite severe constitutional prohibitions, seek ways for Ottawa to engage itself in education issues. Education's ascendancy reflects the widespread view that global economic competition requires nations to have well-educated workforces: education is the new basis for the wealth of nations ('Education and the Wealth of Nations' 1997). The knowledge-based economy's need for skilled workforces requires schools to focus on a core curriculum (Economic Council of Canada 1992). The long-revered neighbourhood school has been scrutinized for its effectiveness and outcomes compared to its global counterparts. Analysts have begun to devise indicators of educational quality and to develop measures of accountability for educators and their managers.

More than economics has made education the lightning rod of controversy. Diverse expectations of education systems, many far removed from traditional concerns, underlie discussions about schools and their role in society. Schools, for example, are called upon to handle violence and provide safe working and learning environments; to feed hungry kids; to integrate students with special needs into regular classrooms; to address problems of literacy; to develop curricular materials sensitive to race, gender, and sexual orientation; and to establish students' mastery of the core curriculum and the newest trends in computer literacy. Increasing uncertainties about education were manifested in the 1990s by the ten provincial and two territorial governments, which established major reviews (Manzer 1994).

Within the context of urban Canada—where over three-quarters of Canadians live and where enormous shifts in demographic characteristics and economic circumstances have occurred in the last three decades—this chapter considers the recent extensive changes in educational governance; with that as a background, the issues of equal educational opportunity, multiculturalism, school violence, and fragmentation of the public school system are taken up.

Education Under Stress

Caplan (1995) noted the extraordinary number of reform proposals heard by Ontario's Royal Commission on Learning. Some called for the 'full-service school', which addresses a wide range of issues, social and educational (Rusk, Shaw, and Joong 1994). Others, less expansively, prescribed, say, a specific approach to language learning (Nikiforuk 1993) or restoration of the classical curriculum (Emberley and Newell 1994). One keen observer of Canadian education argued that six philosophies underlie debates about education: progressive, cultural, technocratic, traditional, individualist, and egalitarian (Holmes 1992). Underlying debates about these educational philosophies is the central issue of 'the core function of the school within the pluralist democracy: Is it to serve essentially the purposes of the state, or those of the parent?' (Holmes 1992: 154).

The 1990s' fiscal crisis of contracting revenues and expanding expenditures, faced by all Canadian governments, complicated educational debates. The traditional language of educational politics—'we need more resources'—was met by the demand to deliver programs with fewer resources than were available the previous year. Provinces began to meld ministries dealing with education and training, to merge school boards, and to force schools to cut expenditures.

Cost-saving in education was not surprising, given both the size of the enterprise and demographic changes. In 1995, primary and secondary education consumed 4.6 per cent of Canada's gross domestic product, an investment that put Canada in the top rank of industrialized nations. Declining enrolments (in 1995, one Canadian in five was enrolled in elementary and secondary education, compared to one in four in 1970), combined with significant increases in spending per pupil, number of educators, and average educator salaries (along with declines in pupil–educator ratios), propelled the drive for fiscal restraint (Gendron 1997).

But education is more than an industry. Schools embody the central values of a society, and education debates mirror fundamental societal issues. Along with health care and income maintenance and security, public education is a pillar of the modern welfare state. It also represents the first extension of the state into what had been a private (that is, family or religious) matter. That extension, which occurred more or less without rancorous debate, except in Manitoba and Quebec, was motivated by the need to foster social order and economic growth (Prentice 1977); only latterly has education been justified as a means of encouraging individual self-development.

Three different dimensions structure educational conflicts. The first focuses on the individual's capacity for learning. Does the education system mould the individual to perceived ends? Or do the individual's abilities, interests, and inclinations structure what teachers and schools offer? The second concerns how public investment in education is justified. Is the system designed to create an academic elite built on the mastery of an exacting curriculum of traditional academic subjects? Or is the goal to generate a technologically proficient workforce able to compete in the global marketplace? Education's social role is the third dimension. Schools, being a principal socializing agency, integrate those from diverse backgrounds, whatever they be, into a compatible and harmonious whole. As conserving institutions, schools pass social values from one generation to the next. Critics of schools see the integrating and conserving functions as camouflaging the real nature of schools, which reproduce rather than change societal inequalities. Indeed, schools, legitimators of the socio-economic differences of society, are essentially political institutions (May 1994). These perspectives are not easily aligned: a recent study of Canadian 'exemplary' schools concluded that the schools saw 'success in both academic and social terms and there is often a tension between the two' (Gaskell 1995: 278).

A series of soundings of public opinion in Ontario indicate that there had been a slow but consistent decline from 1979 to 1998 in the proportion of respondents who saw improvement in elementary and high school education (Livingstone, Hart, and Davie 1999). A British Columbia study reported that employers, post-secondary instructors, and the general public give low appraisals to the performance of high school graduates (Gardner 1996). Many commentators pointed to the middling performance of Canadian students in various international tests (Robson 2000).

Changes in the public's estimation of education may mean that Canadians nowadays are less predisposed to accept uncritically the reassurances of educators. Or, indeed, education very well may have deteriorated. Whatever the explanation, Canadians are considerably less confident about their schools than was the case a generation ago. In the 1990s, pointed questions about educational governance, so taken for granted that it was almost ignored in public commentary, began to be heard, with significant changes being effected.

Educational Governance in Canada

Mackinnon straightforwardly describes the state's primary role in education:

> To the schools the state gives no power of their own; and the teaching profession is kind of a low-drawer civil service, trained, licensed, hired, inspected, and directed by the state. No other activity, institution, or profession is in this extraordinary position; education in North America is now the most completely socialized activity in North America. (1960: 4)

Correlated with the primacy of the state has been the low politicization of educational issues, which have been the quiet work of insiders—politicians, bureaucrats, and teachers—with parents and community groups, who, despite various structures of political representation, are outsiders and generally marginalized (Lewington and Orpwood 1993). Manzer, referring to the first seven decades of the twentieth century, put the matter cogently: 'Educational politics, policy, and administration became increasingly isolated in educational policy communities that were hierarchically structured. At the apex they were dominated by sub-governments of premiers, ministers of education, and senior officials of departments of education' (Manzer 1994: 146).

The five salient features of Canadian educational governance contour how issues are addressed and how programs are implemented. The leading characteristic is the provinces' predominant role. Canada's system stands out from all others, except for Switzerland, because of the national government's minor role in education.[1] The few groups interested in expanding Ottawa's importance in education, such as the Canadian Education Association and the Canadian School Trustees' Association, have been unsuccessful, although in the 1990s, studies on the problem of dropouts and the development of indicators of educational performance were undertaken by the Council of Ministers of Education. For the most part, groups interested in educational policy organize along provincial lines and think about educational policy in provincial terms.

Publicly funded denominational schools, the second feature of educational governance, issue from Section 93 of the Constitution Act, which was designed to protect the educational privileges of religious and cultural minorities that existed at Confederation. Subsequent political accommodations and legislative enactments have led to seven types of publicly supported denominational schools across the land.

Ontario's denominational schools have been the source of enduring political controversy. Until 1984, when Premier William Davis extended full funding to Roman Catholic schools beyond grade 10, the issue had been a major difference between his Progressive Conservative Party and the opposition parties. The status of denominational schools in Newfoundland and Labrador became highly controversial when the provincial government sought to change Term 17 of the 1949 Terms of Union of the province with Canada, which guaranteed four denominational school systems (Catholic, Pentecostal, Seventh Day Adventist, and, since 1968, schools formed out of a combined Anglican, United Church, Presbyterian, and Salvation Army base). In a 1995 referendum, despite claims by Catholic and Pentecostal leaders that the new system would reduce their heretofore constitutionally protected schools' religious character without appreciable cost savings, voters approved a constitutional amendment to merge the twenty-seven existing boards into ten interdenominational boards.

The third characteristic of educational governance pertains to the language of instruction. Canada's bilingual character led governments to be concerned with ensuring that students are taught in their mother tongue and have the opportunity to study the other national language. Since 1981, New Brunswick has constitutionally guaranteed English- and French-speaking students the right to be taught in their own language. In the 1990s, Quebec's schools, historically divided along denominational lines, were restructured as the Parti Québécois government established linguistically based school boards. In other provinces—the exceptions being New-foundland and Alberta—legislation provides for instruction in the minority language where numbers warrant.

The fourth element of educational governance is the existence of locally elected school boards. Only two countries in the world, Canada and the United States, have community representatives (trustees) who play at least some role in determining educational policies and providing citizens some measure of local control. Trustees in most provinces (except for Nova Scotia and New Brunswick) are elected; in New-foundland and Labrador, they are either elected or appointed. Generally, trustee elections are non-partisan, although forms of group-based elections have occurred in the larger cities. Almost all school-board elections have low voter turnouts and high re-election of incumbents.

The 783 boards across Canada in 1994 varied enormously in size; the average enrolment per board was 6,484, with a range from 1,844 (Saskatchewan) to 12,048 (Ontario); enrolment per school, with an average of 326, ranged from 30 in Alberta to 368 in Ontario (Ontario, Royal Commission on Learning 1995, 4: 114).

School boards, usually not very prominently placed in public discussion, were much criticized in the 1990s. Principal failings of boards were the relatively high power of school bureaucrats, relative to (the many) elected trustees; the declining quality of education; and the 'near absence of financial controls' (Bennett 1994: 13).

The view that Canadians were overrepresented was first acted upon in relation to school boards, which were subject to amalgamation in various provinces. Alberta, British Columbia, Manitoba, and Newfoundland reduced the number of boards. New Brunswick, having already cut its boards from 42 to 18 in 1992, abolished them entirely in 1996. The Ontario government, in 1996, as part of the education system's restructuring, reduced boards from 129 to 72 and drastically narrowed their autonomy. Changes in school governance in Metro Toronto, which had had an unusual two-tiered system with divided responsibilities, resulted in one large regional board.

Ironically, while school boards—the voices of the local community—were being merged or eliminated, every province has introduced school parent advisory councils (sometimes connected to district and provincial structures). The premise underlying such councils is that present modes of political representation provide inadequate means for parents to be involved in their children's education. Councils will 'substantially increase the ability of parents and school personnel to influence educational policies and make schools more responsive to the demands of their environment' (Rideout 1995: 12). Three primary concerns, however, have been identified. First, will councils be only advisory to the school's principal (thus duplicating existing home and school associations), or will they have any decision-making role? Second, if councils have responsible rather than advisory roles, to whom are they accountable? Third, as boards are reduced in importance and replaced by parent councils, who represents local taxpayers and the wider community? The uncertain standing of school councils and loss of community input has led the New Brunswick government to re-examine school governance in the province (New Brunswick 2000).

How monies are raised for educational purposes constitutes the fifth element of educational governance. The two main sources of funds are grants from the province and real property taxes raised at the municipal level. In 1994/95, these two funding sources produced 77.5 per cent of money spent on education; the national government and private sources provided other funds (Kitchen and Auld 1995).

Provinces vary enormously in the ratio of educational costs covered by provincial grants and property taxes. For some time in three provinces—Prince Edward Island, New Brunswick, and Newfoundland—only provincial revenues have been used for elementary and secondary education. Alberta announced in 1994 that it would begin to collect all property taxes and redistribute them to school boards, with uniform mill rates set by 1997. In Quebec, the bulk (over 75 per cent) of educational expenses is paid out of provincial revenues. Ontario's Common Sense Revolution, the rallying cry of Mike Harris's Progressive Conservative government, had education reform as one of its priorities, with financing being a central concern. Queen's Park, for the first time, had 'responsibility for determining how money was to be raised, how much money was to be raised, and how funds were to be distributed to schools across the province' (Gidney 1999: 244).

In other provinces, education funding is shared between the provincial government and local school boards, which, using the municipality as the tax collector, impose a levy upon local property for educational purposes, often representing over 50 per cent of the local tax bill.

The upshot of these five features of educational governance is that the ten provincial education systems are extraordinarily complex and diversified. Canadians are often said to live in a highly provincialized political system; it is probably the case that more diversity occurs in education policies and governance than in any other major policy field. Gaskell points out that 'provinces and territories vary in the grade levels they define as secondary education, in the degree to which they have centralized structures, in how they provide minority-language and religious schools, and in the amount of school choice they offer parents and students. Schools also differ in size, organizational structure, programs and services, and community context' (Gaskell 1995: 1).

Moreover, there are considerable variations in per student education expenditures by province, as shown in Table 15.1.

No doubt provincial differences are due to many factors. One of the most important is the economic resources available to provincial governments. Generally, per student spending is lower in the poorer provinces (Newfoundland and Labrador, Prince Edward Island, and Nova Scotia) and higher elsewhere; but the pattern is not linear (with Quebec and Manitoba—'have-not provinces'—having a higher ranking than the 'have' province of Alberta), suggesting that other factors account in part for differences in education spending.

These are likely to be found in a province's political culture, especially the degree to which education is seen to be either a common good or a means of providing for individual social mobility or economic development. The institutionalization of

Table 15.1: Provincial Education Expenditures per Student, 1996/1997

Province	$
Quebec	7,032
British Columbia	6,882
Ontario	6,649
Manitoba	6,620
New Brunswick	6,156
Alberta	5,848
Saskatchewan	5,637
Nova Scotia	5,366
Prince Edward Island	5,148
Newfoundland and Labrador	5,108
Canadian average	6,045

Source: Trevor W. Harrison and Jerrold Kachur, eds. *Contested Classrooms: Education, Globalization, and Democracy in Alberta* (Edmonton: University of Alberta Press and Parkland Institute, 1999), 184.

interest groups concerned with the extent of the state's commitment to education is also a significant factor. Such groups are generally likely to favour more rather than less spending, and to the degree that they are successful, there will be increases in the proportion of governmental resources apportioned to education.

Changes in educational governance in general have been in the direction of amalgamation of systems, weakening of local control, and enhanced provincial control (Carney and Peters 1995). Opportunities for participation in education policies by the local community have been severely circumscribed, perhaps meaning that the policy heterogeneity of Canadian education will be diminished. Will there be a return to the old system of policy-making, in which provincial politicians and bureaucrats are dominant, confronted only by the teacher unions?

Equal Educational Opportunity

John Porter, at the close of his classic study of Canadian society, *The Vertical Mosaic*, argued that Canada 'has a long way to go to become in any sense a thorough-going democracy' (Porter 1965: 557). The failure to develop education systems that lowered class barriers to educational achievement was an integral part of the explanation. Porter's interpretation points to one of education's crucial functions in modern society, that of providing students with equality of educational opportunity (Porter 1979). Because families vary in their capacities or willingness to advance their children's education, state intervention is imperative in order to offer children opportunities to attend school with minimal family costs. Otherwise, it is argued, the bright child born into a poor family that is unable or unwilling to pay for education is denied the opportunities that a similar child born into a well-to-do family (or a poor family committed to devoting its resources to education) would have.

Equality of opportunity is justified on two other grounds. First, post-industrial societies require technologically proficient, specialized, and adaptable workforces capable of meeting the labour, research, and management needs of knowledge-based economies. Education is seen as the engine of economic growth fuelled by the provision of equal educational opportunities that lead to long-term and well-paid jobs. Second, the language contained in human rights codes is directed toward equity, that is, equal or comparable treatment. For example, Ontario's Human Rights Code states, 'Every person has a right to equal treatment in respect to services' (R.S.O. 1990, c.H.19, s.1). Accordingly, the province is obliged to provide students with access to comparable levels of education, although the measurement of same is problematic (Kitchen and Auld 1995).

Coleman (1969) found that the concept of equal educational opportunity contains four provisions: (1) 'free' education up to a given level (the principal entry point to the labour force); (2) a 'common' curriculum for all children, regardless of background; (3) children from diverse backgrounds attending the same school; and (4) fiscal equality across schools within a given locality. Application of Coleman's interpretation to Canada identifies some important barriers. First, the existence of denominational schools results in different educative processes. Canadian students also experience different curricular emphases and orientations from province to province (Hodgetts 1968). A third difficulty arises from reliance on local taxpayers for educational dollars; the potential for inequalities exists because two communities with comparable school-age populations may differ greatly in their capacity or willingness to raise funds for comparable education programs.

Provinces have responded to differences in fiscal resources in three ways. The easiest route is for the province to assume responsibility for funding of education. But even this is not without debate. Alberta's move in 1994 in this direction (as much motivated by the desire to control costs as by any other factor) prompted opposition from urban boards because monies would flow to less affluent rural areas. An alternative policy is equalization programs that reduce differences in the fiscal resources available to school boards. Each board's fiscal capacity is calculated and a formula is developed whereby monies are redistributed from well-off districts to poorer ones. Some provinces—Alberta (until recently), Saskatchewan, and Prince Edward Island—have adopted a variation of equalization known as *foundation funding*, whereby the provincial government establishes a minimum per-student expenditure level and provides funds to boards falling below that level (Giles and Proudfoot 1994).

The third approach has been to create consolidated school districts, on the premise that larger, better-equipped schools are able to offer more educational opportunities than are their much smaller predecessors. Consolidation has a price.

The smaller school offered students a close-knit community and participation opportunities that are not readily available in larger and more anonymous schools (Ontario, Royal Commission on Learning 1995: 4:114). The development of large secondary schools, with enrolments of well over 2,000 students, first in urban then in rural areas, meant that pressure developed to have programs that met students' diverse educational needs. Accordingly, students were streamed into academic or vocational programs on the basis of grades and aptitude tests. The empirical evidence about the impact of school consolidation is mixed. Coleman and LaRoque (1990) have argued that resources are negatively linked with indicators of educational achievement, with ethos, or underlying value consensus, being a very important factor. In this vein, the 'exemplary schools' project concluded that there 'is universal recognition—by policy makers, professionals, students, parents and communities— that *the* essential element in a successful school consists in the values and attitudes of the teachers' (Gaskell 1995: 279).

Considerable evidence suggests that educational opportunities have been structured by socio-economic characteristics of students' families. Analysis of census data from 1941 to 1961 pointed to some narrowing in educational attainments between occupational groupings but 'disparities . . . in access to education remained unchanged' and 'the pattern of class inequalities in access in 1961 was not essentially different from that of 1941' (Manzer 1994: 190). More recent studies reveal some weakening of the relationship between social origin and educational attainment, especially at the elementary and secondary levels, although social class still made a major contribution to differences in attainment (Guppy, Mikicich, and Pendakur 1984). On the other hand, Grabb (1992) linked educational attainments not to social backgrounds, but to individual talent and motivation. Fournier, Butlin, and Giles report that 'only about 7 per cent of Canadians acquired less education than their parents' (1995: 26) and about one-quarter experienced no change. Analysis of whether change in intergenerational educational attainments was due to structural mobility (that is, to overall upgrading of educational levels) or to circulation mobility (that is, individual abilities and merit) concluded that each variable accounted for about one-half of change; but the probability of a person entering post-secondary studies is very much a function of whether or not at least one parent has had post-secondary education (Fournier, Butlin, and Giles 1995). Another study reported that 'the data strongly suggest that the socio-economic status of the father's occupation is associated with the children's educational attainment' (de Brouker and Lavallée 1998: 25). Analysis of youth literacy scores and socio-economic status revealed a strong correlation, with the greatest difference between groups evident in Ontario (Willms 1997). Effects of socio-economic status may be subtle: higher-status parents are more likely to be involved directly in the school, while lower-status parents are more likely to work with their children at home (Norris 1999).

Radwanski (1987) argued that one-third of Ontario students entering high school did not graduate and presented evidence that there were considerable class differences in school continuance. The solution was to replace streaming 'by provision of a single and undifferentiated high-quality educational stream for all students' (Radwanski 1987: 163), which would contain highly specified and common goals, and province-wide departmental examinations at the elementary and secondary levels.

The irony is that both the practice of streaming and the Radwanski proposals flow out of a desire to bring about equal educational opportunities for each and every student in the system. Advocates of streaming argue that students, not having equal learning abilities or academic interests, require programs that address their various needs. Proponents of the single-track system claim that various streams lead to differentiated outcomes and economic opportunities. Yet the single-track system creates enormous pedagogical problems for teachers, who must try to meet the needs and interests of heterogeneous classes of students. And are the academic aspirations and interests of all students served by a program that does not distinguish between students' varying capabilities, interests, and motivations?

The point is that commitment to equal educational opportunity has no necessary policy route. This is so because equal educational opportunity contains three different interpretations of desirable policies: maximization of students' life chances, equalization of least- and most- advantaged children's life chances, and allocation of resources according to children's abilities and motivations (Guttmann 1988). Each interpretation has problematic policy effects. For example, maximization means the adoption of programs directed to improving life chances of children without specifying spending limits. Education is not society's only concern, but maximization requires great utilization of societal resources—and the denial of other social goods—that no society would likely support.

Policies designed to equalize life chances between children pose similar problems. Are we required to allocate enormous resources to those children from the poorest families in order to provide them with opportunities equal to those enjoyed by children of the richest families? Is it necessary to move dollars from the bulk of children to favour children who have physiological or psychological learning disadvantages in an attempt to raise the latter to the level of the former? Affirmative answers to such questions require an enormous shifting of resources (with concomitant denial of other interpretations of equal educational opportunity). Maximization and equalization policies require state intervention in family affairs in order to address systematically the family differences responsible for educational attainments. These policies violate the idea of family autonomy far beyond the limits tolerated by any liberal-democratic society (Guttmann 1988).

The third interpretation of the principle of equal opportunity—in which the state commits educational resources to children commensurate with their abilities and motivations—is the dominant policy route. The commitment is problematic inasmuch as the apportionment of educational resources on the basis of merit results in providing 'the least educational resources and attention to those children who have relatively few natural abilities and little inclination to learn and the most to those children who have relatively many natural abilities and high motivation' (Guttmann 1988: 113).

This results in programs that reproduce the educative capacities of students, negating other interpretations of the principle of equal educational opportunity.

Canadians and educators alike support the idea of equal educational opportunity. But studies of the relationship between social class and educational attainment indicate that Canada has made limited progress in attenuating the impact of class on how students do in school. To achieve that laudable goal would require a much greater singlemindedness of purpose and allocation of resources than hitherto has been the case. There is little to suggest that such purpose and commitment will be forthcoming, even looking beyond the fiscal crises of recent times, which have exacerbated the problem of equal educational opportunity. At the same time, the concept itself has been contested as the social role of eductation has come under scrutiny in relation to multiculturalism.

Multiculturalism and Education

Canada's population has changed enormously since World War II. In 1951, about one-fifth of Canada's population was non-French and non-British. By 2000, primarily as the result of immigration policies that brought about 'ethnic-blind' procedures for the admission of immigrants, the proportion was almost 40 per cent, with recent arrivals mostly located within larger urban areas. Gidney succinctly sums up the change:

> By 1996 close to half of Metropolitan Toronto had been born outside Canada; one in ten had arrived in the previous five years. In the same year, more than half of all visible minorities in Canada lived in Ontario; almost all of them—1.3 of 1.7 million—lived in the Toronto census area, where they constituted a third of the population. (Gidney 1999: 179)

As Canadian communities absorb diverse peoples, their schools have sought appropriate responses. Do they encourage assimilation or differentiation? How do schools respond to the increasing pluralism of their communities? The test of well-established but culturally monolithic practices is exemplified by schools' removal of religiously oriented Christmas events in favour of pageants celebrating snow and the winter solstice. Another sign was the controversy in Ottawa in 1994 concerning the school year's beginning. The school board, having postponed school openings to avoid conflict with a Jewish holiday, heard from Muslims who wanted the 1995 school opening postponed to avoid conflict with their holy-day observances. The board refused but maintained its recognition of the Jewish holiday (Sweet 1998).

The federal government's 1971 multiculturalism statement, produced in good measure because the 1960s' Royal Commission on Bilingualism and Biculturalism had inadequately addressed multicultural issues, marked the beginning of political responses to the emergence of 'non-charter' (i.e., not British or French) peoples. Foremost among these was the Canada Multiculturalism Act of 1987, which committed Ottawa, amongst other things, to promote 'the full and equitable participation of individuals and communities of all origins in the continuing evolution and shaping of all aspects of Canadian society and assist them in the elimination of any barriers to such participation' (S.C. 1988, c.31, s.3(1)c).

Not surprisingly, Ottawa's increasing commitment to multiculturalism legitimated the interests of multicultural groups seeking programs that would address their specific needs and aspirations. Provinces, however, faced the brunt of pressure to develop multiculturally oriented policies and programs because so many pertinent matters fell in their jurisdiction. Some found such initiatives contentious because they were seen as contradicting the bilingual and bicultural character of Canadian society. Others perceived that multiculturalism meant that the social practices and institutions of the dominant culture were being transformed by responding to the preferences and demands of what are labelled minority groups or special interests.

Multiculturalism has come to mean that all peoples—whether Native, 'charter group', or new arrivals—comprise equally the sociological reality of Canada. Schools, in being called upon to develop programs that address that reality, have seen one important assumption of education theory challenged: that they should be part of the process of assimilating minority groups into the dominant group's culture, whether it be French or English (Mazurek 1983). Now the concept of equal educational opportunity extends to respect for, recognition of, and equitable treatment of differences.

The standing of religious practices in the schools exemplifies what has happened. Many provinces have allowed (or required) religious exercises with a Christian (or Judeo-Christian) character, leading many to see the school as a religious institution. Ontario, with the most stringent requirements, mandated that opening exercises included 'the reading of the Scriptures or other suitable readings and the repeating of the Lord's Prayer or other suitable prayers' (Ontario 1980: 155–6). No exemption was allowed, though many boards apparently did not adhere to the statutory requirements (Commission on Private Schools in Ontario 1985). In 1989, the Ontario Court of Appeal ruled that the province's requirements regarding religious exercises violated the Charter of Rights and Freedoms' protection of freedom of religion. In 1999, Saskatchewan, following a ruling by the province's Human Rights Commission, suspended the opening of schools with the Lord's Prayer. Saskatchewan thus joined Manitoba, British Columbia, and Ontario in banning the use of prayers in school.

Boards, responding to the increasing pluralism of their communities, court decisions, and provincial directives, have developed policies regarding the recognition of religiously and culturally significant days. The Waterloo County Board of Education's policy (1993) required schools, in concert with their communities, to develop programs recognizing 'days of significance' (which included Thanksgiving, Halloween, Christmas, Valentine's Day, and Easter) that 'are not perceived to force inclusion or be exclusionary and are balanced with recognition of other cultural events'.

Language education illustrates another dimension of the demand by multicultural groups for inclusion in educational programs on the grounds of cultural preservation. Many groups wanted to have regular classes taught in their mother tongues; in Ontario, the government's response in the 1970s and 1980s was a Heritage Languages program that allowed for after-hours instruction (Gidney 1999).

Immigration is a joint federal and provincial responsibility, with Ottawa having paramountcy in the event of conflict. Because educational costs are borne primarily by provincial governments and local taxpayers, some have called on Ottawa to assume (some) responsibility for financing programs designed to address the educational needs of recent immigrant groups. This would be a remarkable venture, given the provinces' constitutional responsibility for education and the certain opposition from Quebec, if not from other provinces, fearful that Ottawa would expand its influence in education. On the other hand, cuts to English as a Second Language programs—particularly in Ontario, when the province cut back its education funding—have meant that many young Canadians will be inadequately prepared for a most demanding economy (Bullock 2000). The Canada Multiculturalism Act declares that government policy is to promote 'full and equitable participating of individuals and communities of all origins in the continuing evolution and shaping of all aspects of Canadian society and assist them in the elimination of any barrier to such participation' (S.C. 1988, c.31, s.3(1)c). Not having competency in either of the two official languages is one such barrier.

The purported effects of multicultural education programs have attracted an enormous outpouring of rhetoric. Bullivant documented three 'quite dubious claims' (1981: 236) commonly asserted to justify such programs: that children's educational achievements improve by learning about their cultural and ethnic origins; that equality of opportunity will be improved by learning about cultures, traditions, and so forth; and that such learning will reduce prejudice and discrimination. He found that there is little evidence to support these claims. Moreover, to justify multicultural education as a way of establishing and enhancing tolerance is to overlook the intolerant nature of many cultural groups. Multicultural education policies may allow the propagation of certain attitudes, such as female subordination or ethnic hostility, which run counter to the goal of tolerance (Kach and DeFaveri 1987).

Multiculturalism and education contain an enduring tension if one conceives of the relationship through the prism of assimilation and differentiation. There is pressure to integrate newcomers as quickly as possible, because social mobility and economic functioning demand absorption into the dominant culture. Those who do not do well academically are seen as suffering from some deficit that the schools are expected to address. The alternative view wants to preserve and recognize cultural pluralism, both for its own sake and for the sake of the educational attainments of children, whose ethnic backgrounds and socialization processes result in differences, as opposed to deficits, in learning. Critics of multiculturally oriented programs, such as Bullivant, argue that to the extent that these programs focus on lifestyles and folkloric issues rather than on life chances, they allow dominant social groups to perpetuate themselves while purporting to improve the lot of children coming from ethnic communities.

Across the country in the 1990s, schools, especially in urban areas, responding to the increased heterogeneity of their communities, developed a variety of anti-racism programs intended to attenuate stereotypical thinking, confront racism, and generally make schools more inclusive. Nonetheless, representatives of visible minority groups complained that schools essentially remained bastions of white society, with racism being more subtle and systemic than overt and specific. Institutions insensitive to cultural differences, to the point of being essentially assimilationist in character, were perceived to account for the academic difficulties that many visible minority students were perceived to have suffered.

One solution is to institutionalize differentiation. Dei, in a study of minority groups and school dropouts in Ontario, having acknowledged that 'educational reforms must be informed by the common good of society' and that 'the idea of the *community* and *social responsibility* [should be] at the centre of public schooling in Canada' (1995: 146), recommends that 'one predominantly Black junior high school should be set up in each of the six Metropolitan Toronto municipalities' (1995: 156). Such 'separation' does little to promise that various cultural groups will develop understanding, tolerance, and cooperative attitudes toward others. Moving from assimilationist to differentiated institutions poses, yet again, the pluralist dilemma.

An alternative perspective is found in examining the school as an institution inherently political in character and reflecting the power relations of society. If one conceives of a school that has programs, processes, and values oriented toward enhancing cultural pluralism while maintaining high academic standards, then the debate has a different dynamic: the school directs itself to empowering minority groups and the poor. May's (1994) account of Richmond Hill school in New Zealand is especially illuminating. Located in an inner-city area, with students drawn widely from European heritages to Maori and Pacific Islanders, the school, animated by its leaders' explicit understanding that it was both a political and educational institution, successfully married diversity and excellence over a period of almost twenty years. It did so because commitment to social change and democracy infused both its curriculum and its processes of learning, teaching, interaction, communication, policy formation, community participation, evaluation, and counselling. Richmond Hill also speaks to the difficulties of the task; nonetheless, its mission seems to have successfully incorporated cultural pluralism and equal educational opportunity.

Violence in the Schools: School and Society Intersect

In response to increasing cases of drug use and possession, weapons possession, and violence—including assaults on students and teachers—and seeking understanding of the causes of violence and policy alternatives, various educational stakeholders formed, in 1990, the Canadian Association for Safe Schools, an organization whose existence would have been hardly imaginable just a few years earlier. The perceived depth of the problem is seen in educators' looking at the design plans for new schools from the perspective of how to monitor activities and protect students, teachers, and staff and wondering what to do in old schools.

Ontario, in 1993, required school boards to develop policies, plans, and procedures for dealing with school violence. The 'violence-free schools initiative' of the Waterloo County Board of Education (1995), over 160 pages long, in signalling to educators the need to be cognizant of the Young Offenders Act, the Criminal Code, and provincial child welfare legislation, pointed to the increasing complexity of the educational enterprise (Roher 1997). A cornerstone of the Ontario government's

Violence-Free Schools Policy (Ontario, Ministry of Education 1994) was 'zero-tolerance', which had two critical components. First, those involved in severe cases of violence will be expelled. Second, special programs for those expelled will be established. The province's policy underscores the argument that the issue of school violence extends beyond prevention and punishment. The public school echoes the social problems of its community, and society has an obligation to meet the educational needs of all students, even those who transgress social norms (British Columbia Teachers' Federation 1994).

The severity of expulsion, however, and variations from school to school, raised questions of due process and Charter rights. One specific concern was the denial of appeals for expulsions. More generally, as Canada entered the new century, the ability of schools to offer safe and secure environments continued to be tested by disruptive behaviour and violence, sometimes leading to death. In 2000, Ontario moved to implement a new Code of Conduct in its schools; standardized rules, procedures, and penalties (most noticeably, the right of teachers to suspend violators) were accompanied by the right to appeal expulsions (Ontario, Ministry of Education 2000).

The imperative to think about the 'school in society' will be seen again when considering the fragmentation of the public school system.

Fragmentation of the Public School System

Canadian education is marked by institutional diversity. Nonetheless, the extensive control of education by the state means that parents have little say about the education their children receive, outside denominational schools in some provinces. There is, then, a form of monopoly, one defined by geography: a child receives the quality and kind of education that the neighbourhood school offers. Those who want their children to attend another kind of school must pay for the education of their choice.

It is always difficult to pinpoint the time and place of the origins of a movement. One thing, however, is clear: over time, there has been increasing dissatisfaction with state-centred education systems, leading parents to call for options. Wilkinson (1994) identified three factors behind the movement for parents to have more choice in their children's education: hostility about the perceived impenetrability of education bureaucracies, worry about values imparted to young people, and concern about the quality of education, especially given international economic pressures. In the United States and across the industrialized world, the demand for choice in schools has spread quickly (Hepburn 1999), with more and more signs that Canada has not been immune.

One manifestation of the trend is the expansion of private or 'independent' schools in Canada. In 1993/94 there were about 1,500 such schools, 300 more than ten years ago; about half had religious affiliations. Enrolments slowly but steadily increased from 1971 to 1994 to about 5 per cent of all elementary and secondary students (Pagliarello 1994). Some provinces—Alberta, British Columbia, Manitoba, and Quebec—have legislation providing for public funding for independent schools, provided that they adhere to provincial curriculum and educational guidelines. Another sign of dissatisfaction with public education has been the spread, albeit slow, of home-schooling, in which parents or guardians educate their charges by choice (Smith 1996). With positive court decisions and more jurisdictions providing financial assistance to home-schoolers, the phenomenon will probably spread (Luffman 1997).

Some urban school systems have responded to perceived rigidities by establishing open-boundary policies, in which parents may choose between schools depending upon program availability and space limitations. Some systems allow school-based governance, whereby principals, teachers, and staff, sometimes with community involvement, develop programs and priorities that respond to local needs. In Edmonton, for example, the school system has developed a wide range of alternative schools and programs.

Alberta has led the way in the development of charter schools, which 'are established by groups of like-minded parents and teachers who ask for permission to establish and operate a school which is run according to that school's founding document—its charter' (Gardner 1996, 32). Charter schools may serve students with particular needs or offer programs based on a specific philosophy, curriculum, or pedagogical methodology. Alberta's limited experience with charter schools suggests that parents and teachers are satisfied with levels of student achievement (Bosetti et al. 2000).

The extension of funding to Roman Catholic secondary schools in Ontario in the 1980s precipitated an inquiry into the relationships between the provincial government and independent schools, with special emphasis on funding (Commission on Private Schools in Ontario 1985). More recently, Holmes has argued that the increasing heterogeneity and heightening divisiveness about education in the pluralist democracies, of which Canada is an exemplar, point to enhancing existing choice opportunities for parents while maintaining a strong system of public education (Holmes 1992).

Three arguments were identified by Shapiro as justifying the extension of public funds to such schools. Parents who send children to independent schools bear 'double taxation', inasmuch as they pay both education taxes and tuition bills. Shapiro rebutted this argument: an education tax is not equivalent to a tuition charge; rather, it is a levy intended to pay for a common good as identified by society, with no right of opting out (Commission on Private Schools in Ontario 1985).

The second argument is that parents should not only 'be able to choose school environments that affirm and extend their own values but they also have a prior right to select the kind of education they believe to be appropriate for their child[ren]' (Commission on Private Schools in Ontario 1985: 46). Because choice is of considerable value in a democratic society, this claim was given some validity; however, parental choice is not a prior right, 'but one whose claims must be measured against the competing claims of other social policies and goals' (Commission on Private Schools in Ontario 1985: 48).

The third argument identified by Shapiro was that one religious group (Roman Catholics) was provided with an educational option—public funding of denominational schools—that other groups, especially other religiously defined ones, were denied. The Commission, accepting the constitutional context of Roman Catholic schools, found that situation to be discriminatory and made a number of detailed recommendations to allow for limited public funding to independent schools, whether defined in religious or non-religious terms (Commission on Private Schools in Ontario 1985). In 1996, a group of Ontario parents argued before the Supreme Court that their equality rights under the Canadian Charter of Rights and Freedoms were violated by the provincial government's unwillingness to extend public funding to the religious schools their children attended. The Court ruled that the claims had no legal foundation, putting the issue squarely in the political arena ('Adler v. Ontario' 1996). In 1999, the United Nations ruled that full funding for Catholic but not other religious schools was in violation of its Convention on Human Rights.

Shapiro considered three claims in support of the status quo. One is that public funds, under continuing restraint, should not be expected to bear the strain that would result from the extension of funding to independent schools. Second, increased fragmentation of Canada's education systems will result in the formation of more homogeneous schools, which will erode common acculturation experiences and lessen social cohesion. Third, public funding of independent schools will result in different types of schools: the public system as it is commonly understood in Canada and a multiplicity of independent schools receiving public funds. The existence of so many different types of schools challenges the concept of equality of educational opportunity. An independent school, which almost by definition can provide the specialized and focused education deemed to be in a student's interests, need not take all who appear at its door. The public school, by contrast, must enrol all applicants, for whom, on an individual basis, it has much greater difficulty providing the precisely defined and well-focused education close to the student's interests. On the other hand, the public school has the capacity to override deficiencies that students bring with them arising from their familial, class, and ethnic backgrounds. The public system's capacity to provide educational opportunities will be diminished to the extent that academically strong students exit the public system to attend independent schools. The risk, then, in the public funding of independent schools is that society's capacity to offer its members (in the aggregate) equal educational opportunities will be weakened, although certain individuals might secure advantages otherwise not available (Commission on Private Schools in Ontario 1985).

Conclusion

Canada's schools have been subjected to enormous pressures in recent years. There is no reason to think that the future will be different. Emerging social problems and issues will continue to affect schools and educational policy-making. As the number of school-age people falls, both absolutely and relatively, there may be less public support for funding of schools, especially as health and pension requirements of aging populations dominate political life. The cry for increased accountability and the demand for provincial, if not national, standards to ascertain the educational attainments of students will create pressures for provincial authorities to assume more and more control over education. Governance changes mean that countervailing voices to provincial policies are muted, if not silenced, so the ability of local communities to provide input into educational policies is weakened. Parents will look to advisory councils for opportunities to influence schools, but whether they will be allowed to be part of decision-making is uncertain. The movement to independent schools, open-boundary policies, and charter schools will continue, in response to the pressure from parents for more participation in the education of their children. The impact of parental choice upon school outcomes is considerable. Brown, on the basis of his study of three British Columbia schools, concludes,

> The evidence gathered suggests strongly that parental choice of public schools makes an important difference in the lives of children, parents, and educators. Parental choice among public schools is associated with a number of very positive attributes that serve our children, their families, and our entire society. They include high levels of academic learning, civility, and parental involvement. (Brown 1999: 98)

On the other hand, consider a proposal to provide enhanced choice in education. After arguing in favour of open boundaries, school councils (with decision-making roles), specialized schools, and tax-supported home-schooling, Gardner (1996) calls for the establishment of charter schools. In this system of extraordinary choice by parents, what does society do with those parents who are not sufficiently interested in their children's education to consider the choices before them or who want their children to attend the neighbourhood public school? To what extent does that school have the resources to mount educational programs that satisfy provincial criteria and work toward the goal of equal educational opportunity? The well-to-do presumably can easily arrange for children to attend their school of choice. Does society help the poor to meet the transportation costs that are part of a system of choice?

The question of socio-economic differences also arises in relation to calls for schools to meet specified academic outcomes. Schools differ in their communities—rich or poor, educationally committed or not—and in how parents prepare and nurture children for their school years. The future Canadian school will be measured in terms of its preparation of children for the global economy, its incorporation of diverse peoples and cultures, and its ability to respond to heightened parental expectations for participation and choice. What, then, will be the meaning of *public* in public education (Barlow and Robertson 1994)?

Careers in Education

Many young people consider a career in teaching, but competition for places in faculties of education is intense. Academic excellence in university, motivation, love of subject, and temperament are important factors for admission. One significant preparatory experience is to volunteer in schools and in the community. Another is to become a peer tutor.

Education is more than teaching classes or subjects. Some career options include guidance (program choices, careers, psychological counselling), coaching, curriculum design, and administration. Many adults volunteer in schools as part of their commitment to community.

Note

1. For example, in the 1994/95 school year, the federal government contributed $6.7 billion dollars to education (excluding contributions to Established Programmes Funding and official languages programs), representing 11.8 per cent of money spent on education (Perry 1995).

References

'Adler v. Ontario'. 1996. *Supreme Court Reports* 3: 609–726.

Angus Reid Group. 1999. 'Canadians' Assessment and Views of the Education System'. Toronto. (March 3).

Barlow, Maude, and Heather-Jane Robertson. 1994. *Class Warfare: The Assault on Canadian Public Education*. Toronto: Key Porter.

Bennett, Paul W. 1994. 'What's Wrong with the Present School Board System?' *Municipal World* (September): 12–17.

Bosetti, Lynn, et al. 2000. *Canadian Charter Schools at the Crossroads: Final Report of a Two-Year In-Depth Study of Charter Schools in Alberta*. Kelowna, BC: Society for the Advancement of Excellence in Education.

British Columbia Teachers' Federation. 1994. *Task Force on Violence in Schools: Final Report*. Accessed 7 February 2001: http://www.bctf.bc.ca/education/Health/ViolenceInSchools/solutions.html

Brown, Daniel J. 1999. *The Impact of Parental Choice on Three Canadian Public Schools*. Kelowna, BC: Society for the Advancement of Excellence in Education.

Bullivant, Brian M. 1981. *The Pluralist Dilemma in Education: Six Case Studies*. Sydney, Australia: George Allen & Unwin.

Bullock, Carolyn. 2000. *Ontario Cuts to English as a Second Language*. Ottawa: Caledon Institute of Social Policy.

Caplan, Gerald. 1995. 'The Report of the Royal Commission on Learning, 1995'. *ORBIT* 26(2): 2–5.

Carney, Robert, and Frank Peters. 1995. 'Governing Education'. In *Canadian Metropolitics: Governing Our Cities*, ed. James Lightbody. Toronto: Copp Clark.

Coleman, James. 1969. 'The Concept of Equality of Educational Opportunity'. In Harvard Educational Review, *Equal Educational Opportunity*. Cambridge, MA: Harvard University Press.

Coleman, Peter, and L. LaRoque. 1990. *Struggling to Be 'Good Enough': Administrative Practices and School District Ethos*. London: Falmer.

Commission on Private Schools in Ontario. 1985. *The Report of the Commission on Private Schools in Ontario*. Toronto: The Commission.

de Brouker, Patrice, and L. Lavallée. 1998. 'Getting Ahead in Life: Does Your Parents' Education Count?' *Education Quarterly Review* 5(1): 22–8.

Dei, George J. Sefa. 1995. *Drop Out or Push Out? The Dynamics of Black Students' Disengagement from School*. Toronto: Ontario Institute for Studies in Education.

Economic Council of Canada. 1992. *A Lot to Learn: Education and Training in Canada*. Ottawa: Ministry of Supply and Services.

'Education and the Wealth of Nations'. 1997. *Economist* 342(29 March): 15–16.

Emberley, Peter, and Waller R. Newell. 1994. *Bankrupt Education: The Decline of Liberal Education in Canada*. Toronto: University of Toronto Press.

Fournier, Élaine, George Butlin, and Philip Giles. 1995. 'Intergenerational Change in the Education of Canadians'. *Education Quarterly Review* 2(2): 22–33.

Gardner, Don. 1996. *Change and Choice: A Policy Vision for British Columbia*. Vancouver: The Fraser Institute.

Gaskell, Jane. 1995. *Secondary Schools in Canada: The National Project of the Exemplary Schools Project*. Toronto: Canadian Education Association.

Gendron, François. 1997. 'Funding Public School Systems: A 25-Year Review'. *Education Quarterly Review* 4(2): 27–42.

Gidney, R.D. 1999. *From Hope to Harris: The Reshaping of Ontario's Schools*. Toronto: University of Toronto Press.

Giles, T.E., and A.J. Proudfoot. 1994. *Educational Administration in Canada*. 5th ed. Calgary: Detselig.

Grabb, E. 1992. 'Social Stratification'. In *Introduction to Sociology: A Canadian Focus*, 4th ed., ed. James J. Teevan. Scarborough, ON: Prentice-Hall.

Guppy, Neil, Paulina D. Mikicich, and Ravi Pendakur. 1984. 'Changing Patterns of Educational Inequality'. *Canadian Journal of Sociology* 9: 319–31.

Guttmann, Amy. 1988. 'Distributing Public Education in a Democracy'. In *Democracy and the Welfare State*, ed. Amy Guttmann. Princeton, NJ: Princeton University Press.

Hepburn, Claudia Rebanks. 1999. *The Case for School Choice: Models from the United States, New Zealand, Denmark, and Sweden*. Vancouver: Fraser Institute.

Hodgetts, A.B. 1968. *What Culture? What Heritage? A Study of Civic Education in Canada*. Toronto: Ontario Institute for Studies in Education.

Holmes, Mark. 1992. *Educational Policy for the Pluralist Democracy: The Common School, Choice and Diversity*. Washington, DC: Falmer.

Kach, Nick, and Ivan DeFaveri. 1987. 'What Every Teacher Should Know about Multiculturalism'. In *Contemporary Educational Issues: The Canadian Mosaic*, ed. Leonard L. Stewin and Stewart J.H. McCann. Toronto: Copp Clark.

Kitchen, Harry, and Douglas Auld. 1995. *Financing of Education and Training in Canada*. Toronto: Canadian Tax Foundation.

Lewington, Jennifer, and Graham Orpwood. 1993. *Overdue Assignment: Taking Responsibility for Canada's Schools*. Toronto: John Wiley.

Livingstone, D.W., D. Hart, and L.E. Davie. 1999. *Public Attitudes towards Education in Ontario 1998*. Toronto: Ontario Institute for Studies in Education.

Luffman, Jacqueline. 1997. 'A Profile of Home Schooling in Canada'. *Education Quarterly Review* 4(4): 30–47.

Mackinnon, Frank. 1960. *The Politics of Canadian Education*. Toronto: University of Toronto Press.

Manzer, Ronald. 1994. *Canadian Public Schools and Political Ideas: Canadian Educational Policy in Historical Perspective*. Toronto: University of Toronto Press.

May, Stephen. 1994. *Making Multicultural Education Work*. Toronto: Ontario Institute for Studies in Education.

Mazurek, Kas. 1983. 'Multiculturalism and Schools: A Critical Analysis'. In *Racial Minorities in Multicultural Canada*, ed. Peter S. Li and B. Singh Bolaria. Toronto: Garamond.

Neu, Dean. 1999. 'Re-investment Fables: Educational Finances in Alberta'. In *Contested Classrooms: Education, Globalization, and Democracy in Alberta*, ed. Trevor W. Harrison and Jerrold L. Kachur. Edmonton: University of Alberta Press.

New Brunswick. 2000. *Let's Discuss Public Education Governance*. Fredericton, NB: Department of Education.

Nikiforuk, Andrew. 1993. *School's Out: The Catastrophe in Public Education and What We Can Do about It*. Toronto: Macfarlane Walter & Ross.

Norris, Christina. 1999. 'Parents and Schools: The Involvement, Participation and Expectations of Parents in the Education of Their Children'. *Education Quarterly Review* 5(4): 61–80.

Ontario. 1980. *Revised Regulations of Ontario 1980*, regulation 262, Sections 28 and 29, III, 155–56. Toronto: Queen's Printer.

Ontario. Ministry of Education. 1994. 'Violence-Free Schools Policy'. Accessed 7 February 2001: http://mettowas21.edu.gov.on.ca:80/eng/document/policy/vfreeng.html

———. 2000. 'Ontario Releases Code of Conduct and Takes Action for Safer Schools'. Press Release. (26 April). Toronto: Ministry of Education. Accessed 7 February 2001: http://www.edu.gov.on.ca/eng/document/nr/00.04/code.html

Ontario. Royal Commission on Learning. 1995. *For the Love of Learning: Report of the Royal Commission on Learning*. Toronto: The Commission.

Pagliarello, Claudio. 1994. 'Private Elementary and Secondary Schools'. *Education Quarterly Review* 1(1): 42–50.

Perry, David B. 1995. 'Education Financing in Canada: An Update'. *Canadian Tax Journal* 43(1): 222–7.

Porter, John. 1965. *The Vertical Mosaic*. Toronto: University of Toronto Press.

———. 1979. 'Education, Equality, and the Just Society'. In John Porter, *The Measure of Canadian Society: Education, Equality and Opportunity*. Toronto: Gage.

Prentice, Allison. 1977. *The School Promoters: Education and Social Class in Mid-Nineteenth Century Upper Canada*. Toronto: McClelland & Stewart.

Radwanski, George. 1987. *Ontario Study of the Relevance of Education and the Issue of Dropouts*. Toronto: Ontario Ministry of Education.

Rideout, David. 1995. 'School Councils in Canada'. *Education Canada* 35(2): 12–18.

Robson, William. 2000. 'Publicly Funded Education in Ontario: Breaking the Deadlock'. Paper presented to the 'School Choice: Dispelling the Myths and Examining the Evidence' conference in Mississauga, ON, April 1, 2000, sponsored by the Fraser Institute.

Roher, Eric. 1997. *An Educator's Guide to Violence in Schools*. Toronto: Canada Law Book.

Rusk, Bruce, Jean Shaw, and Peter Joong. 1994. *The Full Service School*. Toronto: Ontario Secondary School Teachers' Federation, Educational Services Committee.

Smith, D.S. 1996. 'Parent-Generated Home Study in Canada'. *Canadian School Executive* 15(8): 1–5.

Sweet, Lois. 1998. *God in the Classroom: The Controversial Issue of Religion in Canada's Schools*. Toronto: McClelland & Stewart.

Waterloo County Board of Education. 1993. 'A Guideline for Use in Planning for the Recognition of Religious and Cultural Days of Significance in Schools'. Waterloo, ON: Waterloo County Board of Education.

———. 1995. *Violence-Free Schools Initiative: Policies, Guiding Principles, Procedures, Guidelines, Resource Documents*. Waterloo, ON: Waterloo County Board of Education.

Wilkinson, B.W. 1994. *Educational Choice: Necessary but Not Sufficient*. Montreal: Institute for Research on Public Policy.

Willms, J. Douglas. 1997. *International Adult Literacy Survey: Literacy Skills of Canadian Youth*. Ottawa: Statistics Canada.

Index